# Strategic Planning Kit

FOR

# DUMMIES®

2ND EDITION

# Strategic Planning Kit FOR DUMMIES® 2ND EDITION

## by Erica Olsen

WILEY

John Wiley & Sons, Inc.

**Strategic Planning Kit For Dummies®, 2nd Edition**

Published by
**John Wiley & Sons, Inc.**
111 River St.
Hoboken, NJ 07030-5774
www.wiley.com

WILEY

# About the Author

**Erica Olsen** holds a BA in Communications and an MBA in International Management from Thunderbird School of Global Management. She's frequently tapped to lecture at the University of Nevada in Reno and the University of Phoenix in Reno on management and planning topics. She hosts workshops and has spoken at conferences nationwide.

As one of the developers of MyStrategicPlan, Erica has stripped strategic planning of its fate as a static document. With her online strategic planning system, any organization, regardless of size and budget, can build a plan in a matter of weeks (or even days). After completing the plan, the online system actually helps organizations execute the plan instead of just shoving it on a shelf. Her team developed MyStrategicPlan because they believe in inspiring big ideas and creating the laser-like focus to achieve them.

MyStrategicPlan is just one of several services offered by Erica's company, M3 Planning. M3 also does on-site strategic planning facilitation and retreats, as well as market research consulting. Over the last several years, M3 has developed and reviewed thousands of strategic plans for organizations across the country.

In addition to authoring *Strategic Planning Kit For Dummies,* 2nd Edition, Erica has coauthored *Strategic Planning Made Easy: A Practical Guide to Growth and Profitability* (M3 Planning, Inc.) and contributes regular columns to local, regional, and national business publications.

When Erica isn't lecturing, writing, or planning, she's alternately kayaking, backcountry skiing, rock climbing, biking, running, or bagging peaks around the Western Hemisphere with her husband, Gregor.

Erica always enjoys hearing from her readers. If you have questions about your strategic planning or if you have a success story to share, please contact her through any of the following methods:

E-mail: erica@mystrategicplan.com
Website: www.mystrategicplan.com
Blog: Strategically Speaking, www.mystrategicplan.com/blog

# Dedication

To all the business owners, executive directors, and managers in this world who have a big vision: May you successfully reach that big, hairy, audacious goal.

# Author's Acknowledgments

My sincere thanks and appreciation goes out to everyone who had a hand in putting this book together. The journey was an amazingly wonderful and enlightening experience, and I'm grateful for the remarkable opportunity to author this book. I must recognize a few specific people.

To my book brain trust, who provided ideas, recommendations, and suggestions at every turn — thank you for making this book as good as it could be. I want to specifically thank Alissa Schwipps, Michael Lewis, and technical editor Clint Burdett, for all your help. I would also like to thank the graphics and layout teams at John Wiley & Sons, Inc., who made this book come to life and the marketing teams who brought this book to business owners and managers everywhere. And a special thanks to Howard Putnam, author of The Winds of Turbulence (Howard D. Putnam Enterprises), for his kind words.

To our strategic planning clients who've all contributed to this book through their examples, questions, suggestions, and experiences — thank you for the opportunity to work with your organizations. Working with you is a pleasure and gift to everyone at my company.

Thank you to my great friends for sticking by my side even when I was buried in my writing. You're a continual source of encouragement. Special thanks go out to my friends and colleagues who made this edition fabulous, specifically Milan Sperka and Connie Armstrong, and to the rest of my team, Russell Persson, Vanessa Lindeberg, Cammy LoRe, Kim Perkins, Kristin Larsen, Shannon Forster, and Elsa Ozuna-Richards.

To my family, who's the best family in the world, thank you for supporting me in everything I do. My brothers Ryan and Brett, you provided needed distractions in between my deadlines and kept me focused on what mattered. Grandma and Grandpa Olsen (aka G & G), you instilled the entrepreneurial spirit in our family; to you I'm eternally grateful. Aunt Marlene, you're an amazing mentor; thank you for sharing your knowledge and wisdom with me. Mom, you're a one-of-a-kind business partner and mentor; thank you for taking care of the business and our clients when I was facing looming deadlines. Dad, you added needed clarifications, answers, and content ideas whenever I needed them; thank you for dropping everything to help me. You're as much the author of this book as I am. You're the best.

Most importantly, I want to thank my husband, Gregor. Your unfailing support for everything I do doesn't go unnoticed. I couldn't accomplish any of what I do without you.

## Publisher's Acknowledgments

We're proud of this book; please send us your comments at http://dummies.custhelp.com. For other comments, please contact our Customer Care Department within the U.S. at 877-762-2974, outside the U.S. at 317-572-3993, or fax 317-572-4002.

Some of the people who helped bring this book to market include the following:

*Acquisitions, Editorial, and Vertical Websites*

**Senior Project Editors:** Alissa Schwipps, Christina Guthrie

*(Previous Edition: Tim Gallan)*

**Acquisitions Editor:** Michael Lewis

**Copy Editor:** Jennette ElNaggar

**Assistant Editor:** David Lutton

**Editorial Program Coordinator:** Joe Niesen

**Technical Editor:** Clint Burdett, CMC

**Vertical Websites:** Jenny Swisher, Marilyn Hummel

**Editorial Manager:** Christine Meloy Beck

**Editorial Assistants:** Rachelle S. Amick, Alexa Koschier

**Cover Photos:** © iStockphoto.com / Mark Stay

**Cartoons:** Rich Tennant (www.the5thwave.com)

*Composition Services*

**Project Coordinator:** Sheree Montgomery

**Layout and Graphics:** Laura Westhuis

**Proofreader:** Toni Settle

**Indexer:** Cheryl Duksta

---

**Publishing and Editorial for Consumer Dummies**

    **Kathleen Nebenhaus,** Vice President and Executive Publisher

    **Kristin Ferguson-Wagstaffe,** Product Development Director

    **Ensley Eikenburg,** Associate Publisher, Travel

    **Kelly Regan,** Editorial Director, Travel

**Publishing for Technology Dummies**

    **Andy Cummings,** Vice President and Publisher

**Composition Services**

    **Debbie Stailey,** Director of Composition Services

# Contents at a Glance

Introduction .................................................................... 1

## Part 1: Kicking Off Your Strategic Planning Process ....... 7
Chapter 1: What Is Strategic Planning Really? ....................................... 9
Chapter 2: Why Strategic Planning Works .............................................. 23
Chapter 3: Getting Set Up for Successful Planning ............................... 35

## Part II: Determining Your Core DNA and Envisioned Future ............................................... 53
Chapter 4: Identifying Your Strategic Issues ......................................... 55
Chapter 5: Focusing on What You Do Best ............................................. 75
Chapter 6: Developing Your Mission, Values, and Vision ..................... 91

## Part III: Sizing Up Your Current Situation ................... 111
Chapter 7: Assessing Your Business and Its Capabilities .................... 113
Chapter 8: Seeing Your Business through Your Customers' Eyes ....... 131
Chapter 9: Researching the Market to Find New Customers ............... 147
Chapter 10: Identifying Your Opportunities and Threats .................... 169

## Part IV: Mapping Your Organization's Path to the Future ................................................... 191
Chapter 11: Strategizing for Growth and Sustainability ...................... 193
Chapter 12: Establishing Your Strategic Objectives, Goals, and Actions .............. 211
Chapter 13: Putting Your Plan into Action ........................................... 237

## Part V: Living and Breathing Your Plan ..................... 261
Chapter 14: Execute, Execute, Execute: Putting Your Plan to Work ...... 263
Chapter 15: Scenario Planning: Answering the What Ifs ..................... 283
Chapter 16: Value-Creating Strategies for Entrepreneurial Organizations ............. 295
Chapter 17: Sustainability for the Social Sectors ................................. 305

## Part VI: The Part of Tens .................................... 319

Chapter 18: Ten Tips to Keep Your Strategic Plan from Hitting the Shelf.............321

Chapter 19: Ten Ways to Ruin Your Strategy Meetings
and How to Avoid Them....................................................................325

Chapter 20: Ten Ways to Maintain Momentum in
Your Planning Process (And Life).................................................331

## Appendix: About the CD .................................... 335

## Index .................................................................. 343

# Table of Contents

## *Introduction* ...................................................... 1

About This Book ..................................................... 1
Conventions Used in This Book ................................ 2
What You're Not to Read ......................................... 2
Foolish Assumptions .............................................. 2
How This Book Is Organized ................................... 3
    Part I: Kicking Off Your Strategic Planning Process ....................... 3
    Part II: Determining Your Core DNA and Envisioned Future ............ 4
    Part III: Sizing Up Your Current Situation ..................... 4
    Part IV: Mapping Your Organization's Path to the Future ............... 4
    Part V: Living and Breathing Your Plan ........................ 4
    Part VI: The Part of Tens ..................................... 5
Icons Used in This Book ......................................... 5
Where to Go from Here .......................................... 6

## *Part 1: Kicking Off Your Strategic Planning Process* ........ 7

### Chapter 1: What Is Strategic Planning Really? ................... 9

Clearing Up the Confusion about Strategic Planning ............... 10
    Defining strategy ......................................... 10
    Understanding the importance of a strategic plan .............. 12
    Implementing the strategic management process ............... 12
    Identifying the components of a solid strategic plan ........... 13
    Answering the most frequently asked
        strategic planning questions ............................ 14
Identifying the Levels of Strategic Management ................. 17
Getting Acquainted with the Strategic Plan's Key Elements ....... 17
    Vision: Bringing things into focus .......................... 18
    Strategy: Explaining the value you deliver ................... 18
    Goals and objectives: Empowering employees ............... 19
    Execution and evaluation: Ensuring success ................. 19
Seeing the Signs: Why You Need This Book ..................... 19

### Chapter 2: Why Strategic Planning Works ..................... 23

Strategic Planning Is Most Used Tool by Executives ............. 23
Not Having a Plan Is Too Risky ................................ 25
A Plan Is Required to be a High Performer ...................... 26
    What makes great companies great .......................... 26
    What successful CEOs are spending their time on ............ 27

Everyday Decisions Drive Long-Term Results.......................................28
    The day-to-day impact ...................................................................28
    The bottom-line impact....................................................................29
Agility Is a New Competitive Advantage................................................30
Everyone Is Part of Something Bigger....................................................31
Tribal Knowledge Is Passed on to the Next Generation .......................32
You Can Clearly Explain (and Remember) Your Strategy.....................32
A Strategic Plan Eliminates Wasted Time and Money .........................33

**Chapter 3: Getting Set Up for Successful Planning . . . . . . . . . . . . . . .35**
Previewing the Elements of a Strategic Plan.........................................36
    Where are we now?...........................................................................37
    Where are we going? ........................................................................38
    How will we get there? .....................................................................38
    How will we measure our progress?................................................39
Before You Begin: Assessing Your Planning Readiness .......................40
    Are we ready?....................................................................................40
    Is the climate right? .........................................................................40
Taking a Look at the Strategic Planning Process and Time Frame........41
    Phase 1: Determining your core purpose
        and envisioned future................................................................42
    Phase 2: Assessing your strategic position ...................................42
    Phase 3: Developing your strategies and priorities......................43
    Phase 4: Cascading your strategies to operations ........................44
    Phase 5: Aligning your people and financial resources ...............45
    Phase 6: Executing your plan ..........................................................45
Selecting Your Planning Team ................................................................46
    Getting everyone involved...............................................................46
    Determining who's involved when ................................................48
Going It Alone or Hiring a Facilitator .....................................................49
    Running the planning sessions yourself .......................................49
    Using a facilitator.............................................................................50
Smoothing Out Your Process...................................................................51

**Part II: Determining Your Core DNA
and Envisioned Future....................................................... 53**

**Chapter 4: Identifying Your Strategic Issues. . . . . . . . . . . . . . . . . . . . .55**
Reviewing What Happened Last Year......................................................56
    Recognizing what you achieved......................................................56
    Understanding why you failed ........................................................57
Evaluating Your Products and Services .................................................57
    Picking the winners .........................................................................58
    Dumping the losers...........................................................................60

Putting Your Portfolio Together (In the
  Market Attractiveness Framework).............................................60
    Evaluating market attractiveness and business strength..............60
    Creating your own matrix...........................................62
Looking at Your Financial Performance ..........................................63
    Understanding the financial dynamics of your business...............63
    Sorting out three-year trends......................................67
    Trailing your numbers over 12 months ..............................68
    Evaluating your numbers............................................70
Seeing the Underlying Forces of Your Industry...............................71
Creating Your Short List of Strategic Issues ...............................72

**Chapter 5: Focusing on What You Do Best** ........................**75**
Appreciating Your Competitive Advantage ....................................75
    Taking the 30-second competitive advantage challenge...............76
    Knowing what competitive advantage isn't...........................77
    Realizing what competitive advantage is............................77
    Discovering why having a competitive
      advantage is so important .......................................78
Uncovering Your Advantages ................................................79
    What's your distinct purpose?......................................79
    How do you make money?.............................................80
    Why do customers buy from you?.....................................82
Pinpointing Your Competitive Advantage.....................................83
    Perusing a few examples............................................83
    Stating your competitive advantage succinctly.....................84
    Putting your advantage to the test................................84
    Breaking away from the pack........................................86
Using Your Advantages Now..................................................87
    Implementing your advantages......................................88
    Measuring your advantages .........................................88
    Putting your advantages in your plan..............................89

**Chapter 6: Developing Your Mission, Values, and Vision** .........**91**
Building Your Strategic Foundation.........................................92
Assessing Your Mission.....................................................93
    Elements of an effective mission statement.........................93
    Evaluating your current mission statement..........................95
    Writing a new mission statement ...................................95
Fine-tuning Your Organizational Values.....................................97
    Elements of effective organizational values .......................97
    Creating or updating your organizational values ..................98
    Acting on your organizational values...............................99

Visioning: Focusing in on Your North Star...............................101
Elements of an effective vision statement.....................102
Imagining your future — vividly.....................................102
Creating or updating your vision statement
and vivid description.....................................................104
Futurecasting: Looking to the Future......................................105
Getting into the right frame of mind for futurecasting...............105
Leaving your assumptions at the door...........................106
Working a strategic thinking exercise..........................106
Finalizing Your Strategic Foundation......................................107

## Part III: Sizing Up Your Current Situation .................. 111

### Chapter 7: Assessing Your Business and Its Capabilities ........113

Establishing a Starting Point: Identifying
Your Business's Strategic Position.....................................114
Evaluating Your Company's Capabilities .............................115
Human capital: Having the right people in the right positions ........115
Organizational capital: Getting a feeling
for your corporate culture..............................................117
Knowledge capital: Knowing what you already know..................118
Examining Your Resources ....................................................120
Processes: Connecting Your Capabilities and Resources.....................121
Operational processes .....................................................122
Customer management processes ...................................123
Relationship management processes...............................123
Innovation processes .......................................................124
Other important process areas........................................125
Checking Your Profit Margins.................................................127
Identifying cash creators .................................................128
Detecting cash drains.......................................................129

### Chapter 8: Seeing Your Business through Your Customers' Eyes .....131

Getting to Know Your Most Valuable Customers....................132
Identifying the 80/20 customer .......................................133
Figuring out the lifetime value of your customers .................133
Determining Why Your Customers Are Your Customers......................136
Measuring satisfaction by the numbers..........................137
Obtaining feedback without using a survey....................139
Spending time talking to your customers........................139
Focusing on How You Deliver Value to Your Customers.....................140
Considering different business models............................141
Using a business model to create value..........................142
Framing out your business model ..................................145

## Chapter 9: Researching the Market to Find New Customers......147

Gathering Information about New Markets...........................148
Identifying your information needs...............................148
Locating information sources.....................................149
Creating Your Target Markets.........................................152
Dividing your market into groups.................................152
Visualizing your target customer.................................155
Focusing on the Most Attractive Markets............................157
Defining an attractive segment...................................157
Evaluating your target customer groups...........................158
Standing Out from the Crowd: Your Positioning Statement............159
Writing your positioning statements..............................160
Perusing examples of positioning statements......................161
Reaching Your New Target Markets...................................162
The Four Ps: Neither a soul band nor a legume....................162
The cycle of (product) life......................................163
Staying Market-Focused.............................................165
Gathering relevant information...................................165
Sharing what you know............................................166
Responding to what you've discovered.............................167
Putting It All Together: Organizing Customer Information...........167

## Chapter 10: Identifying Your Opportunities and Threats..........169

Starting Your SWOT Analysis........................................171
Seeing the Future..................................................172
Finding Opportunities in Your Operating Environment................173
Identifying your economic indicators.............................173
Watching important social shifts.................................175
Staying on top of technology trends..............................176
Monitoring political winds.......................................177
Flexing with demographic movements...............................178
Tracking Your Industry.............................................179
Looming new competitors..........................................179
Threatening substitute products..................................181
Bargaining power of suppliers....................................181
Bargaining power of buyers.......................................182
Duking it out with your competitors..............................182
Analyzing Your Competition.........................................183
Identifying your competitors.....................................184
Gathering competitive intelligence...............................185
Isolating what you really need to know...........................185
Seeing the competitive field.....................................186
Evaluating Your Market.............................................188
Summarizing Your Opportunities and Threats.........................188
Finishing Your SWOT Analysis.......................................189

## Part IV: Mapping Your Organization's Path to the Future .................................................. 191

### Chapter 11: Strategizing for Growth and Sustainability .......... 193

Understanding the Difference between Strategy and Tactics ............... 194
    Strategy versus tactics ................................................................ 194
    The levels of strategies ............................................................... 195
Business Unit Level Strategies: Choosing
    Your Leading Strategic Focus ..................................................... 195
    Applying your strengths to a business unit level strategy ........... 196
    Discovering why you don't want to be stuck in the middle ........ 200
    Choosing the right business unit level strategy for you ............. 201
Market Level Strategies: Strategizing How to Grow ........................... 202
    Concentrating on market penetration ........................................ 203
    Delivering with product development ........................................ 204
    Extending scope with market development ................................. 205
    Stepping out with diversification ............................................... 206
    Deciding how to execute your growth strategy .......................... 208
Summarizing Your Selected Strategies ............................................... 210

### Chapter 12: Establishing Your Strategic Objectives, Goals, and Actions ............................... 211

Firming Up Your List of Strategic Alternatives .................................. 212
    Paring down your SWOT .............................................................. 213
    Identifying strategic alternatives ............................................... 214
    Sorting through your other alternatives .................................... 216
Evolving Alternatives into Priorities ................................................. 217
    Sorting out internal and external alternatives ........................... 217
    Creating a short list of external priorities ................................. 218
    Compiling a short list of internal priorities ............................... 220
    Gut checking your priorities ....................................................... 221
Balancing Your Strategic Priorities .................................................... 222
    Financial priorities: If we succeed, how will
        we look to our shareholders? .................................................. 223
    Customer priorities: How do we provide
        value to our customers? .......................................................... 224
    Internal priorities: What processes must we
        excel in to satisfy our customers? .......................................... 225
    Employee priorities: How must our
        organization grow and improve? ............................................ 225
Turning Strategic Priorities into a Road Map for Your Vision ........... 226
    Finalizing your strategies ............................................................ 227
    Writing your long-term strategic objectives .............................. 228
    Making your short-term goals SMART ........................................ 229
    Mapping your strategy ................................................................ 230
    Building your road map ............................................................... 232

Assembling Your Strategic Plan ............................................234
Evaluating Your Strategic Plan ............................................235

## Chapter 13: Putting Your Plan into Action . . . . . . . . . . . . . . . . . . . .237

Managing Performance with a Scorecard..................................237
   Pegging your measures ..............................................238
   Aiming at your targets................................................239
   Building your scorecard ..............................................241
Cascading Goals to Annual Action Plans..................................243
   Tips for cascading one level...........................................244
   Tips for cascading multiple levels.....................................245
   Getting down to cascading business...................................245
   Avoiding land mines in cascading ....................................247
Ensuring Your Plan Makes Cents............................................249
   Estimating revenue and expenses .....................................251
   Contributing to the bottom line.......................................253
   Projecting your financial future .......................................254
   Forecasting with indicators............................................255
Making Your Plan a Living Document........................................256
   Piecing out your plan by audience ....................................256
   Using a performance management system............................258

# Part V: Living and Breathing Your Plan..................... 261

## Chapter 14: Execute, Execute, Execute: Putting Your Plan to Work . . . . . . . . . . . . . . . . . . . . . . . . . . . . . . . . .263

So You Have a Plan — Now What? .........................................264
   Avoiding the pitfalls...................................................264
   Covering all your bases................................................265
   Making sure you have the support....................................266
   Determining your plan of attack .......................................267
Holding People (Including Yourself) Accountable to the Process........268
   Appointing a strategic plan manager .................................268
   Syncing individual action plans with compensation..................269
   Coaching for achievement.............................................271
Heartbeat of Your Management Process: Strategy Reviews................272
   Understanding the difference between strategy and
     operational reviews ................................................272
   Holding effective strategy review meetings ..........................273
   Using a scorecard to measure progress ..............................274
Mastering the Art of Communicating Strategy .............................275
   Making sure everyone buys in .........................................276
   Rolling out the plan ....................................................276
   Continuing communication ............................................277

Keeping Your Plan Working for You .........................................278
Accepting change — the only constant ..........................278
Adapting your plan as necessary.................................280

**Chapter 15: Scenario Planning: Answering the What Ifs ........283**
Grasping the Concept: What Is Scenario Planning? ..................283
Tackling Your Short-Term Uncertainties...............................284
Identifying immediate risks ........................................285
Constructing possible alternative outcomes ..................285
Confronting Your Longer-Term Futures...............................287
Thinking about the big what ifs ..................................287
Building alternative futures........................................288
Connecting scenarios to strategy ................................290
Considering Example Scenarios .........................................291
Shell energy scenarios to 2050....................................291
Cisco's Internet scenarios to 2025................................292
Chatham House's food futures scenarios......................293

**Chapter 16: Value-Creating Strategies for**
**Entrepreneurial Organizations............................295**
Establishing an Owner's Vision ..........................................296
Knowing your true endgame ......................................296
Deciding whether to publish your endgame .................297
Creating a Sellable Business...............................................297
Understanding what creates value .............................298
Valuing your business ...............................................298
Ensuring Your Business Continues after You Leave...............300
Planning for transition ..............................................300
Considering how you want to exit your business .........301
Preparing for a smooth exit........................................302
Gathering additional resources ..................................304

**Chapter 17: Sustainability for the Social Sectors ..............305**
Moving from Profit to Sustainability ...................................306
Getting Your Board on Board the Planning Effort................306
Defining the role of the policy board ..........................307
Being tight on the ends and loose on the means...........307
Planning for Government Entities .......................................308
Recognizing how government planning works ..............308
Getting set up for government planning.......................310
Determining what sustainability means for
government entities ...............................................311
Planning for Nonprofit Organizations .................................312
Redefining competition with the MacMillan Matrix.......313
Mapping out nonprofit strategies ...............................316

## Part VI: The Part of Tens ................................. 319

### Chapter 18: Ten Tips to Keep Your Strategic Plan from Hitting the Shelf. .................................... .321

Getting Everyone Involved from the Start ................................ 321
Deleting the Fluff ................................................................. 322
Appointing a Strategy Manager .......................................... 322
Creating a Strategic Plan Poster (Real and Virtual) ............ 322
Hooking Achievement into Incentives ................................ 323
Using a KISS ....................................................................... 323
Holding a Monthly Strategy Meeting ................................. 323
Using a Scorecard ............................................................... 324
Leading by Example ............................................................ 324
Celebrating Your Success — Whenever You Feel Like It ..... 324

### Chapter 19: Ten Ways to Ruin Your Strategy Meetings and How to Avoid Them ....................................... .325

Refusing to Use a Facilitator .............................................. 325
Neglecting to Conduct Any Research Before the Meeting ... 326
Inviting Everyone ................................................................ 326
Holding an Annual Retreat .................................................. 327
Getting through the Agenda No Matter What ...................... 327
Forgetting to Explain the Process ....................................... 328
Assuming Everyone Thinks Like You ................................... 328
Ignoring the Elephant in the Room ..................................... 329
Ending on a Low Note .......................................................... 329
Overlooking Life after the Meeting ...................................... 330

### Chapter 20: Ten Ways to Maintain Momentum in Your Planning Process (And Life) ..................... .331

Create Your Picture of Success and Make It a Reality ........ 331
Pick a BHAG ....................................................................... 332
Eliminate Your Energy Drains and Recharge Yourself ........ 332
Conquer Your Fears — Concentrate and Be Brave .............. 332
Take Control of Your Finances ............................................ 333
Create a Brain Trust ........................................................... 333
Find the Time ...................................................................... 333
Highlight Small Wins ........................................................... 334
Let the Process Evolve ........................................................ 334
Be Committed ..................................................................... 334

## Appendix: About the CD ................................................ 335

System Requirements ............................................................... 335
Using the CD .......................................................................... 336
What You'll Find on the CD .................................................... 336
Troubleshooting ...................................................................... 341

## Index .............................................................................. 343

# Introduction

*You* have two choices when it comes to running your organization: (1) Be intentional about the path your organization follows or (2) turn on autopilot. Turning on autopilot is kind of like hopping into your Hummer, turning on the satellite navigation system, and following the directions from your home to Las Vegas. Computers aren't the best at making decisions, so you may get to Las Vegas eventually, but are you going to Las Vegas, New Mexico, or Las Vegas, Nevada? If you plot your course before you set off, you're more likely to get to the correct destination.

If you're running your organization without a plan, you're just using the navigation system and not paying attention to how you're getting there. An astonishing 90 percent of businesses are running without a plan. That 90 percent is hoping that the navigation system doesn't fail and that it correctly assumes the end destination. But because you're reading this book, you're ready to run the show, and you're close to joining the elite 10 percent that know a strategic plan is important.

## About This Book

This book is about getting from Point A to Point B more effectively and efficiently and having more fun along the way. Part of that journey is the strategy and part of it is the planning, development, and execution.

Strategic planning isn't about taking on additional work; it's about taking all those numerous daily decisions and making them part of an integrated process. Whether you want to be more effective and efficient or you want to make more money, have a bigger community impact, or move your company from good to great, this book is for you! No more thinking that strategic planning is daunting. This book, and the accompanying CD, makes the process easy, straightforward, rewarding, and fun.

*Strategic Planning Kit For Dummies,* 2nd Edition, brings everything business owners, executive directors, or managers need to take their organizations to the next phase of business growth. The book presents a practical set of strategic planning tools and guides you through an integrated strategic planning process that I break down into six phases.

In this book, you discover how strategic planning is the key element to your growth through a no-nonsense approach. Each part contains relevant content, real-world examples, and useful worksheets. On the CD, you'll find blank, printable versions of several of these worksheets and templates that help you identify your SWOT (strengths, weakness, opportunities, and threats), your competitive advantage, and your road map for success. I also provide some helpful links to short videos on my website that guide you through the steps of the planning phases.

Strategic planning has been overcomplicated by jargon, competing semantics, and consultants of the world (me included!). In reality, *strategic planning* is a business concept that's useful to all businesses and organizations, no matter their size or resources. Use this book as your reference — whether you're part of a large organization or a small one — to create a strategic plan that gets you to your destination.

# Conventions Used in This Book

The following conventions are used throughout the text to make concepts consistent and easy to understand:

✔ All web addresses and e-mail addresses appear in `monofont`. Some web addresses may break across two lines of text. If that happens, know that I haven't put in any extra characters (such as hyphens) to indicate the break. So when typing these addresses into your web browsers, type exactly what you see in this book, pretending as though the line break doesn't exist.

✔ New terms appear in *italics* and are closely followed by a definition.

✔ **Bold** is used to highlight the action parts of numbered steps and key words or phrases in bulleted lists.

# What You're Not to Read

Although I hope you read every word I've written, I understand that your life is busy and that you want to read only the need-to-know info. You can thus safely skip the sidebars — those shaded gray boxes that contain text. Sidebars provide supporting or entertaining info that isn't critical to your understanding of the topic. I use them to go off on tangents or present extended examples, so you can skip them if you want.

# Foolish Assumptions

As I wrote this book, I made some assumptions about you, my reader:

✔ **You're a decision maker.** You hold the position of business owner, manager, executive director, department head, or team/group leader.

✔ **You can influence change in your organization.** Whether you have the final say, you have a strong enough position to influence the course of your business.

✔ **You want to see your organization grow and be sustainable!** Growth is different for every organization. But the underlying premise is you want your organization to do more and be around longer.

✔ **You can see the edges of your strategy, but you need to fill in the detail.** Most organizations know what general direction they're headed in, but they need to turn the generalities into specifics.

✔ **You have a plan, but it's sitting on the shelf gathering dust.** Or you have a plan, but it's halfway completed.

✔ **You want to get everyone on the same page.** I hear this phrase with almost every client I work with, so I assume it applies to you, too. The need to get your whole company focused and pulling in the same direction is a great motivator to do strategic planning.

Although all these assumptions may not apply to you, am I at least close? I wish I could predict the future of your business, but alas, I haven't been granted that power. A strategic plan helps to take out the uncertainty and allows you to shape the future *you* want. And I'm here to help you with your steps along the way.

# How This Book Is Organized

*Strategic Planning Kit For Dummies,* 2nd Edition, is divided into six parts. A quick review of the Table of Contents and the following descriptions of the parts give you a solid overview of the entire book.

## Part 1: Kicking Off Your Strategic Planning Process

The chapters in this part are packed full of who, what, how, and why you should care. You look at a number of concepts in this part, including the strategic planning process, who should be involved, how long it takes, the right time for lanning, the differences between business plans and stratgic plans, and much more.

If you're looking to convince your boss or team members about the importance of strategic planning, look no further than Chapter 2.

## Part II: Determining Your Core DNA and Envisioned Future

Hold on a second. Don't move past this part too quickly; I know you want to. Whether your organization has been around for 2 years or 200 years, you have important knowledge to build your strategic plan on. I like to call that knowledge *tribal knowledge.* Chapter 4 asks you to identify your strategic issues. Chapter 5 digs in to the hard subject of what you do best and helps you identify, develop, and sustain your organization's competitive advantage. Chapter 6 includes a discussion about mission, vision, and values. Additionally, Part II provides you with advice on making sure that the foundation of your business is solid.

## Part III: Sizing Up Your Current Situation

Part III focuses on collecting information that's critical for your strategic decision making. Organizations can't plan without gathering the right data, so Chapter 7 looks at assessing your business and its capabilities; Chapter 8 focuses on seeing your business through your customers' eyes; Chapter 9 takes a look at finding new customers; and Chapter 10 assesses your opportunities and threats. I provide a set of tools for synthesizing the data so you have the right information as you head into strategic decision making in the next part.

## Part IV: Mapping Your Organization's Path to the Future

The main reason you need to do strategic planning is to look into and plan for the future. In this part, you determine how to grow and be sustainable by looking at the different types of value-creating strategies, as well as the more specific strategies surrounding growth, integration, and diversification. Most importantly, you identify and evaluate opportunities and select a strategy to move in that direction. Then I take this section a step further and show you how to operationalize your plan.

## Part V: Living and Breathing Your Plan

No matter how good the plan, if it sits on the shelf, it's going to be useless. In this part, I focus on the execution of your plan and best practices on how to move from a plan to execution. Not all organizations are created equal — quite the opposite, actually. To address specific organizational concerns, you find in this section tips for government and nonprofit strategies as well as entrepreneurial companies. Lastly, seeing the future more clearly is how to constantly adapt and tweak your plan. Scenario planning in Chapter 17 helps you keep the future in focus.

## Part VI: The Part of Tens

Need some quick tips, a shot in the arm, or just a good laugh? The Part of Tens is a collection of hints, reminders, observations, and warnings about what to do and not to do. These chapters focus on giving you a quick set of guidelines for three key areas: facilitating strategy meetings, getting your plan done, and executing the strategy.

Additionally, I provide an appendix that guides you through the software requirements for installing and using the CD. I also give you an overview of all the worksheets and templates on the CD, which is designed to help you through each and every step of your strategic planning.

# Icons Used in This Book

Throughout the book, the following icons appear in the left margins to alert you to special information.

This symbol marks an important truth that's worth repeating. Taking note of these ideas can help you make progress with your strategic plan.

The information next to the Tip icon always includes a helpful hint to keep your strategic plan moving forward as smoothly as possible.

Any information next to this icon is something you want to be wary about. Watch your step when you see a Warning icon. The info can include mistakes others made that you can learn from or moments where you have to weigh the cost of doing one thing over another.

This symbol indicates a concept or work area where the outcome goes into your strategic plan.

Are you an experienced strategic planner? If so, these icons are for you. Take your planning to the next level by employing the ideas highlighted with this icon.

To assist you, I've included editable versions of the handy worksheets and templates on a CD so you can easily start your planning process.

# *Where to Go from Here*

This book is as much about strategy development and execution as it is about the plan itself. If you want to spend time on strategy development, go to Parts II, III, and IV. On the other hand, if you just want to put your plan together, go to Parts I and V.

Another approach to tackling this book is to consider your own thinking and education style. What gets you excited? How do you like to think? Here's a detailed approach for navigating through this book, based on your skills and personality:

- ✔ **Big-picture thinkers:** You may love Chapters 5, 6, 11, and 17 because they're future-oriented and focus on what's possible.

- ✔ **Analytical minds:** Chapters 4, 7, 8, 9, 10, and 17 are for those of you who always look at the what ifs. These chapters look at how to use data from your internal and external environments to develop a list of possible strategies.

- ✔ **Detail-oriented folks:** If you're thinking, "How are we going to do this?" then head to Chapters 12, 13, and 14 to put the pieces together.

- ✔ **Social butterflies, team builders, and crowd pleasers:** Check out Chapters 2, 3, 19, and 20 for ideas to build consensus and get everyone's input.

However you approach your plan, I recommend you start a strategy notebook to capture your thoughts as you move through your planning process. I guarantee you'll stumble across a section of text or an idea that you don't want to lose, so if you jot it down in your notebook, you won't have to go back and find it. In several places, I refer to the notebook as a place to work through some actions and exercises.

Regardless of how you find your way around *Strategic Planning Kit For Dummies,* 2nd Edition, I'm sure that you can develop a strategic plan that fits your team's approach and organization's style. I invite you to share your stories, experiences, vision, and successes with me and other readers on my blog at www.mystrategicplan.com/blog. I look forward to hearing from you. Happy strategizing!

# Part I
# Kicking Off Your Strategic Planning Process

The 5th Wave          By Rich Tennant

Frankly, I liked it better when we ran around barking like heck and scaring them into the pen.

## In this part . . .

*H*aving a strategic plan is the best way to bring focus and direction to your organization. The chapters in this part make you a strategic planning convert. In this part, you discover what strategic planning is and why it's important. You also dive into the steps of the strategic planning process, including who should be involved along the way and how you create a business process instead of just an event.

# Chapter 1

# What Is Strategic Planning Really?

*In This Chapter*

▶ Figuring out what a strategic plan is

▶ Checking out the key parts of a strategic plan

▶ Getting the most out of your strategic planning process

▶ Heeding the warnings that you need a strategic plan

*W*hat will your business be like in three years? Do you have a road map to get from today to your envisioned tomorrow? Will you be a few steps closer to realizing your vision by next year? No one can predict the future. But if you don't change anything, the future won't be any different than the past.

One sure-fire way to impact your company's future (and profitability) is to dust off a timeless tool — the strategic plan — and intentionally drive your organization forward. No one strategic model fits all organizations, but the planning process includes certain basic elements that all businesses can use to explore their vision, goals, and next steps of an effective strategic plan. A good strategic plan achieves the following:

✔ Reflects the values of the organization

✔ Inspires action to achieve a big future

✔ Explains how you'll win in the market

✔ Clearly defines the criteria for achieving success

✔ Guides everyone in daily decision making

Effective leaders aren't sitting around waiting for something to happen. They're anticipating what lies ahead. Managers and business owners aren't waiting for their competitors to swoop in and put them out of business. Instead, they're using their strategic plans to get ahead of the game. So the fact that many people avoid strategic planning because they consider it complex, costly, and time-intensive is just odd. Most of the time, businesses shelve the plan before it can be implemented, even knowing that some other company may invade their market.

Strategic planning doesn't have to be mysterious, complicated, or time-consuming. In fact, it should be quick, simple, and easily executed. And strategic planning isn't just something you cross off your list of to-dos — you must create a culture of strategic thinking, so your strategic planning doesn't become an annual retreat but, instead, a part of daily decision making.

In this chapter, I explore the ins and outs of strategic planning by answering common questions related to strategic planning, discussing the strategic levels of management, and introducing the key elements of a successful strategic plan.

# Clearing Up the Confusion about Strategic Planning

Many people are confused by the terms *strategy, strategic plan,* and *strategic planning.* Well, I'm here to help you get a clear picture. For the moment, forget what you've heard about this subject. I promise that strategic planning makes a huge difference to your organization both tangibly and intangibly, so keep reading!

In the following sections, I not only define what strategy is and how it relates to strategic planning, but I also show you why a strategic plan is important and how you can implement one in your organization by digging in to the key elements of planning.

## Defining strategy

*Strategy* means consciously choosing to be clear about your company's direction in relation to what's happening in the dynamic environment. With this knowledge, you're in a much better position to respond proactively to the changing environment.

The fine points of strategy are as follows:

- ✔ Establishes unique value proposition compared to your competitors
- ✔ Executed through operations that provide different and tailored value to customers
- ✔ Identifies clear tradeoffs and clarifies what *not* to do

✔ Focuses on activities that fit together and reinforce each other

✔ Drives continual improvement within the organization and moves it toward its vision

Knowing what strategy is can also be explained by looking at what strategy *isn't*. Dr. Michael Porter, the leading strategy guru and professor at Harvard University, says strategy *isn't* the following:

✔ Agility

✔ Alliances/Partnering

✔ Aspirations

✔ Best practice improvement

✔ Downsizing

✔ Execution

✔ Flexibility

✔ Innovation

✔ The Internet (or any technology)

✔ Learning

✔ Mergers/Consolidation

✔ Outsourcing

✔ Restructuring

✔ A vision

## Surprising strategic-planning stats

Consider the following statistics from the Balanced Scorecard Collaborative (I cover the Balanced Scorecard in Chapter 12):

✔ 95 percent of a typical workforce doesn't understand its organization's strategy.

✔ 90 percent of organizations fail to execute strategies successfully.

✔ 86 percent of executive teams spend less than one hour per month discussing strategy.

✔ 60 percent of organizations don't link strategy to budgeting.

So what's the upshot of these surprising revelations? Strategic planning matters to the life of your business.

## Understanding the importance of a strategic plan

Simply put, a *strategic plan* is the formalized road map that describes how your company executes the chosen strategy. A plan spells out where an organization is going over the next year or more and how it's going to get there. Typically, the plan is organization-wide or focused on a major function, such as a division or a department. A strategic plan is a management tool that serves the purpose of helping an organization do a better job, because a plan focuses the energy, resources, and time of everyone in the organization in the same direction.

If you're thinking, "Hey, I've got this great book on business plans, so I'll just use that to form my strategic plan," be aware that strategic plans and business plans aren't the same concepts.

A *strategic plan* is a management tool that C-level managers need to master and is for established businesses and business owners who are serious about growth. It also does the following:

- ✔ Helps build your competitive advantage
- ✔ Communicates your strategy to staff
- ✔ Prioritizes your financial needs
- ✔ Provides focus and direction to move from plan to action

A *business plan,* on the other hand, is a planning tool for new businesses, projects, or entrepreneurs who are serious about starting a business. A business plan

- ✔ Helps define the purpose of your business
- ✔ Helps plan human resources and operational needs
- ✔ Is critical if you're seeking funding
- ✔ Assesses business opportunities
- ✔ Provides structure to ideas

## Implementing the strategic management process

In order to create a strategic plan you can execute, you have to implement a strategic management process. The planning process typically includes several major activities or steps. People often have different names for these major activities. They may even conduct them in a different order. Strategic planning often includes using several key terms as well. See Chapter 3 for specific guidelines and checklists to help you with your process.

Don't be concerned about finding the perfect way to conduct a strategic planning process. (Perfection doesn't really exist, does it?) Modify the info in this book to fit with your organization's culture and timing.

The difference between strategic planning and strategic management can be profound to an organization when understood. *Strategic planning* usually refers to the development of a plan. *Strategic management* refers to both strategy development *and* execution. Strategic management is a business process. Strategic planning is an event. Although I refer to strategic planning throughout this book, understand that I mean developing *and* executing because every executive I know wants to drive results. And you do that by instilling a business cycle from developing to implementing to adapting and then repeating.

## Identifying the components of a solid strategic plan

Several different frameworks can help you develop your strategic plan. Think of the frameworks as different lenses through which to view the strategic planning process. You don't always look through two or three lenses at once. Normally, you use one at a time, and often you may not know that you're using certain frameworks embedded in your process. If you're trying to explain to your planning team how pieces of the puzzle fit together, first you must understand the following components of the strategic plan:

- ✓ **Strategy and culture:** Your organization's culture is made up of people, processes, experiences, ideas, and attitudes. Your strategy is where your organization is headed, what path it takes, and how it gets there. You can't have strategy without culture or vice versa. Your culture is like your house, and if it's not in order, the best strategy in the world can't take your company anywhere.

- ✓ **Internal and external:** Similar to the strategy and culture framework, you have an internal and external framework. The strategy is external because you gather information from your customers, competitors, industry, and environment to identify your opportunities and threats. (I discuss how to identify your opportunities and threats in Chapter 10.) Through employee surveys, board assessments, and financial statements, you identify your company's strengths and weaknesses, which are internal. (See Chapter 7 for more info on finding your strengths and weaknesses.)

- ✓ **The Balanced Scorecard perspectives:** Businesses use the Balanced Scorecard framework to develop goals and objectives in four areas (instead of departments): financial, customers, internal business processes, and people. The financial, internal business processes, and people areas are internal. The customer area is external. Chapter 12 elaborates on this framework and the Balanced Scorecard.

✔ **Market focus:** Growth comes from focusing on your customers and delivering superior value to them consistently year after year. Built in to your strategic plan is a market-focus framework because of how critical this aspect is to your organizational growth. Chapters 8 and 9 show you how to make your current customers happy and how to find new customers.

✔ **Where are we now? Where are we going? How will we get there?** Because it's easy to confuse how all the elements of a plan come together and where they go, this framework is a simple yet clear way of looking at the whole plan. I explain this framework in Chapter 3.

## Answering the most frequently asked strategic planning questions

Strategic planning can create a ton of questions. If you already have a long list of questions, you're not alone. The following sections provide the answers to the most commonly asked questions.

### Who uses strategic plans?

Everyone uses strategic plans — or at least every company and organization that wants to be successful. Companies in every industry, in every part of the country, and in most of the Fortune 500 use strategic plans. Organizations within the nonprofit, government, and small to big business sectors also have strategic plans. See Chapter 2 for statistics on how widely strategic planning is used as a management tool.

### Does every strategic plan include the same elements?

A strategic plan usually consists of the following elements:

✔ A mission statement and a vision statement (see Chapter 6)

✔ A description of the company's long-term goals and objectives (see Chapter 12)

✔ Strategies the company plans to use to achieve general goals and objectives (see Chapter 12)

✔ Action plans to implement the goals and objectives (see Chapter 13)

The strategic plan may also identify external factors that can affect achievement of long-term goals. Plans may vary in detail and scope (depending on how big the organization is), but for the most part, a strategic plan includes these basic elements.

## Just exactly what is strategic planning?

The term _strategic planning_ refers to a coordinated and systematic process for developing a plan for the overall direction of your endeavor for the purpose of optimizing future potential. For a profit-making business, this process involves many questions:

- ✔ What's the mission and purpose of the business?
- ✔ Where do we want to take the business?
- ✔ What do we sell currently? What can we sell in the future?
- ✔ Who shall we sell to?
- ✔ What do we do that's unique?
- ✔ How shall we beat or avoid competition?

The central purpose of this process is to ensure that the course and direction is well thought out, sound, and appropriate. In addition, the process provides reassurance that the limited resources of the enterprise (time and capital) are sharply focused in support of that course and direction. The process encompasses both strategy formulation and implementation.

## What's the difference between strategic planning and long-range planning?

The major difference between strategic planning and long-range planning is emphasis. _Long-range planning_ generally means the development of a plan of action to accomplish a goal or set of goals over a period of several years. The major assumption in long-range planning is that current knowledge about future conditions is sufficiently reliable to enable the development of these plans. Because people assume the environment is predictable, the emphasis is on the articulation of internally focused plans to accomplish agreed-on goals.

The major assumption in strategic planning, however, is that an organization must be responsive to a dynamic, changing environment. Therefore, the emphasis in strategic planning is on understanding how the environment is changing — and will change — and on developing organizational decisions that are responsive to these changes.

## Does every company need a strategic plan?

Every endeavor or enterprise already has a strategy. These strategies range from some vague sense of the desires of the owner to massive, overly sophisticated master plans. So the question isn't whether every company needs a strategy but rather whether the company's strategy needs to be well thought out, sound, appropriate, and doable. The answer is yes.

### We're highly successful already, so why should we plan?

Success is strong evidence that a company has had a sound and appropriate strategy. Note the past tense. There's absolutely no guarantee that yesterday's sound and appropriate strategy will continue to be successful in the future. Indeed, assuming so without adequate study poses great danger. Therefore, no matter what your past or current successes are, you need a strategic plan.

### Can a smaller company afford the time for strategic planning?

Experience shows that the top management team devotes approximately 2 to 4 percent of its time to practical strategic planning. In reality, structured strategic planning isn't something more to do; it's a better way of doing something already being done. Indeed, in the long run, you save time. Chapter 16 talks specifically to small and privately-held businesses.

Strategic planning can become a time trap. You can get caught in a long slog of planning if you get too mired down in the details. From the outset, you need to establish that the plan is a living document and isn't written in stone. Doing so helps you avoid strategic planning becoming a time trap.

### Why plan in a world that's highly uncertain?

Your efforts in forward planning can become pointless, especially if you fear that the plan may be overwhelmed by unanticipated events and developments. Uncertainty is, indeed, a major problem in forward planning. However, the greater the uncertainty, the greater the need is for good strategic planning because you want to try to be ready for the unknown. Chapter 15 helps you deal with your uncertainty in strategic planning.

### How can we be confident that our planning will be successful?

Even in the presence of a structured strategic planning process, formulating unsound, inappropriate strategies and/or failing at implementation is quite possible. But this book helps you avoid these many pitfalls. Flip to Chapter 15 to discover how to move from uncertainty to certainty in your planning. Strategic planning is worth the effort because it helps you run your organization better. You can be confident that the information and best practices outlined in this book result in a successful strategic planning process. I promise!

### What is strategic thinking?

Strategic thinking means asking yourself, "Are we doing the right thing?" It requires three major components:

- Purpose or end vision
- Understanding the environment, particularly of the competition affecting and/or blocking achievement of these ends
- Creativity in developing effective responses to the competitive forces

# Identifying the Levels of Strategic Management

After you've decided that strategic management is the right tool for your organization, clarifying what you intend to achieve with the outcome of the planning process is critical to a successful process. Strategic planning means different things to different people, so agreement is critical to reaching the desired end state. Here are four different levels of strategic management, each building on the previous one:

- ✔ **Level 1 — Articulated Plan:** The plan has established the mission, vision, goals, actions, and key performance indicators (KPIs) for the next 24 to 36 months.

- ✔ **Level 2 — Strategic Differentiation:** The plan has a strategic focus on delivering a unique value proposition developed from a clear understanding of market position and customer needs.

- ✔ **Level 3 — Organizational Engagement:** Everyone knows the strategic direction, understands his role, and commits to accountability. An execution/governance process is in place.

- ✔ **Level 4 — Organizational Transformation:** High-performing team, driven by shared values, consistently drives decision making based on the agreed-upon strategy with data, structure (organizational and process), and systems in place to support the activity.

As you're getting ready to embark on your strategic management process, pass these levels around to your management group. Gain consensus and agreement on which level your organization is working toward.

# Getting Acquainted with the Strategic Plan's Key Elements

A company's strategic plan is the game plan that management uses for positioning the company in its chosen market arena, competing successfully, satisfying customers, and achieving good business performance. Most business owners and executives have countless excuses for not having a formal strategic plan. I've heard everything from "We're too new" to "We're not big enough" to "We've never had one; why start now?"

If these excuses sound familiar, check this out: Studies indicate that roughly 90 percent of all businesses lack a strategic plan. Of those that have a plan, only 10 percent actually implements it. So if you're part of the 90 percent, ask yourself these questions:

✔ Can our company be more focused?

✔ Can we deliver more value?

✔ Can our employees be more efficient?

✔ Can our company be more successful?

I'm guessing that the majority of you answered *yes* to all the above (and that's okay). In the following sections, I help you understand how each part of a strategic plan can change how you answer the questions.

## Vision: Bringing things into focus

You get results from what you focus on. Everyone knows this fact, but most companies are busy tending to the urgent problems of the day and not focusing on key long-term issues. Unless your staff can focus on a common vision, the company can't go anywhere. A strategic plan helps direct energy and guide staff toward a shared goal in an ever-changing world.

Orit Gadiesh, chairman of Bain & Company, says, "In the current environment, companies can't afford *not* to have a set of guiding principles — a vision that communicates *true north* to the entire organization." Can your company be more focused? Yes, and to help find your true north, check out Chapter 6.

## Strategy: Explaining the value you deliver

A strategy provides the vehicle and answers the question, "How do we provide value to our customers better than our competitors?" A good strategy focuses on efficiency through the following:

✔ Achieving performance targets

✔ Outperforming your competition

✔ Achieving sustainable competitive advantage

✔ Growing your revenue and maintaining or shrinking your expenses

✔ Satisfying customers

✔ Responding to changing market conditions

Basically, strategies keep your whole company acting together while strengthening the company's long-term competitive position in the marketplace. See Chapters 8 and 9 for creating more value for your customers.

## Goals and objectives: Empowering employees

Goals and objectives make up the road map that empowers your employees to be more effective (and you, too, for that matter). Don't let these elements be just a paragraph on the break room wall or bullet points in a memo; let them shine as primary guidelines for leading the organization to higher levels of performance. Goals and objectives provide the framework for independent decisions and actions initiated by departments, managers, and employees into a coordinated, company-wide game plan. Head to Chapter 12 to develop your goals and objectives road map.

## Execution and evaluation: Ensuring success

A strategic plan is a living, dynamic document. It drives your business and must be integrated into every fiber of your organization so every employee helps move the company in the same direction.

All the best missions and strategies in the world are a waste of time if they aren't implemented. To be truly successful, the plan can't gather dust on the bookshelf. You know what shelf I'm talking about. If you ran a white glove over the shelf, you'd find layer upon layer of dust. You really should clean more often.

Okay, so, no, strategic planning success isn't about cleaning; it's about keeping the plan active so it doesn't gather that proverbial dust. Know what your end result looks like and where your milestones should be. Plan your near term actions and evaluate your progress each quarter. Are you where you thought you'd be if you'd been on target? Or, if you're off target, how far are you off? The course correction to put you back on track becomes your next action plan.

When your company has a clear plan and acts accordingly to the plan, you're going to go from where you are to where you want to go, ensuring your success. Check out Chapter 14 for more on this topic.

# Seeing the Signs: Why You Need This Book

Planning for the future is important, but very few businesses actually do it. Instead of listing the benefits of business planning and strategic planning (see Chapter 2 for those), I opted to include some warning signs that tell you whether you need a new strategy for your strategic planning process. So if any of the following statements apply to you, you need this book.

- ✔ Someone asks where your business will be in one year, and you don't have an answer. You ask your partners or management team the same question, and you hear wildly different answers.

- ✔ You have some idea where you want to go in the next year, but you don't have any idea what you're going to do to make next year a reality.

- ✔ Your company won't hit its revenue goals this year. Although many reasons may exist for the shortfall, you're not sure how to grow the top line.

- ✔ Your brochure, website, sales collateral, and so on have inconsistencies. You can't understand the content. More importantly, neither can anyone else. You find that when you explain your business to a potential client, you tell different stories about how you provide value.

- ✔ You're ignoring your competition. You don't know who your number-one competitor is and what it's doing, who its clients are, what products it offers, what its pricing is, or what its key message points are. When your customers ask you to explain why your company is different, you don't have a good response.

- ✔ Everything on your to-do list is a priority. You don't know where your time is best spent.

- ✔ Friends and colleagues can't refer you because they aren't sure exactly what value your business provides and to whom. They often ask, "What is it you do again?"

- ✔ You're presented with a business opportunity and are unsure how to evaluate whether it's something your company should pursue. In fact, you normally pursue all opportunities for fear you may miss the big one.

- ✔ You enjoy what you do, but you aren't passionate about your business. You'd quit everything and follow that passion tomorrow if you could.

- ✔ Your business development consists largely of attending networking events, but you spend most of your time talking to people you know. You rely solely on word-of-mouth for new customers.

- ✔ You don't know why your customers buy from you. The majority continues to do business with your company, but you're not sure what keeps them coming back. You've never really asked.

- ✔ You find your clients contracting with other companies for services you provide. When asked, they say they didn't know you offered those services.

- ✔ You ask your employees what success looks like, and they don't have a consistent answer. And your incentive plan doesn't sync up with performance expectations.

- ✔ You complain when your customers call because you just don't have time to talk to them. You notice your staff complaining, too.

✔ You don't do market research or solicit customer feedback because you (think you) know your market. You've been in the industry for years and you (think you) know customers' need and wants.

✔ You determine your pricing by looking at your competitor's prices and discounting slightly. All your prices are based on your competitors' offerings.

✔ You can't articulate what your company does best but find that it's a good point of discussion at a cocktail party.

✔ You're asked why you're in business, and your only response is *profit*.

Do any of these statements sound familiar? If so, it's time to get serious about your business and get focused. Having a strategic plan and a succinct strategy that brings clarity and focus to your organization ensures that your time, resources, and actions aren't wasted. If every part of your organization isn't pointed in the same direction, you can end up going in circles and frustrating yourself and your employees. Why not get strategic now and make it your most successful year ever!

# Chapter 2

# Why Strategic Planning Works

*In This Chapter*

▶ Discovering why strategic planning is a leading management tool

▶ Avoiding failures by making plans

▶ Leading by example with good strategic goals

▶ Achieving better results with your strategic plan

*S*uccess isn't a matter of chance but rather a matter of choice. This concept really encapsulates why having a clear strategic direction and strategic plan with a focused implementation process in place is important. Business success isn't going to happen by accident. You must look into the future and create a plan for wherever you're trying to go. Forget about failure rates and all that garbage. If you aren't intentional about the direction of your business or department, you aren't likely to get there.

This chapter provides several reasons why you should care about strategic planning. If you or your boss need convincing, I cover the statistics as well as the intangibles in the sections that follow. A peek at what high-growth organizations are doing can show you how planning impacts your growth.

# Strategic Planning Is Most Used Tool by Executives

During the past dozen years or so, you may have witnessed an explosion in the use of management tools and techniques — everything from Six Sigma to benchmarking. Keeping up with the latest and greatest, as well as deciding which tools to put to work, are key parts of every leader's job. But picking the winners from the losers is tough. As new tools appear every year, others seem to drop off the radar. Unfortunately, there's no *Consumer Reports* for management tools, so choosing and using tools can become a risky and potentially expensive gamble, leaving many leaders stymied.

In 1993, Bain & Company, a leading management consulting company, launched a multi-year research project to get the facts about management tools and trends. The objective of the study was to provide managers with information to identify and integrate tools that improve bottom-line results as well as understand their strategic challenges and priorities.

Bain assembled a database that now includes nearly 10,000 businesses from more than 70 countries in North America, Europe, Asia, Africa, the Middle East, and Latin America. The *Bain & Company's 2011 Management Tools* survey received responses from a broad range of international executives. To qualify for inclusion in the study, a tool had to be relevant to senior management, topical as evidenced by coverage in the business press, and measurable.

The results? Out of all the tools included in the survey, 65 percent of respondents used strategic planning. But despite dropping to second place behind the practice of benchmarking, strategic planning is still a long-time favorite tool, having been used by more than half of the companies in every survey since Bain started this project. Not surprisingly, the most popular tools are the ones that create the highest satisfaction ratings. Respondents were most satisfied with strategic planning out of all 25 tools. See Figure 2-1 for details.

| | USAGE | SATISFACTION |
|---|---|---|
| Benchmarking | 67% | 3.86 |
| **Strategic Planning** | **65%** | **4.07** |
| Mission and Vision Statements | 63% | 3.99 |
| Customer Relationship Management | 58% | 3.92 |
| Outsourcing | 55% | 3.70 |
| Balanced Scorecard | 47% | 3.90 |
| Core Competencies | 46% | 3.88 |
| Change Management Programs | 46% | 3.80 |
| Strategic Alliances | 45% | 3.94 |
| Customer Segmentation | 42% | 3.95 |
| Supply Chain Management | 39% | 3.89 |
| Knowledge Management | 38% | 3.76 |
| Total Quality Management | 38% | 3.97 |
| Business Process Reengineering | 38% | 3.85 |
| Mergers and Acquisitions | 35% | 3.88 |
| Satisfaction and Loyalty Management | 32% | 3.91 |
| Enterprise Risk Management | 30% | 3.87 |
| Scenario and Contingency Planning | 30% | 3.82 |
| Social Media Programs | 29% | 3.73 |
| Shared Service Centers | 28% | 3.77 |
| Downsizing | 25% | 3.52 |
| Open Innovation | 21% | 3.84 |
| Price Optimization Models | 21% | 3.86 |
| Decision Rights Tools | 17% | 3.86 |
| Rapid Prototyping | 11% | 3.86 |

**Figure 2-1:**
Most widely used management tools.

So what does this study tell us? Strategic planning is used by companies worldwide with very high satisfaction rates. Strategic planning is consistently rated the number-one or -two management tool year after year. Strategic planning isn't just a management fad likely to blow away, but it will guide you as you run our organization day after day. Importantly, here are a few key insights from the study that are good to remember as you move to using strategic planning:

- ✔ Management tools are much more effective when they're part of a major organizational effort and are consistent over time.

- ✔ Managers who switch from tool to tool undermine employees' confidence. Decision makers achieve better results by championing realistic strategies and viewing tools simply as a means to achieving a strategic goal.

- ✔ No tool is a cure-all. As you can see from the variety of tools listed, not just one is a silver bullet, but rather a combination of the right tools yields the best result.

For more information on this study, check out `www.bain.com/management_tools/home.asp`.

# Not Having a Plan Is Too Risky

If organizations fail to anticipate or prepare for fundamental changes, they may lose valuable lead time and momentum to combat them when they do occur. These fundamental elements of business are customer expectations, employee morale, regulatory requirements, competitive pressures, and economic changes, and they're always in flux. Many times businesses achieve a level of success and then stall. Strategic planning helps you avoid the stall and get off the plateau you find yourself on.

Accidental success is dangerous. Succeeding without a plan is possible, and plenty of examples exist of businesses that have achieved financial success without a plan. If you're one of them, consider yourself lucky, but ask this question: "Could we have grown and become even more successful if we'd organized a little better?" I'm willing to bet your answer is yes.

Another danger is that the lack of a strategic plan negatively impacts the attitude of an organization's team. Employees who see aimlessness within an organization have no sense of a greater purpose. People need a reason to come to work everyday (besides the paycheck). Lack of direction results in morale problems because, as far as your employees are concerned, the future is uncertain, unpredictable, and out of control. These depressing conclusions can only be seen as a threat to employment, which negatively impacts productivity.

To avoid these dangers, you need to get rid of the naysayers (including possibly yourself). Questioning the value of strategic planning is normal because planning can be intense and costly, but if the attitude that planning isn't necessary becomes part of your corporate culture, it can prove deadly. So look out for the warning signs of indifference:

✔ Leadership indifference

✔ Confusion among the employees

✔ Complacency of stakeholders

✔ Short-term thinking

✔ Lack of unity

✔ Deeply entrenched traditional perspectives

In the rest of the chapter, you discover why strategic planning can help you navigate troubled waters. If you don't have the problems in the preceding list in your organization but need more proof or ammunition to get those around you to see the benefits of planning, you can find the backup you need in the next sections.

# A Plan Is Required to be a High Performer

High-performance organizations have fundamental differences that set them apart from other organizations. Anecdotally, these companies are better than their competitors at everything they do. They work more diligently and incessantly to improve faster than their competitors.

Tons of studies out there dig in to the hows and whys of companies that are ahead of the pack. But instead of getting lost in the details and differences of these studies, take a look at the basics, which I cover in the following sections.

At the end of the day, high-performance organizations accomplish extraordinary results, and they do it with ordinary people. If you keep waiting for extraordinary people to come along and make things happen, you're going to wait a long time. Instead, your goal should be to transform your organization in such a way that your people are capable of delivering high performance every minute and every hour of every day.

## What makes great companies great

Becoming the best at something is often achieved by modeling the behaviors of winners and putting those behaviors into practice. Here are the characteristics of a high-performance company:

✔ Has a purpose that focuses the energy of all its members (typically, that purpose is to be the best there is or ever was)

✔ Simultaneously and continuously maximizes the self-interests of all
   its stakeholders

✔ Outperforms all others (by any measure) not because of what propels
   it but in spite of any and all obstacles that impede it

✔ Makes it possible for ordinary people to perform in an extraordinary
   fashion

✔ Transforms its people into owners of the organization's destiny

✔ Is a healthy organization committed to being great, no matter what it takes

✔ Knows that the execution is more important than the strategy

Whereas a strategic plan is the means, growth and high-performance are the
ends to those means.

An example of a high-performance company is a mid-sized graphics and print
shop in Georgia, which was recognized as one of the best in the industry.
The owner attributes the company's success to the employees' dedication
to the mission, which includes total focus on customer solutions. According
to the owner, the employees practice the mission, not just preach it. To support that action, the company enables all employees to be responsible and
accountable for serving its customers. Not to mention that the employees are
proud of their work and take rightful ownership of their accomplishments. To
that point, they perform extraordinary work.

# What successful CEOs are spending their time on

Have you ever wondered what the guy next door is doing all day? Or, more inter-
estingly, what are the CEOs of growing organizations spending their time on? If
you could just be a fly on the wall in the offices of some of the Inc. 500 CEOs, I bet
you'd discover quite a bit about what it takes to grow an organization.

The Inc. 500, produced annually by *Inc. Magazine,* comprises the top CEOs
of the business world. To be eligible for Inc. 500, companies have to be independent and privately held, have grown from at least $100,000 in net sales in
Year One to $2 million by Year Four. In summary, they're the fastest growing
privately-held organizations in the United States today. The majority of the
Inc. 500 CEOs spend an average of 60 hours a week building their business.
(Knowing this should be a relief to you if you're putting in such long hours
and often think you're all alone.)

Although these CEOs are characterized as hardworking, they're not workaholics, because they set goals first and take action second. Most importantly, they
take the time to reward themselves and others based on the achievement of
the goals and action. Workaholics, on the other hand, usually take action first,

set goals second, and don't necessarily celebrate successes. If you're one of those workaholics out there, consider the strategic planning process as a way to help you set goals and focus on actions you can celebrate.

The Inc. 500 CEOs regularly spend 50 to 90 percent of their time on strategy and business development. Obviously, an organization isn't going to be a high-growth organization if time isn't spent on both active strategy and business development. Granted, 50 to 90 percent is quite a large margin, but it gives you an idea of how these Inc. 500 CEOs spend their time. Take a look at how you're spending your time each day, and figure out what it really takes to be part of a high-growth company.

# Everyday Decisions Drive Long-Term Results

Everyone wants better results, right? Those results may be to earn more money, to use resources better, to create a more effective and efficient team, to improve your work and life balance, to achieve sustainability, and so on. And strategic planning helps. As I discuss in the following sections, the benefits to strategic planning are intangible and show hard bottom-line return on investment (ROI).

## The day-to-day impact

Every day your work impacts aspects of your business. Following these tips can help you realize the true day-to-day impact of having a strategic plan in place:

- ✔ **Spend more time on high impact, high-growth activities.** These activities are where you want to spend as much time as possible. With these maneuvers, you spend less time spinning your wheels.

  Think back on the past month: Were there any projects or activities you were part of directly or indirectly that didn't actually move the organization forward because they were dead-end opportunities? I bet there were. Get rid of this dead weight as fast as possible!

- ✔ **Identify true opportunities versus false starts.** If you know what you're best at and where you want to go, you can more quickly identify true opportunities. Strategic planning helps you put the boundaries on your business. When you ignore extraneous distractions, you use your resources more effectively and more quickly to grow your organization.

- ✔ **Be proactive instead of reactive.** Being in a reactionary mode all the time puts you one (or more) step behind your competition. Make sure that your strategic plan maps out proactive choices to propel your company forward. But be sure to react to customers when they provide feedback or comments that aren't in sync with your way of business.

A complaint that I hear from a lot of clients is that they feel like they're always trying to catch up. If you're out of breath, stop running and get ahead of the change curve. If you have a strategic plan in place and you're working on key strategic activities, you have a little more time to think about how to take advantage of market movement instead of always reacting to what's going on in your environment. Internal advancement, such as in your career as a leader, can come from being involved in strategy development and using it as a true guide to your work.

✔ **Achieve your vision for success.** You started your organization for a reason. You likely have a vision for your business. If you want to achieve your vision for success, you have to specifically figure out how you're going to get there. Having a strategic plan makes success intentional.

✔ **Increase employee commitment.** Strategic planning increases employee commitment — especially in this tight labor market. Helping your employees see the vision that you have for success and growth helps you work toward that goal.

## The bottom-line impact

As business owners, you care about what falls to the bottom line, and so do I. A major reason my company focuses on strategic planning is because it does make a financial difference. To verify this, in 2004, we conducted a research study of strategic planning and strategy execution of 280 firms in the U.S. The following list provides the results of that study and explains what you can expect to achieve as well. (*Note:* To the reader who needs talking points to convince his or her management that strategic planning is profitable, this section is for you.)

✔ **Impact on sales volume:**

- Of those firms whose top management had a high commitment to execute strategic planning, 80 percent reported that their sales volume increased during that year.

- Of the firms whose top management had a lower commitment (average or below) to execute strategic planning, only 59 percent reported that their sales volume had increased during the year.

- From another perspective, firms whose top management had a high commitment reported 12 percent greater increase in sales volume than did those with a lower commitment.

✔ **Impact on net income:**

- Of the firms whose top management had a high commitment to execute strategic planning, 33 percent reported that their net income had increased during the year.

- Of those whose top management had a lower commitment (average or below) to execute strategic planning, only 19 percent reported that their net income had increased during the year.

- From another perspective, firms whose top management had a high commitment reported 11 percent better net income than did those with a lower commitment.

✓ **The role of being proactive:**

- Of the organizations whose top management was proactive, 78 percent reported that their sales volume had increased during the year.

- By contrast of those who were more reactive, only 60 percent reported that their sales volume had increased during the year.

If you compare these stats to the Inc. 500 growth organizations (covered in the "What successful CEOs are spending their time on" section earlier in this chapter), you notice that these figures aren't actually that high. Many of the Inc. 500 companies realized 100 to 200 percent growth over five years. However, the percentage increases are *in addition to* the growth you're already projecting. Therefore, strategic planning helps you either make up part of your growth expectations or is an addition to your projections.

# *Agility Is a New Competitive Advantage*

Is being agile on your list of competitive advantages? Can your business react and change its game plan based on either customer feedback or shifts in market, all while keeping that end vision in focus? A successful business has the ability to assess any given situation and decide how to proceed based on the findings.

The ability to adapt quickly is the name of the game in today's business climate. When everyone on your team is on the same page and is pulling in the same direction, you can easily absorb shifts, make changes, and innovate on the fly. If you don't have a clear direction in your strategic plan, your team may not know how and what to adapt to.

We've all been around long enough to know that markets shift and things don't always stay the same. A business leader's responsibility is to anticipate change. So as you work through your strategic management process, take note. Although you're preparing a five-year plan, remember that you'll need to change things up a bit as you travel down that road to success. You'll likely come across a lot of forks in the road, and you'll be a more sustainable organization if you're better equipped to take the necessary turns to get to Point B. Keep this point in mind: Good businesses don't change strategies every month; they change the tactics to execute a strategy.

Many firms underestimate the buy-in needed to make change happen. Change initiatives need approximately 75 percent of recognizable support from key leaders and managers. If at least a majority of the staff and stakeholders are on board with the strategic management process, then getting everyone else on the same page when the tactics to get to your vision need to shift will be much easier. Identifying what will change, what will stay the same, and why the change is important helps this process along and helps alleviate any fears your staff may have of what may happen as a result of the change.

# Everyone Is Part of Something Bigger

Gallup conducted a study of more than 80,000 managers in 400 companies to determine the most successful managerial behaviors. From that study, they drilled in on 12 key focus areas or traits that best correlate with business success, including the following:

- ✔ Aligning each employee with the mission
- ✔ Letting employees know what's expected
- ✔ Tapping in to the talents of employees
- ✔ Talking with employees about their progress

The process of strategic planning achieves the outcome of *aligning each employee with the organization's mission.* Although this study reinforces common sense, remember that everyone wants to be able to make a difference and have an impact every day.

To keep a good employee base, consider the following:

- ✔ Help the people in your organization understand how their day-to-day work impacts the larger mission of the company through a variety of ways, from engaging different groups in the planning process to linking performance to the broader mission. See Chapter 7 for more ideas.
- ✔ Provide your employees with the support they need, such as timely communication and the best tools and work environment, to do their jobs. Doing so goes a long way.
- ✔ Be sure to link your employee training programs to your overall strategy. Then everyone can be part of the process of helping the company succeed.
- ✔ Find the right skill sets for the job. We all know that a square peg never fits into a round hole.
- ✔ Appreciate your staff and, by all means, challenge them. Then be sure to fairly reward them, and they'll be more likely to stick around. Rewards are often monetary, but they can also be non-monetary, such as providing teams more autonomy or freedom to work differently.

As you're going through your strategic management process, remember these ways to be proactive in order to navigate through all the competition and achieve sustainability.

# Tribal Knowledge Is Passed on to the Next Generation

You don't need to predict the future but do plan for it and lay a roadway to get there. An organization that plans thoroughly has overall succession planning built in as part of its planning process, or as an outcome of the process. According to FranklinCovey's "The Greatness Challenge" campaign, by 2018, 60 percent of experienced U.S. leaders will leave the workforce. Because of this, succession planning is often one of the top strategic initiatives in organizations today. Although positional succession planning is also important, corporate succession planning comes in the forms of a plan and a planning process that transfers tribal knowledge and decision making to the next level of leaders. Bundled in that idea is the importance most all employees put on wanting to advance to the next level and gain more authority and responsibility.

So strategic planning not only sets the corporate direction but also functions as real-time succession planning throughout the organization.

# You Can Clearly Explain (and Remember) Your Strategy

Let's face it: The clock is moving faster than ever (or so it seems). If you want to catch a potential customer's attention and keep your employees motivated to come to work every day, be ready to know your strategy. In summary, a strategy

- Establishes unique value proposition compared to your competitors
- Is executed through operations that provide different and tailored value to customers
- Identifies clear tradeoffs and clarifies what *not* to do
- Focuses on activities that fit together and reinforce each other
- Drives continual improvement within the organization and moves it toward its vision

Consider the following example that Harvard Business School professors David Collis and Michael Rukstad developed to clearly state Edward Jones's strategy: "To grow to 17,000 financial advisors by 2012 by offering trusted and convenient face-to-face financial advice to conservative individual investors who delegate their financial decisions through a national network of one-on-one financial adviser offices."

By crystallizing your strategy, you're better able to be succinct when talking to your employees and customers about your company. And doing so helps you look better than the competition in their eyes. Being precise and having a flow to your strategic planning process helps you stand out from the crowd when giving that pitch. But remember, standing out from the crowd takes going through the strategic management process, which facilitates making hard choices about your future direction.

# A Strategic Plan Eliminates Wasted Time and Money

Stop for a moment and reflect on the hundreds of meetings and projects you and your team worked on over the past three months. How many of those instances weren't directly tied to a strategic initiative? Or better yet, what percentage of your team's time was spent working on something that turned out to be a dead end or yet another rabbit trail? Don't misunderstand me, taking risks means risking failures. However, a good strategic plan helps reduce the potential for false starts. Ideally, you want to align your human and financial resources as closely as possible with your strategic direction to eliminate wasted time and money.

A FranklinCovey study evaluated the characteristics of 52,000 managers across hundreds of organizations. More than 400,000 of the managers' associates were asked to rank the managers. The areas where managers scored the lowest included:

- ✔ Prioritizing work so time is spent on the most important strategic issues
- ✔ Providing clear expectations with employees that align to the strategy
- ✔ Wasting an inordinate amount of time because of poor strategic planning

As your organization is getting prepared to invest in strategic planning, consider that strategic planning eliminates wasted time and money, along with the eight other reasons discussed in this chapter. Ultimately, strategic planning yields organizations a multitude of tangible and intangible benefits when done correctly and for the right reasons. Keep all these reasons in mind as loose outcomes for your process.

# Chapter 3

# Getting Set Up for Successful Planning

## In This Chapter

▶ Understanding the elements of a strategic plan

▶ Going through the strategic planning process

▶ Picking a team to plan with

▶ Calling in help: Choosing a facilitator

▶ Ensuring a smooth planning process

**S**trategic planning can seem just as confusing as accounting, where debits and credits are exactly the opposite of their definitions. (Forgive me if you're a CPA.) Strategic planning doesn't need to be counterintuitive. And understanding how all the parts of a plan work together makes it less confusing.

Planning doesn't have a set rule book, so no common language exists. People refer to objectives as goals and to goals as objectives. Mission gets confused with vision, and no one seems to know where strategies actually fit in. Then you have indicators, measures, metrics, targets . . .

This chapter (or book for that matter) won't stop the debate between semantic differences. But in this chapter, you do look at the elements of the strategic management process and what it involves, assess whether you're ready to begin, determine what the best practices for executing your plan are, and discover how to spot the pitfalls inherent in the process.

# *Previewing the Elements of a Strategic Plan*

Not to oversimplify the planning process, but by dividing a strategic plan into four areas, you can clearly see how the pieces fit together. The four pieces of the puzzle are found in these questions:

✔ Where are we now?

✔ Where are we going?

✔ How will we get there?

✔ How will we measure our progress?

Each area has certain elements to show you how and where things fit. I introduce the elements in the following sections. For a bird's-eye view of this discussion, see Figure 3-1.

**Figure 3-1:** The elements of a strategic plan.

**HOW** ARE WE GOING TO GET THERE?

Strategic Objectives/Priorities

Goals

Action Items

**WHERE ARE WE NOW?**

Strategic Review

Mission

Values

Competitive Advantage

Org-Wide Strategies

**WHERE** ARE WE GOING?

Vision

**HOW** WILL WE MEASURE OUR PROGRESS?

Scorecard/Key Performance Indicators

What matters most is having a strategy and, therefore, an effective strategic plan. An effective plan and execution process require the following attributes:

✔ **Purpose-driven:** A plan based on a mission and a real, true competitive advantage is key. Without it, what's the point of the plan or the organization?

✔ **Integrated:** Each element supports the next. No objectives are disconnected from goals, and no strategies sit all alone.

- ✔ **Systematic:** Don't think of the plan as one big document. Instead, give it life by breaking it into executable parts.

- ✔ **Dynamic:** The plan isn't a static document but a living one.

- ✔ **Holistic:** All areas of the organization are included. Don't plan based on departments first because you risk limiting your thinking. Plan by thinking about the organization as a whole entity and then implement on a department-by-department basis.

- ✔ **Understandable:** Everyone gets it. If anyone, from the top of the organization to the bottom, doesn't understand the plan or how he or she fits in, it won't work.

- ✔ **Realistic:** You can implement the plan. Don't over plan. Make sure you have the resources to support the goals you decide to focus on.

## Where are we now?

As you think about where your organization is now, you want to look at your foundational elements (mission and value) to make sure that nothing has changed. More than likely, you won't revise these two areas very often. Then, you want to look at your current or strategic position, which is where you look at what's happening internally and externally to determine how you need to shift and change. Here are your foundational elements:

- ✔ **Mission statement:** The mission describes your organization's purpose — the purpose for which you were founded and why you exist. Some mission statements include the business of the organization. Others explain what products or services the organization produces or customers it serves.

    Does your mission statement say what you do? Why does your organization exist? See Chapter 6 for more information about creating your mission.

- ✔ **Values statement and/or guiding principles:** This statement clarifies what you stand for and believe in. Values guide the organization in its daily business with its employees, customers, partners, and community.

    What are the core values and beliefs of your company? What values and beliefs guide your daily interactions? What are you and your people really committed to? See Chapter 6 for a detailed discussion of values and principles.

- ✔ **SWOT:** *SWOT* is an acronym that stands for *strengths, weaknesses, opportunities,* and *threats.* These elements are crucial in assessing your strategic position with your organization. You want to build on your company's strengths, shore up the weaknesses, capitalize on the opportunities, and recognize the threats. (You may or may not choose to include your SWOT in your strategic plan but as supporting documentation.) See Chapters 7 through 10 for more on SWOT.

# Where are we going?

The elements of the question *where are we going?* help you answer other questions, such as these: What will my organization look like in the future? Where are we headed? What is the future I want to create for my company? Because the future is hard to predict, you can have fun imagining what it may look like. The following elements help you define the future for your business:

- ✔ **Sustainable competitive advantage:** Sustainable competitive advantage explains what you're best at compared to your competitors. Each company strives to create an advantage that continues to be competitive over time. What can you be best at? What makes you unique? What can your organization potentially do better than any other organization? See Chapter 5 for more on advantages.

- ✔ **Vision statement:** Your vision is formulating a picture of what your organization's future makeup will be and where the organization is headed. What will your organization look like 5 to 10 years from now? See Chapter 6 for more on refining your vision.

# How will we get there?

Knowing how you'll reach your vision is the meat of your strategic plan, but it's also the most time-consuming. The reason your vision takes so much time to develop is because you have a number of routes from your current position to your vision. Picking the right one determines how quickly or slowly you get to your final destination.

The parts of your plan that lay out your road map are as follows:

- ✔ **Long-term strategic objectives:** Strategic objectives are long-term, continuous strategic areas that help you connect your mission to your vision. Holistic objectives encompass four areas: financial, customer, operational, and people. What are the key activities that you need to perform in order to achieve your vision? See Chapter 12 for more info.

- ✔ **Strategy:** Strategy establishes a way to match your organization's strengths with market opportunities so your organization comes to mind when your customer has a need. This section explains *how* you travel to your final destination. Does your strategy match your strengths in a way that provides value to your customers? Does it build an organizational reputation and recognizable industry position? See Chapter 11 for info on different strategies.

✔ **Short-term goals/priorities/initiatives:** Short-term goals convert your strategic objectives into specific performance targets. You can use goals, priorities, or initiatives interchangeably. In this book, I use goals to define short-term action. Effective goals clearly state what you want to accomplish, when you want to accomplish it, how you're going to do it, and who's going to be responsible. Each goal should be specific and measurable. What are the one- to three-year goals you're trying to achieve to reach your vision? What are your specific, measurable, and realistic targets of accomplishment? See Chapter 12 for more on goal setting.

✔ **Action items:** Action items are plans that set specific actions that lead to implementing your goals. They include start and end dates and appointing a person responsible. Are your action items comprehensive enough to achieve your goals? Head to Chapter 13 for a discussion on action items.

✔ **Execution:** In executing the plan, identify issues that surround who manages and monitors the plan and how the plan is communicated and supported. How committed are you to implementing the plan to move your organization forward? Will you commit money, resources, and time to support the plan? See Chapter 14 to put your plan to work.

## How will we measure our progress?

You have your vision in sight and now you're heading down the road toward it. How will you know whether you're hitting those mile markers or whether you've steered off course? Every plan needs some check in from time to time.

Some important progress measures include:

✔ **Scorecard:** A scorecard measures and manages your strategic plan. What are the *key performance indicators,* or *KPIs,* you need to track to monitor whether you're achieving your mission? Pick five to ten goal-related measures you can use to track the progress of your plan and plug them into your scorecard. For help with using scorecards to measure your progress, head to Chapter 14.

✔ **Monthly/Quarterly Business Reviews (M/QBR):** A group check in from time to time allows all team members a chance to report on the status of their action items and make adjustments to their goals if deemed necessary.

✔ **Financial assessment:** A financial assessment helps you determine whether your strategic plan makes financial sense. Do the estimated revenue projections exceed your estimated expenses?

# Before You Begin: Assessing Your Planning Readiness

If you're embarking on this strategic planning journey for the first time, assessing whether you're ready before you start is wise. Successful strategic planning and implementation require a keen understanding of how well your organization can adapt to this new process. Introducing it at the right time is key to successful adoption.

## Are we ready?

This point in your planning is where being brutally honest with yourself is critical. Companies that jump in to planning because they assume they're ready will likely fail somewhere mid-plan and derail the whole process.

You can avoid getting in over your head by honestly answering the questions in the Readiness Assessment on the CD. Review these key areas to assess your readiness.

Ideally, you want to answer all the questions with a *yes.* But that may not be possible. In my opinion, having a *burning platform,* or a reason, to get strategic is important. Typical reasons include wanting to grow, trying to manage uncontrolled growth, or addressing the need for cost containment. If your organization doesn't have a reason to plan, strategic planning isn't going to be very effective. At the end of the assessment, decide whether strategic planning is a go or no-go. If your decision is a no-go, make a quick action plan to solve the problem where you determined your company isn't ready. If your decision is a go, you can feel confident that your organization can move through the planning process, barring any unforeseen circumstances that may pop up.

## Is the climate right?

Strategic planning is doomed to failure when certain circumstances aren't in place. If you're aware of what you need to make the process work well, you're more likely to be successful. If you're in the middle of a planning process, review the following list to make sure you have a climate for planning. Go down the list and check off any items that are true for your group. When you can check them all off, you know you have a climate that's right for planning.

- ✔ No high-impact decisions in the next six months (mergers, management changes, and so on)
- ✔ No serious conflict between key players

✔ Top-level commitment to process

✔ Staff understands the purpose of planning

✔ Adequate resources (staff time and money)

✔ Organization has been around for at least a few years

✔ Commitment to implement key strategies

✔ Successful outcome of the process identified

✔ An organizational climate that inspires forward thinking and rewards creativity

✔ Agree on common language and time frame

# Taking a Look at the Strategic Planning Process and Time Frame

In order to put a plan together that gets you from Point A to Point B effectively and efficiently, you need a system in place to help you achieve the end result. This process is continuous and cyclical, and in a disciplined mode, it requires a focus and pattern to stay on track and be productive while enjoying the journey along the way and learning from it. Having a good strategy dictates how you travel the road you've selected, and effective execution makes sure that you're checking in along the way. Planners take a critical, unbiased look at what has worked before and what hasn't. Gather info from any past planning experiences and use this section to help you run a smooth planning process.

No two companies are alike, and no two strategic planning processes are the same. In this section, you find the six phases necessary to create and execute a successful strategic plan. On average, this process can take between three and four months. However, you may decide to fast-track your process or slow it down. Move at a pace that works best for you and your team and leverage this process as a resource. No matter how it works for your company, remember that the process is continuous, not linear (see Figure 3-2).

**Figure 3-2:**
The strategic planning process is a continuous process.

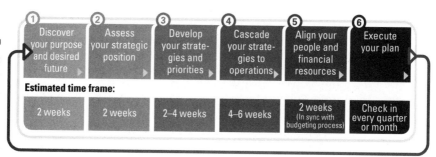

| ① Discover your purpose and desired future | ② Assess your strategic position | ③ Develop your strategies and priorities | ④ Cascade your strategies to operations | ⑤ Align your people and financial resources | ⑥ Execute your plan |
|---|---|---|---|---|---|
| **Estimated time frame:** | | | | | |
| 2 weeks | 2 weeks | 2–4 weeks | 4–6 weeks | 2 weeks (In sync with budgeting process) | Check in every quarter or month |

The following sections provide an overview of the strategic management process to get you started.

# Phase 1: Determining your core purpose and envisioned future

A mission, vision, and values can sound abstract, esoteric, and downright fluffy to a lot of people. However, they're important to building a strong foundation of consensus for your organization. Take the time to articulate these elements on the front end so you have a crystal clear strategic direction, and you'll be more successful when writing goals and objectives.

To efficiently move through this phase, don't confuse mission and vision. *Mission* is a statement about your core purpose (why you exist) and is best stated in the present tense. *Vision* is a statement about your desired state (where you want to go) and is best stated in the future tense. Although you may find values interspersed throughout both your mission and vision, an effective *values statement* clearly delineates the guiding principles of your organization (how you want your staff to behave and interact). Because these three statements are foundational to an effective plan, take the time you and your team need to get them right. However, don't get stuck on being a wordsmith and lose momentum in your planning process; rather focus on intent and allow the statements to be drafts until everyone is comfortable stamping them final.

The duration of this phase is estimated at two weeks. During this time, you answer these business questions:

- ✔ Who are we and why do we exist?
- ✔ Where are we going and why?
- ✔ What are the strategic topics and issues we need to address through this process?
- ✔ What is already determined that we need to build off of?

The chapters in Part II guide you through Phase 1.

# Phase 2: Assessing your strategic position

To assess your strategic position, take a look at the industry or market you're operating in. Also, look at your company culture — teamwork, leadership, climate for action, as well as your employees and their skills and capabilities. This culture is the scenery surrounding your organization. In this phase, you begin collecting and analyzing this information and data and use it to assess your strategic position.

Before you jump in to this phase, determine as a team how wide and how deep you want to go with collecting and analyzing information. A good rule is this: You need the right information and data, not too much or too little, to feel confident in making strategic choices and decisions. The methods to collect that information include conducting web research on macro, market, and industry trends; sending out customer and employee surveys; and acquiring information about your competitors through secret shopper, trade shows, or industry reports. Making sense of the data comes from synthesizing main themes into a SWOT, which is a handy 2-x-2 matrix of your strengths, weaknesses, opportunities, and threats. In Phase 3, you use your SWOT to make strategic decisions.

The duration of this phase is estimated at two to four weeks. During this time, you answer the following business questions:

✔ What are our strengths, weaknesses, opportunities, and threats?

✔ What is our position in the competitive landscape?

✔ What are the political, economic, social, and technical trends that may impact our organization?

Flip to Part III to dig in to this phase.

## Phase 3: Developing your strategies and priorities

In the previous two phases, you addressed where you are and where you're going. Now, you're going to focus on how you'll get there. Use your SWOT to stay grounded and realistic as you build a road map from where you are today to where you want to be. Ultimately, this SWOT and your competitive advantage will help you develop your organization-wide strategies, goals, and objectives. As you develop your strategy and set your goals, make strategic choices about what to do and what *not* to do. Remember that being strategic is about making those hard choices. A mark of a good strategic plan is one that's clear and focused (not too many goals and objectives) as well as balanced — telling a strategy story about how your entire organization is linked and aligned to drive key performance indicators.

Spend time uncovering your competitive advantages based on an understanding of your strategic position. Your competitive advantages are the essence of your strategic plan because strategy is about being different — deliberately choosing to perform activities differently or to perform different activities than competitors to deliver more value to your customers.

The duration of this phase is estimated at two weeks. During this time, you answer these business questions:

- ✔ What is our base for competing and delivering value?
- ✔ What are we best at? What makes us unique?
- ✔ What are the *big rocks* — strategic objectives — we need to reach our vision?
- ✔ What must we accomplish over the next one to three years to achieve our strategic objectives?
- ✔ What are we not going to do?

Chapters 11 and 12 take you through Phase 3.

## Phase 4: Cascading your strategies to operations

By the time organizations get to the point of cascading their strategy, many are tired and worn out from all the work leading up to it. But don't stop yet! Cascading action items and to-dos for each short-term goal is where the rubber meets the road — literally. Moving from big ideas to action happens when strategy is translated from the organizational level to the individual. This point is also when the planning circle widens, and departments and individual contributors join in and develop their short-term goals and actions to support the organizational direction.

Fundamentally, in Phase 4 you move from planning the strategy to planning the operations and from strategic planning to annual planning. That said, the only way to execute strategy is to align resources and actions from the bottom of the organization (individual team members) to the top (the CEO) to drive your vision.

The duration of this phase is estimated at four to six weeks. During this time, you answer the following business questions:

- ✔ How are we going to reach our vision at a functional level?
- ✔ Who must do what by when to accomplish and drive the organizational goals?

Use Chapter 13 to set up Phase 4 for your team and anyone else you're adding to the process.

# Phase 5: Aligning your people and financial resources

Now that you've established a clear direction and the road map to get there, your planning team is ready to align the strategy to resources. Specifically, in Phase 5, you align financial resources and people to the strategy. Accomplishing this task can be simple or complex, depending on how detailed your team wants to get. The simple approach is to review your goals and objectives and look for any areas where you need additional budget or people to successfully accomplish the activity. The more complex approach is to align each goal or objective to a budget line item and review your organizational structure for skill and capability gaps.

After you've completed your alignment, you're ready to roll out your plan to the whole organization.

The duration of this phase depends on your budgeting process. During this time, you answer these business questions:

- ✔ Do we have our resources aligned to our business objectives?
- ✔ Do we have the right people to execute the strategy?
- ✔ What are our communication methods, channels, and frequency?

Chapter 13 is your resource for this phase.

# Phase 6: Executing your plan

Executing your strategic plan is as important as — or even more important than — your strategy. The majority of organizations that have strategic plans fail to implement them (the most common reason being that resources aren't shared between departments). Don't be one of those organizations that spends hours preparing a strategic plan only to let it sit on a shelf. Guiding your work in this phase is a 12-month schedule that spells out the details necessary for a successful plan execution.

You remain in this phase of the strategic management process until you embark on the next formal planning sessions where you start back at Phase 1. Remember that successful execution of your plan relies on appointing a strategic plan manager, effectively driving accountability, and gaining organizational commitment to the process.

The duration of this phase lasts until you need to formally update your plan, starting again at Phase 1. During this time, you answer these business questions:

> ✔ What is on and off target — what do we need to adapt in our plan?
>
> ✔ What emerging strategic topics do we need to identify and solve?
>
> ✔ What can we do to be more effective as a team?

Check out Chapter 14 for all your Phase 6 resources.

Getting lost in the phases can happen before you know it. Use the Strategic Planning Process Checklist on the CD as your quick guide for each phase of the process. The checklist can help keep you and your team on track and ensure your plan is comprehensive and complete.

# Selecting Your Planning Team

The values and vision of your organization are embedded in the strategic framework. As a result, involving the whole organization in at least part of the planning process is vital. Although everyone can't be involved in every part of the process, each person plays a role. In the following sections, I give you some guidelines for the different people in your organization and who should be involved when.

## Getting everyone involved

Yes, you want everyone involved (at certain times). The next few sections show you how to include everyone in a way that isn't a recipe for disaster. As you begin your planning process, you first need to identify who will be on the planning team. From there, you can begin determining who will be department leads (if your organization structure calls for this level), and what team members to include.

### The role of the CEO

The CEO naturally assumes a prominent role on the planning team, setting the vision, driving that vision, and enforcing results. If strategic planning isn't the CEO's passion, it'll never happen. Only the CEO has the force to drastically change the company's alignment. However, during the strategy development part of the planning process, the CEO should remain in the background so other members' ideas can emerge.

You can't overemphasize the visibility of the CEO in the strategic management process. The CEO should attend as many planning sessions as possible, including the annual, quarterly, and monthly meetings.

### The planning team members

The planning team's ideal size is 9 to 15 members with an outside facilitator and an internal coordinator. Planning team members should represent different segments of the company — not just the top-level employees, such as the vice presidents, division and department heads, and other executive level managers who report to the CEO. A team consisting of operating, marketing, and sales personnel brings balance when it comes to considering internal and external needs.

Search out key players from your employees, board members, and top management who can help you strategize. Figure out how to get them involved. If some employees can't take part in person, share early drafts of the plan with them and get their feedback as the process continues. Make sure that you tap your big-picture thinkers as well as get a diverse set of perspectives.

### Everyone else, regardless of position

Employees who have a chance to contribute feel they're making a difference. Being part of the strategic management process is exciting, so make sure that everyone has this opportunity. Employees always have different perceptions from top management on how the business is run. You'll be amazed at the outstanding ideas that come from your employees. To help ensure planning success, the team must solicit its opinions in a confidential, risk-free atmosphere.

Try the following ideas to gather employee information:

- ✔ **Small group meetings:** If you have an open and honest company culture, small groups are a good way to get input from your staff. The benefit to bringing groups together is synergy that results from the discussions and brainstorms.

- ✔ **Anonymous surveys:** Anonymous online surveys allow every employee to voice his or her own opinion, without being influenced by others.

- ✔ **Assessments:** Numerous staff assessments are available that evaluate everything from satisfaction to specific actions and strategies. See Chapters 7, 8, and 9 for more on these tools.

### Non-employees

Consider the input of people who don't work for your company. These folks include customers and suppliers who frequently have unique insights into your business. Customers can identify problems the plan should address, and they may have ideas about how to improve overall effectiveness. Suppliers can offer alternatives to operational problems that hinder delivery of products or services to customers. Although gathering info from these non-employees may not feel comfortable, if you can make it happen, you'll find it very worthwhile.

### The strategic plan manager

The CEO must appoint a respected member of the staff to champion the strategic plan. The strategic plan manager's responsibility is to keep the process moving forward, monitor progress, and alert decision makers if the company strays off strategy or performance.

Although the strategic plan manager position may add responsibility to a staff member's current role, managing the strategic plan is critical to the organization's success, so appoint someone who's seeking additional responsibility and is looking to move up in the organization. This role is a fabulous leadership development opportunity.

## Determining who's involved when

The next question to ask is, "Who should be involved at what stage in the planning process?" Running a strategic planning process democratically isn't the best way to go. Set expectations before you jump in to the process so no one feels blind-sided or left out.

Figure 3-3 maps the different stages of the planning process to the different groups of people who should be involved. *Note:* Use this chart as a guide to develop your own planning team.

As you can see in Figure 3-3, the CEO and strategic plan manager are involved in just about every step of the process. Other groups take part where needed.

| ① Discover your purpose and desired future | ② Assess your strategic position | ③ Develop your strategies and priorities | ④ Cascade your strategies to operations | ⑤ Align your people and financial resources | ⑥ Execute your plan |
|---|---|---|---|---|---|
| **Who should be involved?** | | | | | |
| Planning team, Plan leader, Executive team | Plan leader, Executive team, Planning team, Staff, Marketing team/Sales force, and Customers | Plan leader, Executive team, Planning team | Executive team, Planning team, Department managers, Individual team members | Finance team, Department heads, HR team | Plan leader, Executive team, Planning team, Department managers, Individual team members |

**Figure 3-3:** Your strategic planning team.

# Going It Alone or Hiring a Facilitator

In an age of facilitators, organizational leaders, and planners for everything under the sun, hiring a helper doesn't come cheap. You need to consider three costs to your company for strategic planning:

- ✔ The value of your participants' time — more precious than ever in this time-starved world

- ✔ The cost of any facility rental, AV equipment, travel, food, and lodging

- ✔ The opportunity cost if, following your meeting, plans and decisions aren't carried out or your team's behavior doesn't change for the better

Add up these actual and figural costs, and you can easily see how strategic planning represents a real investment. One way to maximize your investment is to engage the services of a professional facilitator. Obviously, not every meeting calls for a facilitator, but your annual retreat can probably use one.

In the following sections, I show you how to run planning sessions yourself as well as how and when to hire a facilitator.

## Running the planning sessions yourself

For any planning sessions that you choose to run yourself, be sure to follow these best practices: have a clear agenda, require participants to come prepared, start and end on time, and manage the conversation in the room.

To run strategic planning sessions, you want to gather a set of facilitation techniques for different parts of the process. Some of my favorite facilitation exercises and methods include the following sources:

- ✔ **Best Practices for Facilitation:** This source is the second in The Grove's Facilitation Guide Series and is a user-friendly manual of 176 field-tested group practices. The resource proves invaluable to facilitators, managers, team leaders, and consultants looking for facilitation alternatives, such as virtual team work, graphic templates, agenda design, and group decision making. You can purchase the book at store.grove.com/product_index.html.

- ✔ **International Association of Facilitators (IAF) (**www.iaf-world.org**):** This website is the recognized source for credible and valuable professional help for practicing facilitators. On this site, you can find tons of resources related to the facilitation of best practices.

✓ **Post-it Brand Products** (www.postit.com)**:** This website provides immediate access to sticky notes of all sizes. A strategic planning meeting without sticky notes is like an ice cream sundae without the cherry. You can do it, but it's boring (and doesn't taste as good — the cherry, not the sticky notes). In all seriousness, the use of sticky notes can help you gain consensus quickly, keep important ideas and topics posted on poster board–sized notes, and allow for quick brainstorming.

# Using a facilitator

Facilitators bring a fresh perspective to the process. They keep the discussion on track and encourage all team members to act as equals. An outside facilitator levels the playing field between CEO and team members. In an atmosphere of informality, team members can address any issue within the organization without fear of unjust reprisal. The CEO should be involved when appropriate for his leadership, knowledge, and guidance.

### Deciding whether a facilitator is a good idea

So just when should you use a facilitator? Check out the following important instances when considering enlisting a facilitator:

✓ **When you want to participate yourself:** For the most part, facilitating and participating at the same time are impossible. Some people can do both effectively, but most can't. If you're the boss, forget it. You can't effectively facilitate because people still react to you as their superior.

✓ **When you need to address sensitive issues, including conflict:** An outsider's perspective can diffuse heated exchanges and channel intense emotions into constructive problem solving. Consider solving the conflict with the involved parties and bringing the rest of the team together after the problem has been resolved.

✓ **When your team is stuck:** A skilled facilitator uses sensitivity to raise issues that are being avoided and to point out dysfunctional behaviors that are being denied. In this scenario, the aid of the helper gets the team moving to a new level of functioning.

✓ **When your group must deal with complex issues and a variety of viewpoints:** A seasoned facilitator brings a wealth of group processes and activities to scope issues, generate options, make decisions, and build consensus.

### Finding a good facilitator

Facilitation is different from public speaking or training. It's not about having solid content, good platform skills, or an understanding of adult learning principles. Instead, facilitation involves working with groups of people in the moment. The job requires being tuned in at all times to what's happening and being able to suspend or change the process accordingly.

When selecting a professional to guide your session, look for the following characteristics:

✔ An understanding of organizational issues (industry knowledge isn't necessary)

✔ Superb communications skills

✔ Ability to offer insight and empathy while conducting himself with authority and credibility

✔ Experience in running strategic management processes

✔ Conflict management skills and confidence about handling conflict

✔ Ability to help you clarify your outcomes and a commitment to helping you reach your desired outcomes

✔ Honesty and fairness (Don't look for total objectivity. Anyone worth using has opinions; you just want her to make a clear distinction between opinions and facts.)

✔ Understanding of group process theory (A good facilitator is able to apply concepts such as leadership, group norms, team development, systems theory, dialogue, and experiential learning to the design and facilitation of your meeting.)

✔ Logic, self-discipline, and the ability to operate systematically

✔ A style that suits your organization

By using an experienced facilitator in the right situations, you almost certainly accomplish more in your meetings, delve deeper into critical issues, and then resolve them. Equally important, participants leave with positive feelings, stronger cohesiveness, a sense of accomplishment, and a renewed belief in the team. Overall, a facilitator helps you get the job done more quickly because his role is to move the process to conclusion.

# Smoothing Out Your Process

Strategic planning is a process that you want to flow smoothly, but I've had to face the facts: When I plan for a smooth ride, it never goes that way. Something always throws a wrench in the plan, making it an unpredictable process. Fresh ideas at an afternoon meeting may change decisions made earlier in the day.

I don't want you to get frustrated, so I've included the following tips to help your process move along with less uncertainty:

✔ **Think about execution before you start planning.** A strategic plan that sits on the shelf is a colossal waste of time and energy (of which no one has extra to give away). Outline your ideas on how you see the plan being implemented. Even better, talk to your key employees and get everyone's buy-in on executing the plan before you actually put the plan together. Consider reading Chapter 14, which focuses on execution.

✔ **Determine whether you want a top-down or bottom-up planning process.**

- A top-down approach involves the board and executive team setting the vision and long-term goals and the staff developing the short-term goals and actions.

- A bottom-up approach works with the staff developing the whole plan and submitting it to the board and executives for approval.

Normally, organizations end up somewhere between these two extremes. Deciding who takes the first pass at developing the vision and long-term goals is what's important because these are the guidelines for the rest of the plan.

✔ **Commit to a schedule.** Set a very specific deadline for when the plan needs to be completed. Additionally, set the schedule for ongoing strategy meetings and reporting.

Use a large desk calendar to map out the whole year as you embark on the planning process.

✔ **Make everyone feel included.** Not everyone will have a seat at your strategic table, so openly communicate who's involved in what step of the process and why. Explain how everyone's input is being solicited and used.

✔ **Celebrate success.** No matter what you do or where you are in your strategic planning agenda, end your planning days on a high note. Do something fun, such as play a quick game, run through a fun exercise, or go out to dinner.

I can't emphasize enough how important celebrating success is because there never seems to be enough time to have fun. Never let your strategic planning sessions end on a low note where everyone is feeling overworked and brain dead.

✔ **Don't over plan.** One of the biggest mistakes in strategic planning is becoming overly ambitious and overwhelming the company with the amount of work that needs to get done. When you're done putting your plan together, put it away and come back to it a week later. Make sure that it still makes sense and you haven't planned the company into oblivion.

# Part II

# Determining Your Core DNA and Envisioned Future

The 5th Wave                    By Rich Tennant

Excuse me, Hannibal, but would crossing the Alps on, ohh let's say— MOUNTAIN GOATS severely compromise your vision?

## In this part . . .

A great strategic plan is based on your organization's core, which encompasses your purpose, mission, values, and competitive advantage. You may have developed your core during your years (or months) of operation, but in this part, you take what you already know about your company, customers, market, and competitors and develop stage one of your strategic plan. You take stock of last year to determine what strategic issues you need to address, and then you develop or revise your mission, vision, and values. You also examine your competitive advantage to establish what your organization does that's unique and better than the rest.

# Chapter 4

# Identifying Your Strategic Issues

## In This Chapter

▶ Reviewing last year's successes and failures

▶ Determining your profitable products and services

▶ Using the Market Attractiveness Framework to build your portfolio

▶ Evaluating your financial performance and industry structure

▶ Recognizing and addressing your strategic issues

*D*on't you always hate it when your mom (or grandma) says, "Back in my day . . ." Yeah, yeah, I know. You walked everyday to and from school uphill both ways in a perpetual snowstorm. God bless her for trying to share her past, but it always sounds so difficult. The future is much more exciting than the past. The future is where the action is. It's moving. It's shaking. It's sexy and bright. The past just slows us down, like getting stuck in molasses or running under water. Or is it?

Learning from your past can save hours and hundreds of dollars spent on fruitless activities. Ignoring your past can be costly because you aren't adding to your knowledge base. Instead, you're just continually trying new things. By taking a good look at your past performance, you can move faster into the future by avoiding roadblocks and pitfalls you've already encountered to identify strategic issues you need to address during your planning process. Strategic *issues* are critical unknowns that are driving you to embark on a strategic planning process now. These issues can be problems, opportunities, market shifts, or anything else that's keeping you awake at night and begging for a solution or decision.

In this chapter, you look at your past performance and the marketplace to uncover your strategic issues. You don't have to spend too much time wandering down memory lane, but taking a few hours by yourself or with your team to work through the exercises in this chapter may pay high rewards in the future. With a short list of strategic issues that you want to solve during this process, you're able to develop a strategic plan that addresses what's critical to your organization right now.

# Reviewing What Happened Last Year

Because you're not a new organization, you've accumulated invaluable information about your past activities, customers, employees, and financials that can help prevent do-overs. Tap in to that invaluable resource to review last year's performance, including dusting off last year's strategic plan. Ideally, you've been using it monthly or quarterly, so carrying key items forward should be simple.

As a first step in your strategic planning process, use the questions in the following sections to guide your review of last year. Conduct the review either individually, by requesting that employees respond to the set of questions from the lists in the next sections, or as a group, by facilitating the discussion in a regularly scheduled staff meeting. You can add this information to your SWOT, which is covered in Chapters 7 and 10, and begin a list of strategic issues.

After you've identified your successes and failures, look at what goals and objectives continue into the current planning year. Create a notes page and label it "Goals and Objectives," and then start a list of potential items you want to include in this year's plan.

## Recognizing what you achieved

Everyone wants to feel successful and recognized for a job well done, but human nature is to brush by achievements. By listing what you achieved last year as an organization, you help motivate and inspire your team to work smarter and harder in the coming year. Additionally, why not try to replicate what worked well last year? Here are some questions to get the conversation started:

- ✔ What goals did we achieve? Why?
- ✔ What hurdles or challenges did we overcome? How?
- ✔ What new customers did we acquire? How?
- ✔ Who joined our team?
- ✔ What were the bottom-line results we achieved? (See "Looking at Your Financial Performance" later in this chapter for more discussion of this area.)
- ✔ What projects were successful? Why?
- ✔ What have our customers said about us — both positive and negative?

List your successes on a white board and leave them posted for a few weeks. Ask your employees to add to them as they see fit. By displaying your successes, you let your team know that last year's achievements were important. Dig in to the hows and whys of your actions to make the list as specific as possible. When you have your list, use it to guide your planning efforts in the coming year. You can add the achievements to your list of strengths in your SWOT (see Chapters 7 and 10).

## Understanding why you failed

Success and failure are like peanut butter and jelly; you can't have one without the other. You likely didn't achieve everything you expected to last year. You may even have a goal or project that rolls over from one year to the next. You've identified it as important, but you can't seem to move the ball down the field. Now is the time to figure out why.

As with your successes (discussed in the previous section), use the following questions to identify last year's failures and determine what you need to do this year to prevent a repeat performance.

- What lessons did we learn last year?
- What decisions from the past year would we change?
- What goals or projects did we not accomplish? Why?
- What roadblocks or hurdles do we keep stumbling into? Why?
- What challenges did we fail to meet over the past few years? Why?

Use the responses to these questions to fill out the weaknesses section of your SWOT (see Chapter 7). Pull out the ones that may need a deeper dive and add those to your strategic issues list.

# Evaluating Your Products and Services

By looking at the financial performance of your products and services over the past several years and matching it up with market attractiveness, you can identify which products and services to use to grow. Every organization has a portfolio of products or services that it offers to its customers. That portfolio needs to be managed just like your personal investment portfolio. In the financial world, you buy and sell stocks and bonds to yield the highest return. When an investment is no longer generating a positive return, you ask your investment advisor to sell it and find something else that's performing with a better return.

Managing your product or service portfolio is no different. Although you probably don't have as many products or services as you do stocks or bonds and you're likely to move slower between deciding when to buy or sell, the principle is the same. You want to invest in products and services that are doing well and divest the ones that aren't.

Without a doubt, every company has one or more products or services that are losing money. The big issue is that most businesses don't know which of their products and services are winners and which ones are losers.

The primary reason for not being able to figure out the difference between winners and losers is that the monthly financial reports are consolidated. They don't shed light on how each product in your portfolio is performing. You want to be sure that you're selling a product or service for less than it costs to produce it, which is called your *gross profit.* To get beyond your gross profit, you have to dig deeper.

## Picking the winners

You may look at this section and think, "Who doesn't pick winners?" Unfortunately, many organizations produce unprofitable products and services for a variety of valid reasons. Strategic planning is about driving the right decisions, based on facts, even if they're unpopular or political land mines. Read on to learn how to factually assess your products and services to ensure that you have winners.

Determine the period of time for your review before you start. You may choose to look at last year's performance alone, but it may not provide you with enough history. If possible, look at how each product and service has performed over the past three years.

Before you start on this exercise, remember that some products or services may still need to prove themselves and others may be integral to another item in your portfolio. And some clients generate enough revenue that they help even out work flow. So while you assess the profitability of each product or service, pay attention to how it interacts with the rest of your portfolio. In some instances, it may be enough for the product just to contribute to overhead costs.

Open a new Excel spreadsheet and determine your winners and losers by following these steps (see Figure 4-1 for an example):

1. **Create a column, starting with Column B, for every primary product or service (or client) you provide.**

2. **Label the first line in Column A "Sales," and then list all the expenses down the left-hand side below sales.**

   List all expenses directly related to producing the product or service (also called *cost of goods sold*), and then label the next line "Gross Profit."

   You can include all the components of selling and marketing each of your products or services, such as advertising, marketing, commissions, royalties, and so on.

**3. Fill in each line on the schedule for each product or service.**

You may have to do some digging because some numbers may not be readily available. If you can't find the number, make an educated guess. Make sure that when you add up the columns, you end up with numbers that agree with your income statement.

**4. Add all the expenses lines and subtract this sum from your sales line to determine the gross profit for each product you sell.**

You may be shocked to find a lot more of your products, services, or clients have a negative or smaller gross profit than you thought.

**5. Repeat this process for each of the past three years.**

Add the gross profit lines for each product and year together. Use a separate spreadsheet for each year.

**6. Identify which products, services, and clients are winners and which are losers.**

Are the winners' profits growing, staying the same, or declining?

The larger the gross profit, the bigger a winner it is. See Figure 4-1 for an example of how to build your spreadsheet. Refer to this figure to pick out which products, services, and clients this company should keep and which ones it should eliminate.

Service companies may want to evaluate your service lines and your clients. Which of your larger clients are profitable, or winners, and which are losers? Follow the same preceding steps to make this determination.

| PRODUCTS/SERVICES/CLIENTS | | | | |
|---|---|---|---|---|
| | **A** | **B** | **C** | **D** |
| Sales | $125,000 | $275,600 | $230,400 | $426,500 |
| Expense #1 | 55,000 | 81,000 | 55,000 | 281,000 |
| Expense #2 | 12,500 | 46,000 | 55,000 | 155,000 |
| Expense #3 | 7,250 | 1,500 | 27,850 | 12,500 |
| Expense #4 | | 1,500 | 22,000 | 12,500 |
| Gross Profit (sales minus expenses) | $50,250 | $145,600 | $70,550 | <$34,500> |

**Figure 4-1:** Building your spreadsheet to identify winners and losers.

## Dumping the losers

Consider eliminating those products or services that are losing money or firing clients that are losers (not losers themselves, but who aren't making you money). Look at how much money you can immediately put to the bottom line by not engaging in activities that are losing money.

Don't forget that some products may experience seasonality issues and some may be complementary products or services. Evaluate your findings with your specific business issues in mind.

Another option is to consider raising the prices of products, charging higher service fees, or increasing rates to your clients. Alternatively, you can run through the problem-solving activity in the previous section to determine whether you can find a way to make the losers profitable. The key is to not get caught up in trying to save something just because you or your staff like it or because you think you should be able to make money on it. Know when to cut your losses.

# Putting Your Portfolio Together (In the Market Attractiveness Framework)

After you've determined which products or services make money and which ones take money (see previous section), evaluate which ones to invest in by looking at how attractive the market is.

A widely used tool for conducting a portfolio analysis is the Market Attractiveness Framework, which provides a structure that works with your products and services as listed in the previous section. The framework looks at your portfolio based on the strengths of each product or service and its market attractiveness. Check out Figure 4-2 to see the framework in action. This example provides a good picture of where a company should invest to yield the biggest growth in the upper-right-hand part of the matrix.

## Evaluating market attractiveness and business strength

The method of using the Market Attractiveness Framework is to fit your products or services in one of the three areas (as the example shown in Figure 4-2).

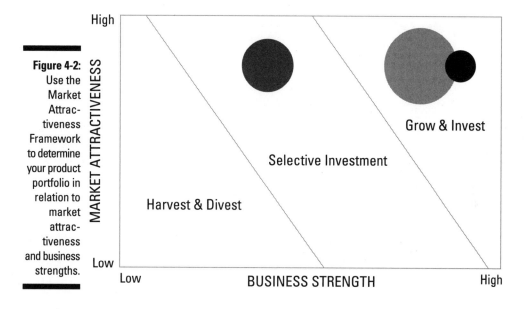

**Figure 4-2:**
Use the
Market
Attrac-
tiveness
Framework
to determine
your product
portfolio in
relation to
market
attrac-
tiveness
and business
strengths.

Determining what factors make a market attractive and what are product and/or service strengths can be difficult to pin down. A healthy dose of intuition is also helpful when determining where to place your products and services in the framework. Based on where these items fall, you can use the recommendations listed in the following sections to help guide your planning efforts.

### Factors that affect market attractiveness

Although any assessment of market attractiveness is necessarily subjective, just use your knowledge and best judgment. The following key factors may also help determine attractiveness:

- ✔ Market size
- ✔ Market growth
- ✔ Pricing trends
- ✔ Intensity of the competition
- ✔ Overall risk in the industry
- ✔ Opportunity to differentiate products and services

The more attractive the item, the higher up you place it on the vertical axis of the framework. The less attractive it is, the lower you plot it.

### *Factors that affect business strength*

A key business strength is product or service profitability. Start with the analysis from the "Picking the winners" and "Dumping the losers" sections. The more profitable a business is, the stronger its product or service is. But profitability isn't everything. Consider these other factors as you plot your products and services on the framework:

- ✔ Product or service uniqueness
- ✔ Brand recognition
- ✔ Market share growth or decline
- ✔ Customer loyalty
- ✔ Relative cost position (cost structure compared with competitors)
- ✔ Production capacity
- ✔ Distribution strength
- ✔ Record of innovations

Determine the business strength of each product or service. The stronger it is, the further to the left you place it on the horizontal axis. The weaker it is, the further to the right you plot it.

## *Creating your own matrix*

After looking at business strength and market attractiveness (see the "Evaluating market attractiveness and business strength" section earlier in the chapter), you can put together your own framework similar to Figure 4-2 and arrange every primary product or service somewhere in the three areas. Based on where each product or service falls, the following guidelines help develop goals for your strategic plan.

Build your own matrix, using the Market Attractiveness Framework on the CD. The following options relate to each of the numbered boxes:

- ✔ **Grow and invest:**
  - • Focus your resources and efforts on maintaining and growing products or services in this box.
  - • Work on improving some of your weaknesses and building your strengths.
- ✔ **Selective investment:**
  - • Include in these boxes products or services that are either in a highly attractive market or capitalize on a business strength.
  - • Modify your activities to eliminate weaknesses.

- Keep these products or services and concentrate any investments in promising areas with limited risks.

- Build on the competitive position you've managed to secure.

- Invest in areas that build on this advantage and help you move products or services in this box to Box 1.

✔ **Harvest and divest:**

- Focus on maximizing your profits while reducing costs.

- Limit your investment in products or services in this box.

- You may want to divest any products or services in this box.

- Cut costs and don't invest.

List actions you develop from this exercise on the *Goals and Objectives* note page. Identify those actions that need additional research and add them to your strategic issues list.

# Looking at Your Financial Performance

The financial health of your organization is critical to your corporate growth. Therefore, evaluating your financial situation is part of your strategic planning process. Want to know how your business is *really* doing? Evaluate your financial performance by looking beyond the numbers on your balance sheet and income statement. By themselves, these statements are informative, but they aren't nearly as informative as the relationships between the numbers.

## Understanding the financial dynamics of your business

Instead of evaluating your past financial statements, analyze the financial ratios. Financial ratios are derived from pulling two numbers from your financial statements and dividing one by another. Doing so helps you create a ratio that eliminates any problems of comparing one company to another. With ratios, you take out any size difference so you can compare apples to apples. Additionally, you can compare your ratios to your industry averages to determine whether you're doing well. Most industry associations compute these ratios. I provide more sources in the later "Evaluating your numbers" section, or you can contact your association to see what they can provide you.

Dealing with financials statements and numbers can be daunting. But don't worry. You don't need to track and monitor everything, but just track key numbers that help you understand the financial dynamics of your business. When tracked and measured regularly, these key financial ratios allow you to

✔ Get a more accurate understanding of your company's financial performance.

✔ Compare performance against the prior year, current budget, and your industry as a whole.

✔ Establish benchmarks to see where you're going and how you're doing.

To make interpretation and management of these ratios easy, I group them into four categories: liquidity, risk, profitability, and productivity. In the next four sections, I use a fictional company, Konas Corp., to illustrate the ratios. Don't worry if your numbers aren't as large as Konas's are. The size of the ratios, not the numbers, is what counts.

### Checking your liquidity

Of primary importance to all organizations is the ability to pay their bills on time every month. The difference between your current assets (those you intend to convert to cash within a year) and your current liabilities (the obligations you have to pay within a year) is your liquidity. Your liquidity is the safety net that protects you from a financial crisis. You need to look at the following two ratios:

✔ **Current ratio:** The current ratio looks out over a 12-month time horizon and measures the cash available to meet current liabilities. The current ratio is determined by looking at your balance sheet and dividing current assets by current liabilities.

With $300,230 in current assets and $200,100 in current liabilities, Konas's current ratio is 1.5, which means that for every dollar of obligation due in the next 12 months, the company expects to have $1.50 to meet those obligations. You should shoot for a ratio of about 2.0.

✔ **Quick ratio:** The quick ratio is a tighter test of your ability to pay your bills. It uses assets that convert to cash within 60 to 90 days rather than 12 months, typically involving only cash and current receivables.

Konas has $271,000 in cash and receivables. Dividing by $200,100 (current liabilities) yields a quick ratio of 1.35. For every dollar in obligations, the company has $1.35 in quick cash to meet them. You want your quick ratio to be higher than a 1.0.

Konas may be a little concerned because its current ratio is less than 2.0, but with a quick ratio exceeding 1.0, it has a reasonable cash position.

### Gauging your risk levels

The mix of your debt and equity indicates your risk level. Although other ratios fall into this group, your debt-to-equity ratio is the key to figuring your risk of how leveraged you are or aren't.

Debt-to-equity ratio says a lot about the general financial structure of your company. This ratio measures the relationship of liabilities, or other people's money, in the business to the owners' or shareholders' money in the business. Often, banks are the largest component of other people's money and watch this ratio very closely, hoping to see plenty of equity to support the debt. To calculate debt-to-equity, you divide total liabilities by owner equity.

Konas has $110,000 in total liabilities and $389,000 in owner equity, for a debt-to-equity ratio of 0.28. In other words, for every dollar Konas's owners have put into their business, other people have put in 28 cents. The other people can feel fairly safe with a cushion this comfortable, meaning the company isn't over leveraged. Companies should be concerned when liabilities outweigh equity. That said, every industry has a debt-to-equity ratio that's considered acceptable, and what's considered acceptable in one industry may not be in another industry, because some businesses require higher capital investment than others.

### Monitoring your profitability

Profitability ratios tell you how well you create financial value for your company. Although net profit is your bottom line, profitability is what you're aiming for year after year. In the previous section, you looked at gross profit by product or service. Here, you look at the profitability of your company as a whole, which includes net profit margin and return on equity (ROE):

- ✔ **Net profit margin:** Net profit margin is calculated by dividing gross sales into net profit. If your net profit margin is low compared to your industry, that means your prices are lower and your costs are too high. You aren't efficient. Lower margins are acceptable if they lead to greater sales, more market share, or future investments, but make sure that they don't go too low. High margins are typically never a bad thing. Watch this ratio each year and use your industry average as a gauge to monitor your performance.

- ✔ **Return on equity (ROE):** ROE measures how much profit comes back to the owners for their investment. This ratio is calculated by dividing net profit by the owner's equity investment.

Konas has a net profit of $65,000 and gross sales of $778,000 for a pre-tax profit margin of 8.3 percent. In other words, the company is making 8.3 cents on every dollar. The owners of Konas have an equity investment of $294,000 in the company, so with a net profit of $65,000, their ROE is 22 percent. This percentage means that the owners make almost 22 cents on every dollar invested in the company as equity. A 20 percent ROE is a reasonable return for risking $294,000.

### Measuring your productivity

The ratios in this section give you a good picture of how productive your company is in using its assets to generate profit. Ratios in this group should be benchmarked against your industry to determine how well you're performing and where you may find areas of improvement.

Check out these ratios:

- ✔ **Sales to assets:** Sales to assets measures how productive your assets are. Look at what you've invested in to generate sales and how productive those investments are. You calculate this ratio by dividing gross sales by total assets.

  My fictional company, Konas, has gross sales of $778,000 and total assets of $1,120,000, for a sales-to-assets ratio of 0.69. This ratio means that for every dollar the company invests in assets, it generates 69 cents in sales. This may be considered a rather inefficient use of assets. The management of Konas should launch an investigation: Possible reasons for this low ratio include too much production capacity or old assets. Konas should outsource production and sell assets.

- ✔ **Return on assets (ROA):** ROA is another measure of how profitable the company assets are. You calculate ROA by dividing net profit by total assets.

  With a net profit of $65,000 and total assets of $1,120,000, Konas's ROA is 5.8 percent. This percentage means that the company makes almost 6 cents of net profit for every dollar invested in assets. This ratio should be interpreted in light of the overall risk, and in this instance, the owners of Konas may consider putting the money in a CD and collecting the interest instead of assuming risk with so little return.

- ✔ **Inventory turnover:** Inventory turnover measures how many times you sell what's on your shelves and/or in your warehouse (in the case of a service company, inventory is time, so this ratio isn't used). Turnover is calculated by dividing cost of goods sold by the cost of the inventory.

  Konas has a $423,000 cost of goods sold and $115,000 of inventory, for an inventory turnover ratio of 3.67. Dividing 365 days by 3.67 indicates it takes 99 days for Konas to sell everything in the warehouse. The faster inventory turns, the less it costs and the more efficient operations are. A smart business owner strives to keep inventory turning faster than his or her industry peers.

- ✔ **Receivable turnover:** Receivable turnover is the ratio of the number of times that accounts receivable amount is collected throughout the year. A high accounts receivable turnover ratio indicates a tight credit policy. A low or declining accounts receivable turnover ratio indicates a collection problem, part of which may be due to bad debts. To determine the collection time on accounts receivable, divide total sales by accounts receivable.

  Konas has gross sales of $778,000 and $178,000 in receivables, for a ratio of 4.3 times a year. After dividing this number into 365 days, it takes Konas 84 days to collect its receivables. This number should be closer to 45 to 60 days.

✔ **Accounts payable (A/P) turnover:** This ratio shows how many times in one accounting period the company turns over (repays) its accounts payable to creditors. A higher number indicates either that the business has decided to hold on to its money longer or that it's having greater difficulty paying. A lower number indicates the company is paying its creditors quickly. To calculate the accounts payable ratio, divide the cost of goods sold by accounts payable.

A/P turnover for Konas is $49,000, with cost of goods sold totaling $423,000, for an A/P ratio of 8.6 times a year. So Konas pays its vendors, suppliers, and others about once every six weeks. Although not bad, wouldn't you want to be paid in 30 days? Thirty days is the ideal time frame, so Konas should strive to pay its vendors promptly.

## Sorting out three-year trends

Armed with information about how to calculate financial ratios (see the section "Looking at Your Financial Performance" earlier in this chapter), you want to set up a spreadsheet that shows financial trends ideally for the past few years. If you don't have complete financial data, put together ratios for the years that you do have information on.

Using a clean spreadsheet, follow these steps to get started. You can reference Figure 4-3, where I added in the data based on the previous sections, for an example:

1. **List financial ratios down the left-hand side and the three years across the top.**

2. **Calculate each ratio for each year based on the formulas provided in the previous sections.**

3. **Label the farthest column to the right (the one after the most current year) "Benchmark."**

4. **Enter the benchmark number based on the few recommended levels provided in the previous section, your desired targets, or industry benchmarks.**

5. **Identify which ratios are performing above or below the benchmark.**

6. **Determine possible corrective action and list your ideas on the *Goals and Objectives* note page.**

   Use the information from the previous section to determine corrective action based on ratios that may not be close to your benchmark or your target.

| KONAS CORP | | | |
| 2009 | 2010 | 2011 | Benchmark |
|---|---|---|---|
| 1.6 | 1.4 | 1.5 | 2.0 |
| 0.26 | 0.25 | 0.28 | 0.24 |
| 21% | 21% | 22% | 20% |
| 0.68 | 0.67 | 0.69 | 0.90 |

*FINANCIAL RATIOS: Liquidity, Risk, Profitability, Productivity*

**Figure 4-3:** Financial ratio worksheet example, using benchmarks to identify areas of improvement.

## Trailing your numbers over 12 months

You need a dynamic way to look at your performance month after month because you'd like to see whether you're growing or shrinking. The Trailing 12 Months (T12M) chart, developed by Kraig Kramers — founder of CEO Tools — can help you track monthly sales for your last 12 months. T12M charts graphically tell you whether you're improving or slipping.

Take a look at both Figure 4-4 and Figure 4-5. Figure 4-4 is an ordinary monthly chart. This type of chart is often misleading and shows little other than season-ality. On the other hand, Figure 4-5 (a T12M) shows a true trend line on sales, gross profits, or whatever key data you use these charts to track.

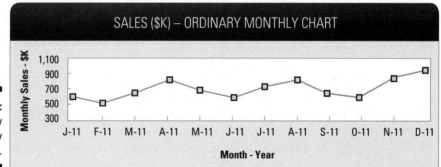

**Figure 4-4:**
An ordinary
monthly
sales chart.

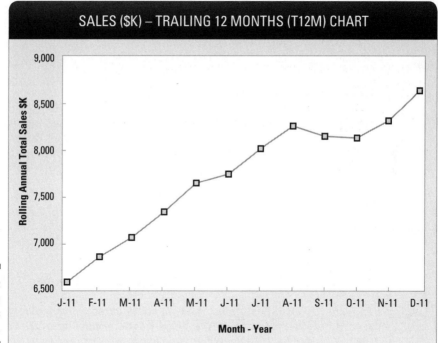

**Figure 4-5:**
A Trailing
12 Months
chart.

Ready to create your T12M? Open a new Excel spreadsheet and follow
these steps:

1. **Label Column A "Month/Year" and list the months in chronological
   order, starting with the oldest date first.**

   For example, label January 2011 as J-11, February 2011 as F-11, and so on.

2. **Label Column B "Monthly Sales" and enter the monthly sales for each corresponding month.**

   In the J-11 column, enter your January sales. In the F-11 column, enter your February sales, and so on.

3. **Label Column C "TTM Sales" and add the first month's sales to the second month's sales in the same row next to the second month's sales.**

   Move down one row, add the sum above it (the first two months) to the sales in month three. This number is a simple 12-month sum that moves forward one month (and down one row) at a time. You're adding the current month to the running total in the row above.

4. **Select Insert and then click Line Chart.**

   Use the line chart to graph Column C. You should see a trend line going up or down similar to that in Figure 4-5.

5. **Evaluate your T12M chart.**

   If your trend line is going up month to month, that indicates positive performance. If your trend line is going down, that means you're performing worse than in previous months.

For additional information on the tool, check out Kraig Kramers's website www.ceotools.com, where you can print a version with a full explanation. (Click New Tools Catalog, scroll down to Trailing 12-Month Chart, and click the PDF symbol to bring it up on your screen and print it.)

By watching your T12M month to month, you can immediately see whether you need to take corrective action and when. If your trend line is moving upward, that means keep on doing what you're doing — growing!

## Evaluating your numbers

Evaluating your ratios against those in your industry provides an objective look at how you're performing. It helps you determine how other companies similar to yours are doing. When you have industry numbers to compare your company to, you can see whether you're performing better or worse than other companies. With that information, you can take corrective action or keep on doing what you're doing.

For access to industry benchmark sources, check out the following online sources:

- ✔ **BizStats** (www.bizstats.com): BizStats is a free online resource that provides industry averages for numerous different ratios.

- ✔ **BizMiner** (www.bizminer.com): This site provides reports of financial ratios by industry.

✔ **Dun & Bradstreet (D&B)** (www.dnb.com)**:** D&B publishes a report called *Industry Norms and Key Business Ratios.* You can find the link to it online under the site's Solutions and Risk Assessment sections.

✔ Financial-data services:

- Standard & Poor's: www2.standardandpoors.com

- Value Line: www.valueline.com

- Moody's: www.moodys.com

# Seeing the Underlying Forces of Your Industry

The industry (or industries) you operate in have significant impact on your future because underlying forces that you can't get away from exist in every industry. As you're identifying your strategic issues, use the matrix discussed in this section to think about what those forces are and what may be changing.

The following categories are evaluated from high to low or growth to decline and provide a quick overview of your industry structure. For a more detailed environmental and industry scan, flip to Chapter 10.

Using the Industry Structure matrix on the CD, complete your own assessment to identify forces and the impact that they could have.

✔ **Life cycle stage:** All industries go through periods of growth, maturity, and decline. An average life cycle lasts 70 years. Maturity is the longest stage at 40 years with growth and decline at 15 years each.

✔ **Regulation level:** The amount of governmental regulation and policy that supports or prevents company operations can be high, medium, or low.

✔ **Revenue volatility:** A higher level of revenue volatility implies greater industry risk. Volatility can negatively affect long-term strategic decisions, such as the time frame for capital investment.

✔ **Technology change:** Technology change is the degree to which technological change impacts continued competitiveness and required capital investments.

✔ **Capital intensity:** Capital intensity is an indicator of how much capital is used in production as opposed to labor. The level of capital intensity can be high, medium, or low. High is a ratio of less than $3 of wage costs for every $1 of depreciation; medium is $3 to $8 of wage costs to $1 of depreciation; low is greater than $8 of wage costs for every $1 of depreciation.

- ✔ **Barriers to entry:** Barriers to entry can be high, medium, or low. High means new companies struggle to enter an industry, while low means a firm can easily enter an industry.

- ✔ **Industry globalization:** Industry globalization is an indicator from low to high of how companies are fulfilling production demands and driving down costs. Product companies are likely to feel higher pressure over service companies.

- ✔ **Concentration level:** Concentration is identified as high, medium, or low. High means few big players account for the majority of revenue; medium is revenue that's concentrated in more than a few big players but isn't fragmented. Low means the industry is fragmented.

- ✔ **Competition level:** This level is the degree to which companies compete against each other for customers within the market. Concentration and competition levels tend to follow the same trend from high to low.

Pulling in external research is highly recommended to bring in a third-party view. Resources include IBISWorld (www.ibisworld.com), Morningstar (www.morningstar.com), and MarketResearch.com (www.marketresearch.com). While all these resources provide fee-based industry reports, the information ensures that you're not planning in a vacuum and you're objectively looking at the industry structure.

# Creating Your Short List of Strategic Issues

Throughout this chapter you work through a series of exercises and exploration that generate a long list of issues you need to address or solve during your planning process, including the following:

- ✔ Past history — lessons learned
- ✔ Current products and services attractiveness and profitability
- ✔ Financial performance to assess the health of your organization
- ✔ Industry structure to uncover underlying dynamics

Naturally, all issues aren't created equal. To focus your efforts, pare down your list to the select few that you think have the potential to have the biggest impact on your organization during your planning period. Typical strategic issues include answers to the following questions:

✔ How will we grow, stabilize, or retrench in order to sustain our organization into the future?

✔ How will we diversify our revenue to reduce our dependence on a major customer?

✔ What must we do to improve our cost structure and stay competitive?

✔ What is our new value proposition given that our customers are buying substitute products and we have new competitors?

✔ How and where must we innovate our products and services?

✔ Our industry is moving toward commoditization; what should we do?

Gain consensus with your planning team around the short list of strategic issues. After you have agreement, identify when you'll address the issues during your planning process. Where necessary, review and update your planning schedule from Chapter 3.

# Chapter 5

# Focusing on What You Do Best

*In This Chapter*

▶ Determining unique strengths that are the basis for your strategic plan

▶ Identifying what activities are core to your company's growth

▶ Knowing what activities set you apart from your competition

▶ Figuring out how to develop and sustain your competitive advantages

*B*usinesspeople and laymen alike throw around the term *competitive advantage* like it's the most common phrase in the English language. The term is not only widely overused but also widely misunderstood. You aren't alone if you've ever wondered what a competitive advantage really is and what you do with it.

Think of your competitive advantage as your organization's DNA — a collection of genes and attributes that makes you unique. When you're capitalizing on your uniqueness, you're healthy, fit, and successful. When you aren't, you feel uncomfortable and slow, and you're exerting more effort than you should.

In this chapter, I strive to not only clear up any confusion you may feel but also help you uncover your competitive advantage and show you how to use the advantage in your planning process and for business sustainability.

## Appreciating Your Competitive Advantage

What's the number-one attribute Warren Buffett — arguably one of the most successful investors in the world — looks for in a company? "Sustainable competitive advantage," he once told an interviewer. Buffett often says, "It's the moat that protects your company." If one of today's most successful businessmen puts competitive advantage at the top of his list, you should, too. But what is it exactly?

Your *competitive advantage* is what you, your company, or your department does better than anyone else. It's what makes you unique. It's *why* you're in business, and more importantly, why your business continues to prosper over time. The sustainable part refers to your ability to continue to do those activities over a long period of time. And, yes, you can have more than one advantage, and you can develop advantages as well. You don't have to possess them all at this moment.

I can't emphasize enough the importance of understanding your competitive advantage. When you really have it nailed down, it helps you and your staff recognize the following:

✔ Which opportunities to pursue and which to pass by

✔ Where to allocate resources and where to cut back

✔ How to do what you already do well even better

✔ How to know the difference between an opportunity and a distraction

✔ When to outsource (to another department or externally) and when to keep the job in-house

Your competitive advantage(s) is the foundation, the cornerstone of your strategic plan. Throughout your planning process, you evaluate every part of your plan to determine whether it supports or detracts from your competitive advantage. In the process, you discover what draws customers to buy the product or service from you instead of the competition.

Knowing how to define your competitive advantage is the first step toward applying it to your organization. Ninety-five percent of all companies don't know their competitive advantages, let alone how to use them to communicate a compelling reason to choose their product or service. If Warren Buffett examined your company, would he find what he's looking for? You'll find out in the following sections.

## Taking the 30-second competitive advantage challenge

Here's a 30-second test to determine whether you know your competitive advantage. A test already? I know; you feel like you're in school again, don't you? Don't worry — it won't hurt. Ready?

> I meet you at a local networking event, and you introduce yourself.
>
> "Hi, I'm Bob Jones with ABC Company."
>
> "Hi, Bob. Nice to meet you. Tell me a little about your company. What's your company best at?"
>
> . . . 29, 30. Time's up!

Can you answer my question in less than 30 seconds, succinctly and with clarity? If yes, go ahead and skip to Chapter 6. If not, don't worry, you're in good company. Honestly, this question is hard to answer; a majority of businesses are trying to figure out what they do best. Try to narrow your focus more than you're comfortable with. By the end of this chapter (if you read the whole thing), you should be able to share your competitive advantage with confidence and shout it from the rooftops.

## Knowing what competitive advantage isn't

Often starting with what something isn't is easiest. So your competitive advantage isn't a list of your strengths. (Not to downplay strengths, because they're important, too — especially in Chapter 7.) But if your competitive advantage list only comprises strengths, it's not very *competitive,* now, is it? You have to be better than your competitors in order to have a competitive advantage. In *Creating Competitive Advantage: Give Customers a Reason to Choose You Over Your Competitors* (Crown Business), author Jaynie Smith provides an example of what a competitive advantage isn't.

A management team from a mid-sized financial services group reported that its competitive advantages included the following:

- ✔ Good reputation in the community
- ✔ Skilled staff
- ✔ Outstanding team and well-respected leader
- ✔ Knowledgeable
- ✔ Strong client list and loyalty
- ✔ Flexible and responsive

Blah, blah, blah. You've heard all this before and so have I. Can't you say these things about almost any professional service firm? This list of strengths shows you why bulleting your strengths isn't what comprises your competitive advantage.

## Realizing what competitive advantage is

A competitive advantage is something you do that's unique. To compete, you must have a *unique* advantage. If you peek at the list in the previous section, you notice that it doesn't include unique qualities — basically anyone in business today needs to achieve that level of competency just to be in the game.

Specifically, a competitive advantage comes from leveraging a company's unique skills and resources to implement a strategy that competitors can't implement as effectively or copy. Read on to see how Jaynie Smith provides an example of what a real competitive advantage is.

When the financial services firm (introduced in the previous section) went through the exercises described in the upcoming section "Uncovering Your Advantages," it uncovered its competitive advantages. Here's what it came up with:

- ✔ Ranked in top 10 percent of money managers who beat Standard & Poor's nationally
- ✔ Fastest-growing American Funds money manager three years in a row
- ✔ Only firm ever featured by American Funds in its advisory newsletter

That's more like it! Wow! Doesn't that say a lot more about the competitive advantage than a good reputation and a skilled staff? This transition from a general to specific, well-thought-out list is the one you need to make when explaining the competitive advantage of your organization or department.

Here are a few more examples provided by Jaynie Smith from businesspeople who answered the question, "What is my company best at?"

- ✔ Sandy, owner of an interior design firm, determined she was best at increasing real estate developers' sales ratio by 35 percent and was the only design team chosen by the top-ten luxury developers in the state.
- ✔ A clothing manufacturer named Joe said he was the best at wearable clothing because "our clothes fly off the racks."
- ✔ The emergency service division of a county in Washington is the best at providing disaster management and response and recovery efforts for all agencies within its service territory because of its skilled people and emergency response equipment.

The remaining sections of this chapter focus on helping you identify and articulate your competitive advantage. I provide more specific examples throughout the chapter.

## Discovering why having a competitive advantage is so important

Although you can put together a strategic plan without a clear understanding of your competitive advantage, you'd be missing the boat. Your goals, strategic objectives, and action plans tend to change and shift over time. Your competitive advantages, after you've identified them, endure and grow stronger, helping your company be sustainable. Other elements of your plan tend to morph. But what makes your company unique is that your competitive advantages stay constant.

Founding your strategic plan on the basis of your competitive advantages is the most important thing you can do as a leader of your business or department. The leading organizations in this world have a razor sharp understanding of their competitive advantage. Everything they do builds and nurtures their DNA. You don't have to be a Fortune 100 company to be that effective.

# Uncovering Your Advantages

No company or department can be all things to all people. Some businesses try and quickly realize that they're spending time and resources on activities that aren't profitable.

What are the sources of your success? What makes your company or department unique? Is your success tied to your ability to innovate new products or services, your ability to respond quickly, your brand and community reputation, or the creative power of your marketing and sales department? Many sources likely contribute to your success.

Ultimately, *you* know what makes your company unique. You live it day in and day out. However, for your uniqueness to be useful in strategic planning, you need to state what you know to be absolutely true about your company. Your list of competitive advantages should make someone say, "Wow, I want to do business with you." To get your list of wows, you need to look at your business from different perspectives. I show you how in the following sections.

Be brutally honest — your insights can be instrumental in moving your company to the next level. Think about this process of uncovering your uniqueness like an exercise in genetic exploration. You know your department or company has unique genes. So go find them.

## What's your distinct purpose?

Your organization exists for a very specific reason, and most likely its purpose is different than any other company out there. Companies are founded for reasons as varied as something to do during retirement to making the world a better place. Unfortunately, sometimes business owners lose sight of why they started their business. If that's you, here are a few questions to consider in determining your purpose:

- ✔ Why was our organization started?
- ✔ What business are we really in?
- ✔ Why does our business exist? Or what would be different in the world if we didn't exist?

To jump-start your thinking, here are some examples of distinct purposes from organizations large and small:

- To solve the growing diabetes crisis
- To capitalize on a real estate growth trend
- To work for myself
- To provide quality window and door products better than anyone else
- To make fitness a way of life for everyone by making it fun, easy, and accessible
- To make my community a better place to live, work, and recreate through publicly accessible open space
- To provide people with a great place to work
- To be the perfect clown

An excellent way to uncover the purpose of your business from a different perspective is to talk with your employees. What do they think the distinct purpose of your organization is? To capture your staff's impression of your business's purpose, use the Employees Business Purpose Questionnaire located on the book's CD. The responses from your employees will help you uncover your competitive advantage. You may be amazed at the insightful comments you receive back from your team. Consider filling out the questionnaire yourself because your answers may also surprise you!

## How do you make money?

If I asked you how you make money, more than likely you'd reply by explaining the types and number of products or services you sell. Although that answer is technically correct, I want you to look at your revenue generation from a different perspective. For the moment, resist looking at your income statement. Hey, I said resist! Put that paper down! No peeking.

Instead of looking at the old income statements, you're going to gain new insight into what really drives your profit. Think about your revenue in terms of profit per X. Here are some examples:

- Profit per customer or client
- Profit per customer visit
- Profit per employee
- Profit per household
- Profit per product or service
- Profit per product or service line
- Profit per region
- Profit per billable hour

You may be tempted to look at this list and decide that several of these examples are your profit engines. The challenge, however, is to determine which one is actually the *best* revenue driver for your business. That's to say, they may all bring money into the business, but one will have the biggest impact. Looking at your revenue generation from this perspective is just like panning for gold. You don't need to change your activities, but you may need to look at your pan from a different angle to see the nugget.

Your profit engine is unique to your business. The following list of attributes makes up a good profit engine. Use this list as well as the previous examples to identify yours.

- **Broad measure:** A good profit engine is broader than a typical financial metric, such as number of products sold or number of customers per day. An example of a broad measure profit engine is selling the best family-style meal in Lakeside at a profit.

- **Customer focused:** A profit engine should add to the customer experience and increase your customer focus. For example, by looking at your services from your customers' eyes, you may realize that instead of profit per product or service, your profit engine is profit per customer.

- **Improves resource sharing:** You only have so much time, money, and resources. If you can share your resources, you're increasing their use and your company's output. For example, a consultant only has so many hours in the day. Instead of looking at profit per hour, she can look at profit per client. Even further, if this consultant has a special methodology she uses in her consulting, her profit engine may be profit per number of uses (books, speaking, training other consultants, licensing, and so on).

## Pegging profitability

Sam, the owner of a chain of regional retail auto parts stores, thought his focus should be on profit per store. Although the profitability of a particular location is crucial, profitability isn't the only variable that counts. As a result of understanding what makes a good profit engine (as explained in the section "How do you make money?"), Sam discovered that looking at the profit per customer is an even better measure of profitability. Now instead of stores competing, they collaborate.

Sam now provides a far superior customer experience than his competitors because stores aren't fighting for customers. Customers get appointments quicker, and their cars are repaired faster.

Also, Sam can share assets, such as people and parts, between all the stores. Sam's improved customer experience is a newfound competitive advantage. His scope of services isn't matched by any of his competitors.

Strategic planning is often about doing what you're already doing but tweaking it slightly. In this case, you can see how looking at profitability by customer instead of store can be a competitive advantage. The retail store now makes decisions that support the customer being the profit center instead of the store. Having a single focus on profitability can help hone your attention when trying to identify your key areas of uniqueness.

How does identifying your profit engine relate to uncovering your competitive advantages? Understanding what drives profitability in your organization helps you to pull out what's really a competitive advantage and what's just nice to have. The sidebar "Pegging profitability" provides an example.

As you evaluate your business, consider what one measure drives your revenue. Use the Project Engine Worksheet on the CD and the example in Figure 5-1 to develop your top three possible profit engines and evaluate them against the criteria provided. Select the profit engine that best meets all three criteria.

**LIST YOUR TOP THREE POSSIBLE PROFIT ENGINES.**
**USE THE THREE CRITERIA TO DETERMINE YOUR BEST PROFIT ENGINE.**

| Profit per *product line* | ☒ Broad Measure | ☐ Customer Focused | ☐ Improves Resource Sharing |
|---|---|---|---|
| Profit per *customer visit* | ☐ Broad Measure | ☒ Customer Focused | ☐ Improves Resource Sharing |
| Profit per *billable hour* | ☐ Broad Measure | ☐ Customer Focused | ☒ Improves Resource Sharing |

**Figure 5-1:** Revving up your profit engine.

# Why do customers buy from you?

Nothing in business ever happens if money doesn't exchange hands. More than likely, your organization has been around for several years because it provides a product or service that people want or need. Ideally, you're performing some market research and asking your current customers why they use your services. But I bet you have a general sense of what it is that drives people to buy from you. Here are some questions to ask yourself to determine what's bringing customers through your door:

- ✔ How do we help our customers? What need do we meet?

- ✔ Are our clients referring our business? Why or why not?

- ✔ If we're being referred, what part of our business do our customers talk about?

- ✔ What area of our business is growing? What product or service line sees the most action in terms of sales?

Even better than answering these questions yourself is asking your customers to answer the questions. Pick your top ten accounts and ask them to respond to the Customer Business Purpose Questionnaire located on the CD. Anonymous responses yield the best results, so ask a colleague or an intern to make the calls on your behalf. Similar responses from different individuals guide the development of your competitive advantage in Figure 5-2 later in this chapter.

# Pinpointing Your Competitive Advantage

Now that you've asked everyone who's important to your business to define your competitive advantage, you need to summarize the findings and pin-point your areas of uniqueness. Look at the responses to the questionnaires from your employees and customers as well as your own answers to the questions from the previous three sections.

In your strategy notebook (which I discuss in the Introduction), capture the common themes or ideas from your customers, your employees, and your-self. Use a separate page for each one of these perspectives. Collect these thoughts from each employee and customer questionnaires. In the sections that follow, you use this data to develop your own competitive advantage. I also provide some examples of successful competitive advantages to help you narrow down your focus.

## Perusing a few examples

Learning from others can be helpful in identifying your own competitive advantage. Check out the following two examples to see how these organiza-tions define their uniqueness.

Pershing General Hospital is a 125-bed, primary-care facility located in a rural area with no other hospitals within 50 miles. Because the organization oper-ates with almost zero competition, it doesn't need to focus on how to beat out other hospitals. However, it does need to decide what services to offer with its limited governmental funding. By offering services that are based on its com-petitive advantages, it can maximize the funding it does receive. Here's what Pershing's employees and customers said the hospital does the best:

- Provides the one and only, high-quality emergency, primary care, and retail pharmacy within its service area
- Staffs the hospital with personnel who have superior knowledge to support efficient operations
- Offers the best care possible by maintaining its full staff of highly-experienced nurses

Surfrider Foundation is a grassroots, nonprofit, environmental organization that works to protect the oceans, waves, and beaches. With 60 chapters and 40,000 members nationwide, the foundation achieves its purpose through membership dues and grant funding. As with the proceeding example, the foundation must focus on its competitive advantages to maintain its funding and be effective. Here are the themes from the employee and customer questionnaires:

- Defined focus on environmental issues that relate to the ocean and only the ocean
- Committed people who are extremely passionate about protecting the ocean
- Dedicated to maintaining a bipartisanship view to foster broad-based support

## Stating your competitive advantage succinctly

Go back to the fictitious networking event earlier in this chapter in the section "Taking the 30-second competitive advantage challenge." You needed to be able to answer what your company was best at in 30 seconds. Here's a second chance. Look at Figure 5-2 and use the formula (your business name + what you're best at + why) to put your list of unique activities into a succinct statement or bulleted points.

## Putting your advantage to the test

Having an advantage over your competitors isn't enough. For your business to be great, it needs to be sustainable and able to endure the test of time. You have to be able to combat today's fierce market forces and uncertainty. Do you want to know why? Read on.

Think about the graveyard of businesses from the dot-com era. Many of these companies didn't pass the sustainability test. You don't want your company to be a distant memory. In fact, you probably want it to live on past your time. And if you're a department manager, you probably want to see your department continue on instead of being restructured.

Here are the cold hard facts:

- Roughly 70 percent of all new products and services can be duplicated within one year.
- 60 to 90 percent of process improvements (learning) eventually diffuses to competitors.

| FORMULA FOR A COMPETITIVE ADVANTAGE | | |
|---|---|---|
| A statement that explains what your company is best at. | | |
| **Your Business Name** | **+ What you're best at** | **+ Why** |
| Honda | is best at developing precision engines and power trains | because its products are the leaders in reliability and technological advancement |
| Bikram Yoga | is best at productizing the yoga experience and practice | because it's packaged for franchising |
| Google | is best at optimizing searches for any type of information | because it continues to innovate and push technology past what was thought possible |

**Figure 5-2:** Drafting your competitive advantage.

You need to make sure that your competitive advantage is long-lasting and not easy to duplicate. So how do you know *when* you've developed a sustainable competitive advantage? You need criteria to help you gauge your success. Take a look at the following measures to see whether you're on the right track:

- ✔ **Consistent difference:** Customers must see a consistent difference between your product or service and those of your competitors. This difference needs to be obvious to your customers, and it must influence their purchasing decisions.

- ✔ **Difficult to imitate:** Your competitive advantage must be difficult to imitate. You want to have an advantage that your competition can't easily duplicate or don't understand how to copy. Often this advantage comes in the form of people, proprietary knowledge within your organization, or business processes that are behind the scenes.

- ✔ **Constantly improved:** The first two bulleted items in this list must create activities that can be constantly improved, nurtured, and worked at to maintain an edge over your competition. The comparison of Wal-Mart versus Kmart is a great example of how one continued to improve its supply chain management and purchasing, whereas the other didn't. Unfortunately for Kmart, it lost its edge because it didn't constantly improve. Wal-Mart invests in ever-refining its product selection and processes.

Reference Figure 5-3 and use the Competitive Advantage Evaluation form on the CD to quickly evaluate whether your advantage withstands the test of time. The more responses to the right-hand side of the form, the better, but don't worry if you don't pass each one. Think about how you can add to your competitive advantage to make it even more sustainable. When you develop goals in Chapter 12, take action to shore up any areas that may concern you.

## Breaking away from the pack

Developing competitive advantages isn't always easy or straightforward. For many, a competitive advantage is developed by nurturing a strength over time. This process turns the activity or intangible asset into something that's difficult to copy. If you have a strength where you can break away from your competition, spend your energy and resources to develop it further. Here are some great ways to break away from the pack:

✔ **Consistency:** One of the hardest and best advantages is the ability to deliver the same product or service time after time after time. To do so, a company must have rock-solid processes that deliver consistency no matter what.

---

### TESTING YOUR COMPETITIVE ADVANTAGE

Will your customers see a consistent, superior difference between your product/service and those of your competitors?

**No difference** · · · · · · · · · · · · · · · · · **Huge difference**

How difficult will it be for competitors to imitate your advantages?

**Not difficult** · · · · · · · · · · · · · · · · **Very difficult**

Can your company constantly improve?

**Little improvement** · · · · · · · · · · · · · · **Extensive improvement**

**Figure 5-3:**
Putting your advantage to the test.

Think about Starbucks. Everyone says you can get the same cup of coffee in San Francisco as you can in Chang Mai, Thailand, and it's true (I had to find out)! Starbucks delivers high-quality service with consistency time after time, which is an amazing core competency. In the product world, this consistency tends to be easier, but in the service world, people are involved every step of the way. And by nature, businesses are inconsistent. Putting consistency into your delivery can be a solid core competency. The consistency of Starbucks lets it introduce new products to deliver coffee to the consumer.

✔ **Brand development:** Growing and developing your brand over time can be a core competency worth more than all the past years' marketing budgets combined. Developing your brand happens by reinforcing your image in the marketplace through everything you do.

Think Kleenex. You don't say, "Hand me a soft facial tissue"; you say, "Hand me a Kleenex," even if the brand is something else. Coke is similar. Many people refer to all soda products as Coke. Those brands have become the product type they represent.

✔ **Depth of knowledge:** Consider how much knowledge you gain in your business year after year. I like to call it *tribal knowledge.* The longer you're in business, the more that tribal knowledge grows. But it only feeds on itself if you capture your experiences in a systematic way. Just as employees can be a key strength, they can also be a key weakness if they move on without leaving the knowledge with the tribe.

✔ **Continued innovation and improvement:** Some organizations excel at innovation whereas others struggle. Innovation is the ability to develop products and services that your market wants better and faster than your competitors.

Intuit, with its Quicken and QuickBooks products, is a company that fosters continuous improvement based on customer feedback. Improvement for improvement's sake is a black hole. Quicken product sales show how this core competency can be worth the time it takes to develop it. Intuit's software success allows it to cross sell mortgages and other financial services to the customer base.

✔ **Longevity:** The pure staying power of a company over time can be a testament to its strength. Nurturing longevity is difficult but something that can be leveraged if you have it. Family businesses are great examples of firms that can use their market history as a core competency.

# Using Your Advantages Now

Focusing on your competitive advantages can have a tremendous impact on your business. If you have time to work on only one part of the planning process, I recommend spending time to formulate your competitive advantage.

By knowing what you're best at, you can focus on what matters for success and profitability.

You don't have to wait until your strategic plan is complete to put your competitive advantages to work for you. Because your list of advantages are probably things you're already doing, you can start doing them better or even start talking about them to raise the level of awareness in and outside of your company.

In the following sections, I show you how to use and measure your advantages as part of your strategic plan.

## Implementing your advantages

Competitive advantages can be utilized in so many ways outside of just your strategic plan. Get creative with how you can make your advantages come to life. Here are some ideas:

- ✔ **Use your competitive advantages in your marketing material.** Turn them into a tag line. Use them in a press release. Add them to your corporate About Us page on your website.

- ✔ **Communicate the advantages daily.** Include your competitive advantages in your signature line on your e-mail. Add a line in your voice mail greeting or your automated voice attendant.

- ✔ **Tell your employees.** Post your advantages in a common area. Add them to your internal blog.

- ✔ **Refine your advantages by obtaining feedback from your customers.** Ask a few of your best clients whether they agree with your list of advantages. Improve or add to it based on their responses.

- ✔ **Make them better.** Develop a handful of 30-day actions that you and your staff can start working on to make your competitive advantages even stronger.

## Measuring your advantages

Now that you've got it, why not try to find a way to quantify your most important competitive advantage and promote that quality about your company? Do you have the metrics that matter and support monitoring your uniqueness? Find a way to support your claim through numbers that you can use to answer, "Why us?" Establishing a measurement based on a core element of your business elevates the importance in your organization and helps you monitor whether you're sustaining the advantage or letting it slip.

Industry data can be helpful in identifying how to quantify your competitive advantage. Referral statistics and retention rates offer other opportunities. Here are other places to look:

- ✔ Inventory turns
- ✔ Delivery times
- ✔ Return rates
- ✔ Satisfaction rates
- ✔ Guarantees
- ✔ Terms
- ✔ Referral rates

## Putting your advantages in your plan

Your strategic plan needs to include a section that states your competitive advantage. But you can also include it in full or parts of it in other areas of your plan. Here are a few ideas:

- ✔ Include the intent of your competitive advantage in your mission statement. (Check out Chapter 6 for mission statements.)
- ✔ Use the information you collected from your customers and employees to start the list of your strengths and weaknesses. (See Chapter 7.)
- ✔ Develop long-term goals that make your competitive advantage sustainable (Chapter 12).
- ✔ Include measures to monitor your competitive advantage.

Most importantly, you use your competitive advantages as a yardstick for every part of your strategic plan. Chapter 14 asks you to evaluate your strategic plan based on how well each section supports your competitive advantages.

Thinking about what you do best helps you build the strongest foundation possible for your business. When you're looking at your list of competitive advantages, be careful that your strategies do nothing to weaken your company's competitive advantage or take away from the key capabilities that got you where you are. Remember, now that you've identified your DNA, everything should grow from these cells.

# Chapter 6

# Developing Your Mission, Values, and Vision

*In This Chapter*

▶ Laying your strategic foundation

▶ Revamping your organization's mission statement

▶ Clarifying your shared organizational values

▶ Describing your vision

▶ Sharing your strategic foundation with others

*W*hile on vacation, a businessman bought fish from an old fisherman every day. One day he arrived to find the fisherman docking his boat at noon. "Is something wrong?" he asked. A smile wrinkled the seller's leathery face. "By no means. All is well." "Then why are you docking your boat so early?" asked the businessman.

"So I can go to my house, sit on my porch, and sip tea with my wife," the fisherman replied. The man of commerce objected. "But the day is still young. You can still fish." "No need to," the fisherman said. "I've made enough money for today."

"Enough? Absurd. You should keep working." The spry old man stopped and stared at his well-dressed visitor. "And why should I keep working?"

"To sell more fish."

"And why sell more fish?"

"Because the more fish you sell, the more money you make. The more money you make, the richer you are. The richer you are, the more boats you can buy. The more boats you buy, the more fishermen sell your fish, and the richer you become. And when you have enough, you can stop working, sell your boats, stay home, and sit on the porch with your wife and drink tea."

The fisherman smiled. "I can do that today. I guess I have enough."

This story, which you've probably heard in a variety of versions, quickly explains the importance of having a clear mission, vision, and set of corporate values. This chapter walks you through specific exercises to help you identify your organization's mission, vision, and core values.

# Building Your Strategic Foundation

Knowing why you're doing what you're doing (your *mission*), where you're trying to go (your *vision*), and how you're going to go about it (your *values*) are the glue that holds an organization together. You preserve these elements while your strategies and goals change and flex with the market. You may modify your mission, vision, or values over time, but the intent stays unchanged. So just like the fisherman, you, too, will have complete clarity when making critical business decisions that impact your future.

Your mission, vision, and values can sound abstract, esoteric, and downright fluffy to a lot of people, especially those who are burning to move forward with a real-world project. These people don't want to hang back conceptualizing about people's wishes and dreams.

Don't let being pragmatic get in the way of this important stage of building a strong foundation of consensus for your organization. If you don't take the time to articulate mission, values, and vision on the front end, you may pay for it later when you're trying to write goals and objectives without a crystal clear strategic direction.

In this chapter, you develop and revise your mission, vision, and values statements. Following an average time frame for the strategic planning process, this chapter's tasks should take you approximately two weeks to complete. Take a look at your strategic foundation — the core and the future of your business — by using the framework in Table 6-1:

| Table 6-1 | Your Strategic Foundation |
|---|---|
| *Your Core* | *Your Future* |
| DNA: What you do best (competitive advantage from Chapter 5) | Future vision: Where you're headed (vision statement from the "Visioning: Focusing in on Your North Star" section later in this chapter) |
| Core purpose: Why you exist (mission statement; see the next section "Assessing Your Mission") | Future description: What does it look like — your envisioned future (vivid description; see the "Futurecasting: Looking to the Future" section later in this chapter) |

| Your Core | Your Future |
| --- | --- |
| Core values: What you stand for (values statement from the "Fine-tuning Your Organizational Values" section later in this chapter) | |

# Assessing Your Mission

A *mission statement* is a statement of the company's purpose or its fundamental reason for existing. The statement spotlights what business a company is presently in and the customer needs it presently strives to meet. To build a solid foundation for a successful business, having a written, clear, concise, and consistent mission statement is essential. This statement should simply explain who you are and why you exist.

For example, the mission statement of Olsen & Associates Public Relations is, "We create positive relationships for our clients in the communities they serve by identifying and utilizing the appropriate means of communication." If the company doesn't live up to this mission, it has no reason to exist.

I help you develop (or revise) your mission statement in the following sections by first looking at the elements of an effective mission statement and then providing several examples throughout.

## Elements of an effective mission statement

Your mission statement serves as a guide for day-to-day operations and as the foundation for future decision making. Make sure that your statement includes the following criteria:

- **Focuses on satisfying customer needs:** Focus the business on satisfying customer needs instead of spotlighting your product or service.

- **Based on your core competencies:** Base your mission on a competitively superior internal strength or resource that your company performs well in comparison to your competitors. For example, McDonald's core competency is providing low-cost food and fast service to large groups of customers.

- **Motivates and inspires employee commitment:** Your mission statement should be motivating. Don't base it on making more sales or profits but on employees' significant work and how the mission contributes to people's lives.

- **Realistic and clear:** Avoid making the mission too narrow or too broad. A mission needs to contain a purpose that's realistic to avoid *mission* *creep,* or expansion outside of your intended boundaries. Many organizations can go off on tangents that aren't core to their purpose and are unrealistic because their mission isn't clearly defined.

- **Specific, short, sharply focused, and memorable:** Write a precise statement of purpose that describes the essence of the business in words your employees and customers can remember you by.

- **Clear and easily understood:** Develop and write your mission statement so you can quickly and briefly tell people you meet at a party or on an airplane why your company exists. If you keep that concept in mind, your statement can automatically be short and comprehensible. Make sure to give your company team a profoundly simple focus for everything it does as a business.

- **Says what the company wants to be remembered for:** In the end, a mission statement leaves a lasting impression. How do you want the world to think of you? Your statement can provide simple insight into why you do business.

## Examples of world-class mission statements

Mission statements are as varied as organizations. Some meet all the effective criteria listed in the "Elements of an effective mission statement" section, and others deviate completely. Here are a handful of mission statements to get your creative juices flowing. (***Note:*** Some of these mission statements are older versions, which I included to provide effective examples from a diverse range of organizations.)

- **Arthur Carhart Wilderness Training Center:** To preserve the values and benefits of wilderness for present and future generations by connecting agency employees and the public with their wilderness heritage through training, information, and education.

- **Boy Scouts of America:** To prepare young people to make ethical and moral choices over their lifetimes by instilling the values of the Scout Oath and Law.

- **Chitimacha Tribe:** We the people of the Sovereign Nation of the Chitimacha, in order to proclaim and perpetuate our vision, hereby embrace these beliefs: We must preserve and protect our natural resources, our people and all Native Americans. We must

promote a harmonious and prosperous existence among ourselves and within our community. We must maintain the highest level of integrity, honor and authenticity in all our endeavors, and We must always exist as a Nation by preserving our cultural heritage.

- **Starbucks:** To inspire and nurture the human spirit — one person, one cup, and one neighborhood at a time.

- **The Elephant Sanctuary:** A natural-habitat refuge where sick, old, and needy elephants can once again walk the earth in peace and dignity.

- **Fannie Mae:** To provide liquidity, stability and affordability to the U.S. housing and mortgage markets.

- **Google:** To organize the world's information and make it universally accessible and useful.

- **Wal-Mart:** We save people money so they can live better.

- **Marine Stewardship Council:** To safeguard the world's seafood supply by promoting the best environmental choices.

✓ **Marriott Hotels:** To make people who are away from home feel they are among friends and really wanted.

✓ **Merck:** To operate a worldwide business that produces meaningful benefits for consumers, our market partners and our community.

✓ **American Water Works Association, the New Jersey Section (AWWA NJ):** Dedicated to the promotion of public health and welfare in the provision of drinking water of unquestionable quality and sufficient quantity; AWWA NJ must be pro-active and effective in advancing the technology, science, management, and government policies relative to the stewardship of water.

✓ **Rotary International:** To provide service to others, promote integrity, and advance world understanding, goodwill, and peace through its fellowship of business, professional, and community leaders.

✓ **Southwest Airlines:** To provide the highest quality of customer service delivered with a sense of warmth, friendliness, individual pride, and company spirit.

✓ **The Clorox Company:** To improve the quality of life in communities where Clorox employees live and work. Community involvement is an integral part of our business and is carried out through a program of grant making, volunteerism, and leadership in community service.

✓ **University of Phoenix:** To provide access to higher education opportunities that enable students to develop knowledge and skills necessary to achieve their professional goals, improve the productivity of their organizations, and provide leadership and service to their communities.

## *Evaluating your current mission statement*

Many mission statements are works in progress. Others have been handed down over the years to the point that they've lost their relevance. If you have a mission statement, it may be time to dust it off or give it a polishing for updates or total overhauls. Generally, if five years have gone by and you haven't even touched your mission statement, it's definitely time for reviewing, fine-tuning, or even rewriting your mission statement.

The worst thing for your planning effort is to have a mission statement that's meaningless to your staff and other stakeholders. Sit down with your senior staff or management team and evaluate the effectiveness of your current mission statement by using the Mission Statement Worksheet provided on the CD. Collect everyone's thoughts and suggestions, but the final decision on how to change the mission is the CEO's. If you do decide to change it, leave the wordsmithing to one person.

## *Writing a new mission statement*

You've determined the need for a new mission statement. It's okay; I'm here to help you start from scratch or even revise the one you currently have. Use the Know What Game You're Playing Worksheet on the CD to get started.

The three components in the following list can help you craft your mission statement. Consider answering these questions from your customers' perspective, and you'll instantly see an improvement in your responses.

✔ What's the purpose of our business? Why do we exist? (See Chapter 5 for tips on how to answer these questions.)

✔ What activity are we going to do to accomplish our purpose? What are we going to provide?

✔ What do we intend to accomplish on behalf of our customers? Or who benefits from our work?

Follow these steps to create an effective mission statement:

1. **Collect ideas and opinions (either through a group meeting or an individual survey) of your senior staff and key employees about the organization's mission.**

   Ask for responses and input specifically on the three questions listed earlier in this section. If you hold a meeting, just brainstorm and allow everyone's ideas to be collected.

2. **Collate and synthesize the responses, looking for similar themes. Develop several different versions of a draft mission statement.**

   Consider using present tense language so the statement reflects what you are, not what you aspire to become.

3. **Evaluate the different drafts against the checklist in the Mission Statement Worksheet on the CD.**

   Keep the drafts that meet the guidelines in the worksheet and throw out the others.

4. **Circulate the draft statements and ask for feedback.**

   Have the staff vote on its favorite version.

5. **Select the best one and make sure every employee receives a copy.**

   If you're developing the mission statement as part of your strategic plan, consider waiting to communicate the new mission statement until the plan is finished.

The organization's purpose and its final mission statement shouldn't be developed by a committee. Use the process described in this section to solicit ideas and input, but ultimately senior management and leaders set the strategic foundation for an organization.

Don't get stuck on this part of the process. If need be, develop a mission statement or a revised statement that's dubbed as a work in progress or a draft. Many organizations get caught up in developing the most perfect statement possible. This thought process misses the reason for a mission statement in the first place. Although you can use your statement in your marketing collateral or with customers (so you may want to check the spelling and grammar), the mission statement's primary usage is to clearly state the purpose of your organization to your employees and other stakeholders. Sometimes it takes years to perfect the statement for public usage. In the meantime, you have a team that understands why it comes to work every day.

# Fine-tuning Your Organizational Values

*Values* are enduring, passionate, and distinctive core beliefs. They're guiding principles that never change. Values are why you do what you do and what you stand for. Values are deeply held convictions, priorities, and underlying assumptions that influence your attitudes and behaviors. They have intrinsic value and importance to those inside the organization. Your core values are part of your strategic foundation.

Herb Kelleher, former CEO of Southwest Airlines, speaks about core values: "We always felt that people should be treated right as a matter of morality. Then, incidentally, that turned out to be good business, too. But it didn't really start as a strategy. It began with us thinking about what is the right thing to do in a business context. We said we want to really take care of these people, we want to honor them, and we love them as individuals. Now that induces the kind of reciprocal trust and diligent effort that made us successful. But the motivation wasn't strategy, it was core values."

More and more companies are articulating the core beliefs and values underlying their business activities. Strong values account for why some companies gain a reputation for such strategic traits as leadership, product innovation, dedication to superior craftsmanship, being a good company to work for, and total customer satisfaction. A company's values can dominate the kind of strategic moves it considers or rejects. When values and beliefs are deeply ingrained and widely shared by managers and employees, they become a way of life within the company, and they mold company strategy. They're also called *guiding principles.* Either way, focusing on these values or principles will help you create a sustainable company. I guide you through identifying your values in the following sections.

## Elements of effective organizational values

Developing core values can be tricky because you're transferring something that's very personal into a group and business setting. As you're working toward developing a values statement for your organization, beware of the personal and emotional connection most of your team members have with creating the values statement.

Here are some guidelines:

- ✔ **One word isn't enough to convey the real meaning of a value.** Create phrases, but not paragraphs.

- ✔ **Values should be specific, not generic.** More than one word is needed to define specificity.

- ✔ **Some values-driven language may be part of your mission statement.** That's fine, but consider not repeating what you've covered elsewhere.

- ✔ **Values need to be shared.** Although you don't need consensus from everyone in your organization, you do need agreement from senior management.

- ✔ **The list should include between five and seven values.** Values need to be memorable to your staff, so having a few statements is better than having so many that nobody remembers any.

To illustrate these guidelines in action, look at Herman Miller, an innovative furniture company.

- ✔ Rather than using the word *excellence,* Herman Miller chose the word *performance,* and explained what that means this way: "It isn't a choice, it's about everyone performing at his or her own best; we measure it; it enriches our lives and brings value."

- ✔ Rather than using the word *teamwork,* Herman Miller uses the word *inclusiveness,* and describes it this way: "To succeed as a company, we must include all the expressions of human talent and potential . . . when we are truly inclusive, we go beyond toleration to understanding all the qualities that make people who they are, that make us unique, and most important, that unite us."

## *Creating or updating your organizational values*

You don't set or establish core values; you discover them. The exercise in this section helps you focus on discovering shared values within your organization by starting with individual's values and moving up to the organization. You can use this exercise to update your current values statement or develop a new one. Focus this exercise on answering three questions:

- ✔ What are the core values and beliefs of our company?

- ✔ What values and beliefs guide our daily interactions?

- ✔ What are we really committed to?

Evaluate your values by using the Values Evaluation Worksheet on the accompanying CD. Because your values are a key foundational element to your company and strategic plan, you want to be doubly sure they're the right ones.

Here are the steps to developing your organizational values statement:

1. **Solicit a list of five to seven core values from each of your key staff members and senior management team.**

   Ask each person to provide the list of values to you individually through a survey or e-mail by answering the questions earlier in this section. Unlike with the mission and vision exercises, values are best solicited individually instead of in a group to begin with. Request that people explain each value they provide.

2. **Merge the lists provided by combining values that are listed more than once.**

   The purpose here is to develop a draft list of values. You may have more than five to seven at this time.

3. **Bring the group together to discuss the list of values.**

   Ask people to comment on what's listed. Revise and modify until you've generated a final values statement.

4. **Evaluate each value against the checklist in the Values Evaluation Worksheet on the CD for effectiveness.**

   You can do this step as a group or individually.

5. **Put the finishing touches on the values statement and communicate across the company.**

   See the next section for ideas on how to use your values statement today.

Need some ideas to get started on discovering your organizational values? See Figure 6-1 for a bunch of words that you can use to stimulate those gray cells. Give a copy to your values team to help the members generate their individual list.

## *Acting on your organizational values*

Developing a set of values is one thing; living by them is something completely different. Having a values statement that's all talk and no commitment undermines your leadership and the management team's credibility. Following are some ways to bring your organizational values to life:

| | | |
|---|---|---|
| dedicated | customer care | positive |
| consistent | strategic | trustworthy |
| outstanding | training | genuine |
| value | support | real |
| helpful | principles | excellent |
| customer service | beliefs | sensitive |
| image | competent | knowledgeable |
| service | sincerity | synergy |
| relationships | self-confident | maximum value |
| dependable | relationships | stand behind our work / people |
| guarantee | efficient | long-term relationships |
| 100% effort | opportunity | do the right thing |
| dedication | honesty / honest | referrals and customer goodwill |
| commitment | productivity | high expectations of |
| adaptable | performance | family |
| security | ability | no hype |
| trust | professionalism | friendly |
| people | retaining | energetic |
| personal growth | development | loyal |
| company growth | responsive/ness | teamwork |
| respect | integrity | creativity |
| community responsibility | passion | pride |
| continuous improvement | collaboration | entrepreneurial spirit |
| quality | customer expectations | innovation |
| embracing change | rewarding work | high performance |
| environmental responsibility | excellence | leadership |
| energy | enthusiasm | fairness |
| personal responsibility | dedication | independence |
| advocacy | expertise | customer satisfaction |
| openness | employee participation | reliability |

**Figure 6-1:**
Ideas, words, and phrases for your values statement.

✔ **Communication:** Send a letter to every employee; develop a brochure; visit every office to personally explain the values; post the values in a public area.

✔ **Training:** Develop short training sessions about the different value topics. If that sounds like a lot of work, consider holding a brown-bag lunch focused on one of the values. Allow an open discussion about what it means to act on and live by each value.

✔ **Reinforcement:** Engrain your values through performance reviews, in your goal statements, and in your everyday language.

✔ **Rewards/Recognition:** Host contests to give employees a fun reason to discover and integrate the values.

✔ **Hiring:** Use your values statement as a guide in your hiring process. Structure interview questions around each one of your values to ensure that you're bringing people into your company who align with your corporate culture.

✔ **Alignment:** Look at your values and figure out specific ways to align daily activities with the values. For example, if one of your values is innovation, then install a system to reward innovation. If customer satisfaction is a value, then set a policy of a 100 percent money back guarantee.

# Visioning: Focusing in on Your North Star

Forming a strategic vision should provide long-term direction, delineate what kind of enterprise the company is trying to become, and infuse the organization with a sense of purposeful action. Vision serves as a unifying focal point for everyone in the organization — like a North Star. In fact, your vision statement needs to be something you can achieve at some point in the future. Visions are also referred to as *big, hairy, audacious goals,* or *BHAGs,* a term made popular by Jim Collins and Jerry Porras in their *Harvard Business Review* article "Building Your Company's Vision."

A vision statement can be as far reaching as 100 years or as short as 5 years. Some people think that if you're not planning for 20 years in the future, you're being too shortsighted. Others say that the world is changing too quickly to plan more than a few years out. Either way, your vision statement needs to work for your company and the industry you operate in. I recommend developing a vision statement that's far reaching but attainable. If you attain it in a shorter amount of time, congratulations! But if you don't push your thinking out far enough, you find yourself being too tactical in your strategic planning.

Your vision should include:

✔ **A vision statement:** A short, concise statement of your organization's future state

✔ **A vivid description:** A long list of words and phrases that describes what that future state is like

Because the items in the bulleted list go hand-in-hand, you can develop them simultaneously, and I provide all the tools you need in the following sections.

Here are two examples of visions, or BHAGs, that were very lofty at the time they were established:

✔ We will put a man on the moon before the end of the decade and bring him back (President John F. Kennedy).

✔ A computer on every desk and in every home using great software as an empowering tool (Microsoft).

These two statements don't sound so crazy now, do they?

# Elements of an effective vision statement

Your vision statement needs to incorporate many elements. The following list contains elements that you can include in an effective vision statement (you don't have to use *every* one, but keep them in mind when you're writing or evaluating):

- ✔ **Audacious:** Your vision represents a dream that's beyond what you think is possible. It represents the mountaintop your company is striving to reach. Visioning takes you out beyond your present reality.

- ✔ **Capitalizes on core competencies:** Your vision builds on your company's core competencies. It builds on what you've already established: company history, customer base, strengths, and unique capabilities, resources, and assets.

- ✔ **Futurecasting:** Your vision provides a picture of what your business looks like in the future.

- ✔ **Inspiring:** Your vision engages language that inspires. It creates a vivid image in people's heads that provokes emotion and excitement. It creates enthusiasm and poses a challenge.

- ✔ **Motivating:** Your vision clarifies the direction in which your organization needs to move and keeps everyone pushing forward to reach it.

- ✔ **Purpose-driven:** Your vision gives employees a larger sense of purpose, so they see themselves as building a cathedral instead of laying stones.

# Imagining your future — vividly

The vivid description in your vision needs to be just that — vivid. Include a list of ideas, phrases, adjectives, and so forth that thoroughly explain what achieving the vision statement is like. Try to imagine your organization when you reach your vision. Your vivid description explains what it feels like. Your description should be vibrant and engaging and should translate the vision from words into pictures that people can carry in their heads.

Here are some helpful questions to develop a vivid description of your vision:

- ✔ What does our company look like? How many employees do we have? Where are we located? How many offices are at this location? What is the office environment like?

- ✔ Who is on the staff? What are their skills, degrees, and areas of expertise? How does everyone work together? What is the culture like?

- ✔ Who are our clients? How many customers do we have?

# Examples of big, hairy, audacious vision statements

Because seeing what other organizations aim for is always fun (and educational), here's a variety of vision statements:

✔ **Chemtura:** To grow a global portfolio of leading specialty chemical businesses, committed to innovation and the creation of value for our stakeholders.

✔ **DuPont:** To be the world's most dynamic science company, creating sustainable solutions essential to a better, safer, and healthier life for people everywhere.

✔ **Heinz:** To be the world's premier food company, offering nutritious, superior tasting foods to people everywhere.

✔ **National CASA:** In changing the course of children's lives, we envision a changed society. To achieve that vision, in partnership with the CASA/GAL network nationwide, we make two promises to every child who has a CASA or guardian ad litem volunteer: We will work with our network as a highly functioning team to ensure that every child finds a safe, permanent and nurturing home — with their own families where possible or if not, in adoptive families that respect their culture and connections. While we work together toward a long-term solution, we will make each child's current well-being a top priority — at home, at school, and in their communities.

✔ **Susan G. Komen for the Cure:** A world without breast cancer.

✔ **Novo Nordisk:** To be the world's leading diabetes care company.

✔ **Pershing General Hospital:** To become the provider of first choice for our community by being a leader in rural healthcare and offering innovative technologically advanced services.

✔ **Recording for the Blind and Dyslexic:** For all people to have equal access to the printed word.

✔ **North Slope Borough School District:** We envision our students graduate prepared and qualified to excel as productive citizens in the world, and able to integrate Iñupiat knowledge and values with Western ways. Our curriculum is culture-based, our attendance rate is above the state average, our parents and community members are committed to education and meaningfully engaged, more of our teachers are our own graduates and speak Iñupiaq, and our schools reflect who we are as people.

✔ **Mattel:** To be the premier toy brands — today and tomorrow.

✔ **McDonald's:** To be the world's best quick service restaurant experience. Being the best means providing outstanding quality, service, cleanliness, and value, so that we make every customer in every restaurant smile.

✔ **Amazon:** Our vision is to be earth's most customer centric company; to build a place where people can come to find and discover anything they might want to buy online.

✔ What type of projects are we working on? How many products or services are we selling?

✔ What is our industry, business community, or media saying about our company? What are the headlines? What publications or TV stations are we featured on? What awards have we won?

# Creating or updating your vision statement and vivid description

Updating or creating a new vision statement can be one of the most exciting parts of strategic planning. Creating your vision statement can be achieved in a fashion similar to that of creating your mission and values statements.

Follow these steps to create your vision:

1. **Gather your senior staff and key employees together for a one- to two-hour meeting.**

   Visioning is best done in a group setting. If your group is bigger than five people, break into small groups of three to five people to allow everyone to have a voice in the process.

2. **Generate a list of ideas and phrases based on the responses to these three questions:**

   • What will our organization look like five to ten years from now?

   • What does success look like?

   • What are we aspiring to achieve?

   Allow the group to brainstorm, even if some of the ideas are totally wacky.

3. **Ask the group to pair ideas that have similar themes.**

   Identify the ideas that most closely resemble the vision for the organization.

4. **Ask one or two people to develop a draft vision statement based on the condensed list of ideas.**

   The vision statement should be short and use verbs phrases that are forward-looking, such as *to be*.

5. **Ask another one or two people to generate the vivid description based on all the themes identified.**

   When developing the vivid description, use the future tense, such as "We will . . ."

6. **Bring the vision statement and vivid description back to the group.**

   Revise until you have something everyone agrees on.

7. **Evaluate the vision statement against the elements of an effective vision statement (discussed earlier in this chapter).**

   Make sure that your vision is as clear as possible.

Evaluate your vision by using the Vision Evaluation Worksheet on the accompanying CD. Because your vision sets the direction for your entire planning effort, you want to ensure it paints a clear picture of where you want to go.

# Futurecasting: Looking to the Future

In order to make the most of your planning effort and the work you've put into your vision statement so far, put your strategic thinking hat on and envision the future. Companies spend a lot of time predicting what sales will be like in the future, but little time actually thinking about the factors that impact that future. These factors include the following:

- Underlying dynamics
- The sweeping trajectory of new competition
- The way customers evolve
- The collision course one industry may be on with another

Consider starting your annual strategic planning retreat by *futurecasting* — the practice of trying to envision your company's future. Really push your team to think about what will be happening in five or ten years. I walk you through several exercises in the following sections that help you focus your viewpoint on your company's future.

A strategic plan is as much about the *planning* as it is about the *strategizing*. Futurecasting helps you really push your big-picture thinking to develop a strategic plan that's truly, well, strategic.

## Getting into the right frame of mind for futurecasting

Unfortunately, most people can't just jump mentally from now to the future. In this section, I show you a mind-bending exercise that can help your team get its creative juices flowing.

Ask your team the following questions in a group setting. Read the answers after everyone has responded in an open setting. (*Note:* Some people may have heard this series of questions before, so ask those already wise ones to stay quiet.)

- **How do you put a giraffe into a refrigerator?** The correct answer: Open the refrigerator, put the giraffe in, and close the door. This question tests whether you tend to do simple things in an overly complicated way.

- **How do you put an elephant into a refrigerator?** Wrong answer: Open the refrigerator, put the elephant in, and close the door. Correct answer: Open the refrigerator, take out the giraffe, put in the elephant, and close the door. This question tests your ability to think through the repercussions of your actions.

- ✔ **The Lion King is hosting an animal conference. All the animals attend except one. Which animal doesn't attend?** Correct answer: The elephant. The elephant is in the refrigerator, remember? This question tests your memory.

- ✔ **You have to cross a river, but it's inhabited by crocodiles. How do you manage it?** Correct answer: You swim across. Why? All the crocodiles are attending the animal conference. This question tests whether you learn quickly from your mistakes.

According to Accenture Consulting, around 90 percent of the professionals it tested got all questions wrong. But many preschoolers got several correct answers. Accenture Consulting says that this statistic conclusively disproves the theory that most professionals have the brains of a 4-year-old.

## Leaving your assumptions at the door

You're dead in the water if you let your assumptions take over strategic thinking. Ask your team to think about how it solved the brainteaser in the previous section. Relating to that problem, how would your team answer the following questions?

- ✔ What assumptions have you made?

- ✔ What rules have you assumed?

- ✔ How do your own perceptions influence the world you inhabit?

- ✔ How do you see the world and how is your view different from that of other people? What advantages and disadvantages are there of each way of thinking?

With those thoughts in mind, how can you and your team think differently? How would your team answer these questions when imagining the problem from someone else's angle? Have your team think about the following ideas as they relate to a different viewpoint:

- ✔ What happens in other countries, cultures, or companies?

- ✔ How can you change the situation to make a solution work?

- ✔ Visit or read about other people's lives and try to understand why they think the way they do.

## Working a strategic thinking exercise

It's time to apply strategic thinking to your business. Have your team try to answer the following scenario:

What will your company look like and how will it compete in the year 2030 or 2035? What trends do you need to consider in your planning?

Ask your team to come up with a list of ideas, statements, or activities to describe how the world looks in these five areas:

- ✔ Economically
- ✔ Socially
- ✔ Politically
- ✔ Technologically
- ✔ Ecologically
- ✔ Legally

With these lists on the wall, consider which trends apply to your business and which will affect your vision. Use this information as you're developing goals and objectives for your strategic plan (see Chapter 12):

- ✔ How can this trend influence our current customers?
- ✔ How can this trend influence our current core business?
- ✔ How can this trend create new customers?
- ✔ Who are the potential customers?
- ✔ What are our competitors doing about this trend?
- ✔ How fast is this trend developing? What accelerates it or slows it down?
- ✔ What are the risks of committing to this trend? What are the rewards?

# Finalizing Your Strategic Foundation

Now that you've reviewed the first phase of the strategic management process, you can see how all the elements of your strategic foundation — competitive advantage, mission, values, vision, and vivid description — should work together. Remember these elements of your organization don't change, or at least they don't change significantly. Your strategies, goals, objectives, and actions change based on market conditions, but they're always built on your strategic foundation.

Bring all the elements discussed in this chapter together in a strategic foundation sheet like the examples shown in Figure 6-2 and Figure 6-3. This sheet is an excellent document to include in a new employee packet, post in the break room, hand out to every employee, and use in strategy meetings. It gives everyone a bigger sense of purpose and an understanding of what your organization is all about.

| SPEAKSHOP | |
|---|---|
| **Competitive Advantages – Our DNA**<br>*What we do best* | **Vision Statement – Our Future**<br>*Where we are headed* |
| • Operational effectiveness through an open marketplace and operational cost efficiency<br>• Specialization in foreign language services<br>• Supplier and consumer loyalty<br>• Early entry and network effect<br>• Latin America and online education domain expertise | Revolutionize language education and establish a new model for business based on loyal yet independent sellers and customers who improve their communities and geopolitical understanding by developing friendships and partnerships worldwide. |
| **Mission Statement – Our Core Purpose**<br>*Why we exist* | **Vision Description**<br>*What it looks like* |
| Speak Shop's mission is to improve the lives of language tutors and students and to foster intercultural understanding and respect. Speak Shop offers tutors the chance to be entrepreneurial in managing their own tutoring services. Speak Shop provides students with the opportunity to achieve new educational goals, change their careers or prepare for travel abroad. At Speak Shop, students and tutors are active participants in creating a fun, educational and friendly environment. | Make foreign language learning available to anyone anywhere, thereby providing previously unattainable access to education, employment and inter-cultural exchange to a wide range of learners.<br><br>Inspire other companies to link profits and social impact and make them co-dependent.<br><br>Create a business that is as close to human as possible. We will make it clear that we are created by people, for people.<br><br>Constantly innovate effective, practical and fun ways to make a positive impact on people, widening our circle of impact broadly along the way. |
| **Values Statement – Our Core Values**<br>*What we stand for* | |
| High performance should be rewarding (fair competition)<br>We are in this together (community & compassion)<br>Individuals can change their lives (determinism)<br>Liberty and justice for all (freedom & equality) | Help millions of people communicate in other languages and become inspired by their own progress. Show them that they are not so different from each other. Help them understand the reason for their differences. |

**Figure 6-2:**
An example of strategic foundations.

## NORTH SLOPE BOROUGH SCHOOL DISTRICT

| **Mission Statement – Our Core Purpose** *Why we exist* | **Vision Statement – Our Future** *Where we are headed* |
|---|---|
| Learning in our schools is rooted in the values, history and language of the Iñupiat. Students develop the academic and cultural skills and knowledge to be:<br><br>• Critical and creative thinkers able to adapt in a changing environment and world;<br><br>• Active, responsible, contributing members of their communities; and<br><br>• Confident, healthy young adults, able to envision, plan and take control of their destiny. | *We envision.....*<br><br>Our students graduate prepared and qualified to excel as productive citizens in the world, and able to integrate Iñupiat knowledge and values with Western ways.<br><br>Our curriculum is culture-based, our attendance rate is above the state average, our parents and community members are committed to education and meaningfully engaged, more of our teachers are our own graduates and speak Iñupiaq, and our schools reflect who we are as people. |

| **Values Statement – Our Core Values** *What we stand for* | |
|---|---|
| Compassion - Though the environment is harsh and cold, our ancestors learned to live with warmth, kindness, caring and compassion.<br><br>Avoidance of Conflict - The Iñupiaq way is to think positive, act positive, speak positive and live positive.<br><br>Love and Respect for Our Elders and One Another - Our Elders model our traditions and ways of being. They are a light of hope to younger generations. May we treat each other as our Elders have taught us.<br><br>Cooperation - Together we have an awesome power to accomplish anything.<br><br>Humor - Indeed, laughter is the best medicine!<br><br>Sharing - It is amazing how sharing works. Your acts of giving always come back.<br><br>We are a spiritual people. | Family and Kinship - As Iñupiaq people we believe in knowing who we are and how we are related to one another. Our families bind us together.<br><br>Knowledge of Language - "With our language we have an identity. It helps us to find out who we are in our mind and in our heart."<br><br>Hunting Traditions - Reverence for the land, sea and animals is the foundation of our hunting traditions.<br><br>Respect for Nature - Our Creator gave us the gift of our surroundings. Those before us placed ultimate importance on respecting this magnificent gift for their future generations.<br><br>Humility - Our hearts command we act on goodness. Expect no reward in return. This is part of our cultural fiber.<br><br>Spirituality - We know the power of prayer. |

**Figure 6-3:** Another example of strategic foundations.

# Part III
# Sizing Up Your Current Situation

The 5th Wave                    By Rich Tennant

"Our customer survey indicates 30% of our customers think our service is inconsistent, 40% would like a change in procedures, and 50% think it would be real cute if we all wore matching colored vests."

# In this part . . .

Strategic planning is as much about planning and execution as it is about decision making. Good decision making comes from collecting the right data on which to base your decisions. In this part, you figure out how to research the market to find new customers. You dig into what internal and external information is needed to assess your business and its capabilities. You also take a peek at your company through the eyes of your customers.

# Chapter 7

# Assessing Your Business and Its Capabilities

*In This Chapter*

▶ Summarizing your strengths and weaknesses

▶ Evaluating how to hire, develop, and retain your best and brightest employees

▶ Checking out your capabilities and resources and linking them together

▶ Assessing your profit margins

*I*magine you're setting out on a road trip. You hop on Google Maps or turn on your GPS to select the quickest route from your home to your destination. With your trip plan in mind, you consult your friend because he traveled that road before. After you're feeling good about your route, you check your resources against your trip plan to make sure that you have enough time and gas to get there. Then, you assess your fuel-efficient SUV to ensure that it's in working condition and that you've loaded up your most recent podcasts to your iPod. You pack your bags and invite two friends because they're fun to have around.

Sound familiar? This situation may seem too methodical, but more than likely, you went through all those steps before you headed out on the road. Mapping a strategic plan is just the same: Your company needs a road map or plan to make the strategic plan work. This chapter focuses on your SUV (or company). More specifically, this chapter takes a look at the following points:

✔ **How does being on your SUV feel?** How it feels on the SUV is your company culture — teamwork, leadership, and climate for action.

✔ **Are the right people on your SUV and in the right seats? Are you keeping them there?** The SUV passengers are your employees, and the seats represent their skills and capabilities.

✔ **What type of SUV are you driving?** The type of SUV you drive indicates your operations — lean and mean or clunky and gas-guzzling.

✔ **Does your SUV run with the right amount of fuel so you have something left over for your shareholders?** This fuel is your profit margin, which indicates how well you use your resources to get where you want to go.

Using the road trip analogy helps explain the unexplainable in strategic planning. Understanding how your company's resources, capabilities, and processes are used to grow the organization is critical to successfully executing your strategy, growing your company, and ultimately making it sustainable. Often, pinpointing all the things that need to come together to move a company forward is difficult.

This chapter focuses on assessing your company's strengths and weaknesses that define where you stand today. Later, you use this information to guide the goals and objectives in your strategic plan.

# Establishing a Starting Point: Identifying Your Business's Strategic Position

To move from where you are today to where you want to go, you have to determine your *strategic position,* or where you stand today. This process is like taking your SUV into a mechanic for the annual tune-up. You get an assessment of what's working, what's not, what you need to fix, and what can wait.

In this chapter and Chapters 8 and 10, you perform an annual tune-up of your business with the help of a trusted business planning tool: the SWOT. SWOT stands for **s**trengths, **w**eaknesses, **o**pportunities, and **t**hreats. These four categories help you focus on the key factors that define your strategic position.

Your focus in this chapter is on your company's strengths and weaknesses; Chapter 8 looks at your strengths and weakness, too, but through the eyes of your customers. In Chapter 10, you focus on completing your SWOT analysis by identifying your opportunities and threats. You see the SWOT again in Chapter 12 when you develop your company's goals and objectives based on this information.

Use the following steps and tools on the CD to get started:

1. **Use the SWOT Analysis Template on the CD to start your own.**

   By breaking down your internal environment into capabilities, resources, and processes, you have a place to start assessing your company. Without these categories, the task can seem a little daunting. This format ensures that you're looking at your strengths and weaknesses holistically, instead of approaching them haphazardly.

2. **Perform a quick survey of your company's strengths and weaknesses, using the Intangible Assets Questionnaire on the CD.**

   Your organization's strengths encompass everything your company does well, including capabilities, skills, and resources, that you can leverage and draw on to execute plans and actions in your company.

Weaknesses, conversely, encompass everything that's holding your company back from achieving your goals or serving your customers. You can conduct this exercise from either a bottom-up (individuals to managers to executives) or a top-down process. Alternatively, you can choose to focus just on your SWOT development on one or more strategic issues that you identified at the beginning of the process.

3. **Dig a little deeper with the SWOT Analysis Template located on the CD to get more specific about each area.**

   Each section of this chapter is likely to give you insights and ideas about your strengths and weaknesses. Again, the SWOT Analysis Template helps you capture all your thoughts and keep them in order. For example, jot down thoughts about your effective customer relationship processes under *Strengths* and problems with employee retention under *Weaknesses*.

As you answer the questionnaires and track your ideas throughout this chapter, you have a good starting point to summarize and add to your key strengths and weaknesses. (Remember, these ideas can become the basis for goals in your strategic plan.) After you read through this chapter, you should have enough thoughts to fill in the two left-side quadrants on the SWOT Analysis Template. Consider this grid a running list of thoughts about your strategic position as you move through the rest of Part III. You complete your full SWOT at the end of Chapter 10.

# Evaluating Your Company's Capabilities

The first phase of identifying your strengths and weaknesses is looking at your capabilities or intangible assets (*intangible* means incapable of being realized or defined — not having physical presence). These assets point to why organizations are good or not good at identifying and leveraging people, culture, and knowledge.

By breaking down your capabilities into certain areas, which I show you how to do in the following sections, you can start to define your strengths and weaknesses. After they're defined, align them with the strategic direction you want to go. You need people with the skills and knowledge who are motivated and resourceful to make your strategic plan a reality. Otherwise, you just have a bunch of good ideas on a piece of paper.

## Human capital: Having the right people in the right positions

How many times have you heard someone say, "Our employees are our most important asset"? And how often do you feel like your company (or any company for that matter) backs up that statement? The time has come where big and small businesses alike no longer pay lip service to this statement. The trend is to spend more time and money on recruiting absolutely the best people. No matter how busy you are, not hiring anyone is better than hiring the wrong person.

After you have the right people on your SUV, making sure that they're in the right seats means they have the skills and abilities to do their jobs. Just hiring them without training and development is like buying a house and doing nothing to maintain or improve it. You're letting your asset go to waste.

When you get the right people in the right seats, you want to keep them there. Nothing is more harmful and costly than losing good people — harmful because knowledge walks out the door and costly because you have to train someone else. So although hiring the best people is good, hiring the best people and making sure that they're developed with the right skills and abilities is better.

Evaluate how well you do the following management tasks:

- ✔ **Hiring:** Only *you* can answer whether your current hiring process yields good results. Every company has its own unique approach to evaluating potential employees — personality tests, rounds of interviews, special questions, and so on. No one way is superior to another. What really matters is getting the right people onboard. But a great way to see quick results in your company, if you're having employee problems, is to hire slow and fire fast.

- ✔ **Developing:** How effective is your training and development program? Do your employees have the best tools and work environment to do their jobs? You may have a formalized program, but, again, what really matters is that your employees are doing their best work and achieving their fullest potential. If employees really are your most important asset, you need to develop them to realize the full value of your investment.

  Training and development needs to be linked directly to improvement *at work.* Make sure that you're training for the capabilities that your organization needs to move forward. For example, if you want to improve your productivity, send your employees to a time management workshop instead of a team-building ropes course. I'm constantly amazed at how many training programs aren't linked to the overall strategy.

- ✔ **Retaining:** The words *employee retention* hit most business owners in the gut. Managing people can be a hard concept for some people, and retention seems to be the perceived outcome of poor management (which isn't necessarily the case because employees leave for numerous reasons unrelated to their jobs). Nevertheless, do you know the number-one reason people leave their jobs? Not feeling appreciated by their boss. Employees need to feel appreciated, challenged, and fairly rewarded to stick around.

  How's your retention rate? Because you've invested a significant amount of time and money into your employees, retaining them becomes imperative. Otherwise, you let your most valued asset walk out the door.

Obviously, the outcome of not performing these management tasks well is a high turnover rate. However, you don't want to wait until people leave to make improvements. You can evaluate these three areas by surveying employees, conducting exit interviews, bringing in an HR consultant, and monitoring overall employee satisfaction. To complete your view of your employees' capabilities, include customer praises and complaints in your assessment.

GoDaddy.com, the number-one Internet domain registrar in the world, is known for putting its money where it really matters. No $5,000 office chairs or $10,000 conference tables. Founder Bob Parsons invests in the two assets that contribute to profitability: people and technology. Although he focuses on keeping costs down, Parsons doesn't scrimp on employee incentives. He gives away televisions, trips, motorcycles, a car, and even a year's rent or mortgage. Why? Because as his call centers grow, he wants them to be a fun place to work. When his people are having fun, his customers are happy because they get to talk to happy employees. When his customers are happy, production and sales go up.

## Organizational capital: Getting a feeling for your corporate culture

The second phase in the assessment of your company's capabilities is reviewing its organizational capital. Now that you have people on your SUV and in the right seats, answer the following questions:

- ✔ How does it feel to be on your SUV? (How is your work environment?)
- ✔ Do you and your employees like coming to work?
- ✔ Does everyone get along?
- ✔ Is someone driving the SUV? (Who's running the show?)
- ✔ What's your organizational culture like?

Organizations are made up of people, and the people determine what goes on at work. At the end of the day, every person is responsible for how the work gets done and how the organization functions.

Structure, teamwork, management, and leadership dictate how it feels to work in your business environment. Evaluate your organizational capital by looking at the following areas:

- ✔ **Structure:** Structure does serve a purpose — to have an efficient flow of information for action and decision making. Normally, organizational charts look like a bunch of departments cobbled together because businesses grow and morph over time. Is your organization structured to allow everyone to operate effectively? How many signatures do you need to get approval?

- ✔ **Leadership:** *Leadership* is the art of getting people to do what you want because they want to. Leadership comes in many styles, but the end result is the same. Leaders are responsible for setting the vision and the strategy. How's your leadership?

- ✔ **Management:** Managers are responsible for making sure that the work gets done and that employees are performing at their peak level. In your company, the lines between leaders and managers may be blurred. Your leaders may be managers, and your managers may be leaders. Either way, both are just as important in keeping your SUV moving down the road. Is your management team successfully getting the work done and helping your employees achieve their fullest potential?

- ✔ **Teamwork:** How do you build a great team? Numerous theories exist that can easily fill the rest of this book. But nothing gets done in business, except maybe answering the phone, without teamwork. For your evaluation, ask yourself whether the whole is greater than the sum of the parts. Are your people achieving more together than apart?

Each of these areas has industries built around it. If you're looking to dig in to improving one or more of them, look to an outside consulting firm or training course that focuses on the discipline specifically.

Patagonia — an environmentally-conscious, highly innovative outdoor clothing company — is notorious for its enviable culture. Under founder Yvon Chouinard's leadership, the company has reached $240 million in annual sales. The business continues to maintain a complete and total commitment to environmentalism as well as blending work and play. At times, profitability takes a lower priority than upholding the corporate values. The corporate culture emanates from the top through Chouinard's philosophy and leadership style. His thoughts are consistently supported by managers, teams, employee internship programs, and the company's lack of cubicles. Surfing at lunchtime or taking major customers skiing is part of Patagonia's business and its culture.

## Knowledge capital: Knowing what you already know

The third phase in the assessment of your company capabilities is reviewing its knowledge capital. The institutional knowledge, or *tribal knowledge,* as I like to call it, is one of those management fads that come and go. But regardless of what may be hip in the business traditions of today, creating and maintaining an efficient knowledge management system to share information companywide is common sense.

Most companies don't maintain and retain knowledge very well because, by some estimates, up to 70 percent of what employees do is nothing more than reinventing what their organization had discovered previously. And why do you want your people wasting time figuring out what someone else in the company has already discovered? Information is an intangible asset that can be a significant competitive advantage if you can harness it.

At its simplest form, managing your tribal knowledge is figuring out a way to capture everything your organization knows and then creating an easy way for everyone in the company to access and share that knowledge. Here's an easy process to make improvements in the area of knowledge capital:

1. **Identify what information is actually knowledge.**

   *Information* is a lot of data put into context. *Knowledge* is information that's been processed and identified as continually useful to the organization. Knowledge must contribute to your competitive advantage. Identify the key areas of knowledge that make your company run. Think about your core processes, customer service, vendor relationships, client relationships, and so on. Think about what would happen if your key employees left. What knowledge do they have that you need to capture?

2. **Capture the knowledge.**

   You want to translate the knowledge from your employees to a place where the information can be stored and backed up. You can capture knowledge by conducting exit interviews, standardizing processes, successfully using customer relationship management (CRM) systems with complete customer profiles, job shadowing, and so on. By capturing the knowledge, you're formally bringing what's in someone's head into your business — permanently.

3. **Share your findings.**

   I know, I know, too much information exists in this world already. I agree! Everyone is on information overload. But your tribal knowledge is the type of information that should make everyone's job easier. Do you have Google-like search capability in your business data that returns usable results? Figure out ways to share the knowledge in five-minute debriefings at your staff meetings, on a company blog, or in a training manual for new hires.

4. **Use the knowledge.**

   Now that you have leverage, make sure that you use it. Put the knowledge into practice by cross-training current employees, educating new employees if it's within their functional area, and adding to the knowledge base continually. If you've done the other three steps correctly, you should see an improvement in overall productivity.

Identify one or two ways to tackle knowledge management this year. Develop a one-year and a three-year goal for your strategic plan. Knowledge disappearance has been a problem throughout time, and what makes the situation more severe today is that the knowledge that's being lost is more complex, abstract, and difficult to create than ever before. More than likely, knowledge management is an area that can use some improvement in your company. You want to protect the information that your company thrives on.

But don't just listen to me. Listen to Bill Gates, one of the most successful entrepreneurs: "The most meaningful way to differentiate your company from your competition, the best way to put distance between yourself and the crowd, is to do an outstanding job with information. How you gather, manage, and use information determines whether you win or lose."

# *Examining Your Resources*

After your capabilities are sufficiently understood, the next step in the SWOT process is looking at your resources. (Refer to your SWOT analysis if needed.) *Resources* are tangible assets — any physical or quantifiable assets that your organization uses to bring revenue into your business. Some assets, such as your brand, are intangible but still have a quantifiable value to your company, just like your long-standing customer relationships.

From a strategic perspective, you need to look at what tangible assets you have versus what you need to achieve your strategic plan. You may need to come back to this section after you've developed more of your plan. But taking stock of where you are now can be helpful in your planning process. Specifically, you need to look at the following:

- ✔ What tangible assets you have in your company right now that allow you to produce your product or service
- ✔ What tangible assets you need to continue to provide and exceed your current service levels

Create a page titled "Resources." List the assets you have (strengths), the assets you need (weaknesses), and the assets you desire. Consider coming back to this page when you're further along in your plan development.

To help identify your business resources, group them under the following categories:

- ✔ **Financial resources:** These resources include all the items available to finance or pay for your strategic decisions. Existing resources include cash balances, lines of credit, other loans, owner's equity, and credit agreements with your vendors.

- ✔ **Intangible resources:** Your intangible resources are everything that you can't touch or feel but that you know has value to your business. These sources include

  - • **Brands:** Your standing and awareness in the marketplace is your brand.

- **Goodwill:** Goodwill is the difference between the value of your tangible assets and the actual market value of your business.

- **Intellectual property:** When you're managing your knowledge, you actually turn a capability into a resource. Intellectual property also includes patents, trademarks, and copyrights.

- **Reputation:** Your reputation is your standing in your community and your industry.

✔ **Physical resources:** Your physical resources include everything you have and use to deliver your products and services. These resources also include

- Production facilities, which may include buildings, plants, machinery, capacity, investment and maintenance, quality, and organization of your production processes

- Information technology (IT), which includes systems, computers, and critical software in use in the organization and also encompasses integration with customers and suppliers

# Processes: Connecting Your Capabilities and Resources

The next step in the SWOT analysis is looking at the processes. Are you cruising down the road smoothly, or is your SUV coughing and sputtering along, barely making it to the next service station? More than likely, your company is somewhere between these two extremes. And you probably go back and forth between states of high and low performance. It's time to open up the hood of your SUV and find out what's going on in there. In this section, you're looking at the processes that connect your intangible assets to your tangible assets to produce an outcome, which is a current product or service, a new product, customer service, or development and maintenance of relationships with partners and governmental agencies.

When evaluating your internal processes, they need to pass the efficiency/effectiveness test:

✔ *Efficiency* **is doing things right.** Are your processes producing the end result you desire?

✔ *Effectiveness* **is doing the right things.** Are you involved in the processes you should be involved in? If not, these processes are potential areas for outsourcing.

By reviewing your internal processes, you find some that are operating at full efficiency and others that are barely hanging on. Do you have some processes that continually have problems? Are there others that are working just perfectly?

Just like with intangible assets, your processes break down into general business areas. Complete the Operational Processes Questionnaire located on the CD to grasp a better understanding of operational, customer, relationship, and innovation processes. These processes are also described further in the following sections.

## Operational processes

Operations produce and deliver the goods and services to customers. These processes encompass managing your creation of customer value.

Service companies may be tempted to think that processes aren't managed in this area, but consider how you deliver your service. It doesn't happen by magic. You take specific steps to deliver what you do; these steps are your operational processes. Because strategic planning is about improving the status quo, looking at how to improve operations is the key.

Operations management covers four generic processes:

- ✔ **Developing and sustaining supplier or vendor relationships:** Bringing raw material and goods into your company is a set of processes that feed into how you produce products and services. Do you effectively manage your supplier relationships to ensure that you obtain the total lowest cost of the products and services you buy? Are you efficiently sourcing, moving, storing, and inspecting the raw materials you use?

- ✔ **Producing products and services:** At the heart of your operational processes is the production of your product and service. Are you efficient at production, thereby lowering production costs and increasing your asset utilization? Are you effectively producing your product with minimal scrap, error rates, or returns?

- ✔ **Delivering the product or service to your customer:** Just like with managing your suppliers, you also have processes that manage your distribution. Are you efficiently delivering your products or services to your customers? Are you effective at reaching your customers through your distribution channels?

- ✔ **Managing operating risk:** Not all companies have direct operating risk, but most companies are exposed to some kind of risk associated with market fluctuations. Processes in this area deal with effectively and efficiently reducing costs associated with capital costs and taxes.

Erlach Computer Consulting, a small technology service company, improved the one key operational process that nearly doubled the company's revenue in one year. The process? Time tracking. Yes, the process may sound simple, but for Erlach, time is the company's inventory, product, and distribution medium. Starting from the top, management required every employee to track his or her time down to 15-minute increments. The company was tracking time previously, but not with 100 percent compliance. Now that the time is captured, Erlach can account and bill for previously unbilled time. Not only were the employees more conscious of their work day, but also clients were correctly charged for the services they received.

## Customer management processes

Customer management processes cut across all your customers — current and new. In evaluating your performance, written or unwritten, your organization goes through the following processes when acquiring and serving your customers:

- ✔ **Selecting customers:** Are you identifying the right customers whose problems you can solve? (Chapter 9 helps you identify your key customers.)

- ✔ **Acquiring customers:** A quick way to evaluate this process is to look at your customer conversion rate. How many prospects are you turning into customers? How effective is your marketing strategy? Is your message the right one, and does it hit the right people at the right time? What's your sales cycle? Has it improved from last year?

- ✔ **Retaining customers:** Assuming that you've landed the right customers and are able to deliver what you promised, your customers should be sticking with you. While you're acquiring new customers, you still want to take care of the old ones. Word of mouth is also important here. When your customers are highly satisfied, they tell their friends.

- ✔ **Building relationships with your customers:** Are you growing your relationships with your customers, or are they stagnant? You can measure this success by seeing whether your customers are buying more from you year after year.

Scandinavian Airlines realized the importance of managing its customers' relationships by breaking down customer relationship management processes to their most basic, uncomplicated level. Jan Carlzon, CEO, says, "Last year, each of our 10 million customers came in contact with approximately five SAS employees, and this contact lasted an average of 15 seconds each time. Those 50 million 'moments of truth' are the moments that ultimately determine whether SAS succeeds or fails as a company."

## Relationship management processes

Organizations don't operate in an isolated pool with just their employees and their customers. Instead, companies and departments have relationships with the communities they operate in, governmental agencies, and partners such as other companies, industry associations, and maybe even competitors. Your company may need to manage relationships with all or a few of these entities because everyone is a piece of the bigger picture.

These relationships break down into the following areas and processes:

✔ **Environmental sustainability:** If your company impacts the environment (what business doesn't?), how effective are you at managing your resource consumption, water and air emissions, waste disposal, and overall environmental impact?

✔ **Employee well-being and compliance:** How's your employee health and safety performance? Are you efficiently taking care of your employees to minimize any safety accidents or repetitive stress injuries?

✔ **Community contributions:** Are you investing in your community through nonprofit organizations or other community programs? Small organizations tend to take a hit-or-miss approach to this area, meaning that they don't consistently contribute to an ongoing charity. Consider the time and energy savings with a consistent community outreach program.

✔ **Alliance management:** Are you efficiently taking care of the organizations you work with? Do you have a consistent approach to managing these critical relationships? Are you effective with your alliance? In other words, are you working with the right ones?

Maximizing profits is just part of running a big business, according to John Mackey, co-CEO and cofounder of Whole Foods — the nation's leading natural and organic grocery chain with $4.7 billion in annual sales. He feels there's a larger trend toward businesses having a greater responsibility in society. Employees, customers, and shareholders all want their businesses to be good corporate citizens. Mackey believes that profits and being a good citizen go hand-in-hand. He puts his money where his mouth is, with 5 percent of annual net profits going toward charitable causes as well as numerous community programs.

## *Innovation processes*

The fourth part of reviewing your processes involves taking a look at your creativity. If you're not innovating, you're dead. (At least that seems to be the general consensus of the business community, but I've yet to see anyone keel over!) Without innovation, anyone can imitate what you're offering after a period of time. Also, business gets pretty boring if you have the same old stuff. Busting out of the old mold keeps things exciting and employees engaged. Here are the four procedures necessary to make innovation part of your business:

✔ **Identify market opportunities for new products or services.** How effective are you at anticipating customer needs and uncovering new opportunities? What are your customers telling your employees (who speak with your customers most often) about their needs?

✔ **Manage the ideas in your innovation pipeline.** Are you effectively choosing the right products and services to potentially move into full development?

✔ **Design and develop the new products and services that are worthy and that leverage your capabilities.** Are you efficiently moving products and services through the development stages by reducing time and costs? Or do new products languish until they become stale?

✔ **Bring the new products and services to market.** Are you efficiently getting your new product or service in front of your current customers? Do they know about all the offerings you have? What's the time to market for your new products, and how will they sell the first year?

How do you know if you're efficient and effective at innovating in general? Your *new* products and services sell. That's the metric for all the preceding processes.

"Pound for pound, the most innovative company in America is W.L. Gore & Associates," according to *Fast Company,* a well-respected monthly business publication. W.L. Gore is known for its premier brand Gore-Tex, as well as other innovative solutions for the electronics, medical, and fabric industries. How does W.L. Gore do it? It operates on five key philosophies that dictate how the company is run:

✔ **Work in small teams.** With small groups, the company is able to respond and innovate quickly.

✔ **Don't establish rank.** Instead of a rigid chain of command, which can delay decision making, the company eliminated rank. All employees are equal.

✔ **Everyone can lead.** Without rank, every employee has the opportunity to be a leader.

✔ **Take the long view.** Great innovations can sometimes take years, not months. By recognizing this time frame, the company doesn't demand results for quarterly shareholder reports.

✔ **Celebrate failure.** Success requires failure. By celebrating failure, the company encourages employees to test every new idea because you never know which one may be a runaway success.

## Other important process areas

Other process areas are important and support the previously discussed processes. These processes don't stand on their own or exist without a process that tangibly produces results. However, highlighting the following three supporting areas makes every organization run a whole lot smoother.

### Technology

Technology (IT) in and of itself isn't a strategy. Virtually everyone has access to the same technology, so technology can't give you a competitive advantage. What you do with your technology is a different story. Figure out whether it makes you faster or slower. Technology should make every other process in your company run smoothly and more efficiently (if selected and implemented correctly). To evaluate your IT, consider the following two questions:

- ✔ Do your IT systems improve the overall operational efficiency of your organization?
- ✔ Does the technology platform let employees take the best care of your customers?

Not to oversimplify systems and decisions, which can be very complicated, but instead of getting caught up in the details, these questions help you look at the big picture. What's the strategic decision you need to make in order to improve either your top or your bottom line? IT should be regarded as any other expense instead of a cost center. Is your IT yielding a return on investment (ROI)?

### Communication

Another big topic that plagues every organization (and every relationship) is communication. If you can get this right, you can retire tomorrow. That's unlikely to happen, though, so the success of your strategic plan rests on your ability to communicate the plan to your employees. While you're assessing your internal operations, assessing your communication methodology is an important area to review, too. As with the other areas in this section, good communication supports your core processes.

Some of the best corporate leaders in the world can tell you that you can't over communicate. No one ever complains about being too informed. As with your strategic plan and any other critical initiative in your organization, follow these simple guidelines:

- ✔ Make sure that your employees hear and understand your message completely. Having three key points to illustrate your message works the best.
- ✔ Communicate the key message points again.
- ✔ Repeat the message over and over again in different settings so everyone knows and is completely clear on your points.

### Productivity

Improved productivity happens when you work smarter with the resources you have or get the same results in less time. Being busy isn't necessarily being productive. Isn't everyone busy? Who isn't? And you may feel productive, but you're only productive if you're producing results that move the company forward. Your time is a highly valuable asset to your organization, so use it wisely. *High-value activities* — those that are directly related to getting and servicing your business — are the ones that contribute to bottom-line results. Here are some examples of high-value activities:

- Communicating with your clients
- Making sales calls
- Managing your employees who deliver your products and services
- Producing your product or service
- Serving your customers
- Writing proposals

Think about how much time you deal with e-mails that have nothing to do with customer communication, like spam. According to Nucleus Research, the average employee receives 21 spam messages each day. Spam costs U.S. corporations on average $712 per employee per year. Multiply that by the number of people in your company who have desk jobs. Ouch!

E-mail is a low-value activity. What a great way to waste time feeling productive. If you spend a total of two hours out of an eight-hour workday on e-mail, that's 25 percent of your time. Unless that 25 percent of your time is producing at least 25 percent of your total income, it's a low-value activity. Now granted, e-mail can be a timesaver but is only a high-value activity when you're communicating with your customers.

Chris is a sole proprietor who owns Amplitude, an organizational assessment and employee training company. In a day where she isn't doing a full training session, she may write a proposal, go to lunch with a contact from a networking event, make some prospect calls, pay her bills, and organize her files. All these activities are important, yet only writing the proposal and making prospect calls directly brings in business. Chris's productivity improvement comes in making more prospecting calls and spending less time paying bills. In fact, she recently hired an assistant with the extra money she made from one additional sale.

# Checking Your Profit Margins

Are you ready to make more money in your business? Who isn't? Even if you're running a nonprofit or government agency, you're always looking at improving your profit margins. Your *margins* tell you how much is left after you've paid your direct expenses. In the SUV analogy, your margins tell you how much gas is left in the tank when you arrive at your destination. So what's the secret to making more money? Stop doing things that lose money. Now, before you roll your eyes, don't overlook the simplicity of this statement.

Here's a classic example of losing money: A mid-sized, business-to-business software company realized that every dollar of revenue generated from its marketing campaigns cost the business about $1.20. Result: The marketing campaign is costing more than it's worth ($1.00 – $1.20). Attributing marketing dollars directly to the sales generated can be a rude awakening.

Ready for some ideas on how to improve your margins? As you read through the lists of ideas in the following sections, keep adding to your list of strengths and weaknesses.

## Identifying cash creators

As most organizations seek long-term sustainable operating models, cash creators aren't focused on the bottom line; rather they're about moving cash more quickly into and through the organization. Think about how the Great Recession helped people get lean and put some of these practices in place to stay that way.

Here are some ways to identify quick cash creators that yield lasting results in a short time:

- ✔ **Do an expense shakedown.** Take time at least once a year to scrutinize each and every company expense. Remember that old habits die hard. Evaluate your travel expenses, telecommunication expenses, insurance costs, subscriptions, and so on. If the expense doesn't contribute to your company's profitability, eliminate it. You're just about guaranteed to find areas in which costs can be reduced or cut out entirely.

- ✔ **Clip coupons.** Okay, not exactly coupons, but find good deals on business services. Everyone from Costco to Microsoft is catering to the small- to mid-sized business market. Make those companies win your business by comparison shopping. This idea is great when you're talking telephone or cellphone plans, suppliers, or even interest rates on company credit cards.

- ✔ **Increase your prices.** Not everyone can increase prices. But if you can back up your price increase with better products, service, and quality, you're likely to keep all your customers. Most people are accustomed to the idea of getting what they pay for. (I've heard the advice of increasing your prices 10 percent per month until you lose 10 percent of your business. Then stop. You may try it again when you improve your products and services. The concept is interesting, and it may have some value for your business.)

- ✔ **Be clear about your payment terms.** From the get-go, institute a consistent and firm payment process. Most customers appreciate your professional approach if the way you do business is clear.

You may consider letting your clients make payments over time, but the costs of having customers who pay late is significant, not only on the cash side but also on time spent on collections.

✔ **Ask for more business.** Do your current and past clients know about all the services you offer? Not only should you educate your customers annually about what you offer, but you should also ask for more business. Chances are you'll get it. Head to Chapter 8 for more on this subject.

## Detecting cash drains

Most organizations intrinsically know where the drains are. Plugging the drains is more about breaking down institutional barriers than it is about implementing the change itself. Brace yourself for the hard conversations and tough choices, but know that you'll be rewarded in the long run.

Check out the following ways to detect cash drains and improve your margins:

✔ **Fire loser customers.** Remember that you're in business to make money. Customers that are costing you money need to be evaluated. The reality is that some customers aren't worth having, even though you spent time and money getting them. Examples of these types of customers include:

- Those who take up too much of your time compared with the profits they generate

- Those who consistently fail to pay on time

- Those who always want more but don't want to pay more

✔ **Market wisely.** No matter what, marketing can be expensive. Whether you're spending money on a TV campaign or paying your employee's salary while she attends a networking event, you need to make sure that your marketing dollars are well spent. With marketing dollars, you need a tangible ROI. If your marketing strategy can't justify the cost, replace the plan with something better or stop what you're doing and save the money until you can figure out a better solution.

✔ **Break even.** Another common cash drain for service firms is inadvertently charging a lower billable rate than your hourly breakeven rate. The *breakeven rate* is the cost per hour to keep your doors open. If you're selling your time, which is your inventory, for less than your cost of overhead, you have a negative profit margin.

✔ **Keep a "Because we've always done it that way" list.** Do you ever wonder why you do something a certain way? If the answer is, "Because we've always done it that way," you may have found a time- and money-waster in your business. If you find yourself saying "Because we've always done it that way," about a process, put the process on the list to be evaluated.

One of the biggest culprits is producing reports. Check to make sure that the reports you produce are actually being used. Look for other areas where changes can be made or that can be completely eliminated in order to save money.

# Benchmarking your place in the pack

*Benchmarks* are surveys and assessments that help determine how well your company performs compared to other companies in your industry or business size. Following are just a handful of benchmarking tools available:

- **BizStats:** Visit www.bizstats.com for instant access to useful financial ratios, business statistics, and benchmarks. BizStats has effective and understandable analysis of businesses and industries. You can benchmark a business in five seconds for free.

- **Business Report Card:** This assessment helps companies pinpoint strengths and weaknesses, capitalize on an existing client base, develop invaluable networks and alliances, and increase profitability. To see whether you're making the grade, go to the Business Report Card at www.mybusiness reportcard.com.

- **B2B Benchmarking Association:** This association brings together a variety of companies for the purpose of process improvement and identification of Best Practice companies through benchmarking. Check it out online at www.b2bbenchmarking.com.

- **BizMiner:** Check out www.bizminer.com to produce a granular industry statistical report for your industry. The site offers industry financial analysis benchmarks for more than 5,000 lines of business and industry market trends on thousands more. Report access requires an affordable subscription fee.

- **Fintel:** This organization has both free and paid access to a financial benchmarking database of privately-held companies. Two products to help your benchmarking include an industry metric report and a business scorecard. For more information, check it out at www.fintel.us.

# Chapter 8

# Seeing Your Business through Your Customers' Eyes

*In This Chapter*

▶ Realizing the value of your customers

▶ Understanding what makes your customers happy

▶ Developing a strong business model that brings value to your customers

*T*he best part about your business is your customers. You have a group of people who like what you sell, find your product or service valuable, and give you money in exchange for a bundle of benefits. Seeing your business through your customers' eyes is one of the best ways to uncover the strengths and weaknesses of your organization.

When you neglect your customers, you tend to assume that you know them, what they want, and that they'll continue to buy from you. Businesspeople come up with various reasons to neglect their customers (intentionally or not), such as the following:

✔ Customer feedback takes too much time.

✔ Doing customer research is too expensive.

✔ I'm scared to hear what my customers really think.

✔ I don't have time to implement customer recommendations.

✔ Our sales are up, so customers must be happy.

In this chapter, you discover some easy ways to get past these excuses to uncover your current customers' needs and wants as well as create customers for a lifetime. By looking at your operations through your existing customers' perspectives, you can conduct more business with them. And armed with this information, you can make strategic decisions that raise your worth in the eyes of those customers who're most valuable.

# Getting to Know Your Most Valuable Customers

Not everything in this world is created equal, and neither are your customers. Most companies lose about 25 percent of their customers every year for a variety of reasons. Recognizing that you'll lose customers is important, yet maintaining existing clients instead of acquiring new ones is substantially cheaper. With this in mind, organizations get trapped in a continuous cycle of trying to fill a leaky customer bucket.

Here are two reasons for customer leaks:

✔ Businesses spend a disproportionate amount of money trying to keep all their customers happy.

✔ Businesses try to hold on to every customer, which isn't statistically possible, while constantly seeking new customers and neglecting their best customers.

How can you stop your customer bucket from leaking? The key is to focus your time and money on the 75 percent of the customers who're likely to stay with you and are profitable.

Do you need more convincing to keep your current customers happy? Check out these statistics from The Center for Customer Focus that just may persuade you:

✔ For every one complaint, there are 26 silent or dissatisfied customers.

✔ Your buyers aren't complaining; they're just not buying from *you*.

✔ Sixty-three percent of silent customers will switch suppliers.

✔ Unsatisfied customers will express their dissatisfaction to at least nine other people.

✔ Roughly 65 percent of customers are dissatisfied because of the feeling of indifference (everything from a bad attitude to not returning an e-mail) by someone at the company.

✔ Your loyal customers will tell three other people about how great you are.

If you take the preceding list of statistics into account, you just eliminated 25 percent of your most valued customers. Only 75 percent remain, which may be thousands of customers, depending on the size of your organization. The process of building relationships with all your constituents and seeing your business from their perspective can be daunting. But don't worry; you make one more refinement before you identify your most valued customers.

To refine your list and identify those customers you need to focus on, the next sections guide you through two different ways to identify who your most valuable customers are.

## Identifying the 80/20 customer

Many businesspeople have heard about the *80/20 rule,* which states that about 80 percent of company sales come from about 20 percent of its customers. Also known as the *Pareto principle,* this rule was named after the Italian economist Vilfredo Pareto who observed in 1906 that 20 percent of the Italian population owned 80 percent of Italy's wealth. Looking further, he noticed that 20 percent of the pea pods in his garden accounted for 80 percent of his pea crop each year. You can chalk this up to coincidence or sheer luck, but either way, Pareto applied this rule to pretty much everything in his life.

You can argue that the 80/20 rule is totally hypothetical, but when it comes to business, this simple hypothesis can help you identify who your most profitable customers are.

Here's how to find your 80/20 customer:

1. **Determine your total sales for last year or last quarter.**

2. **Run a report of total sales by each customer or account.**

3. **Identify the individual customers who account for the biggest percentage of your sales by dividing the total customer purchase into total sales for the period.**

These remaining customers are your best few. They're the ones that trust you, enjoy your products and services, and are most likely to buy from you again and again. According to Howard Hyden, founder of The Center for Customer Focus, your existing customer base is five times more likely to buy from you than go to an unknown company. Did you know that these 20 percent who've purchased from you once will buy from you again? What's the catch? You have to ask them! One-fifth of your customer base is just waiting for you to follow-up with them and offer them something new. Talk about leaving money on the table!

These customers aren't only the key to your growth but also the lifetime value of your business.

## Figuring out the lifetime value of your customers

Just how valuable are your customers? A calculation called the *lifetime value of a customer* translates value into hard dollars. The outcome of this calculation represents a relatively accurate estimate of your customer's value to your company over the lifetime of that customer's business.

The lifetime value of a customer calculation in this section (illustrated in Figure 8-1) doesn't determine profit but rather the overall customer value that can eventually be realized in the best-case scenario that a customer stays with you forever.

Find out for yourself just how much money each of your customers is worth to you. Use the Customer Value Calculator on the CD, along with the following questions and instructions, to calculate your customers' merit:

1. **What's the average sale or amount of money a customer spends per month?**

   Add up your total dollar sales for a year and divide that by the total number of sales transactions you completed. I recommend using the average sales of your 80/20 customer.

2. **How many times a year does an average customer buy from you?**

   Estimate the frequency of purchase of a normal customer. A typical grocery store customer probably shops 52 times per year, whereas a consulting company may do only one project per year for an average client.

3. **What's the expected number of years a customer will use your services or buy your products?**

   The expected number of years is unique to each company. Think about how long you anticipate maintaining relationships with the majority of your customers. This configuration will give you a good number to work with.

4. **How many people per year does your average customer tell about your company?**

   You may have to make a guess here, but the answer is probably between 3 and 12. Generally, the better your customer service, the higher this number is.

5. **What percentage of these people actually become customers?**

   The average is usually between 20 and 70 percent. This range is pretty large, so pick a percentage that you feel comfortable with given your industry.

6. **What's the lifetime value of your average customer?**

   Using the formula in the Customer Value Calculator on the CD and the example in Figure 8-1, calculate the lifetime value of your customers with and without the impact of referrals.

The example in Figure 8-1 shows you how Strategic Essentials, a personal coaching business, applies the lifetime value of its average customer calculation. If each coaching session is $150 and the average customer has two sessions a month, gross sales per customer are $3,600 per year. Estimating that a customer stays with a personal coach on an average of five years, the lifetime value of this customer, before referrals, is $18,000. Customers that see results from personal coaching will more than likely tell their friends. The power of positive word-of-mouth magnifies the value of each customer. Conservatively estimating that each customer tells four people, and 50 percent of those referrals, or two people, become customers, the gross sales from referrals is $36,000. Therefore, the total lifetime value of a customer is $54,000 (the gross sales per customer plus gross sales from referrals). Wow! Doesn't that change the importance of a $150 per hour client?

Whether your lifetime value figure is three figures, six figures, or more, producing a concrete dollar figure gives you a tangible point around which to design customer strategies.

| CALCULATING THE LIFETIME VALUE OF A STRATEGIC ESSENTIALS' CUSTOMER | Your Estimate |
|---|---|
| 1. Average sale per customer per month | $150 |
| 2. Number of sales per year per customer | 24 |
| 3. Number of years customer buys | 5 |
| 4. Number of referrals from customer | 4 |
| 5. % of referrals that become customers | 50% |
| 6. Lifetime Value before referrals = <br>     Calculation: <br>     Gross Sales per year per customer (1x2) <br>     X Number of years customers buy (3) = | $18,000 |
| 7. Lifetime Value of Referrals = <br>     Calculation: <br>     Referrals who become customers (4x5) <br>     X Lifetime Value before Referrals (6) = | $36,000 |
| **Total Lifetime Value of a Customer (6+7)** | $54,000 |

**Figure 8-1:**
Example of how to determine the lifetime value of a customer.

## Other departments are your customers too

As a department manager, you rely on other departments and groups to get your job done. Thinking about those other departments as customers can help if you need to move from single department thinking to cross-departmental thinking. Besides, departments are always resource constrained. If you grease the skids of your relationships with other departments by thinking about how you provide value to them, you'll be able to see better uses of company resources.

Maybe you can't find money in your budget to implement a new order tracking system, but with the IT department's help, showing other departments the value, you can work cooperatively to benefit everyone. Taking a customer approach to working with other departments can often turn poor relations around. Ultimately, you should be doing things that are good for your department, your company, and your internal customers.

Starting today, build the following ideas into your strategic plan and into your daily activities:

- ✔ **Step up satisfaction.** Now that you can see the importance of customer satisfaction in cold, hard cash, you want to step up the level of customer contentment. Satisfied customers lead to loyal customers, and loyal customers lead to referring customers.

- ✔ **Support the customers who refer business to you.** The impact of positive word-of-mouth has a multiplying effect in the lifetime value calculation and also in the marketplace.

- ✔ **Hang your lifetime value of a customer number in your break room.** Make sure that everyone understands the value of your customers. Keep this number in mind when you're dealing with disgruntled customers or prioritizing your daily activities.

- ✔ **Cut out any activity that signals indifference to your customers.** These activities send your clients packing. You know indifference when you're on the receiving end. Examples include sitting on hold for longer than you want to, delayed replies to e-mails or voice mails, lack of follow-through, and general carelessness.

# Determining Why Your Customers Are Your Customers

It's time to uncover why your customers buy products from your company or use your services. Ultimately, the value you provide is only as good as the benefits the customer receives. Your strategy excels or fails on that perception or lack thereof. If you ask companies what they sell and then turn around and survey their customers to ask what they buy, you'll most likely hear two different answers. Generally, customers give you a different answer or express it in a different way than the company. Quickly query a handful of your customers to see whether this trend holds true for your organization. Here are some questions to ask, crafted to your company specifically:

✔ Who buys our products or services?

✔ What do they buy?

✔ Why do they buy?

✔ When do they buy?

✔ How do they buy?

Take Netflix, an online DVD rental service, for example. Employees may say that Netflix sells a service that allows customers to check out and return DVD rentals through the mail or by streaming DVDs online. Conversely, customers may say that they're buying convenience. In order to see your business through the eyes of your most valuable customers, you have to understand what your customers think they're really buying from you. You have to think like your customers.

Answers to these questions can be found in information and feedback all around you. Some of that information is easy to get and some takes a bit more work. In the following sections, I provide a list of methods you can use to find out why your customers are your customers.

## Measuring satisfaction by the numbers

Measurements and metrics abound in companies today. *Customer-focused metrics* are a quick way to determine customer satisfaction. You can benchmark these metrics off industry standards, but more than likely, you know what you want these numbers to be for your company. Are you hitting or missing the mark? Which metrics are the most important to your customers?

Customer-focused metrics are numbers about activities that are important to your customers. You can measure a lot of different parts of your business; some data is meaningful and some is garbage. But if you want to see your business through your customers' eyes, track the items that they care about. Customer-focused metrics are very company-specific. Ask yourself what your customers find most important. Make sure that you're measuring it. Here are some ideas to get your wheels turning:

- ✓ **Volume by customer or client:** Track customer sales by dollars or units per month and see whether your 80/20 customers are starting to order less frequently.

- ✓ **Growth by customers or clients:** Customers may be growing significantly, but you also need to watch whether the number of orders from them is increasing. If it isn't, you may be missing a valuable growth opportunity.

- ✓ **Referral rate:** This number is the most important for the growth of your company. If your customers are referring you, they're happy. If they aren't, you have a problem.

- ✓ **Time to respond to customer questions and inquiries:** How long does it take you to respond to a customer request? Studies show that the longer the inquiry remains unanswered, the cooler the lead gets by 1 percent each day. Slow response time is a big indicator of indifference.

- ✓ **System-up time:** This factor measures the percentage of time a company's equipment or technology systems are up and running to serve your customers. If the product or service is unreliable, it reduces the value in the customers' eyes.

- ✓ **On-time delivery:** If your product doesn't get to the customer when he expects it, the value of your product is diminished.

- ✓ **Error rate:** How many mistakes are made when entering customer orders or delivering completed projects? Tracking your error rate is a good indicator of customer satisfaction. If your error rate goes up, your customer satisfaction likely goes down. Clearly you don't want that to happen.

- ✓ **Returns/rejects/do-overs:** This indicator focuses on how many products or projects come back to you. If you have to fix a problem project or a defective product, it costs your company time and money. And you probably have an unhappy customer.

- ✓ **Overall satisfaction:** If you collect customer satisfaction data, make sure to monitor it regularly.

Look how you're doing in each of these areas compared with where you want to be. This difference gives you a glimpse of your company's strengths and weaknesses. Determine which customer-focused key indicators you want your business to measure and quantify, establish a baseline of current performance, and then set goals to increase performance in these critical areas. You can obtain your measures through your internal data sources, such as customer surveys, CRM systems, fulfillment systems, and so on. If you don't have a source for a metric you want to track, ask an employee to track it for you until you can set up a system to automate it.

Most organizations know what performance they want to achieve for specific metrics. However, if you're looking for outside validation, check out your industry association. Such associations usually have industry benchmarks.

## *Obtaining feedback without using a survey*

Spending tons of money and months collecting customer feedback can be too overwhelming and cost prohibitive for many companies. But still, obtaining feedback is crucial for the ongoing success and sustainability of your company. You can easily retrieve information during the normal course of your business day.

Here's a list of areas you can easily obtain feedback from your customers without using a stand-alone survey:

- **At the point of purchase:** No time is like the present. Ask for feedback at the moment the transaction takes place. This transaction can be face-to-face, on the phone, or over live chat. Customers may not be as honest at this point, but if you ask a question that isn't directly related to the employee, you're likely to get better answers.

- **Order forms and invoices:** Include a comment box on your forms and a business reply envelope for your customers to send back the information.

- **Online:** Add a Tell Us What You Think link (preferably in the header or footer) on every page of your website.

- **Sales reps:** Set up an easy way for your reps to feed information back into your organization, such as through an internal discussion board or intranet that reps access.

- **Newsletters:** If you send a newsletter, include a question or two. Newsletters can be great tools for finding out timely customer information. Instead of asking service questions, consider asking about your customer's industry or business climate. Make sure to ask only one question — two at most.

- **Telephone:** Make sure that your voice mail tells customers how to give you feedback.

- **Comment cards:** Include comment cards inside your shipments.

- **Support calls:** Your technical and customer service reps hear tons of information from your customers. Set up a general system to collect the feedback these employees hear every day.

Consider Lexus, the luxury car manufacturer: Management requires that every employee, from the top to the bottom, interview ten customers every month. By doing so, the company creates a culture that regularly puts customer information in the hands of every employee.

## *Spending time talking to your customers*

When all else fails, ask your customers why they buy from you. Ask the following questions of your 80/20 customers:

✔ What are we doing that's great? What's working?

✔ What isn't working and needs improvement?

✔ What else would you like to see from our company? What else can we do to make your life easier?

✔ If we ceased to exist, what would you do? What would you be giving up?

✔ If a friend was in search of *(fill in your type of company),* would you refer us? Why or why not?

Sam Walton of Wal-Mart, reportedly spent five days every month interacting with customers in his stores. He also spent every Wednesday morning having coffee with his delivery teams to see what they were hearing from store employees and observing from customers. This amount of dedicated time kept him close to and in touch with his customers' needs and wants. Although I doubt his customer attention was the only reason for Wal-Mart's runaway success, it surely played a big part.

Gathering feedback from a variety of sources results in an objective, comprehensive picture of who your customers are, what they want, and what they value. However, collecting the information is only half of the equation. Ensure that everyone in the company knows what customers are thinking by sharing customer feedback throughout the organization. By spreading the news, everyone will start to make better, more informed decisions. For your strategic plan, you can use the information you collected over the years to make calculated decisions that have broader implications.

# Focusing on How You Deliver Value to Your Customers

For many owners and executives, focus represents the biggest roadblock to corporate growth. The problem isn't exactly a lack of focus but more the tendency to unintentionally focus on the wrong things. Because strategic planning is about focusing on the right things, keep your customers' values in the forefront of your planning efforts. Your company is operating in its sweet spot when you're focused on the following:

✔ What you're good at doing

✔ What you like doing

✔ What the market values you for doing

Connecting the dots between these three elements is critical because organizations can easily lose focus on what their customers and the market truly value.

Unfortunately, the term *value* is one of those undefined and vague business concepts that sound good and important but isn't easy to get your arms around. When the benefits of a product or service outweigh the costs, you have value. Value makes something sweeter, better, stronger, faster. You can have pancakes without syrup, but what's the point? Value is the secret sauce that people want or expect when they do business with you. The result of providing superior value is wildly satisfied customers who keep coming back again and again and bring their friends.

One of the best ways to understand value in your organization is to develop or review your business model. Your *business model* is the framework for how your organization creates and delivers value to its customers and to the business owners. Selecting or redefining the appropriate business model can be critical to business success. And because your business model is a great strategic thinking tool in your planning process, I discuss the different types of business models and the building blocks to creating or redefining one in the following sections. You'll know you understand it when you can sketch it and describe it in just a few sentences.

Unfortunately, business models are often one of the most misunderstood aspects of doing business today. In case you do get turned around in this model, just remember that at its core, a business model helps you determine how the company plans to operate, compete, and generate revenue.

## Considering different business models

A business model can be simple or very complex. A restaurant's business model is to make money by cooking and serving food to hungry customers. An online business model can vary from advertising to selling products to creating a community, or can even be a combination of models. Every industry has a different breakdown of business model types. That said, following are example business models in many industries:

- ✔ **Add-on model:** The core offering is priced competitively, but numerous extras drive the final price. All airlines are an example of this model.

- ✔ **Advertising model:** Although this model may seem outdated, the advertising model is still alive and well. Many Internet companies successfully deploy this model with a freemium model (see description later in this list). Examples are Twitter, Facebook, and Google.

- ✔ **Affiliate model:** An affiliate is simply someone who helps sell a product in return for commission; for example, Amazon uses an affiliate model (and also employs the direct sales model).

- ✔ **Auction model:** Auction models are where the price of the good isn't fixed, each individual assesses the value of the good independently, and final value is determined via competitive bids. Examples include eBay, auction houses, and Priceline.

✔ **Bait and hook model:** The bait and hook model generates disproportionate amounts of the revenue on components, refills, and additional contracts. Examples of this model are ink cartridges for printers and service contracts for cellphones.

✔ **Direct sales model:** Of all the models, this one is the most straightforward as it's simply the direct route to the market. Online services such as Amazon and Dell disrupted this model when they went directly to customers and around distributors, but this model, also known as the *brick and mortar model,* is still valid for many industries. Examples of the direct sales model are Zappos.com and many B2B businesses.

✔ **Distributor/retail model:** Companies that buy and sell physical, financial, and intellectual assets use the distributor/retail model. Examples include Wal-Mart and Charles Schwab.

✔ **Franchise model:** Opening a franchise is essentially buying a working business model in a particular industry. Franchise model examples include McDonald's and Subway.

✔ **Freemium model:** This model offers a scaled-down version of the product or service for free with the intent of moving the customer to the premium version. The freemium model is typically used in service-based businesses. Examples are software as a service (SaaS) or mobile phone apps.

✔ **Manufacturer:** The manufacturer model is a standard business model where an organization creates and sells physical, financial, and intellectual assets. Toyota is an example of this model.

✔ **Pay-as-you-go model:** With this model, actual usage is metered and customers pay on the basis of what they consume. An example of this model is pre-paid cards for cellphones.

✔ **Subscription model:** With the subscription, or *recurring revenue,* model, the aim is to secure the customer on a long-term contract so they're consuming your product or service well into the future. Newspapers have been struggling with transitioning from a model that's mostly advertising to one that's subscription-based. Examples include utility companies, publishers, and online applications.

Highly successfully businesses have shaken up their industries through disruptive business models and combined two of the models in the preceding list or leveraged one model into another industry. Think about how Netflix disrupted the movie rental industry by introducing a direct sales model instead of a traditional distributor/retail model. Consider your industry: Is it on the verge of being disrupted, or are you in the position to be the disruptor?

## Using a business model to create value

The business model consists of nine key building blocks that deliver your value proposition, as shown in Figure 8-2. On the right-hand side of the model, you identify your target customer segments (which I discuss in detail in Chapter 9), how you develop relationships with those customers, and the channels by which you reach them, supported by the revenue streams generated from that interaction. On the left-hand side, you think through what key partners, key activities, and key resources you need to deliver your value proposition to your customers and the cost structure to do so.

Alexander Osterwalder is a guru in business model generation and provides concrete descriptions and questions for each building block in the following list. Start with identifying the customer segment you are serving, followed by an identification of the value proposition to that customer segment. From there, build out the right-hand side, or customer perspective, followed by the left-hand side, or the activity perspective, of the model.

- **Customer Segments:** This part of the framework defines the different groups of people or organizations a company aims to reach or serve. Which customer segments will you be targeting? What problem will you be solving for those customers? For whom are you creating value?

- **Value Proposition:** The value proposition is the bundle of products and services that create value for a specific customer segment. What value will you deliver to your targeted customers? What package of products and services will you deliver? Why will customers buy from you?

- **Channels:** The channels describe how the company communicates with and reaches its customer segments to deliver the value proposition. How will you reach your customers? Through which channels do your customers want to be reached?

- **Customer Relationships:** These relationships are what a company establishes or wants to establish with a specific customer segment. What type of relationship does each of your customer segments expect you to establish and maintain with them?

- **Revenue Streams:** The cash a company generates from each customer segment is its revenue stream. What will customers pay for? How much will they pay? How will they pay?

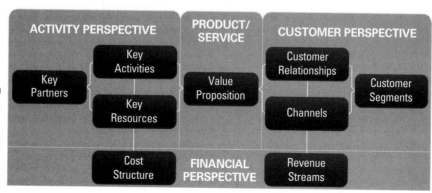

**Figure 8-2:**
The business model framework.

- ✔ **Key Partners:** The network of suppliers and partners that make the business model work are the key partners. Who are your key partners? Who are your key suppliers?

- ✔ **Key Activities:** These activities are the most important things a company must do to make its business model work. What key activities does your value proposition require?

- ✔ **Key Resources:** Key resources are the most important assets required to make a business model work. What are the key resources required to deliver and execute your value proposition?

- ✔ **Cost Structure:** The cost structure describes all the costs incurred to operate a business model. What are the costs of your business model? Which resources and activities are the most expensive? Are your costs less than our revenue?

Calvary Baptist Church, a large congregation with three large campuses, explored a significant strategic shift (using standard business models for churches) in its value proposition during a recent strategic planning process. The planning team asked these questions: "Is our business model changing? Is the way we deliver value to our customers going to be different in the future than it is today based on changing demographics? If it's changing, what would it look like?"

Figure 8-3 illustrates the church's current business model, called the *attractional model,* in which the value proposition is targeted at baby boomers being part of a big corporate body of like-minded individuals. Certainly, other demographics are represented, but the average age of the congregation is 50 to 60. This customer segment expects front desk service to have somebody answer questions. Big congregational offerings and endowments generate revenue. The church staff delivers on the value proposition through two to four large campuses that produce large events weekly. The cost structure of staff and facilities maintenance support these activities.

Figure 8-4 illustrates a possible future business model, called the *missional model.* Under this model, the value proposition targets Gen X and Millennials who want to be part of a small, intimate, relevant community. This intimate community can be established in an attractional model, but it's hard to deliver on given the infrastructure and key activities aren't structured to do so. Specifically, communication networks of hundreds of locations, including schools, homes, and universities instead of massive campuses, distribute the missional model infrastructure. Built-up staff competencies deliver key activities of community building instead of event production. Lastly, the cost structure is centered on technology and revenue streams, like smaller donations and fundraisers.

Assessing and possibly redefining your business model, no matter what type of organization you are, can be a powerful and enlightening part of your strategic management process. Many organizations today are redefining how they deliver value to customers yielding unprecedented success.

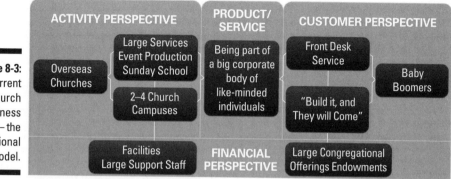

**Figure 8-3:**
The current church business model — the attractional model.

**Figure 8-4:**
The new church business model — the missional model.

## *Framing out your business model*

Ready to frame out your own business model? Grab a hammer and some nails (sticky notes and flip chart) and get going! The Business Model Diagram on the CD helps guide your way.

1. **Gather a small group of diverse perspectives from across your organization to participate in the exercise.**

2. **Use the thought-provoking questions in the previous section for each building block in Figure 8-2 (in conjunction with the Business Model Diagram on the CD) to build your business model.**

   Answer each question by following the flow in the order listed in the previous section.

3. **Document your key assumptions and targets.**

   As you're building your model, keep a list of assumptions you make and future targets you may want to hit as a result of thinking about your organization from the value proposition outward.

4. **Identify what impacts or changes you need to build into your plan to bring your business model to life.**

   Take action on the changes when you construct your road map (strategic objectives, goals, and actions) in Chapter 12.

---

## Need more help?

Looking to dig deeper into the topic of customer relations? The following list of great resources can help you see your business through your customers' eyes:

✔ *Marketing For Dummies,* 3rd Edition, by Alexander Hiam (John Wiley & Sons, Inc.): This reference provides a no-nonsense approach to growing revenue from your current customers.

✔ **Creating Customer Evangelists:** This website is a free resource of articles, newsletters, and blogs by Ben McConnell and Jackie Huba. Check it out at www.creating customerevangelists.com.

✔ **The Center for Customer Focus:** This organization offers customer-focus training and workshops. Several free articles are also available on this topic at www.customer focus.org.

✔ *Business Model Generation: A Handbook for Visionaries, Game Changers, and Challengers* by Alexander Osterwalder and Yves Pigneur (John Wiley & Sons, Inc.): This book is an outstanding reference to use for your business model exercise. Check out the iPad app and other resources at www.businessmodel generation.com.

✔ *The Art of Profitability* by Adrian Slywotzky (Warner Business Books): This book is another great reference for business model designs.

---

# Chapter 9

# Researching the Market to Find New Customers

*In This Chapter*

▶ Investigating new customer markets and picking the best ones

▶ Establishing and targeting your markets

▶ Crafting positioning statements

▶ Deciding how to reach your new customers

▶ Keeping a focus on the market

*A*sking a business whether it wants to find new customers is like asking you whether you want to make more money. Of course you do! Two ways to grow your top line are to increase sales from your existing customers (see Chapter 8) or generate sales from new ones (which I cover in this chapter).

Finding new customers is the role of marketing. After you sift through all the semantics, misused business lingo, and fuzzy concepts, marketing is really pretty simple: Identify who you want to sell to, figure out how to get those people to notice you, and when they do, get them to buy from you. So if marketing is this simple, why does it continue to be confusing? Mainly because most people make it too complicated. At the end of the day, nothing matters until you have a sale. And the only person who can make that decision is the customer. As management guru Peter Drucker says, "The purpose of a business is to create a customer." Period.

The primary reason marketing campaigns fail is because customers weren't offered something they wanted, needed, or valued. The components of a campaign — the product, the product's price, the product's advertising, the sales channels, the salespeople, and the customer service — can contribute to the failure. But ultimately, the problem comes down to the fact that the customer wasn't satisfied.

This chapter focuses on marketing planning elements, which are part of your strategic plan. Additionally, this chapter helps you create a market-focused organization. Whether you're selecting market development or market penetration as potential growth strategies, implementing either of them requires reaching new markets. This chapter also explains how to give those strategies life.

# Gathering Information about New Markets

Good market research ensures that you don't spend a lot of money on marketing campaigns that customers don't jibe with or new products that they won't pay for. To be effective, organizations need good information about their customers' needs, wants, and characteristics. Generally, if the result of your decision impacts the customer, ask the customer for input into your decision before you make it.

 Market research is an entire discipline, which is too overwhelming to cover in depth here. Instead, this section focuses on how to conduct market research for the purpose of making strategic decisions about which target markets to enter. Those markets result in actions within your strategic plan.

## Identifying your information needs

Before beginning any research effort, clearly state your information needs. Undoubtedly, some holes and unknowns about new markets you want to pursue may exist, but you also want to have a better idea of how attractive the potential target market is and whether it identifies with the need you're trying to solve. Ask yourself the following questions about each market you're considering:

- ✔ What market are we trying to serve? How big is our market in terms of number of customers, units sold, or dollar volume?
- ✔ Are there obvious segments in our market?
- ✔ What are the overall trends and developments in our industry?
- ✔ What is the rate of market growth or shrinkage over time? Are there any differences in market growth by time of year?
- ✔ How big are our competitors? What companies have what portions of the market?
- ✔ What products or services do our competitors offer? How do they differ from ours?

✔ How does competitors' pricing compare with ours?

✔ What marketing strategies and tactics does the competition use and to what degree of success?

✔ What are the key factors for success in the market we're trying to serve? Are there any specific media outlets that reach this market directly?

✔ How do customers perceive the problem the offering is intended to solve? How serious do they believe the problem is? What benefits of the proposed offering would be of most importance to them?

✔ How do customers solve the problem today?

✔ What costs do customers incur now to solve the problem?

The list is pretty long, I know, but don't feel overwhelmed. You and your team don't need to answer all these questions. Just focus on the following key steps in processing your answers:

1. **Use the preceding questions to help you identify what specific information you need about potential new markets.**

2. **Clearly state these needs in one or two objectives.**

3. **Use these objectives to guide your research efforts.**

4. **If the information you locate doesn't achieve the stated objectives, file that info somewhere else or delete it.**

## Locating information sources

You know your information needs, but now you've got to go out and find the answers.

Doing market research can be like pulling on a never-ending spool of thread. Sometimes you reach the end of your search and sometimes you don't. At some point, you need to decide whether you've collected enough information to make a strategic decision about which markets to pursue. Weigh the cost of perfect information against the risk of a less-than-perfect decision.

The following subsections provide a list of potential sources. The sources aren't exhaustive, but I do cover the most popular research sources available. Some of the sources are free, and others are quite expensive. I always evaluate the cost of research against the cost of decision. Or in other words, how much insurance do you need or want to buy?

## Internal company information

You may be amazed by how much information you have stored in your company databases, customer relationship management systems, employees, vendors, and distributors. Before you spend any time surfing databases or any money on a research study, start with your internal company information. Look for data that answers the questions in the earlier section "Identifying your information needs."

## Secondary data

Information or data that's already compiled, such as reports, statistics, and white papers, is considered *secondary data*. To get a general understanding of the market and to begin to develop customer profiles, you can easily tap in to secondary sources. Here are some of the best:

- ✔ **Yahoo! Answers:** This service is provided by Yahoo! and allows you to post a question to a stable of qualified researchers. At the time of posting, you set the price you're willing to pay for the information. Average bids range from $5 to $100. Visit the site online at www. answers.yahoo.com.

- ✔ **U.S. Department of Commerce:** The U.S. Department of Commerce provides information about business, trade, and economic information from across the Federal Government. Check out the website at www. commerce.gov.

- ✔ **eMarketer:** This service (www.emarketer.com) provides market research on e-business and online marketing, objective analysis of online market trends, and data from more than 2,000 worldwide sources.

- ✔ **MarketResearch.com:** This source sells market research reports for a variety of industries. It also has the most comprehensive collection of published market research available. Check it out online at www. marketresearch.com.

- ✔ **DemographicsNow:** This company has numerous tools for both business and consumer markets, such as segmentation, customer profiling, site selection, demographic data, and competitive analysis reports. The company's website is www.demographicsnow.com.

- ✔ **Frost & Sullivan:** This business consulting firm provides industry-specific, B2B research and reports for a variety of fields. The online sources are available at www.frost.com.

- ✔ **The U.S. Census Bureau:** The Bureau (www.census.gov) gives you free access to all census data about people, businesses, trade, and much more.

✔ **University Libraries:** Most university libraries provide free access for walk-ins to databases like ABI/Inform, which compile articles from multiple sources where you can search abstracts. If one of your kids is a university or college student, you're paying for that access now. College students often have better access to company data than marketing departments.

A variety of other websites provide business-specific information. Here are a few:

✔ Dow Jones: www.dowjones.com

✔ Factiva: www.factiva.com

✔ Hoover's Online: www.hoovers.com

✔ LexisNexis: www.lexisnexis.com

✔ Standard &Poor's: www.standardandpoors.com/home/en/us

✔ Thomson Research: research.thomsonib.com

✔ U.S. Securities and Exchange Commission: www.sec.gov

✔ Value Line: www.valueline.com

Want to get more specific in your secondary research efforts? The University of California Berkley Library publishes a guide entitled *Finding Information on the Internet: A Tutorial.* Check out this free resource at www.lib.berkeley. edu/TeachingLib/Guides/Internet/Strategies.html.

### Primary data

Whether you have a specific research question, want to evaluate a specific need, or want to test market a product, you may need to go directly to the information source — your customer. This research is called *primary research.* You may also need to conduct primary research if you can't locate a critical piece of information through secondary sources. Primary research includes surveys via e-mail, phone, direct mail, in-depth interviews, focus groups, usability testing, and direct observation.

You can conduct primary research yourself or hire an outside market research agency. Check out the GreenBook directory at www.greenbook. org for a list of market research agencies.

# Creating Your Target Markets

Think about your market as though you're someone who's interested in buying your product or service. You may have some luck reaching some of your customers with a widespread approach, but a targeted approach is more effective. In order to use a targeted approach, you have to aim at a clear target — your ideal market. To create a target, you need to take a sea of customers and group, or segment, them. You then create groups of customers based on similarities; each group becomes a *target market*.

The goal of creating target markets is to target specific customers who have similar needs and wants with the same message, products, and pricing and through the same distribution channels. When done correctly, your target market responds similarly to your marketing efforts.

Look at the following two 24-Hour Fitness customers as an example:

> Tim is a health nut. Working out is his life. He typically uses the facilities five times a week. He's on a program established by his personal trainer and has referred two people to the gym this year already.
>
> Sheila, on the other hand, hasn't set foot in the gym since she joined six months ago.
>
> Membership renewal fees for both Tim and Sheila are due next month. If 24-Hour Fitness uses the same strategy to encourage Tim and Sheila to renew, their tactics may fail. Tim already understands the value and is a satisfied customer. However, Sheila needs substantially more communication to see the benefit. The company may likely lose her.

Clearly, utilizing the same marketing campaign in the preceding example causes a decrease in potential sales and profitability. The same is true with your approaches in the real world. Therefore, you need a more targeted approach to sales and marketing. In the following sections, I show you how to take that approach.

## Dividing your market into groups

What's the best way to divide your large customer base? Find a variable that splits the market into actionable groups.

Most companies first make a product then figure out who to sell it to. The focus is on the product and not the customer, or what the customer wants to buy. By flipping your thinking around, you first look at what customer needs you're trying to satisfy and then which products fit that need. This process helps you isolate customer groups and make educated decisions on which segments offer the most attractive opportunities.

Choosing a variable is like selecting what type of knife to use when preparing dinner. A serrated knife is preferable for cutting bread, a paring knife for halving cherry tomatoes, and a chef's knife for dicing an onion. Each knife has its own specialty. Different knives produce different results. The knife is analogous to the segmentation variable, not the segment itself. You slice and dice markets by using different variables until you come up with the segmentation of your customers that makes the most sense. For example, you can segment a consumer market by product or service benefits sought, demographic variables, geographic variables, psychographic variables, or behavioral variables. But you can't use all of them at the same time, or you'll end up with a market of one.

Segmenting can be confusing and more difficult than it needs to be. Remember, there's no right or wrong way to segment your market. Segmenting requires creativity. Take a shot at creating segments that make sense to you and your business situation. You can always revise your segments at a later date.

The following two sections describe your selection process.

### Benefits

*Benefit segmentation* is based on dividing customers based on their needs. This process is also called *needs-based segmentation.* Simply put, you're trying to solve a need for a customer. Why not group together all the customers who have the same need?

Some marketers argue that using benefit segmentation is the only way to segment a market because people differ only when it comes to paying you for your product based on the benefits your product provides. However, this type of segmentation may not work for your organization, or it may not be as straightforward. Researching your market can provide some insight on how you can segment based on benefits (check out the info in the "Gathering Information about New Markets" section earlier in this chapter for help).

Netflix, an online streaming or home-delivery DVD rental service, divides its customers into three groups based on needs. Group one needs the convenience provided by free home delivery. Group two consists of film buffs who want to be able to access any movie possible. Group three wants the benefit of cheap rentals — they're the bargain hunters who want to watch a bunch of movies for less than $20 per month.

### Descriptors

*Descriptors* are customer characteristics that are significant enough to divide your market. You don't use all the descriptors, but you may use one or two together from the following list:

- ✔ **Behavioral:** Grouping customers by product usage (light, medium, heavy users), brand loyalty (none, medium, high), and type of user

- ✔ **Decision makers:** Grouping customers based on who decides to purchase your product

- ✔ **Demographic:** Grouping customers by age, income level, gender, family size, religion, race, nationality, primary language, and so on

- ✔ **Distribution:** Grouping customers based on where they go to purchase your product, such as in store, online, or through the catalog

- ✔ **Geographic:** Grouping customers by area, such as regions of the country or state and urban or rural

- ✔ **Psychographic:** Grouping customers into cultural clusters, social sets, lifestyle, and personality type

E*TRADE, an online brokerage and bank company, segmented its markets in two ways:

- ✔ The company looked at *behavioral* descriptors, such as usage. It found a large customer segment of day traders who wanted inexpensive and fast trades. E*TRADE developed quick-trade products and bulk pricing to serve this market.

- ✔ The company looked at *demographic* descriptors, specifically income. Through market research, the company discovered that the group of people with $5,000 to $50,000 to invest was a fast-growing segment that was underserved.

Through these descriptors, E*TRADE developed tools to enable the company to profitably serve these customers.

Begin a new notes page for each target customer segment. You may have just a few or you may have a lot. Don't worry about that for now: You can refine your list later. Give each customer group a name and use it to label your page. Then write down the segmentation basis. Did you segment by needs? If so, what's the need? If you segmented by descriptors, what were they? Use Figure 9-3 later in this chapter to guide your notes page structure as you work through the rest of this chapter.

# *Visualizing your target customer*

To visualize your ideal customer, create a customer profile or detailed description of your target customer. Specifically, you want your profile to be so descriptive that you can visualize shaking your customer's hand.

In order to create a detailed customer profile, you need to know your customers' characteristics. Be interested in their likes, dislikes, needs, wants, birthdays, anniversaries, styles, titles, beliefs, behaviors, perspectives, politics, dreams, shoe sizes, and so on. (Okay, I was just kidding about shoe size.)

Check out this list of generic consumer and business characteristics:

- ✔ Consumer characteristics

    - **Demographics:** Age, generation, gender, income, family size, life cycle, occupation, education, religion, race, ethnicity, social class, health

    - **Geographic:** World region, county, state, city, climate, density

    - **Lifestyle:** Innovators, thinkers, achievers, experiencers, believers, strivers, makers, survivors

    - **Personality:** Compulsive, gregarious, authoritarian, ambitious

    - **Usage:** Occasions, benefits sought, user status, usage rate, loyalty status

- ✔ Business characteristics

    - **Demographic:** Industry, company size, location

    - **Environmental:** Economic developments, supply conditions, technological change, political and regulatory developments, competitive developments, culture and customs

    - **Personal characteristics:** Buyer-seller similarity, attitudes toward risk, loyalty

    - **Purchasing approaches:** Location of the purchasing function, decision-making structure, nature of existing relationships, general purchasing and payment policies, purchasing criteria

    - **Situational factors:** Sense of urgency, need of product or service for a specific application, potential size of order

Create a customer profile that requires you to visualize your customers with 100 percent clarity. Table 9-1 presents examples of three grades of customer profiles, from bad to good to better.

| Table 9-1 | Good and Bad Customer Profiles | |
| --- | --- | --- |
| *Bad Example* | *Good Example* | *Better Example* |
| Small businesses located in Oregon | Small businesses located in Oregon that are in the auto industry | Small body shops seeking rapid insurance reimbursement in Oregon |
| All agencies in the marketing industry | All agencies in the marketing industry billing less than $10 million annually | An agency focusing on public relations for local and state government community programs |
| Field sales people constantly on the road | Field sales people earning between $50,000 and $100,000 who're looking to purchase a new car in the next year | Field sales people earning between $50,000 and $100,000 who are image-conscious first movers and are looking to purchase a sports car in the next year |

## Anthropologie's customer profile hits the mark

For an example of a great customer profile, check out what Anthropologie, a national retail store, came up with:

A female about 30 to 45 years old, college or post-graduate education, married with kids or in a committed relationship, professional or ex-professional, annual household income of $150,000 to $200,000. She's well-read and well-traveled. She's very aware — she gets our references, whether it's to a town in Europe or to a book or a movie. She's urban-minded. She's into cooking, gardening, and wine. She has a natural curiosity about the world. She's relatively fit. Her identity is a tangle of connections to activities, places, interests, values, and aspirations. She's a yoga-practicing film-maker with an organic garden, a collection of antique musical instruments, and an abiding interest in Chinese culture.

The Anthropologie customer is affluent but not materialistic. She's focused on building a nest but hankers for exotic travel. She'd like to be a domestic but has no problem cutting corners (she prefers the luscious excess of British cooking sensation Nigella Lawson to the measured perfection of Martha Stewart). She's in tune with trends, but she's a confident individualist when it comes to style. She lives in the suburbs but would never consider herself a suburbanite.

Can you visualize Anthropologie's customers? Without a doubt! Now don't worry if your customer profile isn't this specific. In fact, it probably won't be. Not everyone in Anthropologie's market exhibits all these traits; that would be too narrow. Nevertheless, this example illustrates the power behind really, truly knowing your customers. You can immediately see how this profile helps the company select which products to carry in the store, what messages to use in its advertising campaigns, how to price the merchandise, and what type of customer service drives repeat business.

List the needs and wants for each of your target customer groups. Think about behaviors, motivations, and potential benefits sought. Then list characteristics. If you have a consumer product or service, the major types of characteristics are demographic, geographic, lifestyle, and usage. If you have a business-to-business product or service, the major types of characteristics are demographic, environmental, operating variables, purchasing approaches, situational factors, and personal characteristics. If you have specific companies that you're targeting, write down their names and main contact information.

More than likely, you need to gather additional information about these target customer groups in order to complete your profile. If so, use the profiles to guide your market research efforts, as explained in the previous section.

# Focusing on the Most Attractive Markets

Choosing which target markets to pursue can be challenging because you may want to target all segments, especially those that are growing and appear very profitable, but resist the temptation. Most businesses can't possibly serve all identified target markets (or at least not well). Try to choose between one and three new markets to target at any given time.

Additionally, you want to make sure that your company doesn't enter into segments that you can't support or don't have the resources to provide excellent customer service. You want to focus your energies on the most attractive segments. I show you how to identify attractive markets and then evaluate them in the following sections.

## Defining an attractive segment

If you identified only two or three new markets total, verify that you've identified the most attractive target markets. Use the following checklist to evaluate the attractiveness of each potential segment:

- ✔ **Competitors:** Look at your competitor analysis (Chapter 10 covers this topic in detail). Are you better than the competition? Is the competition getting better or worse at meeting the needs of customers in this segment?

- ✔ **Company resources:** Do you have the right strengths to compete in this segment? Do you have weaknesses that need to be improved and are they fixable? In Chapter 7, you can review your company's strengths and weaknesses. Look at the culture of your organization. Is it consistent with serving this segment?

- ✔ **Segment size:** The sales potential of the segment, in terms of number of units of your product that can be sold or number of customers served, is important in making a segment attractive. Is it big enough to bother with? To find out, use the market research resources provided in the earlier section "Locating information sources." Remember, size is relative. What may be too small to one company may be huge to another. Evaluate where the segment is big enough based on your requirements.

- ✔ **Segment growth rate:** To reduce the risk of losing money when entering a new market, find one that's growing, not shrinking. Although this idea may seem obvious, many companies enter markets that are shrinking. Ideally, you should create a market strategy that allows you to serve a market for a good length of time, recouping marketing expenses and any product or service modifications.

- ✔ **Segment profitability:** You need to know whether focusing on this customer group is feasible. A segment's profitability is important in making a segment attractive. Knowing how profitable is profitable is subject only to your company's requirements. You can estimate revenue for one year with a simple formula:

  Number of customers × average sale per customer × number of sales per customer per year = revenue

  To determine profit from the segment, subtract the estimated costs associated with producing the product or service and reaching the segment. (See Chapter 13 for details.)

- ✔ **Segment accessibility:** Identifying an attractive segment is possible, but there's no cost effective way to reach it. An attractive segment requires that you can reach this group through clear communication channels. To reach the people in this group, you first have to find them. A good indicator of segment accessibility is how easy or hard it is to dig up information in your market research efforts.

- ✔ **Segment differentiation:** Uniqueness is a characteristic of an attractive segment. Will this group respond to product and service offerings differently than other groups you've identified? If not, consider combining two segments. Segment differentiation tends to be obvious. You either see a clear difference or you don't. But you may need to additionally research or test-market your product or promotional message to make sure.

## *Evaluating your target customer groups*

Choices, choices, choices. Narrowing down options is difficult, especially when they all look good. Figure 9-1 provides an excellent example to follow as you evaluate how well each group stacks up against the other. You can use this tool to eliminate markets as well as to prioritize them. To do your own

evaluation, print the Market Segment Evaluation Worksheet located on the CD
and follow these steps:

1. **Write in the name of each segment across the top of the paper.**
2. **Rate each segment on a scale of 1 (poor) to 3 (excellent) against the market attractiveness criteria on the left-hand side.**
3. **Add up each column.**
4. **Focus on the segments with the highest total score.**

Take the segments with the highest total score and use them in Chapter 12 to
develop your strategic goals and priorities for the coming year or years.

| RATE EACH SEGMENT ON A SCALE OF 1 (POOR) TO 3 (EXCELLENT) | | | |
|---|---|---|---|
| | Small Business | Medium Business | Large Business |
| How do you stack up against the **competition**? | 2 | 2 | 3 |
| How are your **company resources** positioned to meet the needs of this segment? | 1 | 2 | 3 |
| What is the **size** of this segment? | 2 | 2 | 2 |
| What is the **growth potential** of this segment? | 3 | 2 | 3 |
| What is the **profitability** of this segment? | 1 | 2 | 2 |
| How **accessible** is this segment? | 2 | 2 | 2 |
| Will this group **respond differently** from other groups to product and service offerings? | 2 | 2 | 2 |
| **Segment Totals** | 13 | 14 | 17 |

**Figure 9-1:**
Evaluating
your market
segments.

# Standing Out from the Crowd: Your Positioning Statement

You've determined who you want to market to, what their needs and wants
are, and that they, as a group, are attractive enough to get your interest.
Now you just have to get their attention! Here's a great analogy from Seth
Godin, author of *Purple Cow* (Portfolio Hardcover), about how to get your
customers' attention:

Cows, after you've seen them for a while, are boring. They may be perfect cows, attractive cows, cows with a great personality, cows lit by a beautiful light, but they're still boring. A purple cow, though: Now, that would really stand out. The essence of the purple cow is that it would be remarkable. Something remarkable is worth talking about, worth paying attention to.

The world is full of boring stuff (like brown cows) and also thousands of competitors, which is why so few people pay attention to what you're trying to communicate and sell. If in doubt, measure the level of market noise in your industry by typing in your business description into Google to see how many companies are doing the same thing you are. (*Strategic planning* returns 70 million results!)

Godin's analogy is simply a visual representation of an age-old marketing concept called positioning. *Positioning* is the space your product or service occupies in the mind of your customers. No matter what, companies consciously or subconsciously influence their position in the customer's mind. You may or may not be positioned the way you want to be. You may also just be a brown cow — invisible and boring. Extremely well-positioned products or services become nouns or verbs, such as Kleenex and Google.

To get customers and potential customers to pay attention, you must clearly position yourself in your customers' mind. To do so, you need a positioning statement that guides all your marketing efforts directed at the target customer group. This positioning statement is the core message you want to deliver in every medium and everything you do.

In the next sections, I discuss positioning statements and how to make yours really shine.

## *Writing your positioning statements*

The purpose of writing a positioning statement is to ensure that all your marketing activities for a customer group are consistent and clear. (And having a positioning statement saves you tons of time in the long run.) Initially, focus on writing a positioning statement that's used only internally. In the future, you may end up using it for other purposes, such as in your marketing collateral, but if you throw that possibility into the mix the first go around, crafting a statement that makes sense may be more difficult. Use your value proposition from Chapter 8 to build your positioning statement. Ready to jump in?

To write your positioning statements, follow these steps:

1. Select the target customer group you want to focus on.

2. Develop a list of needs your customer group has that you intend to meet (if not already included in your customer profile).

3. List your product or service's benefits that uniquely meet these needs.

4. Use the lists of customer needs and product or service benefits to finish this sentence: "When this customer group thinks of my product or service, I want them to think _____."

5. Evaluate your positioning statement to make sure that it's simple, clear, and consistent.

6. Get the word out to everyone by consistently communicating your positioning message in everything your company does for this customer group.

Don't forget: The customer does the real positioning by paying attention and deciding to buy your product or service. What you *do* have control over is assessing what positions exist in the customer's mind and then determining which of those positions you have the best chance of occupying and defending based on your own strengths.

## Perusing examples of positioning statements

Sometimes a positioning statement sounds like a tag line or a slogan. That's fine, but remember that the purpose of a positioning statement isn't to be cute. Instead, its purpose is to help guide all your and your staff's activities associated with a specific target customer group. You can turn your positioning statement into a marketing message in the future.

If you need some inspiration, read through these positioning statements from large and small companies:

- **Mercedes-Benz:** Engineered like no other car in the world

- **Wharton Business School:** The only business school that trains managers who are global, cross-functional, good leaders, and leveraged by technology

- **BMW:** The ultimate driving machine

- **Southwest Airlines:** The short-haul, no-frills, and low-priced airline

- ✔ **Avis:** We are only Number 2, but we try harder
- ✔ **Famous Footwear:** The value shoe store for families
- ✔ **Miller Lite:** The only beer with superior taste and low caloric content
- ✔ **The Heidel House Resort:** The place to reconnect with loved ones
- ✔ **Northern Nevada Business Weekly:** The only source for local business news

# Reaching Your New Target Markets

No matter whether you're targeting 18- to 34-year-old high-income males or 65- to 85-year-old fixed income retirees, you've got to reach them effectively and efficiently. That means finding the right balance of marketing tools and program elements to create and deliver the right product or service to consumers at the right price, right location, right time, and with the right features and attributes. I show you how to do all that in the following sections.

## The Four Ps: Neither a soul band nor a legume

At this stage, you want to bring in your marketing mix. The marketing mix, or the Four *P*s — promotion, place, product, and price — are the combination of actions you have to serve your target market.

Think of each *P* as a leg on a chair. If they don't all support each other, the chair falls over. The same thing is true for your marketing mix. Each element needs to support the other. If any inconsistencies exist, your customers *will* notice.

One of the main keys to the success of any marketing program is creating a marketing mix that's 100 percent relevant and resonates with your target market. The following list covers all four *P*s and how they fit in to the market.

- ✔ **Product:** Your marketing mix is based on and built off your products and/or services. Products are defined as anything that's capable of satisfying customer needs. Make sure that you have a product or service geared toward the need of your target market.

✔ **Price:** Make sure that your price is within the budget of your target market to create that marketing mix that your customers desire. From the customer's perspective, price is the monetary expression of value, and that value is enjoyed by customers. Therefore, value equals benefits minus price. This *P* is one of the easiest *P*s to change. But remember that price really is the only place that actually directly determines revenue generation.

✔ **Promotion:** Just having a good product at a good price isn't enough. These benefits have to be communicated to the customer. Gear your promotional messaging to solve the problems that customers encounter.

You can communicate with your customer in hundreds of ways and more ways are being added every day. (Even manhole covers have logos on them!) The high-level channels include advertising, direct marketing, personal selling, sales promotion, and public relations.

✔ **Place:** This *P* is also known as distribution. Ensure that your distribution efforts are seen by your target market. Place determines where customers can buy or receive your products and services. For product companies, place refers to all the locations a customer can find your merchandise, such as resellers' stores, the company's own stores, a catalog, e-commerce website, or a reseller's website. For service companies, this *P* is often thought of in terms of convenience. How easily can a customer buy services from you? For example, a dry cleaning service increased convenience by centrally locating its operations, offering a delivery and pick-up service, and partnering with several tailors in town.

Estella's Exotic Escapes specializes in high-end, hard-to-find vacation packages. However, half of the packages she offers include mega-chain hotels in places like Cancun and Kona. Her prices are geared toward a large budget, and her ads are in publications that have a subscription base of senior citizens. Do you see the marketing mix chair falling over? The legs of the chair don't support each other. Clearly, this example is over exaggerated, but you always want to make sure that your marketing mix has a message that works together.

## The cycle of (product) life

From a strategic perspective, looking at where your product or service is in its life cycle helps determine actions in each of the Four *P*s related to your target customer groups (see the previous section for info on the Four *P*s).

The following are the four product life cycle phases:

- **Introduction:** This phase provides a period of slow growth with nonexistent profits (because of the extensive promotional costs). Examples include third-generation mobile phones, e-conferencing, and iris-based personal identity cards.

- **Growth:** Growth is a period of rapid market acceptance and developing profits. Some examples of growth are MP3 players, e-mail, breathable synthetic fabrics, and smart cards.

- **Maturity:** This phase is a period of slow growth, level profits, and increasing marketing expenditures to defend the product's position against competitors. Examples of maturity include personal computers, faxes, cotton T-shirts, and credit cards.

- **Decline:** Decline is a period of falling sales and profits. Examples include handwritten letters, checkbooks, and CD players.

Figure 9-2 provides an example to help you develop actions for each of the Four *P*s, depending on where your product is in the product life cycle. To prepare yours, use the Marketing Action Plan Worksheet located on the CD. For each target customer group, follow these steps:

1. **Determine your marketing goal for the target customer group.**

   Flip to Chapter 12 for guidance on writing goals.

2. **Determine what phase of the product life cycle your product or service is in.**

   Use information earlier in this section to determine where your product or service is in its life.

3. **Develop an action plan that addresses product, price, promotion, and distribution.**

   Use the information in Chapter 13 to develop an action plan that supports the goal you developed for this target customer group.

You may not need to take a specific action for each of the Four *P*s. But write down what's happening so you can ensure the marketing mix works cohesively.

| | INTRODUCTION | GROWTH | MATURITY | DECLINE |
|---|---|---|---|---|
| **Marketing objectives** | Create product awareness & trial | Maximize market share | Maximize profits while defending market share | Reduce expenditure & "milk" brand |
| **Product** | Offer basic | Offer new features, extensions, service, & warranty | Diversify brand & models | Phase out weak items |
| **Price** | Usually high; use cost + | Maintain pricing | Match or lower than competitors | Cut price |
| **Distribution** | High expenses | Increase number of outlets | Intensify distribution | Very selective |
| **Promotion** | Build awareness among early adopters | Build awareness & interest in mass market | Stress brand differences & benefits | Reduce level to maintain loyal customers |

**Figure 9-2:** Developing your marketing action plan.

# Staying Market-Focused

The process of researching, segmenting, targeting, and reaching new customers doesn't need to be something you do only when you're focused on finding new customers. In fact, world-class companies have made being market-focused a habit. Being market-focused means taking marketing activities out of just the marketing department and away from initiatives. It means making marketing part of everyone's job.

In the following sections, I explain how being market-focused works and give you tips on staying in the know.

## Gathering relevant information

The key to being market-focused is continuously gathering relevant information about your customers and your market. Most likely, you already gather a significant amount of customer information in meetings and discussions with customers and distributors, from sales reports, through databases, and so on.

When you gather this info, you have to do something with it. Take these tips to heart:

✔ Start collecting the info in a systematic fashion by making a group marketing storage unit, such as a physical filing cabinet or a file on your company server.

✔ Scan the environment for information about government regulation and policies, technological changes, partners and competitors and their activities, and future industry trends. Continual environmental scanning allows you to stay proactive, taking advantage of shifts as they happen, instead of being reactive, and scrambling to keep up.

Sources for info include trade publications, industry events, and your local network. Consider doing this scan quarterly or semi-annually.

## Sharing what you know

When you get a bunch of information, what are you going to do with it? The information you gather should be regularly compiled in a usable form and then shared with employees in various ways. These sharing avenues can include

✔ Brown-bag lunches

✔ Company blogs

✔ Company newsletters

✔ Customer and market databases

✔ Forums

✔ Informal meetings

✔ Internal message postings

✔ Staff meetings

Intelligence needs to be communicated clearly, continuously, and appropriately so your staff can strategically respond to the needs of the market.

## Responding to what you've discovered

Responding to your market is critical to being market-focused. You can generate information and communicate it internally, but unless you respond to market needs, nothing gets accomplished. To be sustainable, your company needs to be driven by the following:

- ✔ An understanding of what your customers want
- ✔ The knowledge of how to meet the customers' needs
- ✔ The delivery of the product or service customers want

Many of you may already be doing most of these activities. Great job! If you aren't, that's okay. Take some action to formalize your process. Studies show that companies that link these activities together achieve greater levels of performance when compared to their competitors. A company that increases its market focus by 10 percent can see a growth of between 17 and 20 percent in overall performance.

Want to evaluate how market-focused your firm is? Check out this free, online assessment tool: www.m3planning.com/survey.

# Putting It All Together: Organizing Customer Information

Businesses that succeed do so by creating and keeping customers. Because marketing plays the key role of making that happen, it has a large part in setting the strategic direction of the organization. But unlike the other sections of your plan, the marketing section starts with a target customer group instead of a goal. See Figure 9-3 for an example of how to organize your customer profile information. Prepare yours by using the Customer Profile Worksheet located on the CD.

You can use the marketing portion of your strategic plan to develop a complete marketing plan, which would include more detail about your markets and your action plans to reach them. However, smaller organizations often choose to have just one plan (a strategic plan) that covers their intended marketing actions.

| | |
|---|---|
| **Example Company:** Hallelujah Acres of Shelby, North Carolina, offers products, counseling, workshops, and conferences to help people attain and maintain optimal health while eliminating sickness and disease and to influence them to adopt a healthier lifestyle based on Biblical principles. | |

| | |
|---|---|
| **Customer Group:** | People with cancer |
| **Strategy:** | Market development |
| **Segmentation Base:** | Need, motivation, and desire to find an alternative cure to cancer because none of the traditional methods are working |
| **Customer Profile:** | *Needs:* Hope, encouragement, education (information), wellness plan, support, accountability to someone <br> *Primary benefit sought:* A non-traditional cure for cancer or relief from pain <br> *Demographics:* All types of non-terminal cancer, any demographic <br> *Geographic:* Located in the southeast region of the United States <br> *Lifestyle:* Survivors, involved in cancer activist and support groups, SAD, misinformed, deceived, bought into the medical establishment, no energy, no hope, depressed, overweight, clogged up over fed and undernourished, toxic and starving <br> *Personality:* Highly motivated, will do anything it takes to get better <br> *Usage:* Very loyal, repeat usage until cured |
| **Segment Attractiveness:** | *Segment Size:* 19,200 <br> *Growth Rate:* 12 percent annually <br> *Profitability:* 960 new customers (5% of market) x $1,200 = $1,152,000 <br> *Accessibility:* Reach through doctors, support groups, associations <br> *Differentiation:* This segment is self-identified. The company is not serving any other group similar to this one. |
| **Positioning Statement:** | When this group thinks of Hallelujah Acres, we want them to think we are the only healthy, alternative solution cancer that really works. |
| **Marketing Objective:** | Reach 5 percent of the southeast cancer patient market with the Hallelujah Acres message by 2007. |
| **Stage of Product-Life Cycle:** | Growth |
| **Product/Service:** | Develop a Hallelujah Acres' cancer-curing kit, complete with cancer-specific books, Hallelujah Acres' Diet products, and DVD movie featuring cured patients. Open Hallelujah Acres' Cancer Clinic in partnership with Oasis Hope Hospital. |
| **Pricing:** | Maintain current product pricing. Segment is not cost conscience. |
| **Promotion:** | Partner with state cancer associations to provide newsletter content, speakers, special promotional offerings to their members. Develop a specific section on the Hallelujah Acres' website for cancer information. Direct mail Hallelujah Acres' brochure with cancer-specific testimonials to target market. |
| **Distribution:** | Sell cancer-specific products on website, through distribution locations. Direct mail product catalogue to target market. |

**Figure 9-3:** Target customer group profile, goals, and action plan.

# Chapter 10

# Identifying Your Opportunities and Threats

*In This Chapter*

▶ Classifying opportunities for and threats to your operating business

▶ Capitalizing on opportunities in your operating environment

▶ Predicting your industry shifts

▶ Sizing up your competition

▶ Rounding out your SWOT analysis

ou're headed down your strategy road with an SUV that's primed and tuned. It's time to look out the windows and check out what's going on around you. How's the landscape? Is it breathtaking or gray? What's happening with the weather, and how are the road conditions? All these factors influence how smoothly you travel down your path to success.

Assume several storms are brewing on the horizon. Three to be exact. Each storm is a little farther away from the next. The closer the storm, the more potential impact it has on your trip. The ones farthest out may or may not impact you, but you keep an eye on them nevertheless. The landscape your company operates in is exactly the same. Your business has three influences. Starting with the outer ring of Figure 10-1, these influences include

  ✔ Your operating environment

  ✔ Your industry, which includes your competitors

  ✔ Your market

Some external influences or factors have more direct impact on your business. Others just take a little longer to get there. By looking at your landscape in three influences, you won't miss anything that may be hiding on the horizon.

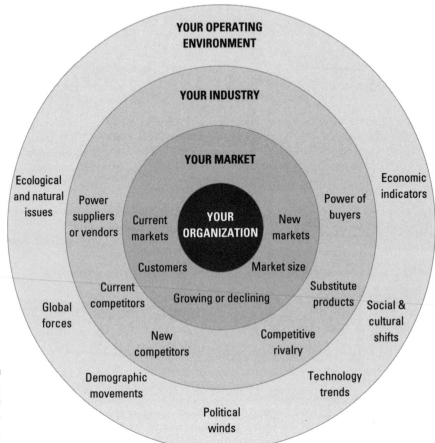

YOUR OPERATING ENVIRONMENT

YOUR INDUSTRY

YOUR MARKET

YOUR ORGANIZATION

Ecological and natural issues

Power suppliers or vendors

Current markets

New markets

Power of buyers

Economic indicators

Customers

Market size

Current competitors

Growing or declining

Substitute products

Global forces

New competitors

Competitive rivalry

Social & cultural shifts

Demographic movements

Technology trends

Political winds

**Figure 10-1:** A view of your environment.

The success or failure of your organization depends not only on your internal capabilities and resources (strengths and weaknesses, which I discuss in Chapter 7) but also on things that happen outside of your control (opportunities and threats). All the info in this chapter helps you identify the forces, issues, trends, and events that can positively or negatively impact your business. What possibilities do you see on the horizon, and where are the minefields?

In this chapter, you identify potential opportunities and threats that may impact your business. You discover some of the larger trends likely to impact all businesses over the next ten years as well as how to spot the ones not covered in this chapter. Lastly, you bring all the pieces of your SWOT together to create a complete picture of your company's strategic position.

# *Starting Your SWOT Analysis*

When responding to opportunities and threats in your environment, you need to react proactively rather than reactively. Being ready for the what ifs can help you determine your strategic position. Figure 10-2 illustrates how these elements fit into your SWOT (also covered in Chapters 7 and 8).

You need to take a quick pulse of your company's opportunities and threats to assess your external situation. To do so, investigate the various areas listed in Figure 10-2 to get more specific about what's happening in your operating environment.

Don't forget to ask for help — getting objective input from others helps you see parts you may have missed. The section "Finishing Your SWOT Analysis" later in this chapter gives you ideas about how to proceed, too. Use the Operating Environment Questionnaire and the Industry Environment Questionnaire on the CD to get your own list started.

| INTERNAL | EXTERNAL |
|---|---|
| **Capabilities:** | **Operating Environment:** |
| ☐ Human Capital | ☐ Political/legal |
| ☐ Organizational Capital | ☐ Environment |
| ☐ Knowledge Capital | ☐ Social |
| **Resources:** | ☐ Technological |
| ☐ Financial Resources | **Industry:** |
| ☐ Physical Resources | ☐ New competitors |
| ☐ Intangible Resources | ☐ Substitute products |
| **Processes:** | ☐ Power of suppliers |
| ☐ Operational Processes | ☐ Power of buyers |
| ☐ Customer management Processes | ☐ Competitive rivalry |
| ☐ Relationship management Processes | **Market:** |
| ☐ Innovation Processes | ☐ Growing, shrinking |
| **Other:** | ☐ Size of markets |
| ☐ Technology management | ☐ New markets |
| ☐ Communication | **Competitors:** |
| ☐ Productivity | ☐ Who they are |
| **Current Customers:** | ☐ Strengths, weaknesses |
| ☐ Customer mix | ☐ Strategies |
| ☐ Satisfaction | ☐ Objectives |
| ☐ Loyalty | |
| ☐ Strength of your value chain | |
| ☐ Strength of your value prop | |

**Figure 10-2:** SWOT Analysis: Determining your strategic position by evaluating your external opportunities and threats.

*Strengths* — *Weaknesses* — *Opportunities* — *Threats*

To capture all your thoughts and keep them in order, create a notes page with a horizontal line in the middle. Label the top section "Opportunities" and the bottom section "Threats." Jot down thoughts about a new market under *Opportunities* and ideas on a competitor's action under *Threats*. (I use this same notation in other chapters when referring to notes.)

# Seeing the Future

How much time do you spend thinking about your company's future? Chances are, not much. Putting out fires and taking care of the day-to-day tasks likely consume most of your time. But to be strategic in your business, you must discover how to spot future opportunities and threats as soon as possible. Yes, you do need to identify the immediate forces at work, but you also want to think about and plan for the future operating environment and industry trends. The value lies in anticipating change before it happens, instead of mindlessly reacting to whatever comes at you next.

What changes should you be thinking about? Answer these questions to get started:

- ✔ Who will our customers be five years from now?
- ✔ How will we reach these customers?
- ✔ Do we regularly improve our product quality and customer satisfaction?
- ✔ What's our company's status as a trendsetter within our industry?
- ✔ Are we aware of new competitive threats on the horizon?
- ✔ Are we focused on catching up to the competition or on innovations in the marketplace?
- ✔ Is management flexible enough to alter our business model as necessary?
- ✔ How does our approach to forward thinking compare to our competition?
- ✔ Are our customers leaving us? Did they tell us why?

Your answers to these broad-reaching questions can tell you a lot about who you are today and what may need to change within your business. The responses can also give you a better sense of the type of resources you need to commit to reaching your organization's future. Make sure to push the boundaries. Think about each area in this chapter in terms of the present but also how it affects you five or even ten years down the road.

# Finding Opportunities in Your Operating Environment

No one has a crystal ball that can peer into the future, but certain trends appear to be in the making and are worth considering now. Although knowing how environmental forces are going to impact your business is difficult, they really do matter. Take the weather, for example: You're subconsciously aware of the force, but not until a big storm comes do you really pay attention. The important part, like everything in strategic planning, is to figure out which trends matter to your business. Huge successes can come from being aware of environmental forces, as I show you in this section.

Your operating environment is influenced by several general areas. These areas summarize the external environment every organization operates in. Refer back to Figure 10-1 to get a clear picture of influences in your operating environment.

Remember your operating environment is the outside circle influencing your business. Some of these trends and issues may even appear to come and go in slow motion. You may not need to watch them religiously, but having an eye on them can be the key to your company's boom — or bust. Although some of these issues may seem ridiculous to you, they may be someone else's reality.

In the next several sections, you discover many opportunities in your operating environment. After you assess your situation, check out the Operating Environment Questionnaire on the CD. The questionnaire can help start your list of opportunities and threats if you're having trouble getting going.

## Identifying your economic indicators

Movements and shifts in the economy affect consumer purchasing power and spending patterns. The state of the United States and world economies can be either an opportunity or a threat for any business, depending on whether your company improves and declines with the economy (real estate) or whether the opposite happens (price of gold). Economic indicators can be frustrating to watch because today's news often contradicts yesterday's report. Nevertheless, the economy is probably one of the biggest influences on your business.

Many economic indicators affect businesses. These areas may not be of the utmost importance for every business, but consider the following list of common economic indicators:

- Overall economic growth or industry growth
- Interest rates
- Government spending
- Changes in employment policies and minimum wage
- Housing costs
- Exchange rates, which impact demand from overseas customers
- Availability of capital
- Consumer confidence
- Average hourly earnings
- Personal consumption expenditures

Even outside trends tend to impact economic indicators. Some of these areas are out of your control and are likely to be huge factors over the next ten years. For more info on economic indicators, check out *Economic Indicators For Dummies,* by Michael Griffis (John Wiley & Sons, Inc.).

Check and see whether you can identify any opportunities or threats for your business in the following list:

- **Aging population:** Percentage of people over the age of 65 will grow in the United States from 13 percent in 2010 to 16 percent in 2020, but the aging megatrend affects all regions of the world — older people tend to be less prone to change.
- **Globalization:** We're rapidly growing in global interconnectedness. Global trade boundaries are quickly evaporating and opening opportunities for goods, services, people, information, technology, fashion, and culture, amongst many others.
- **Technology:** Faster, better, and increasingly more virtual, embedded technologies create data and consumer information at a rate that businesses are required to adapt to with strategic spontaneity in meeting growing demand.
- **Increasing price of oil:** The general consensus is that the era of cheap oil is probably over.
- **Shrinking middle class:** Rich people are getting richer; the number of people in the middle class is shrinking, and the lower class is growing and getting poorer. The result: A larger gap between rich and poor.
- **Increasing natural disasters:** The possibility of more natural disasters is a growing concern. These occurrences not only take a human toll but also upset local and national economies.

A company that provides contract labor to the construction industry forecasts its business based on a leading economic indicator: housing starts. Over the years, the company has refined its planning process to begin making decisions based on changes in this economic indicator with a six months lead time. In other words, when the indicator significantly changed, the company knew it had six months before the impact of that shift would be felt. The company's actions included proactive increase or reduction in workforce.

An appliance services company relies on the economic indicator of durable goods manufacturing to forecast business. As in the preceding example, the company refined its planning and forecasting to understand it had ten months from the indicator change to business impact.

## Watching important social shifts

Cultural and societal shifts are probably the hardest to spot because the results of these forces affect a society's general attitudes, preferences, tastes, and beliefs. Catching, or even better, predicting, a social trend can be a home run for your business. Think about the low-carb craze, the reinvention of coffee as a lifestyle, digital music, outsourcing, offshoring, and so on.

Social indicators include the following issues:

- ✔ Labor availability and types
- ✔ Lifestyle changes, such as working from home or single households
- ✔ Attitudes about work and leisure
- ✔ Education
- ✔ Health
- ✔ Fashion and fads
- ✔ Living conditions

Here's what to watch for or capitalize on:

- ✔ **Virtual learning:** Broadband access is increasingly widening informal learning opportunities less expensively. Online access to credentialing will also increase diversity in learning options to the 500 million young people who don't have access in today's environment. Emerging countries will reap the benefit of online learning as quickly as companies can respond to the demand.

✔ **Individualism:** Playing hand-in-hand with digitization (which makes it so much easier to reach consumers worldwide), individualism accelerates commercialism because consumers can now demand tailored products and services to meet their individual demands.

✔ **Prosperity:** Prosperity is identified as a megatrend across OECD (Organisation for Economic Co-operation and Development) countries that will change the demand for new types of products. We're experiencing a change from agricultural and/or industrial societies to *knowledge* societies in which demand increases for intangible products that offer experiences, services, entertainment, and investment.

## Staying on top of technology trends

Many people believe that the revolutionary impact technology has had on products, processes, and communication systems has just begun — think Twitter, Facebook, and video calls. New technologies and processes continue to change the way organizations operate daily. The problem for most companies is evaluating which advances are truly opportunities and which are simply distractions.

Failure to monitor and address advances may negatively impact your financial position in the market. Areas to watch include government spending on technology, big new discoveries or products, speed of technology transfer, and changes in business processes as a result of technology.

Here are some trends to look for that may be opportunities or threats to your business:

✔ **Acceleration:** Change occurs at startling rates due to the access of information today. Individuals change jobs, relationships, homes, ideas, and interests at a faster rate than ever before. The pace at which products go to market occurs faster, which increases demands on companies to accelerate innovation, development and product introduction to stay competitive and in the forefront of the competition.

✔ **Growth of robots:** Robots are taking on increasingly more complex jobs and assignments and aren't isolated in the simple repetitive tasks.

✔ **Nanotechnology:** This technology is designed and developed to maintain special electrical properties, extremely low friction, and high strength levels. Nanotechnology may, in the future, replace microelectronics and ultimately be the technology that drives microscopic robots used in diagnostic healthcare.

✔ **Mobile everything:** Certainly, the early 2010s will be remembered for how mobile applications transformed the way consumers interface with companies and content. Expect more and more innovation to come around mobile functionality, such as payment processing, cloud computing, and gaming.

With more than 239 million Americans hooked up to broadband in 2010, companies large and small are making serious money by doing everything from working virtually, to offering online services, to distributing anything digital. Skype, the world's fastest growing Internet telephony provider, was sold to eBay for $2.6 billion in 2005 and then sold again to Microsoft for $8.5 billion in 2011. Why the large price tag? It boasted more than 107 million customers worldwide using its service, virtually free. More importantly, the communication platform will be integrated into Microsoft products, such as Xbox and Kinect, Lync (web conferencing service), Windows Phone, and Windows Live, to enhance its Real Time Communication business.

## *Monitoring political winds*

Keeping tabs on your government's policies and legislation on business-related issues is crucial. Decisions made at the federal, state, and local levels can significantly impact how you do business. For example, new taxes can cut into already thinning margins, or tax cuts can improve them. Or changes in labor laws can impact how you handle employees.

Naturally, legislative threats or opportunities can occur on the local, state, and national levels. Monitoring the political winds includes taxes, international trade regulations, consumer protection, environmental policies, the pro- or anti-business attitude of the president, and the biggie — healthcare legislation.

Here's what to expect over the next ten years:

- ✔ **Healthcare consumerism:** Globally, this trend is shifting purchasing power and personal responsibility healthcare in the hands of the consumer. Slowing down the pace or direction of this trend depends on the role the government assumes relative to healthcare coverage.

- ✔ **Security market:** Global government spending in homeland security for 2010 reached approximately $178 billion. In the next ten years, this figure is estimated to jump to nearly $2.7 trillion. Although the United States dominates the market, the list of other countries expanding their security efforts against internal and external threats is growing. Visiongain, an independent business information provider for industries such as Defense, Energy, and Metals, forecasts nine major homeland security markets with high demand for scanning, detection, and protection capabilities.

- ✔ **Government downsizing:** Although downsizing is certainly in process at the federal level, the economic downturn has already forced state and local governments to tighten their belts. The fallout from this action is varied but includes outsourcing non-core services, decreasing service levels of core services such as parks and libraries, and reducing workforce.

One result of healthcare reform is reemergence of Accountable Care Organizations (ACO), which are networks of care providers, such as physicians, hospitals, and ancillary services. The transition of these companies to form or join networks is being driven by legislation that states that in 2012, Medicare must contract with only ACOs. Due to this shift and many others as outcome of federally-driven reform, companies positioned ahead of this trend are more likely to survive and thrive.

## Flexing with demographic movements

Futurists say that you can't understand the future without demographics. Knowing what's going on with demographic changes and movements helps you plan for the demand for your company's products and services as well as labor issues. For example, sometimes seemingly unexplainable lulls or growth spurts, especially in the retail and restaurant industries, can be explained by understanding the changes in the demographics.

Here are the big movements that may impact every U.S. business:

- **Increasing population:** By 2050, the global population is estimated to reach 9.2 billion people.

- **Home healthcare services:** By 2020, nearly 14 million people in the United States will be over the age of 85, and 84 percent of them will want to continue living at home. To do that, more than half will need assistance with daily living activities.

- **Increasing diversity:** Minorities, primarily the growing role of the Hispanics in the United States, will affect business demographics. The population of Hispanic or Latino origin will rise from 12.6 percent in 2000 to just under 25 percent in 2020 and 30 percent in 2050. These statistics represent that one in every three persons will be Hispanic.

- **Greater economic achievement by women:** By 2020, one in every three workers will be a woman. According to the workplace-research group, "Fortune 500 companies with the most women in senior management had a higher return on equity."

- **Generational divide:** By 2020, businesses will have to address the disparity in differing work styles between semi-retired baby boomers and younger generations (Gen X and Millennials). The generational divide is a growing issue in the business culture.

Right at Home has been riding the growing trend of home healthcare services since 1995. The company grew 27 percent in 2010, posting $127 million in revenue with 25,000 clients in the U.S., U.K., and Brazil. Its growth strategy through franchising contributes to the rapid expansion as other savvy business people also want to get in on this trend.

# Tracking Your Industry

An *industry* is a group of companies that sell products or services that are close substitutes of each other, such as the furniture industry, the car industry, or the financial services industry. Knowing the type of industry you're competing in helps you predict changes, movements, or shifts that may impact your business. Also knowing how competitive your industry is can be helpful because some are more cutthroat than others. Harvard professor Michael Porter pioneered the work around looking at industry forces. I use his breakdown as a guide in this section.

What industry does your company operate in? You can most easily identify it by answering the question, "If customers were to purchase elsewhere, what are all the potential options that exist?"

Classify the different types of companies you identify with in small groups until you have a big enough circle to define the entire set. For the most part, identifying your industry is intuitive, but sometimes the nets aren't cast wide enough. For example, a charter sailing company isn't in the cruise industry. Instead, the company is swimming in a bigger pond called the travel and tourism industry.

In an effort to understand the dynamic nature of an industry, you can break any industry into five components or forces: new competitors, substitute products, power of suppliers, power of buyers, and competitive rivalry (see Figure 10-3). These five forces impact every industry in some form or fashion and determine your industry's attractiveness and long-run profitability. I discuss each force in the next sections. As you review the forces, identify whether the force is high, medium, or low in your industry.

## Looming new competitors

The more companies that swim in the same pond and compete for the same customers, the more competitive the industry. Often some competition is better than none. But if jumping in to your industry is easy (for example, restaurants, online services, advertising agencies, and so on), the threat of new competitors is very high. Conversely, if big startup costs and regulatory hurdles have to be crossed — like the construction, airline, and manufacturing industries — you may not feel as threatened. The barriers that exist or that you build determine how big of a threat looming competitors is. Key barriers include the following:

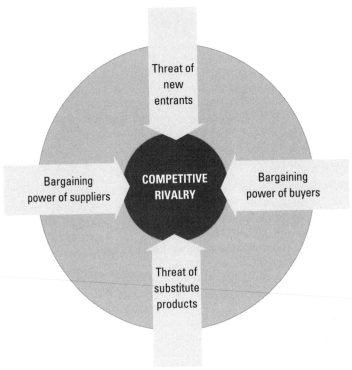

**Figure 10-3:**
Forces
in your
industry.

- ✔ Economies of scale (when more units of a good or service can be produced on a larger scale, yet with, on average, less input costs, economies of scale are achieved)

- ✔ The size of the capital or investment requirements

- ✔ The ease or difficulty of switching from one company to another

- ✔ The ability to access distribution channels

- ✔ The likelihood of retaliation by existing companies

The number of companies developing and selling customer relationship management (CRM) systems grows every year. Companies in this space include Salesforce.com, Sage ACT!, Oracle, and Microsoft with its Business Contact Manager, Intuit. As more and more companies join the party, the current players see the threat of new competitors increasing. The entry barriers are relatively low except one: the difficulty for customers to move from one platform to another. In fact, anyone who's implemented a CRM system knows that the biggest challenge is getting people within the company to adopt the new system. Moving around from one platform to another is a time-consuming process and can kill your business. Because this barrier is so high, the threat of new competitors to established companies is slightly diminished. The opportunity is to grab as much market share as quickly as possible.

# *Threatening substitute products*

With the continual flux of technologies and the speed of development, the threat of substitute products taking the place of yours is greater than ever before. Substitute products can be an area of opportunity or an area of threat, depending on when you catch wind of the change. If you're on top of it, *you* can produce the new product. If you're behind the change curve, you may likely see a decline in demand. The probability that customers will move to a new product or service is based on three areas:

- ✓ The customers' willingness to change or do without (cigarettes)
- ✓ The price and performance of the new product (mail to e-mail)
- ✓ The generic substitution (vacation to staycation)

The popularity of satellite radio has exploded over the past several years, with the two main companies — XM Radio and Sirius — grabbing market share as fast as possible. With more and more consumers tuning in to satellites instead of radio tuners, traditional radio stations are finding their listener base declining rapidly. Who knows the ultimate fate of AM and FM, but media companies are scrambling to reposition themselves because a substitute product is whisking its customers away.

# *Bargaining power of suppliers*

Suppliers or vendors are any companies that provide raw materials, components, or services into your industry. The amount of control your suppliers have over the price of goods you purchase dictates whether this area is an opportunity or threat. The more suppliers, the less control any one company can have over controlling your costs. The power of your suppliers is high when any of the following factors exist:

- ✓ Few suppliers and many buyers
- ✓ Similar products or services but with higher value or cost
- ✓ Suppliers or vendors threaten to integrate forward (like Nike opening its own retail stores called Niketown)
- ✓ Your industry isn't a key customer group for the supplier

AT&T sells many of its telecommunication services through independent sales agents. This distribution channel has facilitated the growth of many small telecommunications consulting companies that resell AT&T products. The commission earned off these products was a primary source of revenue for these agents' businesses. AT&T is one of only a few suppliers of telephony. Because of this fact, losing one of the only suppliers was a huge threat to these companies. And AT&T took advantage of that power by terminating many agent contracts and bringing the accounts in-house. This action was completely legal but destroyed many agents' businesses.

## Bargaining power of buyers

The power of buyers can be summed up in one word: Wal-Mart. Because 10 cents of every consumer dollar is spent at Wal-Mart, any company in the consumer goods industry must contend with the force of its buying power. Buyers in this analysis are people who create demand in your industry. The power of buyers is great with any of the following factors:

- ✔ Many sellers, few buyers

- ✔ Buyers threaten to integrate backwards (a computer manufacturer deciding to produce semiconductors or another component they would normally purchase)

- ✔ Your industry's products are standardized with little differentiation between competing products

- ✔ Your industry isn't a key supplying group for the buyers

## Duking it out with your competitors

The rivalry or intensity at which you compete against your competition can move and change over time as the dynamics of the industry change. Competitive rivalry is an opportunity or a threat, depending on how you handle it.

Do you recognize the intensity of the competition, and are you positioning yourself accordingly? Or are you feeling the pressures, but don't know where they're coming from? The following aspects have an effect on whether you feel the pressure of your industry more or less:

- ✔ **The structure of the competition:** Rivalry is greater when there are many small companies and less when there's a clear market leader.

- ✔ **Growth objectives:** Rivalry is greater when everyone is focused on growth (like biotech) and less when the industry is mature (like publishing).

- ✔ **Exit barriers:** If leaving an industry is expensive or difficult, rivalries tend to be higher.

- ✔ **Degree of differentiation:** This factor is present in industries where products are commodities. *Commodities* are products and services that have no obvious differences, and companies compete on price (like computers, steel, and so on). Rivalry is higher than when competitors can differentiate their products.

> ✔ **The structure of the industry costs:** In industries that have high fixed costs (like manufacturing), competitors tend to cut prices to fill unused manufacturing capacity, which leads to higher rivalry.

# Analyzing Your Competition

Swinging from one extreme to another is easy when it comes to analyzing your competition. Some organizations don't worry about what their competitors are doing and just charge ahead. Others track every move and assess how to react. You want to fall somewhere in the middle.

The reason to do a competitive analysis is to assess the opportunities and threats that may occur from those organizations competing for the same business you are. You need to have an understanding of what your competitors are or aren't offering your potential customers. Here are a few other key ways a competitive analysis fits into strategic planning:

> ✔ **To help you assess whether your competitive advantage is really an advantage:** Your competitive advantage, by its definition, means you have an advantage over your competition. (Flip to Chapter 5 for more on competitive advantage.) If you don't know your competitors well enough, you won't know whether you're really better than they are in the areas you've isolated as your competitive advantages.

> ✔ **To understand what your competitors' current and future strategies are so you can plan accordingly:** You don't want to be crafting the same strategy as they are or you won't be successful. Remember, you want to be unique in the value you provide to your customers.

> ✔ **To provide information that will help you evaluate your strategic decisions against what your competitors may or may not be doing:** By looking at what your competitors are and aren't doing, you may find out whether you're missing something they've already identified. Or, conversely, if you're on to a trend that they haven't noticed, you may need to move faster.

The process of gathering competitive intelligence is like putting together a big puzzle. Each piece individually may not seem that interesting, but when all the pieces are put together, you have a complete and useful picture. In the same vein, if you don't have enough information, the picture is incomplete. In the following sections, I show you how to identify your customers and gather the right amount of info about them.

Before conducting your competitive analysis, decide your basis of comparison. In other words, are you doing the analysis on a product or service? A product or service line? Or on the company as a whole?

## Identifying your competitors

If you're gearing up for a big athletic competition, your training regimen is directly proportional to who you're competing against. You really don't want to work harder than you have to, right? Well, the same idea applies to your business. Certainly, if you're running a for-profit business, you're competing to win. If you're a nonprofit or a department head, you're competing for scarce resources, usually funding. In all cases, you need to know who you're trying to beat so you can position yourself properly.

The clearest way to identify your competitors is to figure out what would happen if you weren't around. Who would supply your customers' needs, and what would customers buy to solve their problems? Also, who's taking away your customers, and whose customers are you taking?

You can group competitors in three categories, as discussed in the next sections.

### Direct competitors

These companies are the ones you need to find out the most about because they're your fiercest competitors. When customers are making purchasing decisions, their products or services always end up on the short list. With this group, you're vying for the same customer dollar. More than likely, you have three or four companies that fall into this category.

### Indirect competitors

These companies offer alternative products and services than what you offer. Usually, you don't worry about these companies too much, but you should keep tabs on what they're up to. Sometimes an indirect competitor can become a direct competitor.

### Substitutes or new entrants

While conducting your competitive analysis, determine whether any substitute products or potential new entrants exit. A *substitute product* is anything that delivers the same set of benefits to your customers as you do but isn't a competing product. For example, DVD rental is a substitute service to cable TV. New companies or entrants coming on the scene may change your industry completely, such as satellite radio has done to the radio industry.

Don't restrict your thinking only to companies similar to your own. Consider firms outside of the realm of possibility, such as those who compete in the industry from a corporate strategic viewpoint. When contemplating the future, you need to envision any number of possibilities.

## Gathering competitive intelligence

In the past, collecting data on your competitors was difficult. Today's over-abundance of information makes this important analysis much easier. Now you can collect data legally and ethically and through a plethora of sources available to you. Check out Table 10-1 for a list of sources.

The sources for competitive analysis are broken into three groups: online, physical, and undercover. Information online is the easiest to secure, followed by physical, and then undercover.

| Table 10-1 | Sources for Competitive Intelligence | |
|---|---|---|
| *Online Sources* | *Direct or Physical Sources* | *Undercover Sources* |
| Corporate website | Pricing, pricing lists | Hire an ex-employee |
| Annual reports | Advertising campaigns | Talk to vendors |
| Press releases | Special promotions | Interview customers |
| Newspaper articles or stories | Brochures, sales kits | Attend their seminars or conferences |
| Analysts reports | Purchasing their products | Attend social events or networking where they're present |
| Government reports | Trade show booth | |
| Online presentations | | |
| Blogs | | |
| Newsgroups | | |
| Patent applications | | |

## Isolating what you really need to know

Undoubtedly, you or someone else probably knows some things about your competitors. However, knowing about the CEO's favorite lunch spot or the receptionist's name isn't going to get you very far.

Here's what you *do* need to care about and know about your competitors:

- ✔ **Their profiles:** Who are they? What products or services do they sell? How many employees are in the company? See Table 10-2 for more ideas.

- ✔ **Their strengths and weaknesses:** What do they do well? What don't they do well or need to improve?

✔ **Their competitive advantages:** What are they best at in the market or industry?

✔ **Their strategies and objectives:** Where are they headed, and how are they going to get there?

Take the time to formalize what you know and what you *want* to know in writing. With this list in mind, you can more easily sort out what's important when you conduct your competitive analysis. You can also make a small SWOT grid for each of your competitors (refer to Figure 10-2 at the beginning of this chapter for an example of a SWOT grid). See Table 10-2 for more specifics on what you need to know about your competitors.

| Table 10-2 | Sleuthing Out Your Competitors |
| --- | --- |
| *What You Probably Already Know* | *What You Want to Know* |
| Overall sales and profits | Sales and profits by individual product or service |
| Expenses levels | Cost of goods sold |
| Organizational structure (number of employees and positions) | Customer profiles |
| Distribution of products or services | New product or service ideas |
| Identity and profile of the senior management | Size of customer database |
| Marketing strategy and messaging | Effectiveness of marketing campaigns |
| Customer retention | Future investment plans |
| | Terms and partnerships with vendors |

## Seeing the competitive field

After you collect data on your competition (see the previous section), what do you do with it? Follow these steps to develop a Competitor Grid (located on the CD) similar to Figure 10-4:

1. **Select the product or service or customer segment to focus on.**

   If your competitors are the same across product or service lines or customer segments, skip this step.

2. **Narrow down your playing field if at all possible.**

   Look closely at your top three competitors or groups of competitors. Add your organization to the list.

**3. Determine your competitors' key strengths and weaknesses.**

The factors can be customer service, pricing, quality, operations, resources, personnel, and so on. Develop a good understanding of likely changes your competitors may make in the near future. Use the information collected during your intelligence gathering.

**4. Summarize each competitor's key point of differentiation.**

Answer the question, "What is XYZ competitor great at?"

**5. Critically review your Competitor Grid to summarize themes to add to your opportunities and threats.**

Add your thoughts to your list of opportunities and threats you started at the beginning of the chapter. You use this information to develop strategies, strategic objectives, and goals in Chapter 12.

If you find your competitors lacking or missing some obvious opportunities, this opening is a perfect chance for your business to fill the void. To do so, you need to figure out the best strategy. Review the different strategies listed in Chapter 8 for ways to differentiate yourself from your competition. Your competitive analysis guides you to select the one that gives you an edge on your competition.

| COMPETITOR | STRENGTH | WEAKNESS | DIFFERENTIATION |
|---|---|---|---|
| Competitor #1 | Huge, well known company with Fortune 100 clients. | Limited personal attention per client | Long-standing reputation and deep knowledge and expertise |
| Competitor #2 | Key high profile clients and they advertise and promote themselves well | Limited service offering | Niche focus with specialty and best-in-class within a single service |
| Competitor #3 | Financial strength with significant venture capital backing | No local office; hard to find on the web | Most innovative in the industry due to financial backing - fastest to market |
| Competitor #4 | Comprehensive office - all services are on-site | Known as the most expensive provider in the market | Face-to-face service in all major markets |
| Themes: | **Threats to us:** Competitors growing stronger through financial backing and brand awareness | **Opportunities for us:** Stay positioned competitively from a price and services offerings | |

**Figure 10-4:** Visualizing your competitive landscape.

# Evaluating Your Market

Referring back to Figure 10-1 in the beginning of the chapter, your market is the ring closest to your company. Trends, changes, and shifts that occur in your market likely have the biggest impact on your company. Your market is a group of customers that you can easily identify who respond to your products or services in similar ways. Your offering satisfies the needs and wants of the whole group.

You need to have a complete picture of your company, so taking a high-level look at your market is important. Based on the information you have available today, you can quickly determine the opportunities and threats that exist in your markets by following a few steps:

1. **List the three to five main markets you compete in. Also list one or two new potential markets.**

2. **Determine whether each market is growing, shrinking, or staying the same.**

3. **Figure out the size of each market, including number of customers, projected dollar size, and number of companies in the market.**

4. **Determine whether serving the market presents an opportunity or whether the market isn't worth focusing on.**

5. **Summarize the markets you want to focus on in your opportunities section of your SWOT.**

Don't worry about being exhaustive in your list because doing so can cripple your planning effort. You need to have enough info to feel comfortable with making decisions based on what you've collected. If you don't feel comfortable with the information you have available today, select one or two items to research further.

# Summarizing Your Opportunities and Threats

Opportunities and threats are external factors — forces that you don't control or your competitor can take advantage of if appropriate. For example, an opportunity may be that the rising number of Hispanic consumers can lead to an increased demand for your product if your company is positioned correctly. A threat may be that the proliferation of technology is making a current product obsolete.

If you answered the questionnaires in the previous sections, you have a good starting point to summarize and add to your key opportunities and threats.

You can translate those thoughts into a grid like Figure 10-2. Right now, you've developed thoughts to fill in the two quadrants on the right side of the grid.

# Finishing Your SWOT Analysis

If you've worked through the last three chapters and collected all the data I've discussed, it's time to make some sense of your list by organizing it in a SWOT format. Remember, the purpose of a SWOT is to help produce a good fit between your company's resources and capabilities and your external environment.

Your SWOT analysis is a balance sheet of your strategic position right now. In the analysis, you bring together all your internal factors, strengths, and weaknesses, as well as your external factors, opportunities, and threats. Strengths and weaknesses are factors that you can control and affect, which you identify in Chapters 7 and 8. Opportunities and threats, which you identify in this chapter, are out of your control; you can either try to take advantage of them or try to minimize them. Follow these steps to complete your SWOT analysis grid:

1. **Construct a grid, using the SWOT Analysis Template located on the CD.**

   Refer to Figure 10-2 for an example of a completed grid.

2. **Review your list of strengths, weaknesses, opportunities, and threats you developed over the last three chapters.**

   Condense similar factors. Eliminate nonessential ones. You want to be able to see a clear picture of your strategic position. If too many factors exist, drawing any conclusions is impossible.

3. **Place your company's strengths and weaknesses in the left side of the grid.**

   Make sure to include only the factors that are *internal* and controllable.

4. **Place your opportunities and threats in the right side of the grid.**

   Make sure to include only the factors that are *external* and out of your direct control.

Be careful not to oversimplify the strength, weakness, opportunity, or threat descriptions. Saying that *poor communications* is a weakness is easy and too broad a comment. Instead, identify specifically which communications cause problems. Is it with customers through the call center, information on pricing disseminated to staff, or something else? Getting specific leads to a solution. This level of detail issue is one reason a skilled facilitator can improve the output of the team.

Before you move on, consider pulling in other people to get an objective perspective of your opportunities and threats. Here are a few approaches to consider:

✔ **Hold a SWOT meeting.** Bring in your key employees and managers to help you complete your SWOT. You can either facilitate the meeting by asking them to think about the areas explained earlier in this chapter, or you can have a free brainstorming session. At the end, get your groups to come to a consensus on what the top five strengths, weakness, opportunities, and threats are. You can use the results to guide your short-term goal development for your strategic plan.

✔ **Form a SWOT team.** Pull together a group of employees and outsiders, such as advisors or industry experts, to do a SWOT analysis. Ask this team to pull in ideas not only by talking to co-workers but also by assessing the competition and your industry to see what you may be missing.

✔ **Go stealth.** Not everyone feels comfortable sharing ideas in front of a group, especially if the opinion isn't a widely shared one. Develop a web-based survey, such as Zoomrang or Survey Monkey, with open-ended questions about the strengths and weaknesses of your company. Make sure that the survey is anonymous and that everyone knows it. I do these surveys with all my clients, and the information people provide is invaluable. You couldn't pay a consultant enough to give you the same ideas.

A well-thought-out SWOT helps you weigh factors against each other to determine what your company should do and when you should do it. In Part IV, you take action on your SWOT analysis by developing goals and objectives around your findings. In the meantime, if you want to take action now, here's how to use your SWOT today:

✔ Build on your strengths.

✔ Shore up your weaknesses.

✔ Capitalize on your opportunities.

✔ Recognize your threats.

Change is the only constant in business. Therefore, assessing your strategic position is as dynamic as the environment you operate in. Know that your SWOT just captures a moment in time, like your balance sheet. Take this tool out every time you go into your strategic planning cycle. I promise it never gets rusty.

# Part IV
# Mapping Your Organization's Path to the Future

The 5th Wave                    By Rich Tennant

POOR STRATEGIC PARTNERSHIP

GOOD HUMOR ChemLAWN

"What'll it be, a cone, a bar, or weed killer?"

# In this part . . .

Undoubtedly (or at least I hope), opportunities for your organization abound. More often than not, you have more to do than you have time to do it. In order to move your organization into the future, you need to select the right opportunities and the right strategies to go with them. In this part, you identify, evaluate, prioritize, and execute your opportunities. You determine how to grow and establish your strategic position against your competitors and develop your road map to growth and sustainability. Lastly, but most importantly, you discover how to put your plan to action.

# Chapter 11

# Strategizing for Growth and Sustainability

. . . . . . . . . . . . . . . . . . . . . . . . . . . . . . . . . . . . . . . . . . . . .

## In This Chapter

▶ Differentiating strategy from tactics

▶ Determining the value-creating strategy for your organization

▶ Growing your business by using current products and developing new ones

. . . . . . . . . . . . . . . . . . . . . . . . . . . . . . . . . . . . . . . . . . . . .

*A*t the end of the day, what's every business trying to do? Grow. Businesses strive to grow more customers, more sales, positive cash flow, larger deal sizes, higher volume, more billable hours, justification for higher prices, and so on. Ask any hardworking entrepreneur what he or she is working on and you're bound to hear a comment related to growth. Growth is why you're in business — to build or create something bigger than yourselves. Because if you're not growing, you're shrinking.

With that said, you don't want to focus on growth for growth's sake because growth is just the means to an end. Your desire to grow must match up with your vision for your organization. Growing rapidly, growing incrementally, or maintaining your current position requires specific strategies.

In this chapter, you discover the different paths for growth and sustainability strategies. You understand how to travel in more than one direction to find partners and acquire others. Lastly, you look at how to evaluate the different growth strategies against each other to get a clear picture of your strategic choices.

One thought to consider: Only 49 percent of executives surveyed say their companies have no list of strategic priorities. According to Cesare R. Mainardi, coauthor of *The Essential Advantage: How to Win with a Capabilities-Driven Strategy* (Harvard Business Press), "Too many companies grab too hastily for what seems like the next answer to growth."

However, on the other side of the coin, if you have too many strategic priorities, you end up with a plan that's just too cumbersome and something you can't manage. So the key to a good plan is having the right strategy recipe.

# Understanding the Difference between Strategy and Tactics

Quite often, people confuse strategy and tactics and think the two terms are interchangeable. Well, unfortunately, they're not. In the following sections, I explain the difference between strategy and tactics as well as provide the three levels of strategy.

## Strategy versus tactics

According to strategy guru Michael Porter, "Competitive strategy is about being different. It means deliberately choosing a different set of activities to deliver a unique mix of value." *Strategy* is the *what* part of the equation and helps you answer the question, "What are we trying to accomplish?" Yet your business design may not be sustainable; you may have trade-offs for how you position your business with customers and competitors. Every business has limited resources and deals with a competitive landscape. The more it does of one thing, the less it can do of another. This concept leads to *tactics,* or the *how* part of the equation. Your tactics help you answer the question, "How are we going to accomplish our goal?" Ultimately, a good way to think about the difference between the two is that strategy acts as a guide to a set of actions that various departments or teams will undertake. Figure 11-1 further illustrates the difference between strategy and tactics.

| STRATEGY (WHAT?) | Quick View | TACTICS (HOW?) |
|---|---|---|
| What | **Quick View** | How & Who |
| Stratos: army, or resources Ago: leading | **Greek Definition** | Taktike: the art of organizing an army, a maneuver |
| To lead your resources, a plan, method, or series of maneuvers or stratagems for obtaining a specific goal or result | **Greek Definition** | A plan for attaining a particular goal |
| Stable, democratic Iraq, through the Surge and Clear-Hold-Build | **Example** | Operation Sinbad including the various ways to advance on a city, to clear a house, and to detect mines |
| Organization-level determiner: Foster the growth of youth to be the strong leaders of tomorrow. | **Organization Example** | Staff-level auctioning: Develop programs that teach civic responsibility and leadership. |

**Figure 11-1:** The difference between strategy and tactics.

Keep this thought in mind: What you're *not* going to do is sometimes just as important as what you *are* going to do. For example, a company decides it's going to target the baby boomer group, so it makes a decision to not target another generation.

## The levels of strategies

Businesses use three levels of strategies in the planning process to help them grow and become sustainable. Figure 11-2 visually explains the following three levels:

- ✔ **Corporate level strategy:** This level answers the foundational question of what you want to achieve. Is it growth, stability, or retrenchment? For more on this strategy, see Chapter 3.

- ✔ **Business unit level strategy:** This level focuses on how you're going to compete. Will it be through customer intimacy, product or service leadership, or lowest total cost? What's the differentiation based on? I discuss this strategy in the next section.

- ✔ **Market level strategy:** This strategy level focuses on how you're going to grow. Will it be through market penetration, market development, product or service development, or diversification? See the later section "Market Level Strategies: Strategizing How to Grow" for more on this strategy.

| LEVELS OF STRATEGY | | | |
|---|---|---|---|
| Corporate Level Strategy | | | |
| Business Unit Level Strategy | | Business Unit Level Strategy | |
| Market Level Strategy | Market Level Strategy | Market Level Strategy | Market Level Strategy |

**Figure 11-2:** Levels of strategy.

# Business Unit Level Strategies: Choosing Your Leading Strategic Focus

It's time to take out your big strategy guns and kick it up a notch. To increase your value to your customers or stakeholders, you need to create something better or different than your competitors. You do this by leveraging your existing strengths — or developing new ones — in the following three ways:

> ✔ Using operational excellence to provide *lowest total cost*
>
> ✔ Using continued innovation to provide *product or service leadership*
>
> ✔ Providing complete *customer intimacy* by knowing their needs and wants

Strengths usually fall into two broad categories: cost advantage and differentiation. When you apply these strengths to a market that's either large and varied or small and homogeneous in its needs, three basic strategies result, as indicated by italics in the preceding list. I explain each strategy in greater detail in the next section.

These strategies are often called *generic* because they're not firm or industry dependent. I call them *business unit level strategies* because they're applied at the business unit level. By consistently executing a business unit wide strategy, or a strategy that consistently guides how you create value, you can provide a product or service that's better than your competition.

Figure 11-3 shows the flow of the business unit level strategy process. In the following sections, I provide an overview of the three business unit level strategies and guide you through the steps to picking one that best fits your business.

## Applying your strengths to a business unit level strategy

Selecting your business unit level strategy really comes down to determining what your customers value the most about what you provide. Your low prices? Your cutting-edge products? Your ability to deliver a service that fits their needs exactly? Take a look at each option in this section to see which strategy is the best fit for your company.

Select a business unit level strategy for each target customer group you serve. For smaller organizations or departments, select one strategy for your whole company. Managing multiple value propositions can be nearly impossible.

### Leading with lowest total cost

Creating value through lowest total cost focuses on appealing to a broad spectrum of customers based on being the overall low-cost provider of a product or service because of the company's focus on efficiency. The company implementing this strategy provides superior value to its customers by offering them lowest total cost. Ultimately, it competes on scale, serving customers who want reliable, good-quality products or services but who want them cheaply and easily.

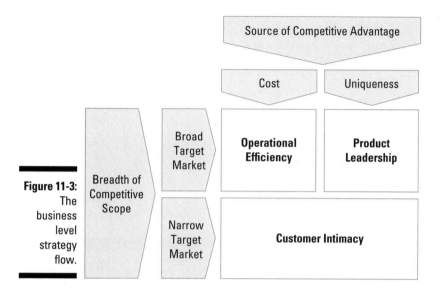

**Figure 11-3:** The business level strategy flow.

A lowest total cost value proposition sounds something like this: "We offer products and services that are always consistent, on-time, and low in cost." Check out these goals if you're executing this strategy:

- ✔ To continually offer the most attractive prices
- ✔ To purchase and source from the lowest-cost suppliers
- ✔ To offer excellent and consistent quality
- ✔ To ensure that our company has a good product or service selection
- ✔ To make buying from our company easy and fast

To reach your goals, you need to master your operational processes. This process includes monitoring outstanding supply chain management, super efficient operations to control costs, cycle time and quality, and inventory management. See Figure 11-4 to get an overview of this strategy in comparison to the other two strategies discussed in the following sections.

Providence Plumbing, a plumbing, heating, and air company, creates outstanding value through a real-time data system. All the company's technicians have powerful handheld data systems that allow them to accept, respond to, and close service orders all in one smooth process. Through this data system, the company cuts down its operational costs by reducing drive time, service order data entry, and error rates due to lost orders and billing costs. The company's customer satisfaction has soared because most service orders are responded to on the same day as requested, customers find little surprise in the final bill, and the company's prices are the lowest across the board.

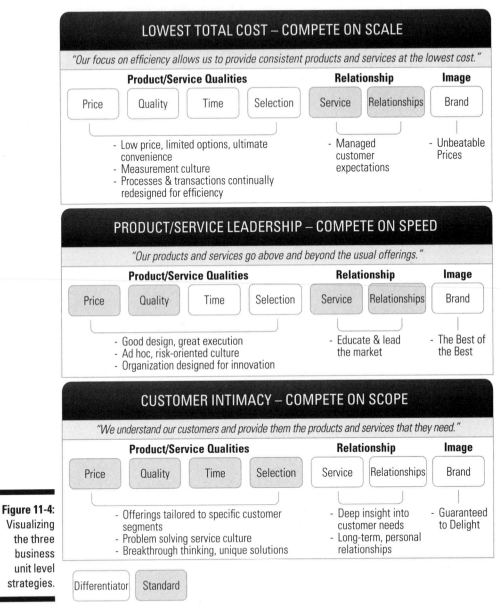

**Figure 11-4:** Visualizing the three business unit level strategies.

Adapted from Drs. Robert Kaplan and David Norton, creators of the Balanced Scorecard

Other companies that continue to offer the best buy or lowest total cost through their excellent internal operations include Wal-Mart, Southwest Airlines, Dell, and IKEA.

## Leading with product/service leadership

This strategy concentrates on creating a unique, innovative product or service line while competing on speed. A company implementing this strategy provides superior value by offering its customers a continuous stream of innovative products or services, regardless of the costs in terms of price or inconvenience. It seeks to identify emerging opportunities and continuously strives to develop and deliver new products and services to market quickly.

A product and/or service leadership value proposition sounds something like this: "We offer products and services that expand existing boundaries past what was thought possible." To execute this strategy, your goals may look like the following:

- To strive to be first to market with new products, services, or functionality
- To always produce leading-edge products and services that exceed the performance of competing products
- To maintain higher prices than competitors because of the superior product
- To reach and educate new customer groups

You need to master your innovation processes and develop an innovation culture to reach your goals. These steps include having a pipeline full of new ideas, using a conversion rate of ideas to production, implementing excellent and quick product development processes, and staffing marketing and sales departments that can bring the product to market quickly. Refer to Figure 11-4 to get an overview of this strategy in comparison to the other two strategies.

Instead of studying Spanish by going to classes or hiring a tutor, students in Guatemala learned from Spanish tutors through Speak Shop, a web-based application that allows video and voice conferencing. The company was first to market with this innovative method to connect students and tutors in their homes or at work. To maintain its first-mover position, the company continues to add functionality, such as quizzes, lesson plans, curriculum, and discussion boards, to enhance its core product.

Additional companies that are always on the cutting edge of their industries with product or service leadership include Intel, Mercedes-Benz, Sony, and Apple.

## Leading with customer intimacy

Creating value by really knowing your customers concentrates on a narrow market segment by a deep understanding of your customers and their perceptions of the value of the product or service you offer. A company implementing the customer intimacy strategy competes on scope, providing superior value by tailoring its products or services to match *exactly* the needs of targeted customers. It serves customers who are willing to pay a premium to get precisely what they want and specializes in satisfying unique customer needs through an intimate knowledge of the customers.

A customer intimacy value proposition sounds something like this: "We provide the best total solution to our customers because we make a practice of knowing exactly what they need." Try to fashion your goals around the following examples:

- ✔ To ensure that our customers feel like we understand them by continually engaging in market research and responding to it
- ✔ To provide customized products and services to meet their needs
- ✔ To stress exceptional customer service
- ✔ To install and effectively use a customer relationship management system
- ✔ To offer and sell a complete solution (selling multiple and bundled products and services)

Develop a customer-focused culture to attain these marks. These procedures include offering as many products and services that your customers are looking to you to provide — meaning that you completely solve the problem or need that your customers have. Refer to Figure 11-4 for an overview of this strategy in comparison to the two previous strategies.

A rapid software development company develops tools for online collaboration. Based on customer feedback, the company develops additional tools and online applications specifically to meet the needs of its growing client base. In fact, this company is so focused on its customers that it provides a free online forum and training for customers to develop their own collaboration tools, using its platform.

More examples of companies that are providing complete customer solutions through customer intimacy include Nordstrom, Goldman Sachs, and Cabela's.

## Discovering why you don't want to be stuck in the middle

If you're tempted to execute all three strategies, think again. That's called *being stuck in the middle*, or *riding the fence*. Executing a stuck in the middle strategy is like being in the middle seat of a five-seat row on a 747. You don't know whether to crawl over the mom with her sleeping baby to the right or over the guy with his laptop to the left. Being stuck in the middle isn't a good place to be!

Selecting only one business unit level strategy to lead with is widely considered one of the best ways to achieve and maintain your competitive advantages. Why? Because if you select two or more approaches and then fail to achieve them, your organization gets stuck in the middle without a competitive advantage. Practically speaking, when it comes to budget time, you need to decide whether you're investing in R&D (product leadership) or eliminating costs out of your supply chain (low cost leadership). You need to do the standard value-creating activities across all strategies, but you need to differentiate yourself with the combined set of activities in these strategies.

That said, another school of thought is that leading with one business level strategy isn't always best because within the same product or service, customers want the best product, lowest cost, and high touch experience. My perspective is that strategic plans are difficult and confusing enough, so to add complications by leading with multiple strategies muddies the water and leads to confusion when hard decisions need to be made. If you must, prioritize what strategy you're leading with and which two are secondary so when it comes to focus, your team is clear about your choice.

## Choosing the right business unit level strategy for you

The basic difference between business unit level strategies are (1) whether a company's market or industry target is broad or narrow and (2) whether the company is pursuing a competitive position (or creation of superior customer value) linked to low costs or product differentiation. To determine the right business unit level strategy for your company, follow these steps:

1. **Answer the question, "Is the market or industry target broad or narrow?"**

   Broad: market scope; a relatively wide market emphasis

   Narrow: limited to only one or few segments in the market

2. **Determine whether the competitive position focuses on lowest total cost or product differentiation.**

   Low costs: Company works to achieve lowest costs of production and distribution.

   Product or service leadership: Company focuses on a product or service offering that's unique from competitors in ways that appeal to buyers.

3. **Based on the results from Steps 1 and 2, make your selection.**

   If the target is broad and competitive position is low costs, then by definition the overall strategy is lowest total cost.

   If the target is broad and competitive position is product differentiation, then the overall strategy is product or service leadership.

   If the target is narrow and competitive position is low costs or product differentiation, then the overall strategy is customer intimacy.

   If the target isn't well defined and the competitive position isn't clear, the overall strategy is middle-of-the-road. Generally, a firm can't be successful at all three strategies and thus jeopardizes performance, which requires clear focus.

# Market Level Strategies: Strategizing How to Grow

Successful growth stems from matching your strengths and weaknesses with the opportunities that exist in your business environment. Your growth strategy is the way in which you position your company to exploit your strengths and opportunities and mitigate your weaknesses and threats. By strategizing how to grow, you're actively deciding how to connect your mission with your vision (see Chapter 6 for more on missions and visions). Your growth strategy answers the question, "How do we get there?"

Keep these key points on growth in mind as you move through this chapter:

✔ Growth begins with your customers in mind.

✔ Growth focuses on opportunities.

✔ Growth looks forward by learning from the past.

✔ Everyone can grow.

Growth comes from either leveraging your market knowledge or leveraging your product knowledge. Figure 11-5 illustrates how you can leverage your market and/or product knowledge to create four different strategies, originally presented by Igor Ansoff in 1957, which still has practical business application today:

✔ Market penetration

✔ Product development

✔ Market development

✔ Diversification

| MARKET | | |
|---|---|---|
| | Existing | New |
| **PRODUCTS** — Existing | **Market Penetration** Focusing on your market and product by niching. | **Market Development** Leveraging your product knowledge to reach new markets. |
| **PRODUCTS** — New | **Product Development** Leveraging your market knowledge to develop new products. | **Diversification** Diversifying by offering new products in new markets. |

**Figure 11-5:** The four areas of growth.

In Part III of this book, you identify your strengths, weaknesses, opportunities, and threats. If you've covered that information, use it to guide your strategy selection in this chapter.

# Concentrating on market penetration

The most common growth strategy is to focus on what you do best by emphasizing your current products in your current markets. This strategy is also called the *concentrated growth strategy* because you're thoroughly developing and exploiting your knowledge and expertise in a specific market with known products.

How do you grow if you're already doing what you do best now? Simple. Do the following:

✔ **Increase present customers' rate of use.** You achieve this goal by

- Increasing the size of purchase

- Maximizing the rate of product obsolescence

- Finding new uses for your product

- Advertising other uses

- Offering incentives for increased use

✔ **Attract your competitors' customers.** You lure customers away from your competitors by establishing differentiation, increasing advertising efforts, or cutting your prices. Look at Chapter 5 to find ways to differentiate yourself from other companies.

✔ **Attract non-users to buy your products.** This process can be done by offering trial uses of your products, adjusting the price up or down, and promoting other uses to attract these customers (check out the following example for details).

Think about Arm & Hammer Baking Soda. You can easily argue that it's not the most exciting product; in fact, it's almost boring. Agree? It's white powder in a box, but the company dominates the market as the number-one baking soda for cooking year after year. But with such a large market share, you may be wondering how the company grows by using its current products. The answer: It finds a new use for an existing product. The company launched a year-long marketing campaign, promoting the use of baking soda as a refrigerator deodorizer, which resulted in a 57 percent increase in sales! Arm & Hammer didn't stop there. Check out the company's website at www.armandhammer.com for a timeline of how it continues to reinvent uses for its core product.

## Delivering with product development

If you have a good understanding of your market, another way to leverage your knowledge is to develop new products and services to meet your market's needs. When you hear the term *product development,* you may think about brand new products, but that's not necessarily the case. Executing a product development strategy can happen by adding more value to your existing product through features, upselling, or cross selling. The best things about this strategy are you've already established yourself in your current markets and you know what your customers want. You have the distribution channels, and you know how to reach them.

Consider the following questions if you're thinking about expanding your product line or developing new products:

- ✔ Will your customers benefit from the added value or new feature? Are they asking for additions to the current product line?

- ✔ Do potential manufacturing, marketing, and distribution cost efficiencies exist from an expanded product line? Can you share current costs across the new products or services?

- ✔ Can your current assets, brand, marketing, and distribution be used with the new product?

- ✔ Do you have the skills and capabilities to develop and produce the products proposed?

After you've given product development some consideration and have decided to proceed full steam ahead, here's how to develop new products and services to meet your market's needs:

- ✔ **Add new features or services by extending your current products.** For example, cellphone companies add on media packages for text messaging, additional ring tones, and Internet access. Here are a few ways to extend your current offering:

  - • Adapt (adapt to other ideas and developments)

  - • Modify (change color, motion, sound, odor, form, or shape)

  - • Magnify (provide more for a higher price or provide stronger, longer, or extra value)

  - • Reduce (make smaller, shorter, or lighter, or make a trial version)

  - • Substitute (swap out other ingredients, processes, or power)

  - • Combine (join other options, products, ideas, or assortments)

- ✔ **Develop additional models and sizes of your current products.** For example, the iPod expanded to the iPod mini and the iPod nano.

> ✔ **Develop totally new products.** In this case, you usually leverage your brand recognition. Some good examples of this development are Gerber producing baby clothes and a CPA firm expanding from tax work into financial planning.

Your success with your current products in a market doesn't guarantee success with new ones. The classic failed product development strategy was New Coke, which Coke introduced in the '80s as a replacement for Coke. Coke assumed that its customers would gravitate toward a newly-developed formula only to realize, too late, that its cola drinkers were fiercely loyal to the traditional flavor. Needless to say, the new product fizzled.

Nowadays, Coke introduces new products along with existing products, even if they overlap (like Coke Zero and Diet Coke — both diet sodas, but one isn't replacing the other). The lesson here is don't trash what's been working just fine when trying something new.

## Extending scope with market development

You can grow by leveraging your product knowledge to reach new customers. More than likely, you've spent time and money developing your product and service offering. Assuming you're happy with your current offering, extending it into new markets is a logical next step. Taking that next step is aptly called a *market development strategy.* If you identified potential new markets as opportunities in Chapter 10, you can use these strategies to reach them.

Here are some considerations to make before executing a market development strategy:

> ✔ Is the market attractive? (To really answer this question, I recommend some form of market research to validate your gut feeling.)

> ✔ Are you willing to commit the required time and resources to reach this new market?

> ✔ Can your business adapt to the new market?

> ✔ Will you maintain your current competitive advantage in this new market?

In the next two sections, I cover the two types of market development strategies.

### Expanding geographically

When you're thinking about expanding, first think about where you want to cultivate new business. Your options are to expand to other regions locally, nationally, or internationally. Geographical expansion works well for a company that wants to expand its service territory because it needs a physical location to serve its customers. Clearly your ability to expand is subject to your ability to finance such an expansion. See "Deciding how to execute your growth strategy" later in this chapter.

Many of the big boys of business, including McDonald's, Wal-Mart, and Home Depot, have exported their operations to other countries. On a smaller scale, many microbreweries have opened up new locations in various metro areas and airports in the United States as a way to expand their geographical reach.

### Reaching into new market segments

You can also grow by reaching a completely new set of customers or market segments. This area is such a popular growth strategy because you leverage the products and services you've developed. (Flip to Chapter 9 for the entire story on new market segments.)

Examples of this strategy abound, such as Bayer aspirin now being sold not only for aches and pains but also for heart attack prevention if taken daily.

## Stepping out with diversification

Sometimes you just need to bust out and try something new — like learning the polka. Or if you're a tobacco firm, buying a packaged-food company; a cola firm entering the water business; or a chemical company going into the spa supply business. All these moves, except the polka of course, are examples of diversification. (The polka would be diversifying your dance portfolio, but that's another book altogether.) *Diversification* is entering new markets with new products. Refer back to Figure 11-5 for how this strategy relates to the others.

Many companies appreciate the need to diversify but few use it as a way of relating to their markets. Fundamentally, this strategy is about creating new products with new product life cycles and making the existing ones obsolete. By doing so, firms launch new products that are developed not just for current customers but for new ones, too.

To execute this strategy, you usually manage a merger, an acquisition, or a completely new business venture. (See "Deciding how to execute your growth strategy" later in this chapter.) Well-known, highly innovative companies include Intel, Google, DuPont, and all the pharmaceutical companies.

A company's diversification strategy can be either related or unrelated to its original business. *Related diversification* makes more sense than unrelated because the company shares assets, skills, or capabilities. But many successful companies, such as Tyco and GE, continue to buy unrelated businesses.

Check out the next two sections for more information on related and unrelated diversification. Figure 11-6 also summarizes the reasons for related and unrelated diversification.

| RELATED DIVERSIFICATION | UNRELATED DIVERSIFICATION |
|---|---|
| Sharing skills and competencies | Interest to the owners or executives |
| Leveraging a brand name | Reducing risk by operating in various markets and product lines |
| Using shared marketing skills and knowledge | Refocusing the company |
| Using sales and distribution capacity | Tax benefits |
| Exchanging manufacturing skills and know-how | Defending against a takeover |
| Access to research and development and new product capabilities | Obtaining liquid assets or other assets needed by the main company |
| Realizing economies of scale | Defending against a takeover |

**Figure 11-6:** Choosing between related or unrelated diversification.

## Related diversification

In related diversification, companies have a strategic fit with the new venture. To make this strategy work, you capitalize on the strengths or competitive advantage you've already established.

Richard Branson, famous for his company Virgin, has more than 300 companies that carry the Virgin name: Virgin Atlantic, Virgin Mobile, and Virgin Galactic — his most recent venture into space travel — are just a few examples. This related diversification strategy works because all the companies share the brand, marketing, public relations, and corporate knowledge.

## Unrelated diversification

Unrelated diversification has nothing to do with leveraging your current business strengths or weaknesses. It's more about not putting all your eggs in one basket. For example, an investor diversifies his financial portfolio to protect against losses. Many entrepreneurs execute this strategy unknowingly by becoming involved in multiple, unrelated businesses. Unrelated diversification is the most risky of all the market level strategies.

Hypothetically, say the owner of a local IT consulting company decided to take over a failing sandwich shop because he always wanted to be in the restaurant business. Clearly, these two businesses are unrelated. But by accident, the business owner is executing a diversification strategy. He's now in the IT industry and the dining industry.

## Growing up (and down)

Another potential way to grow is through *vertical integration* — moving up and down your supply chain. You can integrate forward by setting up operations closer to your customer, such as a clothing company opening up retail stores. Or you can integrate backward by moving closer to your raw material source, such as the clothing company opening a manufacturing plant. Although these strategies are less common than the others discussed in this chapter, they do have some benefits:

✔ **Direct access to supply and demand:** Eliminating the middleman in both directions is forward and backward integration. Getting direct access to your vendors and customers can be a huge benefit for many businesses.

For example, many of the auto manufacturers moved forward by investing in the big car rental firms. Many companies seek backward integration because there's no source for a component they need. For example, when refrigerated warehouses were needed by meat packers, they built them.

✔ **Better control over the quality or availability of the product or service:** Many times, manufacturers need specialized raw material that's a key component in the end product. To gain better quality control and eliminate the risk of not being able to acquire the product, the company buys the vendor, which is *backward integration.*

In order for Sony to guarantee content for its products, the company purchased Columbia Pictures, Tri-Star Pictures, and CBS Records.

✔ **Entry into a potentially attractive business area:** Manufacturers continually fight margin pressures. The best way to get control is to go directly to customers instead of through retailers, also known as *forward integration.*

Companies like Nike have been successful in this area, whereas a company such as Universal Pictures hasn't.

## *Deciding how to execute your growth strategy*

The preceding sections lay out different growth strategies. Now you need to evaluate which path you want to take. But in order to choose a path, you must decide how to execute the strategy.

By matching your growth strategies with your strengths, weaknesses, and opportunities, you can determine which ones to pursue.

The best way to visually see your strategic choices is to create a Product/Market Grid. Developing this grid helps you prioritize and sort your options. Figure 11-7 provides an example; use it along with the following steps to develop your grid.

Use the Product/Market Grid Worksheet located on the CD when you're ready to finalize your grid.

1. **Create a table that lists all your current and potential products down the left column and all your current and proposed markets across the top.**

   Refer to Figure 11-7 for an example of the grid in action. Note how *Current Market #1* and *New Market #1* have the highest priority based on projected market demand.

2. **Estimate the demand for your current and new products in each of the markets by filling in the cells different shades of gray.**

   For example, if the product has a potential high demand, shade the cell dark gray. If the product has a low demand, fill the cell with light gray.

3. **Based on your demand estimations, select your growth strategy.**

   Look at whether you're leveraging your product or your market knowledge in each market. For example, in the column titled *Current Market #1*, there's high demand for the two current products and one new one. To increase sales for the new product, the company will continue to serve the market by executing a product development strategy.

4. **Decide how to execute the growth strategy.**

   You need to base this decision on your knowledge and judgment of the resources you have to execute each strategy. Will you do it yourself, find a partner, or acquire a business? (See previous sections in this chapter on these endeavors.)

5. **Prioritize each group based on which is the best opportunity for your company**.

   Use this information to guide the development of your customer goals and objectives in Chapter 13.

| | Current Market #1 | Current Market #2 | New Market #1 | New Market #2 |
|---|---|---|---|---|
| Current Product #1 | | | | |
| Current Product #2 | | | | |
| New Product #1 | | | | |
| New Product #2 | | | | |
| Growth Strategy | Product Development | Market Penetration | Market Development | Diversification |
| Strategy Implementation | Do it myself | Do it myself | Find a partner | Look at an acquisition |
| Priority | 1 | 2 | 3 | 4 |

**Figure 11-7:** Your market growth strategies.

**Legend – Projected Demand:** ■High demand ■Medium demand ■Low demand □None or N/A

Basing your project demand on market research and past sales is the best way to construct this grid. Although this info isn't always available, do your best to fill in the grid because it provides you with a good idea of how likely one strategy is compared to the others. If you have the time, jump online, talk to your sales people, or hire a market research firm to get the real data to fill in your Product/Market Grid.

Keep your Product/Market Grid handy. You use it again in Chapter 13 to develop your goals and objectives in your strategic plan.

# Summarizing Your Selected Strategies

Now that you've worked through the different levels of strategy, it's time to summarize your decisions so you can start building your road map. Use the Strategy Summary Worksheet on the CD as a checklist to select strategies to embed in your plan.

Although good analysis, effective process, and market knowledge are key components to effective strategy development, they're not the only components. Developing strategic plans isn't easy, even though the process is spelled out and organized. As organizations put the strategic planning process in motion, it tends to take on a life of its own. Apply the concepts shared in this chapter that are applicable and jettison those that don't have relevance. The judgment of leaders and managers can ultimately make the difference between successful strategies and failed ones.

# Chapter 12

# Establishing Your Strategic Objectives, Goals, and Actions

*In This Chapter*

▶ Putting your SWOT to use

▶ Developing your strategies by looking at all the alternatives

▶ Striking a balance among your strategic priorities

▶ Transforming your priorities into strategic objectives and goals

Congratulations! If you've been working through this book from beginning to end, you've made it halfway through the strategic management process. Right about now, you may feel like the process is a little out of control. But don't worry; that's a common feeling that occurs primarily because you've collected so much information, input, and feedback that sorting through it all seems impossible. So much so that it can feel disorienting. So step back and review what you're doing. Strategic planning answers where you are now, where you're going, and how you're getting there.

Visualize a famous bridge, such as the Golden Gate Bridge, Brooklyn Bridge, or Tower Bridge. All bridges have two primary support pillars and a span between the two, allowing one part of land to be connected with another. One of these pillars explains where you are now — your mission, values, strengths, weaknesses, opportunities, and threats. The pillar on the far side represents where you're going — your vision. How you get there is the span, or the road, in between — your strategic objectives, goals, and action plans.

Now because the span between the two pillars is quite long, you need to bridge the gap with long-term strategic objectives and short-term goals. How you build the bridge is your strategy. You can have a different strategy for each section of the bridge, or you can have a consistent strategy for the whole thing — it doesn't matter. But think about the strategy as the *how* and the goals and strategic objectives as the *what.*

The critical part of this analogy is that in order for the bridge to function properly, every element has to support the other, or it collapses. So as you look at the ideas you generated in the previous chapters, some of them help connect the two pillars and some are probably outliers.

Use the following process to develop your road map, which connects your mission to your vision. Where applicable, the time frame for each section of your plan is indicated in parentheses.

- ✔ Evaluate all the strategic alternatives generated by assessing your strategic position.
- ✔ Develop a short list of internal and external strategic alternatives.
- ✔ Create strategic objectives (three to five years).
- ✔ Create short-term goals (one year).
- ✔ Develop action plans based on the goals (next 90 days).
- ✔ Establish who's responsible for carrying out the goals.
- ✔ Select measures to track your progress.

In this chapter, you evaluate your strategic alternatives, priorities, and goals. I use the words *choice, alternative, ideas, possibilities, thoughts,* and *actions* to mean anything that you're considering acting on and including in your strategic plan. So keep that in mind as you read.

# Firming Up Your List of Strategic Alternatives

Being strategic is all about making choices. And strategic choice is about making subjective decisions based on goal information. To do so, you first generate a list of all feasible alternatives. That means *everything*. Don't be shy — put down all your thoughts about potential alternatives for your organization to move from where you are today to where you want to be.

In Chapters 7 through 11, you cast your net wide to determine the actions to take based on your current strategic position. In fact, it probably feels a little messy right now. If you worked through each of the previous chapters, you've more than likely developed a SWOT that's multiple pages in length. In the following sections, I help you narrow your focus through a variety of approaches to create a short list of strategic alternatives.

# Paring down your SWOT

In order to move from a list of possibilities to an actual plan, you need a workable list in each of the four SWOT quadrants: strengths, weaknesses, opportunities, and threats. If your SWOT is overly long or if you have a lot of people involved in your process, consider the following ideas for paring down the SWOT quadrants. (If you don't feel like your SWOT is long, jump to the next section, "Identifying strategic alternatives.")

- ✔ **Create themes.** Simply combine like themes until you have a workable list of fewer than ten per quadrant.

- ✔ **Choose high impact.** With your planning team, ask each member to select the top three SWOT that will have the biggest impact on the future of the organization. Keep the items in each quadrant that have the most votes.

- ✔ **Conduct an opportunity analysis.** Often, businesses have more opportunities than they can reasonably execute on. Using the information you collected on your markets and customers in Chapter 9, determine which of the opportunities have the biggest potential to generate revenue compared to the investment needed to pursue the opportunity. Select those opportunities that have the highest return on investment, or ROI.

- ✔ **Use the Impact/Effort Grid.** If doing a full-blown opportunity analysis is too much, use the Impact/Effort Grid located on the CD as a simple exercise to sort out the best opportunities from the ones that are just good ideas. The *y*-axis indicates *effort* or resources needed to accomplish the opportunity. The *x*-axis indicates *impact* or results expected from the opportunity. For each opportunity, plot which quadrant it falls into.

  In the example in Figure 12-1, an organization would most likely select to pursue opportunity D because it has a high impact with a medium level of effort.

Before you move on, review your SWOT one last time with these guidelines in mind:

- ✔ Keep each quadrant to ten or fewer items.

- ✔ Don't solve your weaknesses; just identify the issue or challenge. For example, *poor communication* is a weakness whereas *need more staff meetings* is a potential solution.

- ✔ Remember opportunities and threats are external alternatives for growth and sustainability. Don't list *improve communication* under opportunities.

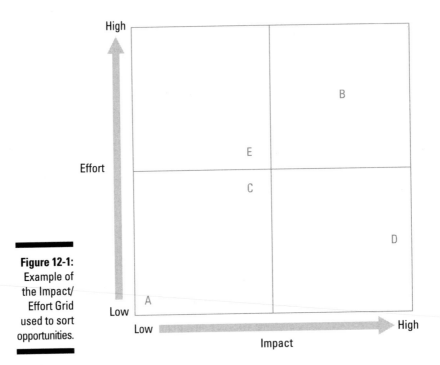

**Figure 12-1:**
Example of
the Impact/
Effort Grid
used to sort
opportunities.

# Identifying strategic alternatives

Now that you have a workable SWOT, you can identify your strategic alternatives or choices. Remember that by itself, a SWOT isn't actionable. But by matching up factors from one quadrant with factors in another quadrant, you can start to identify potential actions based on the SWOT analysis.

The point of matching internal factors with external ones is to identify a fit between organizational strengths and market opportunities. In other words, what opportunities can you take advantage of, based on what you've already got to work with? Also, by matching weaknesses with opportunities or threats, you may see some compelling pairs that are worth pursuing.

Get creative in this exercise! Put down all your ideas, even if they seem ridiculous. Allow yourself and your team to brainstorm. You can pull it back down to earth at the end of the exercise. See Figure 12-2 for a visual.

|  | **Strengths-S**<br>List Strengths | **Weaknesses-W**<br>List Weaknesses |
|---|---|---|
| **Opportunities-O**<br>List Opportunities | **SO Alternatives**<br>Use strengths to take advantage of opportunities | **WO Alternatives**<br>Overcome weaknesses by taking advantage of opportunities |
| **Threats-T**<br>List Threats | **ST Alternatives**<br>Use strengths to avoid threats | **Threats-T**<br>Minimize weaknesses and avoid threats |

**Figure 12-2:**
Creating strategic alternatives for growth.

To develop a variety of choices, work through these steps with yourself or your team. Use Figure 12-2 as a reference for the following steps:

1. **Pull out your SWOT analysis from Chapter 10 (if you've completed that already).**

   No SWOT? Then pull one together for this exercise or jump to the next section.

2. **On a white board or a big piece of paper, draw a matrix similar to Figure 12-2.**

   You can also use the Strategic Alternatives Worksheet on the CD.

   If you have a lot of strengths, weaknesses, opportunities, or threats, you don't have to rewrite them all in the matrix boxes, just work from a handout.

3. **In the box labeled *SO Alternatives*, match internal strengths with external opportunities.**

4. In the box labeled *WO Alternatives,* match internal weaknesses with external opportunities.

5. In the box labeled *ST Alternatives,* match internal strengths with external threats.

6. In the box labeled *WT Alternatives,* match internal weaknesses with external threats.

7. Review all four quadrants and highlight the choices that look the most promising.

8. Use the items you highlighted as a source of potential actions when developing your priorities in the section "Evolving Alternatives into Priorities."

Here are some generic examples of how this exercise works:

✔ Strong reputation (strength) + market growth in a neighboring community (opportunity) = expanded operations in new market

✔ High cost structure in a specific product line (weakness) + arrival of new technology that would reduce supply chain overhead (opportunity) = improved operations through technology investment

✔ Cost advantages through proprietary knowledge (strength) + primary industry is in decline (threat) = entering new industry that leverages cost advantages

✔ Poor employee morale (weakness) + tight labor market (threat) = development of an improved employee benefits package

## Sorting through your other alternatives

In addition to your SWOT analysis, throughout the strategic planning process, you've kept ideas and notes (I hope) about possible actions to include in your strategic plan. But in case your ideas aren't all in one place, use the following list to gather your thoughts about your current strategic position and refer to the chapter listed in parentheses for more information if needed:

✔ Last year's incomplete goals and actions (Chapter 4)

✔ Improvements, modifications, and enhancements to current products and services (Chapter 4)

✔ Improvements to operational process (Chapter 7)

✔ Enhancements to capabilities and resources (Chapter 7)

✔ Action to eliminate cash drains and to improve cash creators (Chapter 7)

> ✔ Ideas to improve current customer value, retention, and loyalty (Chapter 8)
>
> ✔ Opportunities and threats in the environment, industry, and market (Chapter 10)
>
> ✔ Entering new markets and serving new customer groups (Chapter 11)

Look at these different lists and eliminate anything that's unrealistic, unimportant, and excessive. Create a list of choices that are truly important to your organization right now. As with the previous exercise, use this list as a source of potential actions in the next section.

# Evolving Alternatives into Priorities

This section brings you to the scary part of strategic planning. Why scary? Because people are terrified of making wrong choices. If you worked through the previous section, you have some lists of choices, but because you can't do everything, now you have to eliminate some of those choices. Know that every other business owner, executive director, and department manager has come to the same place you're at right now. Although guarantees never exist in business, this section helps you develop your own guidelines to assure that you make the right choices. But at the end of the day, you have to make a decision.

The one concept that most business owners, executives, and managers forget is that the lack of a decision results in more derailments of the mission than any other cause.

## Sorting out internal and external alternatives

Grouping alternatives helps you compare like things when making trade-offs. For example, choosing between investing in new technology or hiring a new person is an expense decision with similar outcomes, whereas choosing between entering a new market or implementing a succession plan isn't directly related. So at this point, you want to divide your choices into two groups — those that have internal implications and those that have external implications.

How do you decide what's internal and what's external? Check out the following definitions:

✔ *Internal priorities* include everything related to productivity and process improvements, such as employees, training, operations, technology, efficiencies, research and development, and anything else that deals with the internal operations of your organization.

✔ *External priorities* include everything that's related to revenue generation, such as entering new target markets, serving new customer groups, developing new products, and partnering with other organizations.

The quickest and easiest way to sort through your list is to highlight internal choices one color and external choices another color. Use the next two sections to move from alternatives to priorities.

# Creating a short list of external priorities

Creating a short list is the last part of synthesizing all your options to the select few for your strategic plan. Ideally, you want to have between three and five external priorities. If you have too many, you may lose focus, and your plan may become too big. More than likely, your lists contain a dozen or so priorities, so you need to eliminate some more.

After you've sorted out your internal and external opportunities (see the previous section), start comparing your external choices to figure out which to take off first. You make this comparison because you need to make some trade-offs. Remember to compare only opportunities that are directly competing (external to external and internal to internal). In other words, making equitable trade-offs requires comparing apples to apples. Internal priorities are competing with other internal priorities, and external priorities are competing against other external priorities.

If you have a hard time limiting your priorities, make a *someday list.* This list contains priorities that are important and that you'll get to *some day.* If you still have too many options, use the paired comparison analysis that follows.

The paired comparison analysis helps you eliminate, limit, or prioritize your alternatives. (You can see an example of this tool in Figure 12-3 and find an editable version of the table on the CD.) This analysis helps you set priorities when multiple demands exist on the same resources — your time and money. The paired comparison analysis isolates choices and removes some subjectivity.

Use the tool and follow these steps to compare each option one at a time:

1. **Use your pared-down list of opportunities and draw a grid, listing each option in both a row and a column header.**

   Assign a letter to each option, as shown in Figure 12-3.

**2. Block out cells on the table that compare an option with itself.**

These cells remain the same. Normally you block out the diagonal running from the top left to the bottom right, as shown in Figure 12-3.

**3. Block out cells that duplicate a comparison.**

These cells are below the diagonal. See the example in Figure 12-3.

**4. With the remaining cells, compare the option in the row with the one in the column.**

For each cell, decide which of the two options is more important. Write the letter of the more important option in the cell and score the difference in importance from 0 (equal importance) to 3 (much more important).

**5. Consolidate the results by adding the total of all the values for each of the options.**

Convert these values into a percentage of the total score to determine rank of importance.

G&G Construction, a small, local construction company, is looking at a variety of expansion options (see Figure 12-3). With limited resources and bonding capacity, the company can pursue only one opportunity at a time. The opportunities include the following:

✔ Expanding into new markets by opening satellite offices

✔ Buying a concrete company

✔ Establishing an exclusive partnership with a civil engineering company

✔ Expanding service line to include custom homes and remodels

| | Expanding into new market (A) | Buying a concrete company (B) | Partnering with an engineering firm (C) | Expanding service line (D) |
|---|---|---|---|---|
| **Expanding into new market (A)** | | A,2 | A,3 | A,1 |
| **Buying a concrete company (B)** | | | C,3 | D,2 |
| **Partnering with an engineering firm (C)** | | | | D,2 |
| **Expanding service line (D)** | | | | |

**Figure 12-3:** Using the paired comparison analysis to identify the best opportunities.

Company executives compare the opportunities. First, they write the letter of the most important option, and then they score their difference in importance. For example, looking at Figure 12-3, when comparing *expanding into a new market (A)* with *buying a concrete company (B),* the executives chose A over B. Then they decided that expanding into a new market was two times more important than buying a concrete company, so they wrote "A, 2" in that cell. They went through the same process for each comparison then added the A, B, C, and D values and converted each into a percentage as follows:

- ✔ A = 6 (46 percent)
- ✔ B = 0 (0 percent)
- ✔ C = 3 (23 percent)
- ✔ D = 4 (31 percent)

*Expanding into a new market (A)* is the most important opportunity, followed by *expanding the current service line (D). Buying a concrete company (B)* is the least important and may come up when the other opportunities have been realized. You can see how the comparison allows each opportunity to be evaluated against the others as well as show the difference in importance between each one.

## Compiling a short list of internal priorities

Instead of using the Paired Comparison Analysis Worksheet for internal alternatives, check out the helpful Goals Grid tool on the CD (also shown in Figure 12-4). Although you can use this tool for many purposes, it's particularly helpful to categorize your internal alternatives into the four basic categories of goal making: achieve, preserve, avoid, and eliminate. Simply sort the internal alternatives by examining the yes and no answers to two very basic questions:

- ✔ Do you want something?
- ✔ Do you have it?

Develop three to five internal priorities based on those items that end up in the *achieve* and *preserve* categories. You may find that some alternatives don't make it through the Goals Grid because they were good ideas that you don't want at all.

**Figure 12-4:**
Sorting out your internal choices with the Goals Grid.

# Gut checking your priorities

Nice work! You've succeeded at funneling everything you've gathered to date into a short list of internal and external priorities. Before you move on, do one last check to make sure that what you've decided to focus on is aligned with the other parts of your strategy.

Here are some guiding principles to keep in mind when evaluating priorities:

- ✔ **Boundary principle:** Evaluate every priority based on whether it's within your mission. Set a rule to require that the opportunity aligns with the organization's core purpose and values.

- ✔ **How-to principle:** Develop a principle that requires you to sketch out how to implement the priority if you took advantage of it before jumping in. If you can't clearly define an action plan for the priority, you know that trying to execute it will go poorly.

> ✔ **ROI principle:** Prioritize options based on how much money you want to see returned within a certain time period. Pull in your finance or accounting people to help you establish this one.
>
> ✔ **Vision principle:** Prioritize some priorities over others based on their connection to reaching your vision. Set a rule to require that all opportunities must help you reach your vision.

Clearly, in the strategic planning process, you seek options and choices. But such decisions occur regularly outside of strategic planning. By establishing rules, you can quickly evaluate whether an opportunity is really an opportunity or a distraction. Develop a set of principles and use it as a litmus test. If the opportunity doesn't pass the test, it's out. Lastly, if the priority isn't clear to those who haven't worked on the prioritization described in the section, it's not going to be accepted.

# Balancing Your Strategic Priorities

Often, business owners and executives fall prey to the allure of setting too many financial goals. Or their goals are exclusively financial. Thinking too much about the financial side of business detracts from the other reasons they're in business, such as employing people, contributing to their communities, or providing a needed product or service. Enter the Balanced Scorecard.

The Balanced Scorecard (BSC) is an excellent management tool that ensures you have a holistic and balanced strategy as well as a way to track performance over time to assess whether goals are being met. I introduce the Balanced Scorecard in this chapter to help you write goals in the four key areas that all organizations must excel in to succeed. Chapters 13 and 14 go into further detail to help you build and develop the rest of your scorecard, including how to track your measures and targets.

---

## The scorecard of success

In the early 1990s, the Balanced Scorecard (BSC) was introduced by Robert Kaplan, a Harvard Business School professor, and David Norton, the founder and president of Balanced Scorecard Collaborative, Inc., as a new way to work with business strategy. Today, more than half of the Fortune 1,000 companies in North America use the BSC, which has become the hallmark of a well-run organization. Many organizations say the scorecard is the foundation of their measurement and management systems.

---

To have a balanced and holistic strategy, organizations must have goals that feed off each other. I describe these perspectives in the following list:

- The **"Financial"** perspective indicates whether the company's strategy is contributing to top- and bottom-line improvement.

- The **"Customer"** perspective is focused primarily on creating value and differentiation when acquiring, retaining, or servicing the customer. This driver deals primarily with gaining and growing customers and market share.

- The **"Internal/Operational Processes"** perspective focuses on the systems and processes that are critical to creating value and, ultimately, customer loyalty. Positive long-term results rely on defining the competencies needed to maximize the effectiveness of those internal systems.

- The **"People/Learning"** perspective focuses on a company's commitment to its greatest resource — people. This area focuses on creating value by developing an environment that fosters learning, innovation, and prioritizing on its "human asset". The premise is that people drive the other three elements to achieve the company's goals.

Take Yogurt Beach, a company with a top-line financial goal to increase the revenue by 10 percent annually: How will the owner achieve her financial goal? Sell more yogurt. In order to sell more yogurt, she must have a great product that's different from the competitor down the street and provide outstanding customer service. And what does she need to do to deliver great customer service? Have efficient processes that deliver yogurt quickly. To excel at quick delivery, she has to have well-trained, friendly employees.

For each perspective, develop at least one long-term strategic objective but no more than five. If you develop too many at the beginning, your plan may become unwieldy. Look at your short lists of external and internal priorities you developed in the previous section. Note which priorities fall where and note the link to other priorities. If you're short in any area, consider developing additional priorities to have a balanced strategy.

# Financial priorities: If we succeed, how will we look to our shareholders?

Goals in the financial area fall into two categories: revenue generation and productivity improvement. A solid strategic plan has one goal in each of these activities. The financial perspective contains priorities that explain how your company looks to shareholders, who are usually owners and investors. By serving your customer well, you increase your revenue generation. By improving your internal business process, you enhance productivity improvement. Your financial goals may include the following:

✔ **Revenue generation:**

- To increase revenue by 10 percent annually

- To increase gross profit by 10 percent annually

- To increase sales by 10 percent annually

✔ **Productivity improvement:**

- To decrease expenses by 5 percent

- To increase net profit by 10 percent

- To improve overall efficiency as measured by output over a period of time

- To improve overall productivity (doing more with what you have)

## Customer priorities: How do we provide value to our customers?

Customer priorities support the financial goals. These goals focus on meeting the needs of the customer through products and services. All your external goals fall into this category. Crafting new and current customer goals is a good way to structure this section. Following are some important long-term strategic objectives for valuing your customers:

✔ **New customer goals:**

- Introduce existing products into a new market.

- Introduce new products to new and existing markets.

- Anticipate future customer needs through customer feedback.

- Expand sales to the global marketplace.

✔ **Current customer goals:**

- Expand sales to existing customers.

- Increase customer retention.

- Increase customer loyalty.

- Cross sell existing products or services to current clients.

- Achieve and maintain outstanding customer service.

- Develop and use a customer database.

- Anticipate future customer needs through customer feedback.

# Internal priorities: What processes must we excel in to satisfy our customers?

Internal business process goals serve several purposes: Support the customer and financial goals, focus on administrative processes that have an impact on creating customer value and satisfaction, and focus on internal management activities and operational functions needed to support the products and services. Look at your list of internal priorities for this section. In Chapter 7, you find all the areas of organization you must look at in order to succeed. You may glean some additional ideas from that chapter. Here are some long-term strategic objectives to prioritize your internal goals:

✔ Acquire enhanced CRM data mining capabilities.

✔ Improve internal processes.

✔ Increase efficiencies through the use of wireless or virtual technology.

✔ Increase community outreach.

✔ Develop and implement a promotional plan to drive increased business.

✔ Establish one new strategic alliance annually.

✔ Improve internal communications.

✔ Redirect or restructure available resources.

✔ Improve distributor and supplier relationships.

✔ Improve marketing, advertising, and public relations.

✔ Capitalize on physical facilities (location, capacity, and so on).

✔ Improve organizational structure.

# Employee priorities: How must our organization grow and improve?

Employee priorities drive everything else in your plan. Without your team, you don't have an organization. These goals focus on developing people, increasing the company's knowledge base, improving through innovation, and discovering best practices. Check out Chapter 7 for additional information on employee priorities. Work on these long-term strategic objectives with your employees:

✔ Continually discover and adopt current best practices.

✔ Align incentives and rewards with employee performance.

✔ Employ professionals who create success for customers.

✔ Develop a broad set of skills useful for customer support.

✔ Develop a team who understands strategy.

✔ Transfer knowledge from your leading-edge clients.

✔ Continually develop a set of best practices in your industry and your clients' industries.

✔ Improve labor relations, human resource development, and training.

# Turning Strategic Priorities into a Road Map for Your Vision

This area is probably the most widely debated part of strategic planning. Having goals, objectives, and strategies are great, but knowing how they all work together (if in fact they do) and if you need them all is another story. I suggest ignoring the semantics and focusing on establishing a time frame. What matters is having a combination of long-term and short-term markers to keep your organization moving in the right direction. Think of the following hierarchy to demystify the terms of your priorities:

✔ **Core values:** Your guiding principles that *rarely* change and that you stick to no matter what vision you're pursuing

✔ **Mission:** The underlying purpose why you're in business in the first place

✔ **Vision:** The big, hairy, bold goal you're headed for, and the concept that everything your company does is focused on

✔ **Strategy:** The guiding statement that explains how you get to your vision

✔ **Three-year strategic objectives:** Intermediate goals that are broad and continuous, that you achieve on the way to your vision, and that explain the activities you need to be in to achieve your vision

✔ **One-year SMART goals:** One-year markers that support your long-term strategic objectives

✔ **Action items:** Items that explain the who and the when (see Chapter 13)

Figure 12-5 illustrates how to use the four balanced scorecard perspectives as well as how strategies, goals, and objectives fit together.

| Overall strategy: Leverage current resources to gain market share. | | | | | |
| --- | --- | --- | --- | --- | --- |
| **Long-Term Strategic Objectives** | | **1-Year Goals** | **Measures** | **Targets** | **Person Responsible** |
| **Financial** | | | | | |
| Establish a financially stable and profitable company. | 1 | Increase our billable hours by 10% over the next 12 months. | # of billable hours | 1.2% increase each month | |
| | 2 | Achieve sales growth of 10% per year. | Monthly sales | 1.2% increase each month | |
| **Customer** | | | | | |
| Introduce current products to two new markets. | 1 | Realize 10% of the company's annual sales from the small business market by end of next year. | # of small business clients | 100 clients | Marketing department |
| **Internal Business Processes** | | | | | |
| Achieve order fulfillment excellence through on-line process improvement. | 1 | Reduce the time lapse between order data and delivery from 6 days to 4 days by this June. | # of days to process each order | 4 days | Shipping department |
| | 2 | Reduce the number of returns due to shipping errors from 3% to 2%. | # of returns due to shipping errors | 2% | Shipping department |
| **Employees & Learning** | | | | | |
| Provide employees with challenging and rewarding work. | 1 | Reduce turnover among sales managers by 10% by the end of the year. | Employee turnover | 10% | Sales department |
| | 2 | Hire and train a human relations director by the end of the year. | Director hired | achievement | CEO |

**Figure 12-5:**
Putting together your strategic objectives, goals, and strategies.

# Finalizing your strategies

Your strategies are the general methods you intend to use to reach your vision. Although strategies are embedded in all elements of your strategic plans, consider listing the top one to two strategies or long-term activities your company needs to pursue in order to achieve its vision.

A strategy is like an umbrella. It's a general statement(s) that guides and covers a set of activities. You can develop strategies for your whole organization, a department, or a specific set of activities. No matter what the level, strategies answer the question of how you do something in simple, clear language that everyone can understand and get behind.

Review your notes from Chapter 11 to identify your corporate and business level strategies.

Here are a few sample strategies:

- **Starbucks:** To build the brand one cup at a time, based on three key ingredients: the quality of the coffee, their retail stores, and selective brand extensions
- **The Boy Scouts of America:** Consistently delivering the youth experience to a growing membership base
- **The Economic Development Authority of Western Nevada:** To move toward economic development and to increase the base of companies contributing to the region's measurable quality of life to ensure long-term vitality of the community

## Writing your long-term strategic objectives

Strategic objectives are the general areas in which your effort is directed to drive your mission and vision. With strategic objectives, the company moves from motive to action. Strategic objectives define what an organization intends to accomplish both programmatically and organizationally. Strategic objectives are articulated as broad categories that are non-measurable and continuous.

To help you write your strategic objectives, think about your answers to the following questions:

- What areas do you need to be involved in to accomplish your vision?
- In what areas will you continue being actively involved in for the next five years?

For example, a nationwide radio station, which broadcasts 24 hours a day, 7 days a week in 235 communities, would answer these questions with a summary of five strategic areas:

- Audience engagement and community development
- Audience reach and usage

✔ Financial stewardship

✔ Operational excellence

✔ People development

Based on these five areas, the organization developed broad, continuous statements that articulated the strategic intent of each one — becoming the strategic objectives.

## *Making your short-term goals SMART*

Realistic goals ought to serve as a tool for stretching a company to reach its full potential; this means setting goals high enough to be challenging to energize the company and its strategy. Short-term goals are immediate mileposts on your way to your vision. Think about achieving them in a one-year time frame. With goals, the company converts the mission, vision, and long-term strategic objectives into performance targets.

For effective goals to track a company's performance and progress, they must state specifics: how much of what kind of performance and by when it's to be accomplished. The goals must be relevant and aggressive yet achievable, and they must be stated in measurable or quantifiable terms. Think SMART when you create your goals:

✔ **Specific:** Goals need to be specific. Try to answer *how much* and *what kind* with each goal you write.

✔ **Measurable:** Goals must be stated in quantifiable terms, or otherwise they're only good intentions. Measurable goals facilitate management planning, implementation, and control. (See Chapter 13 for more on measuring your goals.)

✔ **Attainable:** Goals must provide a stretch that inspires people to aim higher. Goals must be achievable, or they're a setup for failure. Set goals you know you, your company, and your employees can realistically reach.

✔ **Responsible person:** Goals must be assigned to a person or a department. But just because a person is assigned to a goal doesn't mean that she's solely responsible for its achievement. See Chapter 14 for ideas on how to hold your team accountable for goal achievement.

✔ **Time specific:** Your goals must include a timeline of when they should be accomplished.

## Mapping your strategy

Seeing your whole strategic plan — the relationships and dependencies — can be difficult, but doing so is necessary to make sure that your company sees the big picture. Unlike financial plans, with income statements, balance sheets, and cash flow statements, no common or uniform elements exist for describing a company's strategic plan. That's where a strategy map may come in handy.

The creators of the Balanced Scorecard also created the idea of a strategy map. Strategy maps aren't for creating strategy; they only describe strategies. A *strategy map* has several purposes:

✔ To evaluate and make visually explicit the organization's perspectives, strategic objectives, and goals

✔ To visualize the fundamental relationships between each goal

✔ To connect employee learning and internal processes to customer value and financial goals

A benefit of strategy maps is that everyone from the top of the ranks to the bottom can see how he fits into the company. In fact, you can color code the different goals by the department that's responsible to show how each department fits into the overall direction. See Figure 12-6 for an example of a strategy map and how to read it and evaluate your strategy. You're looking for linkages and interdependences. If you have an unsupported goal, it won't be achieved. You should be able to draw at least one arrow, or cause and effect relationship, between one goal and the next.

Look at Figure 12-6 as you read the following example. This company can establish the link between high profits and improved sales training as follows:

✔ If we improve our technical and service skills by sending our staff to continued education classes at least once a year, our staff continues to be highly trained.

✔ If the people in our staff are highly trained, they become problem solvers instead of order takers.

✔ If they're problem solvers, we're increasing the perceived value for services provided by regularly adding value to our customers.

✔ If we continue to add value to the services we provide, revenue increases through improved sales.

Every goal doesn't need to link to every other goal. But you do need to make sure that every goal is connected to at least one other goal. For example, if your goal is to increase overall efficiencies, but you don't list a goal for time management or productivity training or improving your internal process, you won't increase efficiency. Naturally, just stating something doesn't mean that it happens.

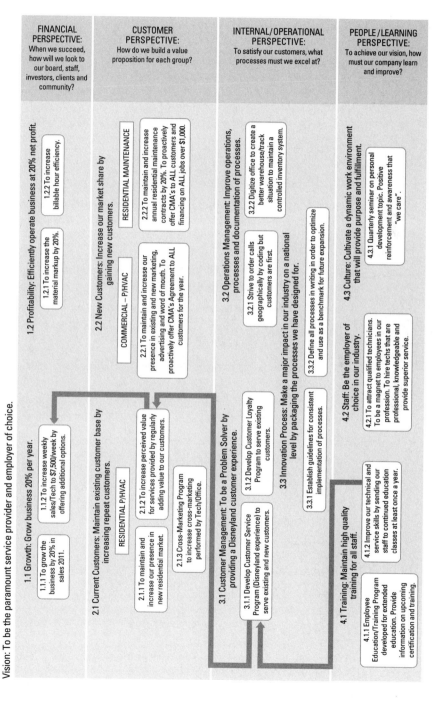

**Figure 12-6:** Mapping your strategy.

Vision: To be the paramount service provider and employer of choice.

**FINANCIAL PERSPECTIVE:** When we succeed, how will we look to our board, staff, investors, clients and community?

**CUSTOMER PERSPECTIVE:** How do we build a value proposition for each group?

**INTERNAL/OPERATIONAL PERSPECTIVE:** To satisfy our customers, what processes must we excel at?

**PEOPLE/LEARNING PERSPECTIVE:** To achieve our vision, how must our company learn and improve?

1.1 Growth: Grow business 20% per year.

1.1.1 To grow the business by 20% in sales 2011.

1.1.2 To increase weekly sales/Tech to $7,500/week by offering additional options.

1.2 Profitability: Efficiently operate business at 20% net profit.

1.2.1 To increase the material markup by 20%.

1.2.2 To increase billable hour efficiency.

2.1 Current Customers: Maintain existing customer base by increasing repeat customers.

RESIDENTIAL P/HVAC

2.1.1 To maintain and increase our presence in new residential market.

2.1.2 To increase perceived value for services provided by regularly adding value to our customers.

2.1.3 Cross-Marketing Program to increase cross-marketing performed by Tech/Office.

2.2 New Customers: Increase our market share by gaining new customers.

COMMERCIAL – P/HVAC

2.2.1 To maintain and increase our presence in existing and new marketing, advertising and word of mouth. To proactively offer CMA's Agreement to ALL customers for the year.

RESIDENTIAL MAINTENANCE

2.2.2 To maintain and increase annual residential maintenance contracts by 20%. To proactively offer CMA's to ALL customers and financing on ALL jobs over $1,000.

3.1 Customer Management: To be a Problem Solver by providing a Disneyland customer experience.

3.1.1 Develop Customer Service Program (Disneyland experience) to serve existing and new customers.

3.1.2 Develop Customer Loyalty Program to serve existing customers.

3.2 Operations Management: Improve operations, processes and documentation of processes.

3.2.1 Strive to order calls geographically by coding but customers are first.

3.2.2 Digitize office to create a better warehouse/track situation to maintain a controlled inventory system.

3.3 Innovation Process: Make a major impact in our industry on a national level by packaging the processes we have designed for.

3.3.1 Establish guidelines for consistent implementation of processes.

3.3.2 Define all processes in writing in order to optimize and use as a benchmark for future expansion.

4.1 Training: Maintain high quality training for all staff.

4.1.1 Employee Education/Training Program developed for extended education. Provide information on upcoming certification and training.

4.1.2 Improve our technical and service skills by sending our staff to continued education classes at least once a year.

4.2 Staff: Be the employer of choice in our industry.

4.2.1 To attract qualified technicians. To be a magnet to employees in our profession. To hire techs that are professional, knowledgeable and provide superior service.

4.3 Culture: Cultivate a dynamic work environment that will provide purpose and fulfillment.

4.3.1 Quarterly seminar on personal development topic. Positive reinforcement and awareness that "we care".

Creating a strategy map is more art than science. Of course, strategies are as individual as companies, so you can modify the guidelines to map your strategy. As you try to map your strategy, check out the Strategy Map Worksheet on the CD, which provides a great framework. Also review the corporate strategy maps in Chapter 11 for reference.

Create your strategy map on a piece of paper and sticky notes first and then transfer the notes into a Word document, using the draw toolbar or a graphic layout program. Use the following steps as a guide to create your map, but don't feel like you have to follow them exactly.

1. **Write your vision statement at the top of the page.**

2. **Draw four horizontal rectangles — one for each of the four perspectives of your organization: financial, customer, internal business processes, and employee learning — stacked on top of each other under your vision.**

3. **Place your three-year strategic objective in the top area of each perspective the objective is associated with.**

   Space the goals out so you have enough room for the next step.

4. **Put your one-year goals on individual sticky notes or in circles under each associated three-year goal.**

   Make sure that the one-year goal supports the three-year goal that it's under. If not, move it to where it does fit.

5. **After all the goals are on your map, draw arrows between the goals to indicate the cause and effect relationship between them.**

   A great way to start this is to look at your financial goal and ask what causes the goal to happen. Go through this type of questioning for each goal except in the area of employee learning because everything stems from your employees.

6. **Take a hard look at your strategy map to make sure that all goals are supported and that they're all integrated.**

   Congratulations! You now have a strategy map for your organization. *Note:* If you're working on a white board, flip charts, and so forth, be sure to take a picture of your finished work. You may need it later!

## Building your road map

As your strategy map tells your interrelated strategy story, your road map shows you mileposts from current to future. Strategy planning is as much about the *strategy*, as depicted in your strategy map, as it is about the *planning*, as illustrated in your road map. I think the road map view is extremely helpful to visualize what needs to be prioritized year-by-year to achieve your vision.

Use the Road Map Worksheet on the CD along with Figure 12-7 and the following instructions to build your road map.

1. **Label the top row with the planning years relevant to your organization.**

2. **Add your long-term strategic objectives to the left-hand column by each perspective.**

3. **Add your year one goals to the next column by each strategic objective.**

| Long-Term Strategic Objectives | Year One Goals | Year Two Goals | Year Three Goals |
|---|---|---|---|
| **Financial** | | | |
| To establish a financially stable and profitable company. | Increase our billable hours by 10% over the next 12 months. | Continue to increase billable hours by 10% by end of 2012. | Reduce operating costs by 10% by end of 2013. |
| | Achieve sales growth of 10% per year. | Achieve sales growth of 12% by end of 2012. | Increase sales by 15% by end of 2013. |
| **Customer** | | | |
| Introduce current products to two new markets. | Realize 10% of the company's annual sales from the small business market by end of next year. | Gain 10% of the company's annual sales from the health care sector by end of 2012. | Maintain 10% increase in annual sales from health care sector in 2013. |
| | | | Grow small business sales by 5% in 2013. |
| **Internal Business Processes** | | | |
| To achieve order fulfillment excellence through on-line process improvement. | Reduce the time lapse between order data and delivery from 6 days to 4 days by this June. | Decrease time lapse to 3 days by end of 2012. | Upgrade and implement new software system. |
| | Reduce the number of returns due to shipping errors from 3% to 2%. | Maintain 2% shipping return error rate. | Strive for less than 1% returns due to shipping errors by end of year. |
| **Employees & Learning** | | | |
| To provide employees with challenging and rewarding work. | Reduce turnover among sales managers by 10% by the end of the year. | Implement profit sharing program by end of 2012. | Provide professional development opportunities for all departments. |
| | Hire and train a human relations director by the end of the year. | Focus on team building through 2 off-site events per year. | Expand team to include PR/marketing director. |

**Figure 12-7:**
Paving your road map.

4. **Add year two and year three goals to the columns where they align with the strategic objective.**

   Ask what you must accomplish in the given time frame to drive your strategic objective.

Most organizations can see the next 12 to 18 months clearly, but past that, the future becomes a little fuzzy. Remember that building your strategic plan is a process, not an event. So if you can't see the next two or three years, don't worry. Revisit your road map during your strategy reviews (see Chapter 14), and you'll eventually find more clarity.

# Assembling Your Strategic Plan

Now it's time to take all the work you've done up to this point and put it together in one comprehensive document. This task may seem tedious, but I bet you can find someone on your staff who loves this type of detail work. So seek that person out to collate everything you've done to date. If you don't have such a person, brew a big pot of coffee and get to work!

Here's why this part of the job is so important:

- ✓ **The strategic direction becomes clear.** Without compiling everything into one document, your plan is just a bunch of different parts. When the parts become whole, you clearly see how you can reach your vision.

- ✓ **Ideas become action.** Up until now, you've developed and collected a bunch of great ideas. By formalizing them into a plan, you can develop action plans and assess the financial viability of your choices.

- ✓ **Gaps are identified.** With everything in one place, stand back and evaluate your plan. Does it make sense? Are your goals supporting one another? Have you missed anything?

If you've kept your notes in your strategy notebook (as I explain in the Introduction to this book), bringing everything together should go quickly. Don't forget to bring together the ideas and input from your team that you've been soliciting throughout the planning process. See the following sample outline for your strategic plan (I included chapter references in case you need to review specific sections):

I. Strategic Foundation and Direction

      Competitive advantage (Chapter 5)

      Mission, vision, values (Chapter 6)

II. Current Strategic Position

    SWOT analysis (Chapters 7, 8, and 10)

    Customer profiles (Chapter 9)

III. Organization-Wide Strategies

    Corporate strategies (Chapter 11)

    Business level strategies (Chapter 11)

    Strategy map (Chapter 12)

IV. Strategic Objectives and Goals

    Long-term strategic objectives (Chapter 12)

    Annual corporate goals (Chapter 12)

    Road map (Chapter 12)

    Corporate scorecard (Chapter 13)

V. Financial Projections and Organizational Structure

    Financial projections (Chapter 13)

    Organization chart (Chapter 13)

VI. Departmental and Individual Action Plans

    Department scorecards (Chapter 13)

    Action plans (Chapter 13)

Note that a strategic plan isn't like a business plan because the strategic plan document is primarily for your internal use. It's not a sales piece for outside critique (except in the case of seeking financing), so you don't need any extra verbiage or fluff. Just make sure the content is easy to read and flow. The preceding outline is merely a recommendation. Feel free to revise and modify to fit your needs.

More than likely you have some ideas, goals, and considerations that aren't part of this plan, but you don't want to lose them. Create a someday list or file. Put all your extra information in this file for your next strategic planning session.

To see a sample strategic plan, check out my website at `www.mystrategic plan.com/examples`.

# Evaluating Your Strategic Plan

Now that your plan is all together in one place, take a step back and evaluate. Did you create the strategy you intended to create? More than likely, you and your team have put a lot of time into the document you now have in front of you. Put it away for a week and don't look at it. No peeking! After working on this document for months, you can easily get so close to the plan that you miss obvious flaws (called the not-seeing-the-forest-for-the-trees syndrome).

When you pick your plan back up, reread it and answer these questions:

- ✔ **Does your plan connect your mission to your vision?** Make sure that all your goals and strategies align with your vision and support your mission. Modify or delete any outliers. You want all your energy focused on reaching your vision.

- ✔ **Is your plan realistic?** Over planning is a common problem. Consider pushing some deadlines out farther than you originally anticipated.

- ✔ **Is your plan integrated?** Make sure that all the elements of your plan support each other. (See "Mapping your strategy" earlier in this chapter for information on developing a strategy map to help answer this question.)

- ✔ **Is your plan balanced?** You developed your plan using the Balanced Scorecard Framework. Make sure that you have a good balance between financial, customer, internal business process, and employee and learning goals.

- ✔ **Is the plan complete?** Identify any holes in your plan or potential activities that are unsupported.

- ✔ **Is the document clear?** Writing down an action item or a goal that makes sense in the moment is easy, but making sure that the action makes sense in six months is crucial. Make sure that every statement is explicit so everyone knows what's intended. Seek someone you trust outside of your organization to review your plan for clarity and consistency.

# Chapter 13

# Putting Your Plan into Action

- - - - - - - - - - - - - - - - - - - - - - - - - - - - - - - - - - - - - - - - -

## In This Chapter

▶ Using a scorecard to measure your progress and track results

▶ Developing action plans for your short-term goals

▶ Cascading goals for buy-in

▶ Assessing the financial viability of your strategic plan

▶ Setting up a management system

- - - - - - - - - - - - - - - - - - - - - - - - - - - - - - - - - - - - - - - - -

*Y*ou've arrived! If you're at this chapter in sequence, you've reached the point where you can actually operationalize and give your plan life. You've developed your business strategy and have a clear road map designed to reach your vision. You've identified what you're best at (Chapter 5), developed your mission, vision, and values (Chapter 6), sized up your internal and external environment (Chapters 7, 8, and 10), determined your growth strategies (Chapter 11), selected new markets to reach (Chapter 9), and established your strategic objectives and goals (Chapter 12). The next step (this chapter) is to put your plan into action and manage it.

As you work through this chapter, remember that C-level leaders and board of directors expect your strategy to be well thought out, concise, persuasive, and easy to understand in just a few presentation slides. Keep in mind that less is more as you write your strategy. Leaders and directors are looking for whether you have the skill to implement the strategy, not how deep you can get into the specifics.

## Managing Performance with a Scorecard

Your corporate scorecard is a tool to help you monitor the progress of your business and your strategic plan.

A scorecard consists of goals, measures, and targets. *Goals* are desired outcomes. You gauge the progress toward attaining a goal by one or more measures. Goals have causal relationships — one action causes another outcome.

Because you've established SMART goals (see Chapter 12), you can more easily pull out or delineate the measures you need to track.

A scorecard goal consists of two pieces:

- ✔ **Measure:** A measure is an end point. It's an explanation (word text) of what you want to achieve. Measures are also the indicators of how a business is performing relative to its goals and whether the overall strategy has been accomplished. For every goal, you should track at least one measure that tells you how you're progressing toward achieving the desired outcome.

- ✔ **Target:** Targets quantify (numeric) the outcome measures. Target measures are the specific numbers you need to hit in order to achieve your goal and can be expressed in weekly, monthly, or annual figures.

I expand on the measures and targets of a scorecard goal and how to build your strategy scorecard in the following sections.

## Pegging your measures

Creating good, solid measures is the first step to developing your scorecard (see Chapter 14 for info on how to use your scorecard).

Measures are quantifiable performance statements, and they must follow certain guidelines. Measures should be

- ✔ Relevant to the goal and strategy
- ✔ Placed in context of a target to be reached in an identified time frame
- ✔ Capable of being tracked period after period
- ✔ Owned by the person who's responsible for the goal

The following are different types of measures:

- ✔ **Efficiency measures:** These measures are productivity and cost effectiveness measured as ratio of outputs per inputs. Examples of efficiency measures include turnaround time per application processed and number of students graduating to number of students enrolled.

- ✔ **Outcomes measures:** These measures are the end result of whether services meet proposed targets or standards and demonstrate impact and benefit of activities. Examples include the percent increase in intern-ships and the application to enrolled yield rate.

✔ **Quality measures:** These measures gauge effectiveness of expectations and generally show improvement in accuracy, reliability, courtesy, com-petence, responsiveness, and compliance. Examples of quality measures include number of audits with no findings or within a range of accuracy.

✔ **Project measures:** These measures show progress against an initiative that has a terminus. The measure is usually stated as the percent complete.

Sometimes the measures are obvious, like number of new customers. Other times, they can be hard to come up with. If you're stumped, ask yourself some of the following questions:

✔ What causes this goal to occur?

✔ What causes increased sales?

✔ What causes operations to improve?

✔ What causes an increase in market share?

✔ What causes customer satisfaction?

✔ What causes employee satisfaction?

See Figure 13-1 for a helpful list of possible measures. For more key perfor-mance indicators, check out www.kpilibrary.com.

Determining measures can be tough work. Don't agonize over finding the best measure. Start with the most obvious and easiest to collect. As you work with your plan over the next several years, you can refine your measures.

## Aiming at your targets

The following are different ways to select your targets:

✔ **Internal benchmarking:** Generally, organizations select targets based on a change leaders want to see from the previous year to the current year. Certainly, the underlying resources and actions need to be in place in order to affect the increase or decrease, which should be spelled out in your action plans.

✔ **Industry association benchmarking:** Instead of looking internally, organizations can set performance targets based on industry standards. Before signing up for an industry performance standard, do your homework to make sure the standard is based on a set of organizations or companies similar enough to yours. If not, the target will be unrealistic or unfair to achieve.

✔ **Competitive benchmarking:** Similar to industry benchmarking, competitive benchmarking is selecting one other company's performance as a target. Depending on the goal and, therefore, associated target, you may not be able to acquire this information. But if you can, competitive benchmarks can be very powerful because they bring out a competitive spirit in employees who you rely on to drive the performance improvement.

✔ **Base lining:** Sometimes you have no historical information and no reliable industry information. If that's the case, go with your intuition to set the target and give yourself the grace to adjust along the way until you do have a reliable base line.

| Financial | Customer | Internal Business Processes | Employee & Learning |
|---|---|---|---|
| • Net sales (dollar growth and percent increase)<br>• Gross profit margin<br>• Pretax earnings (dollar growth and percent increase)<br>• Operating expenses (SGA) as a percent of sales<br>• Receivables turnover<br>• Inventory turnover<br>• Debt-to-equity ratio<br>• Total equity dollars<br>• Operating cash flow<br>• Investing cash flow<br>• Financing cash flow<br>• Ending cash<br>• Earnings per share<br>• ROI, ROE, ROA | • Improving image/reputation<br>• Number of customer complaints<br>• Percentage market share<br>• Number of customers retained<br>• Customer satisfaction<br>• Dollars per account<br>• Time spent with customer<br>• Revenue per customer<br>• Number of transactions per unit time<br>• Average sales dollars per transaction<br>• Customer satisfaction index<br>• Number of customers<br>• Number of new customers<br>• Ratio of new to existing customers<br>• Average sales per customer | • Percentage operating costs<br>• Billable efficiency<br>• Quality of product/service<br>• Defects ratio<br>• New product success rate<br>• Cycle time to deliver<br>• Project turnaround time<br>• Number of defects or returns<br>• Delivery times<br>• Delivery response time to customer<br>• Number of test market trials<br>• Relative product quality<br>• Number of new products<br>• Number of products produced<br>• Average cost per product<br>• Number of products sold | • Employee retention<br>• Employee satisfaction<br>• Number of quality resumes on hand<br>• Employee turnover<br>• Number of ideas in the pipeline<br>• Number of employee suggestions<br>• Percentage of employees who are systems efficient<br>• Average sales per employee<br>• Number of net new positions<br>• Number of relevant trainings attended |

**Figure 13-1:**
A list of common measures.

# Building your scorecard

Although scorecards are effective, they can also be daunting. For your first crack at this tool, consider just building your scorecard for high-priority goals. Identify the top seven to ten goals and associated measures that are most important to your company this year, known as *key performance indicators,* or *KPIs.* So you don't collect too many KPIs, ask yourself this question, "Does the measure directly affect our customers?" Then follow these steps to build your scorecard. In the following years, consider building a scorecard that monitors all your goals.

1. **Identify the right measures.**

   Most of your short-term goals should have measures associated with them. You build your scorecard based on these measures. But just because you picked a measure to track a goal doesn't mean that it's a good measure. Work with your initial measures for several months. If you see that some are meaningless or too hard to track, dump them and find new ones. Ask yourself, "What outcome are we trying to achieve?"

2. **Establish increments that mesh with the targets.**

   In addition to getting the right measures, make sure to get the right time frame and size of measures. For example, if your target is a 10 percent increase in sales over the year, break the target down to a monthly number. For ease of tracking, try to use the same increments for all your measures. If you're reporting monthly, use monthly measures.

3. **Identify the data source.**

   Clearly identify where the monthly number is coming from and who's responsible for reporting on it. Without easy access to numbers, you find yourself doing a ton of extra busy work. If you can't get access to a data source or no data source is available, find a new measure.

4. **Input numbers monthly.**

   Enter numbers every month for each measure. Use the *Year to Date* column to track your running progress. This column should add up or average all the months entered to date.

5. **See the big picture.**

   The primary purpose of KPIs is to give you a big-picture look at the business with a relatively small amount of information. If you aren't seeing the big picture, change the measures. A great way to get a visual is to produce a chart or graph for each measure.

6. **Repeat Steps 1 through 5 for departments and teams, where appropriate.**

   Ideally, your department and teams have their own scorecards that support the corporate scorecard.

ON THE CD

The easiest way to build your scorecard is to use the framework from Figure 13-2 in an Excel spreadsheet. (I provide a blank version of this Scorecard Worksheet on the CD.) If you prefer, see Chapter 14 for a streamlined reporting process.

| GOALS | MEASURES | TARGETS | FREQUENCY | SOURCE | YEAR TO DATE |
|-------|----------|---------|-----------|--------|--------------|
| Increase number of new paying customers by 50% | Conversion of new contacts within 2 months | 50% | Monthly | Customer Relations Management System | 20% |
| Increase number of former paying customers by 25% | Renewing of previous relationships that were inactive | 25% | Monthly | Customer Relations Management System | 12% |
| Improve inventory turns | # of inventory turns per year | 4–6 | Monthly | Enterprise Resource Planning | 2 |

**Figure 13-2:**
An example strategy scorecard.

# Clear goals produce results

Organizations that execute with excellence focus on a handful of clear goals and align the focus of every department and employee to those few goals. Take FranklinCovey Co. and Harris Interactive, Inc., as examples. They conducted a study to test the gap between goal setting and the actual achievement of those goals in various companies. With more than 11,000 respondents, the results shed some light on issues around planning for organizations with multiple levels and departments. Here's what the study found:

✔ **Lack of clarity:** Only one in six workers thinks his organization sets clear goals, and fewer than half say they understand what their companies are trying to achieve. Flip to Chapter 14 for solutions to this issue.

✔ **Wasting time on non-critical tasks:** By their own account, respondents spend only 49 percent of their time on crucial organizational

goals. One hour out of three is spent on urgent but irrelevant tasks, such as checking e-mail. One hour in five is wasted dealing with pointless bureaucracy issues, such as politicking and attending unproductive meetings. By having a strategic plan that everyone buys in to and understands, you can increase time spent on the crucial aspects of your organization.

✔ **No accountability:** Only about 50 percent of all respondents said that they feel accountable for performance. They're rarely, if ever, called on to report progress. Chapter 14 also addresses this problem.

✔ **No line of sight between organizational goals and work:** Only 20 percent of people have clearly defined work goals, and 10 percent clearly understand how work relates to the organization's top priorities.

Don't confuse scorecards and dashboards. Scorecards are often spreadsheets that look like Figure 13-2, focused on tracking the monthly progress of your KPIs. *Dashboards,* in this situation, are the visual representation of your scorecards, often displayed as charts and graphs. You need the data collected from a scorecard to create a strategy-focused dashboard.

# Cascading Goals to Annual Action Plans

By the time company managers get to the action planning part of strategic planning, many are tired and worn out from all the work leading up to this point. But don't stop yet! Setting action items and to-dos for each short-term goal is essential. The next step is to connect those goals with people, deadlines, and costs.

Basically, you're developing an action plan for each goal. An *action plan* explains who's going to do what, when they're going to do it by, and in what order they're going to do it for the organization to reach its goals. The design and implementation of the action planning depend on the nature and needs of the organization.

Although coming up with an action plan for each goal may seem like a monumental task, here are a few ways to simplify the process:

- ✔ **List the concrete steps or to-dos that you need to accomplish in order to achieve your goals.** You don't need to list every single action item for each goal — that may take all year.

- ✔ **Focus on identifying large to-dos that warrant discussion at a team level.** Stay away from big items that are so big that you don't know where to start.

- ✔ **Identify all the actions that need to occur within the next 90 days.** Continue this same process every 90 days until the goal is achieved.

To develop your action plan, take a look at these approaches:

- ✔ **Cascading directly to individuals:** Because every short-term goal is assigned to a person or to department managers, you can have each party develop action items for the goal it's responsible for. Then reconvene as a group and discuss each action plan. The benefit to this approach is speed and personal buy-in. The drawback is you may miss out on group ideas.

> ✔ **Cascading to department managers then to individuals:** With your strategic planning team or a group of staff members who are impacted by the goal, you can identify the next actions for each short-term goal. The benefit of working in a group is the ability to generate a lot of ideas about how best to achieve the goal and cascade it. The drawback is that action planning in a group setting can take a long time.

## Tips for cascading one level

For every short-term corporate goal, identify the following items. These items are listed in logical order and flow to make it easy to develop each one:

> ✔ **Action item or to-do:** Start the sentence with a verb to show the action that's being done. After all the action items are listed, order them based on priority.

> Don't worry about writing action items for your financial goals. All your financial goals are achieved through the rest of the goals in your plan. For example, increasing sales by 10 percent is a function of marketing and sales reaching new customers or selling more to existing customers.

> ✔ **Person or department responsible:** If the action plan requires shared responsibility, make one person the lead.

> ✔ **Start and end dates:** Start dates are important because they allow you to see the duration of an action. Without the start date, you won't know whether you're behind schedule until the end date passes. When establishing an end date, commit to the deadline.

> ✔ **Expense:** Identify an estimated expense if applicable. If dollars are hard to estimate, then estimate the time required.

See Figure 13-3 for visual representation of cascading one level. Also see Chapter 12 for an expanded version of this figure.

| ACTION PLAN | | | | | | |
|---|---|---|---|---|---|---|
| PRIORITY | ACTION ITEM | PERSON RESPONSIBLE | START DATE | END DATE | PROGRESS | EXPENSE |
| **Goal:** Realize 10% of the company's annual sales from the small business market by end of next year. | | | | | | |
| 1 | Gather secondary market research. | Susie | 1/1/11 | 2/1/11 | 50% complete | None |
| 1 | Hold 3 focus groups. | Beth | 2/1/11 | 3/1/11 | 25% complete | $10,000 |
| 2 | Develop a marketing plan. | Beth | 3/1/11 | 4/1/11 | Not started | None |
| 3 | Execute marketing plan. | Beth | 4/1/11 | 12/31/11 | Not started | $100,000 |

**Figure 13-3:** Pulling together your action plan for each short-term goal.

## *Tips for cascading multiple levels*

Cascading goals multiple levels means breaking down the corporate goals into a set of smaller goals relevant to each department and then again to individual goals. A simple way to think about this process is to think about goals spilling over a cliff like a waterfall. Goals must spread throughout an entire organization to be executed, as Figure 13-4 shows.

The department goals describe what each unit needs to achieve. These goals are then broken down further until individuals in the unit have their own performance goals. In this way, progress throughout the organization is measurable.

 Cascading goals isn't an easy or fast process. Be prepared to meet resistance in getting people to get on board. Some may need specific training because they don't know how to develop goals and others may need coaching to enhance their performance.

Reduce waste by 10% across
the company by end of 2012.

**Figure 13-4:**
How
cascading
goals work.

**Manufacturing Dept:**
Reduce scrap by 5% from
widget production by end
of 2011.

**Shipping Dept:**
Reduce returns resulting
from mis-picks by 5% by
August 2012.

**Administration Dept:**
Institute a paper recycling
program to reuse scrap
paper for in-house printing
by end of 2012.

## *Getting down to cascading business*

 Follow these steps to cascade goals in your organization down to as many levels as you choose, including individual players. Use the Cascading Goals Worksheet on the CD for practice.

1. **Select a person to be in charge of managing the cascading process.**

   If you've appointed a strategic plan manager, he's the ideal person for the job.

2. **Create a grid that lists all the corporate goals on the left-hand side and all departments horizontally across the top.**

3. **Identify which departments are responsible for each goal.**

   Some goals may require two or more departments.

4. **Ask each department head or manager to develop department specific goals to support the corporate goals his department has been assigned.**

   See Figure 13-5 for an example. Managers should ask these questions: What must we, as a team, do to support the corporate goals? What must I do to support my team's goals?

5. **Repeat Steps 2 through 4 as needed.**

The planning team should ensure that the department level goals achieve the corporate goal after all department goals are completed. See Chapter 14 for information on communication goals, holding everyone accountable, and tips on execution.

When goals cascade successfully, the results can be dramatic because you get alignment across the entire organization. All the executives at the same level need to agree on how they support the CEO's vision and what they can do to minimize conflict. Cascading goals creates constancy of focus, which gets everybody thinking about his contribution and how he's the foundation for the corporate goals. Be sure to get the agreement in writing. See Figure 13-6 for an example of effective goal cascading in action.

| DEPARTMENTS | | | | |
|---|---|---|---|---|
| **CORPORATE GOALS** | Manufacturing | IT | Marketing | HR |
| 1. Improve net income by 10% by 12/31/11. | X | | X | |
| 2. Improve customer loyalty by increasing retention by 15% by 12/31/11. | X | X | X | |
| 3. Increase employee retention by reducing turnover by 5% by 9/30/11. | | X | | X |
| 4. Improve operational efficiency through the implementation of an ERP system by 6/30/11. | | X | | |

**Figure 13-5:** Spreading goals to different departments.

| CORPORATE GOALS | | IT Goals | |
|---|---|---|---|
| | 1. Improve net income by 10% by 12/31/11. | | N/A |
| | 2. Improve customer loyalty by increasing retention by 15% by 12/31/11. | | 2.1 Train all employees on the new CRM system by 9/30/11 to increase system utilization and reduce customer complaints. |
| | 3. Increase employee retention by reducing turnover by 5% by 9/30/11. | | 3.1 Reduce employee frustration by responding to IT requests within 24 hrs. <br><br> 3.2 Provide remote desktop access to all employees by 7/31/11 to allow employees to work from home. |
| | 4. Improve operational efficiency through the implementation of an ERP system by 6/30/12. | | 4.1 Install Phase One modules of the ERP system by 12/31/11. <br><br> 4.2 Establish a regular training schedule by 10/31/11 for employees to learn the new system and provide feedback for Phase Two. |

**Figure 13-6:**
Translating corporate goals to be meaningful for each department.

# Avoiding land mines in cascading

Some organizations are more political, departmentalized, controversial, or dysfunctional than others. So knowing whether you're heading into a minefield before you take your first step is crucial. But don't despair! Your planning efforts can still be wildly successful.

In the next sections, I cover potential barriers to your planning, so you can (hopefully) avoid these pitfalls and prevent your planning efforts from blowing up.

## Limited budget and resources

If you lead a department, often externally imposed resource and operational constraints severely hinder your ability to plan and act autonomously. For example, your budget may be so constrained that even lining up training for your people to develop staff may not be possible. You're allowed to budget for operational overhead only, and you're only allowed to go off what was done in the past.

If this is your situation, get creative. Be a change agent. Rework your departmental budget, buddy up with other departments, develop a non-expense option to implement your plan, or start your political positioning to get around your roadblocks.

Technology seems to always be a resource constraint and roadblock. For example, the shipping department may not be able to explain why it needs $3 million for a new shipping system, while the legacy system continues to age and create operational drag. The current system still works and gets the job done. The fact that a new system is needed has to be defended early and often. For many groups, getting something like this is a multi-year political battle.

### Alliances and coalitions

Because of resource constraints (see previous section), you must often ally with other groups and departments to get anything long-term done. You may not think that group work is a barrier, but it is because your goals may not align with the other department's goals.

To create buy in, you often have to compromise or co-mingle goals and resources. Think of it like going on vacation alone, versus going on vacation with another family. The competing expectations and agendas often muddy the water, and you end up having a different trip, which often happens to departments that are forced to work together because they can't act alone.

### Conflicting missions

Department missions often clash with other department missions. At the operational level, planning happens in individual groups, whereas organization-wide strategic planning often happens only at an executive level and rarely at an operational level. So there's a huge gap between the folks on the top and the people near the work. Within a system, these groups do whatever they want, and they do it without awareness of the larger whole. The exact opposite happens at the executive level. They plan at a 100,000-foot level but have no idea how to actually execute anything or track progress. Successful organizational leaders have to live in that demilitarized zone between.

### People handling

People are the most important resource in the plan. People add a tremendous amount of value to the equation, but they can also be the biggest obstacle to achieving your goals. When you borrow key players from another department, Murphy's Law states that they won't be available when you need them. Keep other departments aware of when you need their help by communicating frequently.

You'll never be able to do anything alone, so you have to think about others, cater to others, and so on. So sharpen your people-handling skills in all aspects in order to prosper strategically. See Chapter 14 about coaching for achievement.

### Departmental identity

You must be able to know your department's value and identify it for your stakeholders. It may be different depending on the audience. In the organizational environment, the little things matter. Letting another group use your conference room, color printer, laminator, or trucks with a lift-gate result in the right words being whispered in the right ears at meetings you're not invited to. Know what you have to trade and offer.

Also, know what you have that someone else may find valuable. People can go directly to your chain of command and ask for something that causes you a panic and a loss of resources as you struggle to fulfill a last-minute request. Anticipate their needs and desires and incorporate them into your plan. You simply must understand what outsiders find valuable about you and your organization, or you become a leaf in the wind.

### Metrics, metrics, metrics

When you're always asking and pitching for everything you want on a strategic level, you must build in the time, resources, and processes to track everything. Measurements can be an extremely crucial tool to getting what you want. You must be able to prove worth or protection from something that can get you off track at all times. That means you have the data and the fancy reports on tap. You can say, "Gee, boss, we want to help you, but we're already overcommitted by 23 percent. In fact, I'd like more people. So if you can get me the staffing I need, maybe I can take this extra thing on." Hand over a fact sheet that explains it in black and white.

# Ensuring Your Plan Makes Cents

After you've completed your goals and actions, assess the financial viability of your strategic plan. While your action items and goals are fresh in your mind, estimate the costs associated with the implementation of each item.

All the best-laid strategic plans are subject to time and money. In this section, you look at the estimated expenses and the potential revenue. This review helps you make decisions about when to implement certain action items and whether your cash outlay generates the required revenue to meet your financial goals. As with every business, budgets are never big enough to do everything you want to do.

A business can be considered a financial success when it does the following:

✔ Stays in the black and turns a profit

✔ Has a healthy balance sheet (see Chapter 4 on ratios)

✔ Generates good cash flow

✔ Produces a good return on investment (ROI) for its shareholders

Attaining financial success starts with a financial assessment that's based on historical record and future projections. By looking at the past to help plan and predict the future, you can gain much better control over your company's financial performance. A good financial plan gives you a detailed picture of the financial health of your business and the viability of your strategic plan. It also helps you know whether you're getting off track during implementation so you can take action before anything serious occurs — like running out of cash.

To conduct a financial assessment of your strategic plan, take the following steps:

1. **Estimate revenue and expenses.**

2. **Conduct a contribution analysis to determine whether your strategies positively contribute to the bottom line.**

3. **Combine all your numbers in a one-year and three-year financial projection.**

The cold reality is that you're in business to make money. If you're not making a return on your investment (ROI) at some point, you don't have a business; you have an expensive hobby. Ouch! That hurts, I know, but it's the truth. If you don't believe this truth, skip this section. But if you do, your financial assessment concludes with an analysis on your ROI. After all, there's no sense in implementing a plan if it won't yield the desired return.

As an owner, you're either investing in or drawing out of your business. If you're investing for growth, you ought to have a clearly defined payback period and strategic plan to get you through it as fast as possible. Your payback period needs to match up with your owner's vision (see Chapter 6 for more info). Business owners often plan for growth without considering how long it takes to get a payback or developing the action plans to get there.

Looking at how quickly you'll get paid back for your investment forces you to decide whether you're comfortable with the time period. If the time period is too long and the investment is too big, don't invest. Revise your strategic plan by removing a few goals and action items until you develop a plan you're comfortable with. Remember, the plan works for you — you don't work for the plan.

## Estimating revenue and expenses

Expense and revenue estimating is an imperfect science. However, it's meant to give you an idea of the additional cash outlay you need to implement each area of your plan and the revenue you can expect to generate. In the previous exercises of this chapter, you identify potential expenses for action items as well as potential revenue for each target market group you develop in Chapter 9. Here you combine that information with your current operations to get a complete financial picture. Identifying large expenses that may prohibit implementation is important.

### Revenue

An easy approach for estimating potential revenue is to estimate the potential revenue for each target customer group separately (see Chapter 9 for information on finding new customers). Ideally, your market research gives you a rough idea of how much revenue or sales per customer you can anticipate generating. Before you can determine estimated revenue, you need to find out the following information:

Estimated number of customers: _____

Estimated average sale per customer: _____

Estimated number of sales per customer per year: _____

Plug this data into the following formula to determine the estimated revenue in a year:

Number of customers ∞ average sale per customer ∞ number of sales per customer per year = estimated revenue for this year

### Expenses

List expenses associated with any goal or action in the plan that aren't part of your normal operating expenses. Additionally, estimate your current operating expenses by forecasting each item based on how it increases to accommodate for the expected growth.

### Assumptions

As you're thinking about your revenue and expenses, undoubtedly you're making some assumptions, such as the sale price of your products, the cost of materials, your lease payment, and so on. Instead of keeping these estimates in your head, write them down. These assumptions are called *financial assumptions.* You gain the most insight from projecting your financial future when the assumptions that drive the projections are comprehensive and written out.

A list of assumptions is simply a list of givens that you're basing your projections on. Your list should include all revenue and expense assumptions related to running your organization. You use these assumptions in the steps you follow in the "Projecting your financial future" section later in this chapter.

Here are some tips to keep in mind when you develop your assumptions:

- ✔ **Don't overthink this part of your financial analysis.** The goal of developing projections isn't about perfectly predicting the future. Most people have rather foggy crystal balls. Following this exercise can help make your crystal ball a little clearer.

- ✔ **Have a few knowledgeable individuals (your mentors) review your assumptions.** Choose people who will be painfully honest with you. Are you being too conservative or not conservative enough? Are you missing anything that you need to include in your projections?

- ✔ **Consider developing best-case and worst-case scenarios, such as +10 percent growth and –10 percent growth.** Identify which of your assumptions may vary widely and use those to develop a scenario (see Chapter 15 for more on scenario planning). Common scenarios are based on growth rate, number of customers, and product or service price.

- ✔ **Whenever possible, estimate the odds of your scenarios.** No need to break out the statistics book — just answer for yourself which of your scenarios is most likely and why.

If you're not up to developing a complete set of financial projections, you need to at least list the assumptions for the future course of your business. Then construct a contribution analysis to determine the financial impact your strategic plan will have on your organization's profitability. (See the next section, "Contributing to the bottom line," for more on constructing a contribution analysis.)

# Contributing to the bottom line

Just because a market looks attractive doesn't mean that you can serve it profitably. Before your creative folks start churning out cool ads, do a quick contribution analysis. A contribution analysis determines whether a particular target customer group contributes to the overall financial well-being of the company. In other words, is this customer group profitable?

A contribution analysis provides a projection of whether your strategy generates revenues in excess of expenses. If the contribution analysis determines that the dollar investment in the strategy you need to reach this target customer group can't be justified, rethink and adjust your customer and financial goals. See Figure 13-7 as an example. Use the Contribution Analysis Worksheet on the CD and your list of assumptions from the preceding section as a guide to conduct this analysis for each of your target customer groups. Eliminate the groups that don't positively contribute to the bottom line. Use the groups that do contribute to the bottom line in the financial projections you make in the next section.

| | EXAMPLE |
|---|---|
| **Estimated Revenue** (Number of customers × average sale per customer × number of sales per customer per year) | 100 × $1,899 × 2 = $379,800 |
| **Minus Cost of Goods Sold** (Cost of Goods Sold = Unit Cost × number of customers × number of sales per customer per year. If you are a service company, there may not be cost of goods sold.) | $50 × 100 × 2 = $10,000 |
| **Gross Profit** (Subtract Cost of Goods Sold from Estimated Revenue) | $379,800 − $10,000 = $369,800 |
| **Minus Action Item Expenses** (Expenses from action items associated directly with this target customer group.) | $10,000 + $100,000 = $110,000 |
| **Minus Other Direct Expenses** (You may have other action item expenses required to reach this customer group.) | One additional staff member @ $50,000 |
| **Contribution to Bottom Line** | $369,800 − $110,000 − $50,000 = $209,800 |

**Figure 13-7:** Contributing to your financial well-being.

# Projecting your financial future

By putting all your revenue and expense assumptions together and projecting them over three years, you can see in black and white how successful your business can be. Projecting also allows you to grow the business without running out of cash. Growth in sales always incurs additional cash requirements to generate and support the additional revenues. When used properly, financial projections can help you determine what additional assets you need to support your increased sales and what impact those assets and sales have on your balance sheet. In other words, the financial projections indicate how much additional debt or equity you need to stay afloat.

All commonly used financial and accounting system packages come with functions to create financial projections. Use these tools to create your financial projections by plugging in assumptions based on your strategic plan. If your system doesn't allow for projections, use the Financial Projections Worksheets located on the CD.

Your financial projections include forecasting all three of your financial statements. Create projections by month for year one and then by year for the next two years. Follow these steps using the Financial Projections Worksheets on the CD:

1. **Project the income statement.**

   Use the estimated revenue for each target market group that you determine in the earlier section "Estimating revenue and expenses." Plug in the expenses related to your goals and action items and your operating expenses, to determine your net profit (hopefully) or loss.

2. **Project the balance sheet.**

   As sales go up, so do other areas of the business — variable assets (accounts receivable, inventory, and equipment), variable liabilities (accounts payable and accrued expenses) and (hopefully) net income. If your net income plus the increase in variable liabilities equals or exceeds the increase in variable assets, the company has the resources to finance itself. If not, you must bring in additional debt or equity. Use your current balance sheet to determine the various asset and liability accounts in your business.

3. **Project cash flows.**

   Using the information in Steps 1 and 2, project how these numbers impact your cash flow, paying special attention to how much new debt or equity you need to inject into the business and when you need to inject it.

Even the best of the best don't project their financial future with 100 percent certainty. Protect your business by building in a cash flow cushion in case things don't go according to plan. This cash flow cushion, or *compensating balance,* is the act of borrowing or saving slightly more than you need and keeping it in a rainy-day account. Maintaining a compensating balance is a good business practice and can protect you from seasonality, economic swings, and other changes in the business climate.

## Forecasting with indicators

One method of getting a better handle on the future is through extrapolating the past. You can do so by finding a leading indicator that your company's sales revenue lags. For example, an appliance service company may find that an increase or decrease in its revenue may lag behind the change in the economic indicator of durable goods manufacturing by ten months. Thus, the company needs to track the indicator monthly as a viable indicator of the direction of its business. The National Bureau of Economic Research has an extensive listing of economic data at www.nber.org/releases. The St. Louis Federal Reserve Bank's FRED system is also very good and has superb charting capabilities for marco-economic indicators. This information is published regularly and is free to the public.

A few other ideas about indicators you need to understand when projecting or forecasting revenues include the following:

✔ When scanning the future, embrace indicators that don't seem to fit. Remember that you're looking through the lens of today to attempt to understand tomorrow. So don't discount an indicator just because it doesn't make sense at present.

✔ If you hold a strong opinion about a product or an event, don't rely on only one piece of information or indicator. Gather additional information so your projections aren't skewed.

✔ Use the past or your historical perspective to help you connect the dots of the future. However, look back beyond the recent past because, if the recent past was a solid indicator of the future, everyone would get wealthy by relying on the Dow or NASDAQ indexes.

Before moving on to the next section, consider establishing an ongoing forecasting program. Update your forecast monthly or quarterly by scanning the economic and competitive landscape and revising your numbers. Accurate and updated forecasts are critical to effectively implementing and monitoring your strategic progress.

Creating financial projections isn't an easy task, but don't skip this exercise or you'll miss an important part of developing a sound strategy.

Undoubtedly, one of your financial goals is to increase your sales and/or profitability. After you've completed your projections — even if they're rough — double-check that your goals match your numbers. The financials tell you which goals to keep and which ones to cut. Keep the goals with a positive story and revise the ones with a negative story.

# Making Your Plan a Living Document

The bane of any and all strategic plans is that they sit on a shelf and collect dust. Don't entomb your outstanding business strategy in a three-ring binder. Make your plan a living document by using parts of the plan for different audiences. Your audiences may include, but aren't limited to, your board, management team, employees, and banks. You also have different functions in your organization that need different pieces to the plan. For example, a department only needs the goals and action plans assigned to it. The same is true for individuals.

In the following sections, I guide you through creating different versions of your strategic plan for different audiences, and then I show you how to monitor your progress and communicate company direction by using performance management software.

## Piecing out your plan by audience

To make your plan a living document, break it up into several versions, such as the following:

- ✔ **The complete version:** This document has everything and anything you developed in your strategic planning process (yes, even the kitchen sink!). This version includes all the parts listed for assembling your strategic plan in Chapter 12 plus all the support material you collected, such as market research, employee assessments, customer surveys, and so on. Keep all information in one centralized location so you can pull from it in your next planning sessions.

- ✔ **The board version:** The board version is best suited for boards and includes just the high-level stuff, such as the mission, vision, values, strategic objectives, and goals. Exclude the measures, responsible persons, action plans, and so on.

✔ **The bank version:** Banks want a complete strategic plan as well as a narrative description and hard numbers. This version should include

- A complete set of financial projections

- A one-page executive summary

- Bios of key management and staff

- A list of key customers or accounts

- An explanation of financing needs with supporting assumptions

✔ **The management version:** A management version of your strategic plan is your scorecard. Your scorecard periodically tracks the key performance indicators (KPIs). Because the KPIs are tied to goals, your management knows whether you're on strategy. Use those tracking numbers to produce charts and graphs that quickly provide executives with a dashboard of your performance.

✔ **The communication version:** Strategic planning is as much about articulating a strategic direction as it is getting your staff pulling in the same direction. Communicate your strategic plan through your strategy map. Post the map in the break room or another common area so people are continually reminded of the corporate direction.

✔ **The department version:** For department managers to implement their portion of the strategic plan, the corporate plan needs to be translated to a department plan.

✔ **The individual version:** Like with the department managers, individuals need to know exactly what they're responsible for so they can act accordingly. Creating an individual action sheet, which lists an employee's goals and action items, is a great implementation tool. You can use the same sheet as a reporting tool for employees to keep managers informed on their progress.

You probably don't need all these versions, and you may have some special versions based on your company's needs. Either way, you can see how much easier implementing your plan is when employees have the information they need to execute. By creating these different versions, you won't see your plan collecting dust.

As you make use of various sections of the document, you don't want to end up with a set of independent strategic plans. Always make sure that all versions point back to the master document. My company created MyStrategicPlan.com to avoid the issue of versioning and to make it easier to implement a plan by giving people the parts of the plan they're responsible for. You may find the site (www.mystrategicplan.com) useful for your organization and for implementing your own plan.

## Masterful metrics make a measurable difference

Strategy planners want to see lasting, positive results. Whether you're internal to your organization or an external consultant, everyone reading this book likely understands the importance of SMART goals. Chartering actions that are measurable sounds simple enough, but the masterful aspect of a measurable goal is to make sure the metric is aptly suited to reflect non-ubiquitous success.

This detail is important because when you attain goals, you create small wins that deserve celebration. People within your organization must be able to recognize the validity of these achievements. If the measurement of the goal is too weak or non sequitur to a larger communicated vision, you may be giving ammunition to the resistors in your organization.

Almost all types of change create some form of resistance, from at least a small throng of people within the organization. This group of people will harbor skepticism and use it to drive critiques of what's billed as progress. This reaction is human nature to some degree, but a line is crossed when information is manipulated to suggest that the only way things can be "right" is if they fit nicely within the conceptual reality of the scrutinizer.

Leaders need to understand this kind of bias as they move change programs and plans forward. You can see it manifest with a goal's attainment being discredited or unrelated to the true momentum needed. Constructive critiques can make change efforts stronger. If critiques only support pre-existing opinions or reinforce ineffective processes, then you're dealing with a confirmation bias, which only fulfills the status quo. Navigate around this quicksand of consensus because although it looks harmless enough from the surface, it can pull your change efforts downward, slowly but surely.

## Using a performance management system

After you have a strategic plan in place, a powerful tool to monitor your progress and communicate company direction is performance management software. Before you choose a system for managing performance, you want to make sure that you'll get the most out of it. In order to make the most of your software, you need to avoid some common strategy pitfalls by putting in place some of the following time-honored business practices.

- ✔ **Executive sponsorship:** Leadership teams must use and support your performance management software or it can become just another IT program.

- ✔ **Accountability:** Expensive performance management software doesn't ensure success; implementation of your plan depends on solid accountability.

- ✔ **Process first:** The software just supports the strategic management process, so put a process in place and hold those monthly strategy review meetings.

✔ **Rollout training:** Instead of buying a system and expecting it to work, a plan must be in place to encourage adoption and manage the system for success.

Performance management applications or systems come in many shapes and colors. Regardless of your final choice, do note that you'll need to select some type of system to manage your plan if you plan to drive toward continuous execution. Largely, organizations adopt the system that's the best fit for the corporate culture and IT strategy. With that in mind, use the following potential options as a guide to help determine what's best for your organization right now.

✔ **Spreadsheets:** For small plans, you can use spreadsheets or word documents. Consider creating one document that's your strategic plan and a second document that highlights the progress of your strategic plan. A fatal flaw is producing too many documents.

✔ **Web-based applications:** For medium- to larger-size plans with multiple teams and/or departments, use a web-based application for easy access to all planning components. Great systems include MyStrategicPlan.com (shameless plug!), Rhythm, Active Strategy, and Executive Strategy Manager (ESM).

✔ **Enterprise resource planning (ERP) modules:** For organizations that have an ERP system in place, use the strategic management model that's already built-in. Although the deployment can be lengthy and difficult to secure IT resources, the outcome will be stronger because of the direct link to the underlying data. Market-leading ERP systems with these models include SAP, MS Dynamics, and Oracle.

# Part V
# Living and Breathing Your Plan

The 5th Wave          By Rich Tennant

@RICHTENNANT

JUST CAKES

AND PIES

AND ICE CREAM     AND BURGERS

& Deli Wraps

JUST CAKES

Coming Soon!
SALAD BAR

# In this part . . .

This part is where you move from strategy development to execution. You put your plan together in a cohesive, clear document, and then you move to executing the plan. You read about everything from how to empower your employees to holding effective strategy meetings. I also cover scenario planning — how to make the uncertain certain. If you run a governmental agency, nonprofit organization, or small business, this is the part for you.

# Chapter 14

# Execute, Execute, Execute: Putting Your Plan to Work

*I*mplementation is the phase that turns strategies and plans into actions in order to accomplish strategic objectives and goals. Implementing your strategic plan is as important as — or even more important than — your strategy. The critical actions move a strategic plan from a document that sits on the shelf to actions that drive business growth. Sadly, the majority of companies that have strategic plans fail to implement them. According to a *Fortune* cover story, nine out of ten organizations fail to implement their strategic plan for many reasons:

✔ 60 percent of organizations don't link strategy to budgeting.

✔ 75 percent of organizations don't link employee incentives to strategy.

✔ 86 percent of business owners and managers spend less than one hour per month discussing strategy.

✔ 95 percent of a typical workforce doesn't understand their organization's strategy.

A strategic plan provides a business with the road map it needs to pursue a specific strategic direction and set of performance goals, deliver customer value, and be successful. However, the strategic plan is just a plan; it doesn't guarantee that the desired performance will be reached any more than having a road map guarantees the traveler will arrive at the desired destination.

In this chapter, you look at how to set up successful implementation, hold your team accountable, and create a process to monitor and adapt your plan.

# So You Have a Plan — Now What?

For those businesses that have a plan in place, wasting time and energy on the planning process and then not implementing the plan is discouraging. Although implementation may not be the most exciting topic to talk about, it's a fundamental business practice that's critical for any strategy to take hold. As I discuss in Chapter 3, the strategic plan addresses the *what* and *why* of activities, but implementation addresses the *who, where, when,* and *how.* The fact is that both the plan and implementing the plan are critical to success. In fact, companies can gain competitive advantage through implementation if done effectively.

In the following sections, you discover how to get support for your complete implementation plan and how to avoid common mistakes.

## Avoiding the pitfalls

In this section, I provide a list of lessons I learned the hard way. Because you want your plan to succeed, heed the advice here and stay away from the pitfalls of implementing your strategic plan.

Here are the most common reasons strategic plans fail:

- ✔ **Annual strategy:** Strategy is discussed only at yearly weekend retreats.

- ✔ **Getting mired in the day-to-day:** Owners and managers, consumed by daily operating problems, lose sight of long-term goals.

- ✔ **Lack of communication:** The plan doesn't get communicated to employees often enough.

- ✔ **Lack of empowerment:** Although accountability may provide strong motivation for improving performance, employees must also have the authority, responsibility, and tools necessary to impact relevant measures. Otherwise, they may resist involvement and ownership.

- ✔ **Lack of ownership:** The most common reason a plan fails is lack of ownership. If people don't have a stake and responsibility in the plan, it's business as usual for all but a frustrated few.

- ✔ **A meaningless plan:** The vision, mission, and values statements are viewed as fluff and not supported by actions or don't have employee buy-in.

- ✔ **No accountability:** Accountability and high visibility help drive change, which means that each measure, objective, data source, and initiative must have an owner.

✔ **No progress report:** No method is in place to track progress, and the plan only measures what's easy, not what's important. No one feels any forward momentum.

✔ **Not considering implementation:** Implementation isn't discussed in the strategic planning process. The planning document is seen as an end in itself.

✔ **Out of the ordinary:** The plan is treated as something separate and removed from the management process.

✔ **An overwhelming plan:** The goals and actions generated in the strategic planning session are too numerous because the team failed to make tough choices to eliminate non-critical actions. Employees don't know where to begin.

Avoiding pitfalls is easier when they're clearly identified. Now that you know what they are, you're more likely to jump right over them.

## Covering all your bases

As a business owner, executive, or department manager, your job entails making sure that you're set up for a successful implementation. Before you start this process, evaluate your strategic plan and how you may implement it by honestly answering the following questions to keep yourself in check:

✔ How committed are we to implementing the plan to move the company forward?

✔ How do we plan to communicate the plan throughout the company?

✔ Are there sufficient people who have a buy-in to drive the plan forward?

✔ How we going to motivate our people?

✔ Have we identified internal processes that are key to driving the plan forward?

✔ Are we going to commit money, resources, and time to support the plan?

✔ What are the roadblocks to implementing and supporting the plan?

✔ How will we take available resources and achieve maximum results with them?

✔ Are those who need to help and don't work for us going to commit money, resources, and time to support the plan?

You don't need to have the perfect answers to all these questions right now, but just make sure that you give all the questions equal consideration. You don't want to look back six months from now and wish you had identified some big issues that are now threatening your success. If you've identified some red flags, assess whether they're huge obstacles or small ones. If they're big, get them out of the way before you implement, even if it means pushing your timeline out for a while.

## Making sure you have the support

Often overlooked are the five key components necessary to support implementation: people, resources, structure, systems, and culture. All components must be in place in order to move from creating to activating the plan. I touch on these five components in the following sections.

### All hands on deck: People

The first stage of implementing your plan is to make sure to have the right people on board. The right people include those folks with required competencies and skills needed to support the plan. In the months following the planning process, expand employee skills through training, recruitment, or new hires to include new competencies required by the strategic plan. See Chapter 7 for a refresher.

### Show me the money: Resources

You need to have sufficient funds and enough time to support implementation. Often, true costs are underestimated or not identified. True costs can include a realistic time commitment from staff to achieve a goal, a clear identification of expenses associated with a tactic, or unexpected cost overruns by a vendor. Additionally, employees must have enough time to implement what may be additional activities that they aren't currently performing. See Chapter 13 for more information.

### If you build it, they will come: Structure

Set your structure of management and appropriate lines of authority, and have clear, open lines of communication with your employees. A plan owner and regular strategy meetings are the two easiest ways to put a structure in place. Schedule meetings to review the progress monthly or quarterly, depending on the level of activity and time frame of the plan. See the "Adapting your plan as necessary" section in this chapter.

### Plug it in, turn it on: Systems

Both management and technology systems help track the progress of the plan and make it faster to adapt to changes. As part of the system, build milestones into the plan that must be achieved within a specific time frame. A scorecard is one tool many organizations use to incorporate progress tracking and milestones. See Chapter 13 for more information.

### *Make yourself at home: Culture*

Create an environment that connects employees to the organization's mission and makes them feel comfortable. To reinforce the importance of focusing on strategy and vision, reward success. Develop some creative positive and negative consequences for achieving or not achieving the strategy. The rewards may be big or small, as long as they lift the strategy above the day-to-day so people make it a priority. See Chapter 1 for more info.

## *Determining your plan of attack*

Implementing your plan includes several different pieces. Executing a plan can sometimes feel like it needs another plan of its own. But you don't need to go to that extent because I've done it for you! Use the following set of comprehensive implementation steps as your base implementation plan. Modify these steps to make them your own timeline and fit your organization's culture and structure.

1. **Finalize your strategic plan after obtaining input from all invested parties.**

2. **Align your budget to annual goals based on your financial assessment.**

3. **Produce various versions of your plan for each group.**

   See Chapter 13 for ideas on how to use different parts of your plan for employees, management, and your board.

4. **Establish your scorecard system for tracking and monitoring your plan.**

   Check out Chapter 13 for details on building your scorecard and see the later section in this chapter "Using a scorecard to measure progress" for how to use your scorecard to track your progress.

5. **Establish your performance management and reward system.**

6. **Roll out your plan to the whole organization (see the "Rolling out the plan" section for roll-out ideas).**

7. **Build all department annual plans around the corporate plan (see Chapter 13 for more departmental information).**

8. **Set up monthly strategy meetings with established reporting to monitor your progress.**

9. **Set up annual strategic review dates, including new assessments and a large group meeting, for an annual plan review.**

   See the later section "Heartbeat of Your Management Process: Strategy Reviews" for tips on conducting strategy review meetings.

# Holding People (Including Yourself) Accountable to the Process

Accountability is key to successful implementation — hands down. If you and your team don't have to report to anyone on your progress, the plan may find itself farther and farther down your to-do list or at the bottom of your stacks of papers. You don't need an elaborate accountability system, but you do need something everyone understands.

One of the most important pieces to successful implementation is *you*. In addition to your strategic plan manager (covered in the next section), find someone to hold you accountable — a business coach, an executive group, a colleague, an outside consultant, or anyone else outside of your business who advises you.

Don't forget to discuss the consequences for non-performance with your team. Just like rewards, consequences are critical in any action plan. Often, the consequences are removal from the team that's working on the goals. Peer pressure creates such an intense expectation of performance that it causes action, so hold monthly strategy meetings where people have to publicly report on their progress. If you had to give a report in front of your peers, you'd have your act together, right? Just the thought of humiliating yourself in front of the team for non-performance may make you sick to your stomach, so you're going to make sure that you've done your job and are prepared for the presentation.

In the next few sections, you find out about appointing a strategic plan manager, paying for performance, and coaching for success. All these ideas have been tested, and they really work.

## Appointing a strategic plan manager

Charge a key staff member with the responsibility of overseeing implementation of most aspects of the strategic plan. This person is the *strategic plan manager* or *engineer*. This individual makes sure that processes are running on schedule and monitors other staff members responsible for meeting specific goals. He's also responsible for providing monthly reports and facilitating your strategy meetings. In my experience, without a manager, all the good ideas in the world won't go anywhere.

Feel like you need to find a taskmaster? You've got it! A strategic plan manager's job description should include the following:

✔ Is respected in the organization (which allows him to keep you and everyone else on top of their responsibilities)

✔ Understands the strategic planning process and the strategic plan itself

✔ Has a good understanding of the business or organization and has the ability to get along with everyone

✔ Has good attention to detail and is deadline-oriented

Oh, and by the way, the manager can't be you — the business owner or executive. You have enough other stuff to worry about.

## Syncing individual action plans with compensation

A common trend in compensation plans is to pay for performance. No doubt about it; people pay attention when it comes to their own pocketbooks. Linking performance to short-term goals and action items in your strategic plan is a natural connection. Performance-based compensation is a huge way to structure performance plans. Check out *Inc. Magazine's* compensation guide at www.inc.com/guides/hr for ideas on compensation.

Although linking pay to performance is a good way to ensure that your plan gets implemented, it's not the only factor. For additional ideas, check out the nearby sidebar "Creating a strategy-focused organization."

Here are some best practices to make your incentive plan as successful as possible:

✔ Tie incentives to corporate results, team results, and individual performance, where appropriate.

✔ Fit the compensation plan in with your core values and culture.

✔ Simplify a complicated plan so everyone, regardless of education level, can understand it.

✔ Communicate your incentive plan as much as possible.

✔ Involve employees in the process by sending an employee survey before you structure your plan to see what they're looking for.

✔ Shell out incentives in the form of control of one's schedule, cash, time off, company perks, group outings, and so on. Don't be tightfisted: Outstanding results can come from a history of outstanding rewards.

✔ Get your employees energized about the incentive plan by making the plan exciting and motivational.

✔ Share financial and business plans with employees and provide education if they don't understand financial issues.

✔ Don't expect attitudes and behaviors to change overnight: Implementing an incentive program involves a long-term process, not a one-time event.

Remember the purpose of incentive plans is to change behavior and move your whole organization as a team toward your vision. Make sure that your incentive plans clearly link performance to business goals. That link exists to ensure that you reward only those behaviors that lead to accomplishing your business goals.

---

## Creating a strategy-focused organization

Organizations that are strategy-focused are more effective with their resources, have higher employee retention, and make more money because they serve their markets better than their counterparts. And they stay in business longer because they proactively respond to the environment around them. Want to create a culture that's strategy-focused? Here's a list of ideas gathered from a bunch of different organizations:

✔ Be a strategic leader. Lead by example and prioritize your strategic plan over everything else. Stay committed.

✔ Cut out the jargon. Make sure everyone in your organization really understands the plan.

✔ Hang your one-page strategic plan in the break room or another central location.

✔ Involve your staff in the final development of the plan. Ask for and use employee ideas.

✔ Create a *champion,* or owner, for every goal and action. Make strategy everyone's job.

✔ Ask your employees to create the action items to support their assigned goals.

✔ Review the plan with management or the group.

✔ Align the organization with the strategy.

✔ Use a scorecard to monitor progress monthly.

✔ Schedule regular updates. Hold a monthly meeting, one-on-one with the team leaders, where you discuss only strategy. Hold a quarterly full staff strategy meeting to report on the progress.

✔ Challenge underlying assumptions. Revisit and refine the strategic plan three months from now.

✔ Hold yourself accountable through a mentor, personal coach, or business organization.

✔ Link strategy to performance.

✔ Continually scan your environment to identify changes that may impact your strategy.

✔ Reward success! Throw a party when significant goals are reached.

# Coaching for achievement

Think about your favorite Olympic athlete. Do you think the athlete's goal is foremost on her mind every day? You bet it is. That's why you and your manager must act as coaches to get Olympic-level performances out of all your people. Susan Scott, author of *Fierce Conversations: Achieving Success at Work and in Life, One Conversation at a Time* (Berkley Trade), suggests we shift our thinking to "Holding people able."

In addition to focusing on the goal, Olympic athletes are incredibly disciplined. Implementing goals that were set months ago is no different. It requires that same level of commitment and discipline.

Here's where you and your managers need to lead rather than fight fires and do detail work. By acting as a coach, use the strategic plan as your framework to guide your team to high performance. Just like an athletic coach, you need to do the following to motivate and guide your team:

- ✔ **Encourage:** People need to feel like they're doing a good job and are appreciated for their hard work. Coaches say encouraging words to their team members to keep them motivated and engaged.

- ✔ **Support:** Without the right skills and resources, no amount of prodding and pushing will get the job done. Coaches support their team by making sure it has the training, knowledge, and ability to complete the task.

- ✔ **Yell at the right time:** Just like athletic coaches know when to yell, managers need to know when to push their team. A good coach knows when performance is lagging and when to turn on the pressure.

- ✔ **Bring out the best:** Seeing the strengths and weaknesses of your team allows you to bring out the best in your staff. Coaches know how to make people the best they can be.

- ✔ **Monitor performance:** Keeping track of how everyone is performing is another trait of a good coach. With your SMART goals (covered in Chapter 12), you can assist your employees in creating an action plan (if it isn't already established) and keep them on the path toward achieving it. Meet with employees regularly to discuss the status of goal accomplishment.

Coach your team through setbacks or roadblocks. Coach your team for success by recognizing and rewarding employees for achievements.

# Heartbeat of Your Management Process: Strategy Reviews

The monthly or quarterly review meeting is the heartbeat of the strategy management process. In order for a plan to be an effective management tool, it must be up-to-date, guide decision making, and be top of mind. Therefore, consistent review and monitoring of the plan are necessary to know whether you're on or off course and to modify the course if necessary. A monthly or quarterly strategy review is the best way to achieve this outcome.

Over the life of a strategic plan, a company's vision and mission often remain the same, but its goals and objectives probably need revised. Depending on the industry, some businesses can maintain a strategic plan for a year or longer, whereas others have to respond to market changes more frequently. Move ahead with the plan as established, but be prepared to let go and switch strategies as necessary. Take corrective actions quickly to compensate for the dynamic business environment most businesses operate within. In today's ever-changing business environment, who has the time to stop and figure things out? No one. You adapt on the fly and so should your plan. The best way to address this issue is through periodic plan reviews.

In the following sections, I provide a quick look at the differences between strategy and operational reviews, guide you in holding strategy meetings, and show you how to use a scorecard to measure and report your progress.

## Understanding the difference between strategy and operational reviews

Differentiating between a strategy review and an operational review is important. Simply put, an *operational review* is an in-depth look at the big picture, addressing communication issues, operating procedures, profitability issues, and other factors that affect a business, making it unstable. A *strategy review* monitors progress of the company from a strategic level, making sure that the objectives are on track. Table 14-1 breaks down the differences between strategy and operational reviews even further.

| Table 14-1 | Strategy versus Operational Reviews |
|---|---|
| *Strategy Review Meetings* | *Operational Review Meetings* |
| Waypoint level: "highways in the sky" | Runway level: "coming in for landing" |
| Department level conversation about *what* you're working on | Keeping everyone in the loop on *how* your projects are going |

| Strategy Review Meetings | Operational Review Meetings |
|---|---|
| Review of key performance indicators (KPIs) — **are we moving the dial; showing results?** | High-level updates on your projects — **are we on target?** |
| Deep dive into one or two department goals and discuss strategic issues | Escalate issues that require management involvement |
| Take action and adapt the plan | Share travel plans |
| Dept. manager reports out; group discussion/brainstorm | Individual reports out |

# Holding effective strategy review meetings

Holding regular strategy reviews is key to implementing your strategic plan, making the numbers, achieving your company goals, and, finally, making strategy a habit for everyone involved. These meetings give you the ability to manage activities that drive future results and hold people accountable for making sure that those activities happen. More importantly, these meetings allow you to keep your finger on the pulse of your efforts and make any necessary adjustments before it's too late.

So how do you go from holding just another meeting to making these strategy meetings effective and worth everyone's time? Check out the following tips:

- **Schedule the monthly strategy meetings on the same day and at the same time each month.** For example, schedule the meetings for the first Tuesday at 10 a.m. every month.

- **Invite individuals or heads of each department.** Ensure the perspectives at the table are diverse and cross-represented.

- **Make the meeting mandatory — no exceptions.** Having the meeting scheduled for the same day and time every month helps attendees work their schedules around it.

- **Keep presentations to a minimum.** Make sure to have a clock or watch in the meeting room, or assign a person to watch the time for agenda items.

- **Start and end on time and stay on task with an agenda.** See the sample agenda in Figure 14-1.

The purpose of your meetings is for individuals and department heads to give a quick report on where they stand on the measurements identified on their scorecard. Restrict the meeting to reporting on measurements and nothing else, so you can stay on task and remain within the established limit. By following this process, everyone on the management team knows exactly where the company stands in terms of key measurements.

| STRATEGY REVIEW AGENDA | |
| --- | --- |
| Kickoff and meeting setup | 15 Mins |
| Corporate performance review | 30 Mins |
| Department performance review (10 mins per department) | 10 Mins per group |
| Strategic theme or topic (1 or 2 topics) | 30 Mins per topic |
| Wrap up | 5 Mins |

**Figure 14-1:** Sample agenda for your monthly or quarterly review.

Here are some guidelines to use as you establish your meeting structure:

- ✔ **Separate strategy reviews from operational reviews.** Establish a clear separation by (1) holding them on separate days or (2) making a clean break in the meeting from operations to strategy.

- ✔ **Review strategy on a monthly or quarterly basis.** Monthly can seem too frequent for review because strategy, by its nature, is long term. However, quarterly can seem too infrequent and, therefore, strategy won't be top of mind. The solution is to rotate strategy themes and issues monthly. Review one theme per month, so each theme (if there are three) is visited quarterly.

- ✔ **Use open reporting to promote accountability, transparency, and teamwork.** Use goal status and scorecards (see the next section "Using a scorecard to measure progress" for more info).

- ✔ **Create issue-oriented meeting agendas.** Collect strategic issues from your team ahead of time or revisit those that rolled over from the previous strategy review meeting. Pre-prep the issues in order to facilitate a truly strategic conversation.

If problems arise, convene a separate task force team meeting immediately afterward. Task force team meetings should be kept to a time limit, such as 30 minutes, and include only those people who are directly responsible for the measurements or those who can contribute to resolving the problem. The primary purpose of this meeting is to brainstorm ideas and give the appropriate department heads some fresh thinking on how to approach the problem. Everyone puts her best ideas on the table, and the manager in charge goes back and decides which ideas to implement. The following month, the department head reports back to the task force team on the actions he took to resolve the issue.

## Using a scorecard to measure progress

The scorecards you build in Chapter 13 are the link from your plan to progress against your plan. You then track the progress against each goal in your scorecard and use it during your strategy reviews.

Using your scorecard is a step-by-step process that you can implement in your organization. The following list provides steps for using your card. (*Note:* If you don't have multiple departments, ignore the department references.)

1. **Provide each department or individual with its respective scorecard.**

2. **Instruct each department or individual to collect data based on the specific measurement for each goal.**

3. **Ask each department or individual to summarize the data collected for each measurement on its scorecard.**

4. **Direct any questions to the strategic plan manager.**

5. **Request each department or individual to submit individual scorecards to the strategic plan manager for the month.**

6. **Ask the strategic plan manager to update the overall organizational scorecard with the numbers from the department or individual scorecards.**

7. **Request that each strategic plan manager report the status of the overall organizational and department scorecards at the monthly strategy meeting, or request each department head to report the status on his own.**

# Mastering the Art of Communicating Strategy

Good communication unlocks many organizational mysteries, so the fact that communicating your business strategy is critical to your success isn't surprising. When the owner(s), executives, and managers continually demonstrate the link between strategy and specific business decisions, staff members are encouraged to think strategically as well. After the initial goal-setting process is complete, devise a plan for communicating those goals. Your communication plan falls into these three scenarios, which are explained in the sections that follow:

✔ **Waiting until the plan is close to completion to start talking about it:** Instead of waiting, obtain feedback and get buy-in from employees early in the process. By facilitating upfront communication, you head off any resistance that may occur later on.

✔ **Rolling out the plan when you feel it's as close as it'll be to completion:** Consistently communicate the plan to everyone in the organization.

✔ **Continuing to communicate how the execution of your plan is going:** Doing so keeps the plan top of mind and everyone committed to achieving the goals.

In a recent budgeting process in Washoe County, Nevada, one of the county commissioners required that every budget request support the organization's strategic priorities. Now that's top-level commitment! All the departments quickly figured out how to match their initiatives with the strategy.

## Making sure everyone buys in

Don't assume that individuals will automatically buy in to your plan. What may seem clear to the planning team may not be clear to those not as involved in the strategy development. Give employees an opportunity to get involved on the back end of the process by setting up a feedback mechanism, such as a brown-bag lunch question-and-answer forum, a suggestion box, or a one-on-one meeting. Doing so gives employees a chance to respond as well.

By gathering and responding to feedback, you facilitate employee buy-in and build a broader understanding of the organization's goals and objectives. If you don't get people to buy in to the plan, the plan may ultimately fail. You can also take it a step further and share the strategic plan with other stakeholders, like investors, customers, alliance partners, vendors, and so on. An open approach can generate more helpful ideas and suggestions about the future of your business.

## Rolling out the plan

Rolling out your plan can range anywhere from a big, high-profile campaign to a low-key announcement. Whatever you decide to do, make sure to inform everyone in your organization. You may choose to give complete copies of the plan, including background material in appendixes, to certain groups of stakeholders, whereas you may give other groups only the body of the plan without its appendixes.

Here are a few tips for involving people in your plan and having a successful rollout:

- ✔ Consider an annual state of the union message where the finalized plan and vision are rolled out to the entire organization.
- ✔ Make the announcement exciting and get everyone engaged.
- ✔ Give every board member and executive a full copy of the plan.
- ✔ Distribute the entire plan — or at the very least, the highlights — to everyone in the organization.
- ✔ Post your one-page plan or strategy map in a break room or another common area.

- Consider giving each employee a card with the mission, vision, and values statements printed on it.

- Incorporate your strategic plan into the orientation process for new board members and employees.

- Include portions of the plan in policies and procedures, including the employee manual.

- Provide copies of the plan for key partners, such as funders or investors, business coaches, vendors or suppliers, and so on.

## Continuing communication

Launching goals with a major rollout isn't enough. Goals must be visible and repeated to keep the commitment alive. Why not have some fun with your ongoing communication. You can find plenty of creative ways to keep your employees up-to-speed on the status of the plan. Taking it one step further, you can reinforce goals without coming across as a nag by adding humor, inspiring quotes, and customized encouragement to the messages. You can't say thank you enough; keep that in mind when goals are attained.

Here are just a few ways to ensure ongoing communication:

- In monthly e-mail messages

- At surprise coffee breaks

- On computers as screen savers

- In envelopes with paychecks

- In company newsletters or e-letters

- On the bulletin board in a common area

- Through your company blog

- Through your intranet

One client of mine dedicates an entire room to ongoing communication, dubbed *the war room.* The room includes anything and everything about the company's strategy. On one wall is a timeline with sticky notes that display all the different goals and their deadlines. Another wall contains charts and graphs of the company's key performance indicators from the scorecard. And yet another wall contains space for brainstorming and contributing to key strategic issues at hand. The wall also contains an area for capturing items that are hard to measure, such as innovative ideas, customer complaints and compliments, and employee training schedules. The room is updated monthly, and anyone in the organization can walk in and see what's happening with the business.

## How 'bout some reports to go with that scorecard?

For the past two years, a large manufacturing company has used a process whereby each department head turns in a one-page monthly summary linked to the comprehensive corporate strategy. These summaries include the department scorecard and reports of performance on strategy. The reports also explain how well the company's progressing with the defined action plans, what obstacles exist, and what can be improved.

At a monthly meeting, the company starts by defining a series of actionable items based on the monthly reports. From there, action plans are developed and reported back on the one-page summary reports.

The CEO feels the benefits are usually quite substantial. After all, when action items are consistently elevated, department heads know they're responsible for implementing the items as efficiently as possible (that's called *work peer pressure*). The department heads appreciate this process because it raises the bar for everyone and keeps their staff focused on the right things.

# Keeping Your Plan Working for You

A strategic plan needs to adapt to survive changing or unanticipated conditions. A business that develops and executes a strategic plan gains significantly from the experience, and starting with a working model and achieving a tangible plan can be more successful for your business than having no plan at all.

In the following sections, I walk you through how and when to adapt your plan in an ever-changing and fluxing environment.

## Accepting change — the only constant

*Two caterpillars are conversing, and a beautiful butterfly floats by.*

*One caterpillar turns and says to the other,*

*"You'll never get me up on one of those butterfly things."*

What a powerful and fun parable about change. Change, even though we often resist it, is inevitable. In fact, your strategic planning process may trigger changes in your own organization, either in terms of the work done or in the internal structuring of the work. No matter how you present it, people struggle with change. They may need help accepting and adapting positively to the changes. That's where you come in.

Determining which changes require action and which require monitoring is the responsibility of you and your management team. When change is needed, take the following steps:

1. **Make sure that everyone understands the change and why it's necessary.**

   Even if people have been part of the strategic planning process, they may need you to explain the implications of decisions to them afterward.

2. **Respond to people's ideas and feelings.**

   Let people express their concerns and respond to them. If you can't agree, at least be sympathetic about the feelings generated by change.

3. **Develop a planned process of change.**

   Share the process with everyone in the organization or project, so people know what to expect and when to expect it.

Need more information and ideas? Check out the Change Management Learning Center online at `www.change-management.com`.

---

# Change and the Zen archer

While in Japan as a professor (1924 to 1929), Eugen Herrigel experienced Japanese culture and became a student of archery from a skilled and somewhat controversial teacher, Awa Keno. As a master of his venerable technique, Keno became disenchanted with traditional approaches to the practice of archery. He began to refer to long-respected ways of training as "kind of a hereditary disease," which led him to develop his own style of shooting even while being considered a lunatic for doing so. The essence of his style was to hone proper skills as a foundation and then train one's mental and spiritual energy to enter into the absolute way of performance and achievement.

As Keno's student, Herrigel wove his appreciation of Zen Buddhism into his lessons, which inspired his writing for *Zen in the Art of Archery* (Vintage). Here are a few strategic considerations from his approach:

✔ **Transformational culture change can be met with fierce resistance.** Keno wasn't afraid to scrutinize and change ritualized approaches to temple archery, even under great institutional and personal scrutiny. Have you taken stock of your rituals or routines lately to verify their utility in today's environment?

✔ **Foundational training should be approached as a kind of muscle memory.** When training reaches the highest quality possible, achievement becomes a matter of will. What type of muscle memory does your organization need to excel?

✔ **Never underestimate the power of ideas outside of your culture to impact your reality.** The book *Zen in the Art of Archery* was published in post-war Germany, where the concept of Zen was as familiar as sand is to the Arctic. Yet it took hold and continues to influence the way Westerners interpret archery.

Keno was a visionary in the realm of Japanese temple archery. He created a space for the practice of archery that hadn't dared to exist within established traditions. He emphasized the evolution of process into a higher realm of individual awareness, which is what empowerment is all about. While Herrigel's interpretation has its critics, the impact of ideas born from his experience make a difference for readers 60 years later. Takeaway: Lessons in leading change are timeless.

# *Adapting your plan as necessary*

Never lose sight of the fact that strategic plans are guidelines, not rules. Deviating from your plan is okay, but you need to understand why you make a course correction. Figure 14-2 gives a visual decision map to help you determine whether you need to adapt your plan.

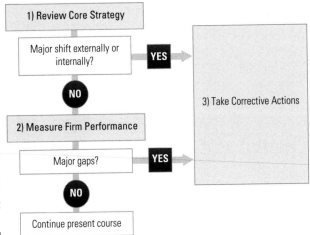

**Figure 14-2:**
To adapt or
not to adapt
your plan.

1) Review Core Strategy

Major shift externally or internally? → **YES** → 3) Take Corrective Actions

**NO**

2) Measure Firm Performance

Major gaps? → **YES**

**NO**

Continue present course

Every three months or so, evaluate the plan implementation by asking these key questions:

- ✔ Will the goals be achieved within the time frame of the plan? If not, why?

- ✔ Should the deadlines be modified? (Before you modify deadlines, figure out why you're behind schedule.)

- ✔ Do we need to renegotiate when folks from other departments are going to be needed? Why?

- ✔ Are the goals and action items still realistic?

- ✔ Should the company's focus be changed to put more focus on achieving the goals?

- ✔ Should the goals be changed? (Be careful about making these changes — know why efforts aren't achieving the goals before changing the goals.)

- ✔ What can be gathered from this adaptation to improve future planning activities?

Adapt your plan according. Always keep copies of past plans and include an updated date in the footer of the document.

Remember that implementation is the most difficult part of the planning process. No one factor from the preceding list makes or breaks the successful implementation of the strategic plan. However, when these areas are considered and acted on, the chances for successful implementation are greatly improved. Most importantly, a business that has a strategic plan and implements it is ahead of 90 percent of the companies that have no plan at all.

# Chapter 15

# Scenario Planning: Answering the What Ifs

. . . . . . . . . . . . . . . . . . . . . . . . . . . . . . . . . . . . . . . . . . . . . .

*In This Chapter*

▶ Planning for short-term risks and uncertainties

▶ Developing potential future operating environments

▶ Linking future scenarios with your overall organizational strategies

. . . . . . . . . . . . . . . . . . . . . . . . . . . . . . . . . . . . . . . . . . . . . .

*B*ecause none of us can predict the future, we have to rely on a combination of instincts and research so we can see the future a little more clearly. Although some consider scenario planning an exercise in mapping uncertainty, I subscribe to the philosophy of Pierre Wack, world-renown leader in scenario planning, who sees it as an exercise in isolating certainties.

In this chapter, I guide you through creating scenarios and possible actions to address short-term or immediate uncertainties as well as building longer-term scenarios for possible future operating environments. In both cases, you explore strategic thinking exercises intended to solidify and refine your core business strategy. Because strategic planning is about making decisions, scenario planning is a tool to help you feel confident that your decisions are the best ones, based on moving from uncertainty to certainty.

# Grasping the Concept: What Is Scenario Planning?

*Scenario planning* is a way of simplifying a complex future by providing the opportunity to ask the what-if questions and to rehearse how you may respond should a certain event or trend happen in the future. Ultimately, no matter how good your plans and research are, all your knowledge is about the past, and all your decisions are about the future. Scenario planning faces up to this dilemma, confronting you with the need to acknowledge that you don't, and can't, know the future. Pierre Wack sums up the outcome that scenarios seek to change our mental maps of the future.

Scenario planning was first developed and used by the U.S. Air Force during World War II. It gained acknowledgement in the business world when Shell Oil utilized scenario planning techniques to predict the oil crisis of the 1970s. For organizations, scenario planning provides an invaluable opportunity to have a strategic discussion around key drivers and critical uncertainties in your operating environment.

Scenarios aren't an end in themselves. They're a management tool to improve the quality of organizational decision making. You may not always have time to do scenario planning, but consider doing a scenario analysis to push the bounds of your thinking. You never know what you may come up with. Use scenario planning in the following situations:

- ✔ When the CEO and her core thinkers need to push their planning horizon far into the future to sharpen their perspectives
- ✔ When you're starting to update your plan and need to re-imagine your vision, especially if the future is less than clear
- ✔ When you're starting from scratch and want a robust way to ensure you're developing a strategic direction that incorporates all the environmental trends
- ✔ When you're trying to get your team to think outside of the box
- ✔ When you want to develop mini action plans for short-term risks

With scenario planning, you're imagining not just one but a variety of future possibilities. All the great opportunities in the world aren't enough unless you have contingencies in place. And remember, you're not only preparing for unexpected threats but also trying to foresee unanticipated opportunities.

# Tackling Your Short-Term Uncertainties

Although big, game-changing driving forces may present an array of opportunities and threats, a number of smaller scenarios hit closer to home — the *what ifs*. These scenarios are short-term uncertainties that tend to keep you up at night. A great way to test the waters of scenario planning is to build out a few scenarios based on one of your known short-term uncertainties or risks.

This exercise can be accomplished in one or two meetings and is much less resource-intensive than the extensive scenario planning explained in "Confronting Your Longer-Term Futures."

In the following sections, I walk you through this exercise by providing example questions to help you identify your immediate risks and giving you the steps you need to build a scenario plan for those risks.

# Identifying immediate risks

To build a set of short-term scenarios, you first have to identify one variable or area of uncertainty. Certainly, you can repeat this exercise numerous times, but for simplicity's sake, I recommend tackling one risk at a time. Ask yourself the following questions to help you identify which variable you want to use:

- ✔ What if sales are flat this year or sales decline by 20 or 30 percent?
- ✔ What if sales increase rapidly, such as 25 percent or more?
- ✔ What if accounts receivable collections slow by 30 days?
- ✔ What if banks increase interest rates by several percentage points?
- ✔ What if our biggest customer goes out of business or we lose our biggest client?
- ✔ What if our competitors actively pursue our accounts?
- ✔ What if we have a major public relations crisis, such as a bad product or a lawsuit?
- ✔ What if we find out that important information from our company found its way into the hands of our competitors?

You may identify with one of these variables. If not, select one that's most pressing to your immediate concerns or uncertainties.

# Constructing possible alternative outcomes

After figuring out what your short-term variable or uncertainty is (see preceding section), you want to develop other possible outcomes — or basically, plan for the what-if scenario. Here are the steps to building a short-term scenario plan:

1. **Define a time frame for the scenario.**

   Some events may occur in 20 years, some in 2. But you can't work with indefinite, open-ended scenarios. For this exercise, your time frame will likely be within the next several years because you're addressing short-term uncertainties.

2. **Establish the primary variable in your scenarios.**

   Use the questions listed in the preceding section to determine your variables. Alternatively, you can use current and future trends outside of the company. Assess ways in which these trends may present opportunities or threats to your business. Check out Chapter 10 for a list of current and future trends.

3. **Clearly articulate the scenario with a problem statement.**

   On a white board, write down "What if _____?" or "What happens if _____?" and fill in the blank. For example: "What if we lose our biggest client, resulting in a 50 percent decrease in revenue?" or "What if a public relations scandal ruins our reputation or brand image?"

4. **Create a compelling headline or working title for the scenario.**

   Something like "ABC Company Takes Its Production In-House" or "Partner in Company X Sued over Malpractice" can work.

5. **Flesh out the details of the scenario.**

   Clarify the exact situation your company would be in if the scenario actually happened.

6. **Develop a trigger point and an action.**

   Know when to execute the action plan if the scenario should occur by having a clear trigger point. (The *trigger point* is when your variable becomes a reality.) For example, a trigger point may be housing starts declining 10 percent per month for 6 months in a row.

   Then write down your action plan by listing in detail the top five steps you'll take. Design these steps to be clear and concise so they're not subjective when put into effect.

If you run several scenarios, you may see a range of choices come up that identify potential threats and opportunities. Many of these choices can go unnoticed if you focus exclusively on your organization's present-day situation.

---

# The butterfly effect

We've all seen and heard the unsettling headlines pointing to a business slowdown in the newspapers and in national news: "Home Foreclosures Skyrocket," "Housing Market Continues Slump," "Disappearing Sales Tax Revenue," and "Credit-market Contagion From US Subprime Crisis Affects Global Economy."

Most of us consider such trends to be too national to have local impact. However, the chatter in our local business community indicates otherwise as people are citing slower decisions with contracts, capital expenditures, and other big commitments. Human nature is to ignore the bad news rather than pay attention to it. Whether you think you're immune to this slowdown or not, consider the ramifications of disregarding such an economic change. Would you sleep better if you had a clear idea how to mitigate real risks in your business operations? One way to mitigate the uncertainty of the present is to plan for the future.

You may be familiar with the *butterfly effect*, which theorizes that something seemingly innocuous, such as a butterfly's wings, may be the catalyst for something larger, such as a tornado. Having a simple action plan for a couple of potential scenarios that may impact you is well worth your time. So if the impossible happens, all you need to do is implement the plan instead of scrambling to figure out what to do. A scenario plan will help you do just that.

# Confronting Your Longer-Term Futures

Scenarios are short, internally consistent narratives of possible futures; they're not predictions. Some uncertainties aren't as pressing as others, such as those that may occur in the far future. In the previous section, you explore how to plan for immediate risks. In this section, I show you how to plan for longer-term uncertainties. Organizations know that longer-term uncertainties exist, but they often don't want to address them because they're not as pressing or as critical today.

## Thinking about the big what ifs

The most significant trends likely to affect the larger world are those forces that are the big what ifs — the *driving forces*. These situations tend to push your thinking and are usually classified as the *big unknowns*. Draw from your research in Chapter 10 for this section. The forces generally fit in one of four categories:

- **Political issues:** You may need to handle electoral concerns, such as who's going to be the next president. Legislative changes can affect tax policies, and regulatory issues can include figuring out what to do if Microsoft were to go under.

- **Economic issues:** Macroeconomic trends and forces shape the economy as a whole. How does the price of crude oil impact the cost of running your business? Microeconomic dynamics are also a factor. What will your competitors do? How does the very structure of the industry change? And within the company itself, will you be able to find the skilled employees you need?

- **Social dynamics:** This area includes specific demographic issues, such as how influential youth may be in ten years, and softer issues of values, lifestyle, demand, or political energy, such as people getting bored with online chatting.

- **Technological issues:** In this category, you deal with direct access, such as how high-bandwidth wireless affects landline telephones; enabling technologies, such as nanotechnology bringing in the next chip revolution; and indirect technology, such as biotech evolving past medicine into mainstream full-body entertainment.

Identifying which of the big what ifs may impact your firm is the key to scenario planning for these forces. Some of these scenarios may seem far-fetched, whereas others are quite a bit more likely.

The goal in scenario planning isn't to create one specific future. Instead, by drawing attention to key drivers and exploring how they push the future in different directions, planners create an array of possibilities that result in the ability to make crucial decisions today. Then you connect the like themes from all the scenarios to your strategy by updating or adapting your plan or developing an entirely new strategic direction.

## Building alternative futures

Ready to step into your future? Use this section as a guide to run scenarios with your team. But first, how many scenarios should you develop? Normally, in the traditional approach, you should create between two and four possible futures for each variable.

Don't feel compelled to develop a complete strategy for each scenario. Instead, take the exercise through the following steps and then refer to the next section, "Connecting scenarios to strategy," to develop your action plan.

If you want to see an example as you review this process, go to www.scenario thinking.org, click Scenario Thinking in Practice, and then click RSM MBA 2010 Scenarios. Although this process is slightly simplified, Figure 15-1, which is the Future of the City Centre 2025 scenario, provides a good look at the outcome.

**Sustainability**

**Green Clusters**
- Steady economic growth
- Government spending in infrastructure
- Community clusters develop
- Inter-cluster transportation
- Online dominant businesses
- Urban agriculture
- Utilize advanced technologies

**Empowerment**
- Economic transformation
- High investment in sustainability
- People move to city center
- Green lifestyle/transportation in style
- Waste in food, cradle to cradle
- Businesses in city center
- Whole Foods Market

**Emotional Value**

**Spiral of Destruction**
- No action on sustainability
- Economic depression
- Edge cities grow city center doesn't
- Corporations decline
- Commodities in demand
- Tension increase leading to war
- No government spending

**Business as Usual**
- No drastic improvement in sustainability
- Recession becomes new normal
- Edge cities decline big cities grow
- Gradual decline in climate stability
- 7.8 billion people on earth
- Economic cycles shorten
- Oil crisis
- Government spends on infrastructure
- Fast paced, high stress life

**Figure 15-1:**
Future of
City Centers
Scenario
2025.

*Developed by Sander de Iong, Secretary General Rotterdam IAB, EDBR*

Here are the straightforward steps to building scenarios:

1. **Establish a clear-cut decision(s) focus.**

   Instead of starting with a view of all the possible trends impacting your organization, identify the major issue or decision you're facing, such as siting of a new plant, entering into a global alliance, entering a new market, or revamping product distribution channels. By tying scenarios to needed decisions, you effectively link them to specific planning needs from the beginning and prevent the exercise from straying off into overly broad generalizations about the future of society or the global economy.

2. **Identify key drivers of change.**

   Identify the primary driving forces that affect your company and industry. (See the previous section "Thinking about the big what ifs" for more info on identifying your drivers.)

   Drivers fall into two categories: predetermined elements or critical uncertainties. *Predetermined elements* are relatively stable or predictable, like demographic shifts. (See Chapter 10 for a list of these trends.) *Critical uncertainties* are unstable or unpredictable, such as consumer tastes, government regulations, natural disasters, or new technologies or products. A critical uncertainty is an uncertainty that's key to the decision you focused on from Step 1. Sometimes phrasing these uncertainties as questions can help you clarify them.

3. **Select the two most important drivers.**

   Don't complicate scenarios by selecting too many drivers. Restrict yourself to formulating three or four scenarios with sharply contrasting futures: (1) the baseline, business-as-usual, world-as-it-is scenario; (2) the scenario that one driver alone dominates; (3) the scenario that the second driver alone dominates; and (4) one with both drivers present. See Figure 15-1 for an example.

   These drivers are the different directions in which a critical uncertainty may play out. Each scenario provides a different answer to the decision. Each answer presents myriad implications that fundamentally change the business environment.

4. **Develop the scenario outline.**

   Give each scenario a creative name. Establish a timeline and brainstorm the future state by writing a short internally consistent story of the future. See the "Considering Example Scenarios" section for examples of scenario names and outlines.

5. **Determine implications of each scenario.**

   Within each scenario, determine the implications for the issue or decision specified at the outset. If one of the scenarios seems unlikely, eliminate it at this time. Discuss with your organization what your decision or business response should be. By doing so, you can rehearse responses to those possible futures and spot them as they begin. Discussing your decision also raises people's awareness of what's going on in the world and their understanding of how they interpret what they see to be pro-active to signals.

6. **Summarize overall strategies.**

Luckily, you don't choose amongst the scenarios or have to rank or rate the probability of them occurring. Rather, you use them all to help form consensus about the world and to recognize which ones are in play at any given time. Move from exercise to execution by identifying and taking action on strategies that work across multiple scenarios.

## Connecting scenarios to strategy

In the beginning of your scenario planning, make a strong connection with scenarios and strategy by choosing a decision or issue (refer to Step 1 from the list in the preceding section) that has significant strategic implications to your organization. After doing that and completing the remaining steps, use one of the following four approaches (listed from easiest to hardest) to con-nect your scenarios with strategic decision making:

- ✔ **Evaluate a specific strategic decision.** For some short-term uncertain-ties, you may need more fully developed scenarios to help you arrive at a definitive decision or action. Decisions may include investing in a new plant or entering a new market. This question is likely the same as you called out in Step 1, but the outcome is clearly defined to help you reach a go or no-go decision based on possible operating conditions devel-oped in the scenarios.

- ✔ **Evaluate your existing strategy.** Determine your strategy's effectiveness in a range of business conditions by testing its success under each of the four scenarios you developed in the "Building alternative futures" section. Identify modifications or shifts that require attention.

- ✔ **Develop your strategy based on a single scenario.** This approach is based on selecting one of the scenarios as a starting point and focus for strategy development and then using the other scenarios to test the strategy's viability and assess the need for tweaks.

- ✔ **Develop your strategy to address all scenarios.** This approach is the most robust to linking scenarios to strategy because it requires the development of a resilient strategy that can deal with wide variations in business conditions found in the four scenarios you developed earlier in the "Building alternative futures" section. You can expect this strategy development to require additional time because a repetitious process is necessary to create a comprehensive yet coordinated strategy.

# Considering Example Scenarios

Major corporations and research firms often develop and share future scenarios specific to an industry's future or to address major global problems. In this section, I provide several examples that may be relevant to your organization. Although you may not be able to use these scenarios in total because they weren't created to solve your specific business issue, often you can use them as inputs to your scenario planning process.

 Want more? You can find an outstanding library of scenarios compiled by Daniel Eramsus, professor and scenario planning pioneer, at www.scenario thinking.org. Since 1996, post-graduate MBA students have published scenarios about the future of the information society online as part of his classes on scenario thinking at the various business schools around the world. This site includes more than 100 scenarios (and growing) on everything from climate change to the future of work.

## Shell energy scenarios to 2050

Shell Oil continues to be the leader in scenario planning, with a specific eye toward the impact of oil on our society, economy, and environment.

Here's a quick overview of the drivers and the two scenarios Shell developed in its "Shell Energy Scenarios to 2025" report:

**Key Drivers:** The three key driving forces are (1) step-change in energy use, (2) supply will struggle to keep pace, and (3) environmental stresses are increasing. World population is set to increase 40 percent by 2050. History has shown that as people become richer, they use more energy.

**Scenario 1 — Scramble:** Under this scenario, policymakers pay little attention to more efficient energy use until supplies are tight. Greenhouse gas emissions aren't seriously addressed until major climate shocks exist.

**Scenario 2 — Blueprints:** Under this scenario, growing local actions begin to address the challenges of economic development, energy security, and environmental pollution. A price is applied to a critical mass of emissions, giving a huge stimulus to the development of clean energy technologies, such as carbon dioxide capture and storage, and energy efficiency measures. The result is far lower carbon dioxide emissions.

Shell provides excellent tools for scenario planning as well as fully developed scenarios at www.shell.com/scenarios.

Check out the Explorer's Guide developed by Shell scenario planners for a detailed guide on how to do scenario planning. Just go to www.shell.com/scenarios and click Scenarios: An Explorer's Guide on the left side of the page.

## Cisco's Internet scenarios to 2025

Cisco and Monitor Global Business Network set out to develop scenarios that answered these questions:

✔ What will the Internet be like in 2025?

✔ How much bigger will the Internet have grown from today's 2 billion users and $3 trillion market?

✔ Will the Internet have achieved its full potential to connect the world's entire population in ways that advance global prosperity, business productivity, education, and social interaction?

In Cisco's Internet scenarios report, titled "The Evolving Internet: Driving Forces, Uncertainties, and Four Scenarios to 2025," it identified the following drivers and scenarios:

**Key Drivers:** Cisco's three driving forces are (1) size and scope of broadband network build out, (2) incremental or breakthrough technological progress, and (3) unbridled or constrained demand from Internet users.

**Scenario 1 — Fluid Frontiers:** This scenario predicts a world in which the Internet becomes pervasive and centrifugal. Technology continues to make connectivity and devices more and more affordable (in spite of limited investment in network build-out) while global entrepreneurship — and fierce competition — ensure that the wide range of needs and demands from across the world are met quickly and from equally diverse setups and locations.

**Scenario 2 — Insecure Growth:** In this scenario, users — individuals and business alike — are inhibited from intensive reliance on the Internet. Relentless cyber attacks driven by wide-ranging motivations defy the preventive capabilities of governments and international bodies.

**Scenario 3 — Short of the Promise:** This scenario consists of a frugal world in which prolonged economic stagnation in many countries takes its toll on the spread of the Internet. Technology offers no compensating breakthroughs, and protectionist policy responses to economic weakness make matters worse — both in economic terms and with regard to network technology adoption.

**Scenario 4 — Bursting at the Seams:** In this scenario, the Internet becomes a victim of its own success. Demand for IP-based services is boundless, but capacity constraints and occasional bottlenecks create a gap between the expectations and reality of Internet use. Meanwhile, international technology standards don't come to pass, in part because of a global backlash against decades of U.S. technology dominance.

If you're interested in the implications and potential strategies from these four scenarios, check out the full report at `http://blogs.cisco.com/emerging/the-evolving-internet/`. Scenario developers provide a set of excellent implications and possible strategies for each scenario that can be readily applied by companies who provide devices, connectivity, software or services, and/or content.

# Chatham House's food futures scenarios

Commissioned by the United Kingdom in 2008, Chatham House commenced a Food Supply Project that resulted in robust scenarios that organizations impacted by global food supply and food prices can use to jump-start their scenario planning. The official title for this report is "Food Futures: Rethinking UK Strategy" and includes the following scenarios:

**Key Drivers:** The driving forces are (1) demand for food is increasing because the global population is rising and major developing economies are expanding, and (2) global supply capacity, meanwhile, is struggling to keep up with changing requirements.

**Scenario 1 — Just a Blip:** In this scenario, high food prices prove to be a temporary blip and soon return to the long-term trend line. However, a possibility exists that if food prices fall back sharply, financial speculation in commodities will operate in reverse and lead to exaggerated food price volatility.

**Scenario 2 — Food Inflation:** With this scenario, food prices stay high for a protracted period. They contribute significantly to inflation, but the economy adapts and the existing food system copes.

**Scenario 3 — Into a New Era:** In this scenario, input prices initially stay high as per capita production falls steadily. In response, the system of food production must shift dramatically so increased yields are delivered efficiently through regenerative, rather than purely extractive, uses of resources.

**Scenario 4 — Food in Crisis:** In this scenario, multiple shocks disrupt food production and supply. Prices skyrocket as stocks plummet, triggering food shortages, famine, and civil panic.

You can find additional information, including summary and full reports that contain implications of each scenario at www.chathamhouse.org.uk.

# Chapter 16

# Value-Creating Strategies for Entrepreneurial Organizations

## In This Chapter

▶ Uncovering your personal vision for your business

▶ Recognizing the value or projected value of your business

▶ Figuring out how your business will continue when you exit

Although publicly-traded companies get all the media limelight, roughly 90 percent of the businesses in the United States are privately held. As a business owner, you have some special considerations in your planning efforts:

✔ What's your endgame?

✔ How do you establish the value or projected value of your business?

✔ How will your business continue when you exit?

Although you may not want to think about some of these questions today, each one influences the strategic direction of your company. Many owners have a difficult time thinking about life after their company. However, your endgame is arguably the most important part of your strategic planning effort. And although you may not share your ideas with your staff, you want to have a clear plan for your departure.

Take a few minutes to consider the legacy you want your business to leave. Will it continue indefinitely or pass to your children or employees? Do you plan on cashing out or will your business just cease to exist?

Many entrepreneurs can't clearly see what their businesses look like without them, so they leave their exit strategy to chance rather than intention. But here's the bottom line: The ownership of your business will be transferred at some point, with or without you. Your death or other unforeseen life changes may force the transfer, but through careful planning, you can leave a legacy of how you want your business to run. The sections in this chapter are specifically related to you, the business owner, and help you put the finishing touches on your strategic plan.

In this chapter, you'll look at your own personal vision, determine the value of your company, and figure out how to plan for your company's survival after you leave. This chapter is intended to be an addendum to the rest of the book. Although everything presented in the previous chapters is completely applicable, this chapter takes planning one step farther for entrepreneurs of small businesses.

# Establishing an Owner's Vision

Business owners have the unique responsibility of determining the strategic direction of an organization based on their personal *endgame* — the final result they want out of their business. An endgame can be anything from continual cash flow, to a business sale, to more time off, to changing the world. Basically, the endgame is the business owner's personal vision.

Because your personal life and your business life are intertwined, you should have a BHAG (big, hairy, audacious goal; see Chapter 6) that runs in tandem with your corporate vision statement. This statement is called the *owner's vision statement* and isn't necessarily shared with your employees but is created specifically to develop a single focus point for all equity shareholders. In the next sections, I walk you through developing your owner's vision statement, or endgame, and figuring out how to communicate that vision to your employees.

## Knowing your true endgame

The great thing about being a business owner is you fully command the ability to lead a group of people to accomplish your dream or vision. More than likely, you started your business because you have a deep passion for doing something better or differently than everyone else. Harnessing and communicating that passion can be two of the most powerful things in business, driving success beyond what you may think possible. Although we all know that it takes more than passion to have a successful business, often we lose sight of what originally sparked us to start our business in the first place.

Simon Sinek, author of *Start With Why: How Great Leaders Inspire Everyone to Take Action* (Portfolio/Penguin), reminds us that "those who inspire are not driven with what they do, they are driven with *why* they do it. Any organization can explain *what* it does; some can explain *how* they do it; but very few can clearly articulate *why*."

As you think about your owner's vision, reconnect with why you started your business in the first place. Why do you spend 60 hours a week doing what you do? What's your endgame beyond money or profit, which are simply the results? After you've answered these questions, identify what personal financial gain you want to see. (See the section "Creating a Sellable Business" for more on identifying the value of your business.)

Many entrepreneurial businesses don't have an owner's vision because their founders haven't looked at life outside of business ownership. An owner's vision — even though it may seem far out — is imperative for anyone who's founded or purchased a business.

Take out a notes page and label it "Owner's Vision Statement." List your ideas related to the questions asked at the beginning of this chapter. As you answer those questions, consider when you plan to exit, how you plan to exit, how much return you want to see, and so on. See the "Creating a Sellable Business" section for more thoughts on exit planning.

## Deciding whether to publish your endgame

Two schools of thought exist on how transparent owners should be with their endgame. One school subscribes to the idea that telling employees what you ultimately want to do with your business, specifically in the financial area, is too personal and may look greedy. The other school adheres to the idea that the more people who share in the vision, the better. I think there's danger in sharing personal financial targets *unless* everyone shares in the success. Depending on your management style and compensation structure, strike the balance that works best for you.

Regardless of your choice, I encourage you to share your *why* so everyone — staff, customers, and partners — can connect with your passion, and you can build a strong strategic plan that reinforces your core purpose.

For a public example of an owner's vision that leads with *why* and shares with everyone who interacts with the company, head over to Yoga to the People at www.yogatothepeople.com and see its vision on the home page.

# Creating a Sellable Business

Building value is essential to having a successful company as well as a successful exit. Jeff Clavier, founder and managing partner of SoftTech VC, shares his outlook that "good things happen to good companies." As such, entrepreneurs should worry about only one thing: building great products that users or clients care about. Then, eventually, a good (to great) outcome will materialize. With that in mind, whether you do or don't eventually want to sell your business, applying the key principles of what makes a company valuable makes great business sense.

In the next two sections, I cover what creates value in a business and how to value yours. I also provide additional resources for this exercise.

## Understanding what creates value

Many businesses are never bought or sold because founders fail to focus on what creates true market value. Often owners get sucked into working *in* the business instead of *on* the business, which results in the business becoming too reliant on the owner. The owner becomes the subject matter expert that everyone, including customers, relies on.

To prevent growing a non-sellable business, try following a few of these value-creating activities:

- Creating a repeatable, consistent product or service offering that doesn't rely on you
- Generating recurring revenue, positive cash flow, and strong, improving profit margins
- Systemizing your sales process and deal flow to ensure reliable sales funnel
- Developing coveted intellectual property, such as brand equity, digital and physical assets, customer database, and patents or copyrights
- Acquiring a diverse customer base to reduce reliance on big customers
- Building and retaining a top-talent team because turnover is difficult and costly
- Grooming the leader who will sustain your business if you disappeared suddenly

See how you're doing on creating value by taking the Sellability Index quiz developed by John Warrillow at www.builttosell.com/siq. Also, if you want to dig deeper into any of the topics in the preceding list, check out John's book *Built to Sell: Turn Your Business into One You Can Sell* (Flip Jet Media, Inc.), which is full of great info that can help you do just that.

## Valuing your business

Few business owners are fortunate enough to sell their company when its value is at an all-time high. Even fewer owners who've sold their companies will ever know how or whether they could've achieved a higher price.

Check out the following sections for how to determine your business's value.

# Inspired by success

In case you don't think selling your business is likely or even possible, here are examples of some entrepreneurial companies who sold their businesses. (I hope you're inspired by their success.)

✔ **Mint.com:** Mint, a free online personal finance service that aggregates all personal financial accounts into a single view, sold to Intuit for $140 million four years after it was founded.

✔ **PushLife:** After just two years in operation, this mobile entertainment startup was acquired by Google for $25 million.

The company built a platform that enabled users to port iTunes and Windows Media player libraries into non-Apple phones.

✔ **TweetDeck:** The popular desktop and cross-platform mobile application for Twitter feeds was purchased by Twitter for $40 million just four years after startup.

✔ **Fundamo:** To expand its reach and access, Visa purchased Fundamo's platform that provides mobile financial services for mobile network operators and financial institutions in developing markets in Africa, Asia, and Latin America for $110 million.

## Establishing a value

Many factors can pique a buyer's interest — strong management, quality products, proven processes — but earnings will always be key. Historical, verifiable, and sustainable earnings that increase year over year are most attractive to perspective buyers. With that in mind, understanding how your business achieves the highest possible earnings becomes the road map to your strategic planning process.

The process begins by measuring how well your business is currently managed in comparison with other similar businesses that have recently sold. For example, when comparing two recently sold companies in your industry with similar revenue, you may find that Company A sold for a multiple of 3.5 times earnings while Company B sold for a multiple of 4.9 times earnings. Further analysis may uncover major differences in such factors as ratio of earnings, salaries, or cost of goods sold in relation to revenue.

## Determining your value

The comprehensive approach to determining your value is to conduct a business valuation that includes market comparisons. First, determine what your revenue or net profit needs to be to make your organization worth selling. Then, have an analyst or valuation specialist research the market and do a *for sale* valuation of your company, not an *estate* or *tax* analysis.

Several major databases are available via subscription, such as Done Deals, BIZCOMPS, and IBA Market Data. Business owners can also get valuations from accounting, consulting, and investment banking firms.

The quick, less scientific way to determine your value is to look up sales of similar companies online. Inc.com's website provides a free valuation service (www.inc.com/valuation). Whichever angle you choose, make sure to include in your owner's vision the dollar value you're shooting to sell your business for.

Armed with the valuation results, identify areas you need to fine-tune and improve to create increased earnings and, ultimately, a higher price when selling your business.

# Ensuring Your Business Continues after You Leave

The fact that you'll leave your business at some point is a given. If you've been ignoring this point, you're not alone. People start and run businesses for numerous reasons, and so much energy goes into that process that most owners never really consider how it may end. The reason most business owners avoid this entire discussion is because it's not the most inspiring topic. Nevertheless, setting a clear exit strategy is imperative to ensuring that your years of hard work pay off in the end. Take the self-assessment using the Exit Planning Assessment on the CD to see where you are with your exit planning.

Planning an exit strategy shouldn't begin when you decide to sell your company. Although setting aside time for planning in smaller organizations is hard because you don't have a person who can dedicate her time to strategic planning, take the time to make strategy part of your culture. After the effects of executing your strategic plan are felt, you'll realize that you didn't have time *not* to do it. I promise.

Knowing your options and a few best practices can make this task seem less intimidating. Check out the following sections on how to make the important transition.

## Planning for transition

The best time to start planning the exit strategy is when your venture is launched or purchased. Any number of front-end decisions and strategies can have long-term impact on the operations.

Don't leave anyone out of the planning process because, in a smaller organization, you run the risk of alienating some people. Although you may not think that including everyone on the staff is appropriate, how will it look if everyone but two or three members is included? Be sure to find ways to engage everyone in the process.

The first phase of your transition is called *exit planning* — directing how to transfer the business when you leave. Exit planning is a key part of your organization's strategic direction because it dictates how you set up your business for the long run. The following list outlines the four different ways you can exist your business. Each one results in a different outcome.

- ✔ **Transfer ownership to a family member.** If you've groomed a relative to take over, this approach is probably your most likely exit strategy.

- ✔ **Sell to employees or other owners.** If you have other owners or a pool of dedicated employees, this approach will most likely ensure your business lives on under its current operating state.

- ✔ **Sell to a third party.** Depending on your business's valuation, this approach may be the most lucrative to you and other owners.

- ✔ **Liquidate.** Probably the most unattractive, this exit strategy is often used when no other options exist.

The second phase of your transition is *succession planning,* which involves determining who runs the business when you depart. Succession planning is necessary for three of the four strategies listed in this section (not liquidation); I discuss succession planning in more detail in the "Preparing for a smooth exit" section.

Consider drafting your own personal vision statement that includes your exit strategy for your business. This statement doesn't necessarily need to be shared with your staff, but it can guide the strategic growth of your organization. When creating your vision, consider the following: Do you want to grow or stay small? If you want to grow, by how much (see the "Valuing your business" section)? What future do you want to create for your business? Being crystal clear about your owner's vision is really important, because if you're fuzzy on your vision, it will never materialize.

## Considering how you want to exit your business

No matter whether you're considering an outright sale or deciding to groom another person to lead the business, think about these critical factors as you start developing your exit strategy:

- ✔ **Timing:** When is the right time? Timing has an impact on the quantity and quality of buyers. You need to decide when the right time is based on your business life cycle. Ideally, you'll exit when you're on the top, not on the downward slide.

- ✔ **Value:** What's an objective sale value or price for your company? Business owners are often unpleasantly surprised at the low value an outside entity places on their business. Get an outside valuation so you won't be surprised when you're ready to exit.

- ✔ **Succession or sale:** What's the appropriate selection process or training sequence to prepare for a smooth transition? The next section, "Preparing for a smooth exit," discusses the elements of finding the right person to take over.

- ✔ **Income tax:** Uncle Sam's cut can play a bigger role than you may like. Maximizing value requires reducing income taxes as much as possible. Talk to your CPA about the best way to handle income taxes.

- ✔ **Separate self (management) from the investment:** How will you separate yourself from the value of the business? You want the investment to stand alone, without your involvement. To do all these things, you need to slowly pass clients, relationships, and responsibility to other employees in your firm. Often, business owners have branded their last name into the business name. If that's true for your business, figure out whether you can eliminate that tie.

- ✔ **Purpose beyond business:** What are you going to do after the transfer? Don't wait until after the sale or exit to answer this question. Have a plan for what you'll do without your current daily activities. For some of you, having a plan for after your business is sold may be easy and for others, not so much. Take care of yourself just as you're taking care of your employees during this time of transition.

## Preparing for a smooth exit

After you've determined how you can exit the business, succession planning helps you determine who runs your business after its transfer. (This phase is relevant for all exit strategies except liquidation.) While you still have ownership and control, adding your input is crucial. No one knows the business better than you, so take advantage of your current situation and aid a successful succession.

To make sure the succession goes smoothly, update or establish your strategic plan so it can be used as the guide for the person who takes over. This guide helps maintain financial stability and future growth of the company. You want your successor to flourish because, undoubtedly, your financial future is intertwined with your business's future success. Therefore, take adequate time to develop a complete strategic plan so your successors have a steering wheel to guide the business safely through the competitive marketplace.

As the owner, you probably have grand ideas and big plans. But remember not to overwhelm your staff by thinking too big or grandiose. Recognize your constraints and create a realistic strategic plan.

Follow these steps to develop a succession plan:

1. **Write a job description for your successor(s).**

   You know the requirements of the position you'll be vacating better than anyone. Make a detailed list of everything you do and then ask your direct reports to comment and add to it.

2. **Develop a training program for your successor(s).**

   You know the needed skills and knowledge to be competent in your current position. Consider having your successor shadow you in your job, making an assistant CEO/leadership position, or creating a management training program. All these options, or a combination of them, achieve the goal of giving your successor the tools he needs to do your job.

3. **Formalize and communicate the plan to all interested parties.**

   No matter who you appoint to take over or whoever your successor is, someone's feeling may get hurt, and you may end up with disgruntled family members or employees. If you communicate your plan with detailed explanations, people may better understand why you made the decisions that you did. Time can resolve sensitive issues. Make sure to also create all necessary legal documents to protect your business decisions.

4. **Create a management letter for your spouse (or significant other).**

   In the event of an untimely transfer, your spouse (if you have one) needs to know how you want to handle the situation, what your current goals are, who can be trusted and relied on in the current management team, and who can compose a dependable board of advisors. Write a statement including all these factors.

   If you don't have a spouse, you should still craft a management letter because you need to explain how you want to transfer your business.

   In either situation, provide a copy of your management letter to your spouse or most trusted confidant as well as your corporate attorney. Consider putting this letter in a safe deposit box as well. The most important point of this letter is to ensure that your intentions are upheld in case you aren't there to oversee the transfer.

## *Gathering additional resources*

Assemble a group of trusted advisors to help protect your assets and future desires. When taking all considerations to heart, developing sufficient responses and eventually setting a solid strategy can be easier with outside expertise and resources. The following free, online resources can also help you start your transition process. These sites are brokerage sites for buying and selling businesses, and they can help owners get started and/or see what valuations similar businesses are earning.

- ✔ www.businessbroker.net
- ✔ www.buysellbiz.com
- ✔ www.thebizseller.com

# Chapter 17

# Sustainability for the Social Sectors

. . . . . . . . . . . . . . . . . . . . . . . . . . . . . . . . . . . . . . . . . . . . . . . . . . . .

## In This Chapter

▶ Shifting from a resource focus to a sustainability focus

▶ Involving your board in strategic planning

▶ Understanding government planning

▶ Thinking about competition in nonprofits

. . . . . . . . . . . . . . . . . . . . . . . . . . . . . . . . . . . . . . . . . . . . . . . . . . . .

$S$trategic planning in *social sectors,* specifically defined as the government and nonprofit organizations, is becoming more and more common for several reasons:

✔ The communities in which people live and work are increasingly complex.

✔ Social issues are more difficult, more interrelated, and more critical to solve.

✔ Community leaders and executive directors are being asked to be more accountable for the performance of their organizations and communities.

✔ As change accelerates, managers need proven management approaches, often borrowing from the private sector, to help them be more effective with their resources.

That said, many nonprofit and government organizations have been crafting strategic plans far longer than the business community. Private organizations have adopted best practices from this field and vice versa. Many of you may not be running a nonprofit or government entity, but you may sit on several boards or committees. This chapter can help you be a better board member by understanding your role in strategic planning.

This chapter is intended to be a supplement to the rest of the book. Although the majority of ideas and concepts presented in the previous chapters are applicable, a few modifications are necessary for effective social sector strategic planning.

# Moving from Profit to Sustainability

Clearly the big difference between for-profits and nonprofits and governments is that pesky little word *profit*. Social-sector organizations are mission-driven, not profit-driven. So instead of the bottom line being strictly money (although that's necessary to keep the doors open), the real reason for these organizations' existence is public and community service.

In his book *Good to Great and the Social Sectors: A Monograph to Accompany Good to Great* (HarperCollins), Jim Collins talks about how social sector organizations should think about their economic engine not in terms of profit but in terms of resources. Collins says, "The critical question isn't 'How much money do we make?' but 'How can we develop a sustainable resource engine to deliver superior performance relative to our mission?'"

Based on Collins's research of hundreds of social sector companies, the resource engine has three components, which can be developed into goals in the Balanced Scorecard areas discussed in Chapter 12:

- ✔ **Time:** How well does your organization attract staff and volunteers to contribute their efforts at normally lower than market wages? Think about developing goals in areas of *people* and *learning*.

- ✔ **Money:** How stable and sustainable is your cash flow? In the Balanced Scorecard areas, cash flow is covered in the *customer* perspective. Do you have solid programs that deliver to keep your cash flowing?

- ✔ **Brand:** How effective are you at developing relationships and emotionally connecting with potential supporters? Managing your brand is part of the *operational* area.

With these components, you can develop revenue goals to create an effective resource engine. (See Chapter 13 for tips on goal writing.) And these types of goals make more sense to your staff and board, instead of talking about profit.

# Getting Your Board on Board the Planning Effort

Your organization's governing or policy board plays an important part in your strategic planning efforts. The degree of influence boards have varies from nonprofit to government organizations. But in some form or fashion, these appointed or elected members are responsible for defining the organization's purpose and mission, articulating the strategic priorities for the planning year, and monitoring the execution of the plan.

In the following sections, I help you figure out what your board members should be doing and how to get to those desirable end results by taking different actions when necessary.

## Defining the role of the policy board

The elected or volunteer governance aspect of both nonprofits and government entities adds another layer to the planning process. Clarifying their role helps leverage the board's expertise as well as streamline a process that can get unwieldy. So what are the roles of the policy board, board of directors, board of county commissioners, the city council, and so on?

Effective policy board members should do the following:

- ✔ Focus their attention on their policy-making role and stay out of the day-to-day.
- ✔ Establish a clear set of priorities for the organization.
- ✔ Hold the staff accountable for achieving the established priorities through regular meetings and tying budget requests to the strategic plan.
- ✔ Listen and acknowledge staff recommendations regarding the execution of the plan.
- ✔ Concentrate their resources on being more effective at policy making.

## Being tight on the ends and loose on the means

Being *tight on the ends* involves building a strong commitment and understanding of objectives and goals of your organization and its board. Although you write the objectives and goals in ink, create the action items in pencil. Allow those who are responsible for the goals — that is, your board — to develop their own methods to best achieve the goals. Hence, be *loose on the means.*

Many strategic planning experts recognize the importance of flexibility and authority in the implementation of a strategic plan. Those people involved in the implementation process need to have enough flexibility and authority to be creative and responsive to new developments — without having to reconstruct an entire strategic plan. Flexibility is important because adjustments are necessary when planning for an uncertain future. An organization's objectives and goals are much less likely and far more difficult to change than the programs and activities planned to achieve them.

Say, for example, that an organization's goal is to increase new customers by 10 percent this month. In order to achieve this goal, corporate headquarters creates a sales promotion as an action item. The local employees realize that a major conflicting event is occurring in their community that may hinder the success of their promotion. Clearly, those responsible for implementing the promotion need to adjust the program plan without changing the original goal (to increase new customers). Among their options are an extended promotion or a new date altogether.

# Planning for Government Entities

Government planning reaches farther than business planning because most plans — whether community cultural plans, regional tourism plans, county plans, or neighborhood development plans — exist outside the realm of any single agency. Therefore, successful planning requires enough authority and resources to assure the plans' intentions are fulfilled. Basically, the majority of for-profit planning takes a single entity approach instead of a community or regional scale approach. When you're planning for a single organization, boundaries, authority, and responsibilities are well defined. When the planning scale expands beyond individual organizations to include a community, different methods are required.

The following sections highlight the key areas where planning for government entities differs from private sector planning.

## Recognizing how government planning works

Because government entities operate as monopolies in most cases, have elected boards that change every four to six years, and provide services that are legislated instead of based on market demand, these organizations must recognize how those factors affect their planning. In the following sections, I show you how to accommodate some factors that affect government strategic planning.

### Leadership

Leaders must win internal and external support for strategic planning. Often the agency that initiates a plan deliberately seeks community leaders outside its own organization to head the planning. This strategy helps demonstrate that the planning is intended to benefit the whole community. Cross-agency cooperation requires leadership and dedication to get the plan completed and executed.

### Governing board

Your governing board is a broadly representative steering committee of between 10 and 15 members, which you put together to oversee the planning. In government planning, a few initiators may identify a larger group of community leaders to form a temporary steering committee. This committee brings more authority and resources to the planning table. Additionally, you can form cross-agency or departmental task forces around key priorities or goals to help facilitate the implementation. Both the steering committee and the task forces help cut across agency and departmental lines.

### Power and politics

Power and political conflict can be volatile enough to derail planning from its course. Here are a few examples:

- ✔ A regional cultural tourism plan can run up against agencies with competing interests.

- ✔ Culture-war based political agendas can erupt in public planning.

- ✔ Public-sector initiatives too closely associated with one mayor or county commission can be dismantled by their successors.

- ✔ Even an uncontroversial issue like arts education can evoke conflict when competitive grants for implementation are at stake.

No simple remedies exist for these conflicts except to be alert for power issues and try to sidestep the politics before getting embroiled in them. Wise planners don't assume that all people have the same interests. Proactive planners identify potential political power bases and get buy-in at the beginning of the process by recognizing the different interests.

### Values and culture

An organization's culture tends to be more homogeneous than not. Members of an organization, although potentially diverse, have much in common arising from their voluntary association with the group. They share many values; if they didn't, they wouldn't join and stay as staff or volunteers.

Cities, counties, and communities, on the other hand, are more diverse than most private or nonprofit organizations. A plan for a varied community must respectfully accommodate those differences if the resulting recommendations are to be taken seriously. Use assessments that reach people in neighborhoods, job sites, and churches, which represent a community more authentically than one where consensus depends on those who speak up at a public hearing in city hall. Be genuinely inclusive.

### Administrative systems

Community-wide planners may need to create the administrative systems that sustain their work. Often the absence of a dependable means of communication or a system for monitoring the development and execution of a strategic plan can derail the process. Set up good, clear administrative systems that keep everyone apprised of the process as well as the results from their hard work.

### Community involvement

Successful government plans consider the community to be the constituents on whose behalf the plans are made. Here are a few suggestions:

✔ Do a community-wide survey or assessment.

✔ Get your various citizen groups involved in developing your plan.

✔ Hold community-wide workshops.

✔ Provide numerous methods for community input, such as an online forum, a discussion board, a primary point of contact, or a hotline.

After all, people undertake government plans to fulfill a community need.

### Central control of implementation

Central control of a government entity plan's implementation can be quite difficult. Assuring action on the policy and program plans that characterize most government and community-based organizations can hit roadblocks if execution isn't centralized. You can achieve centralized control by appointing one or two people within the organization to monitor the execution of the plan. Everyone in the organization needs to know who's acting in an oversight capacity to move the plan along. With central control, implementation is more consistent and smooth because problems can be addressed and solved more quickly.

## Getting set up for government planning

Keeping with the theme from the earlier section, running a streamlined planning process can be challenging due to various stakeholder groups that are involved. Set your agency up for success by implementing some of the following tips and suggestions:

✔ Identify specific agencies charged with implementation of clear outcomes. Doing so only works if named agencies participate in the planning.

✔ Identify a single, coordinating entity charged with overseeing implementation. In some cases, the coordinating agency or group is created to implement the plan.

✔ Involve respected and representative community and business leaders in your process.

✔ Reconvene the planning steering committee periodically to monitor implementation progress. The expectation of a public accounting for results can be a powerful incentive to act.

✔ Plan for the municipality or county to commission a formal evaluation of the plan two to five years after publication.

✔ Widely distribute a well-designed plan. Describe goals in general terms and actively encourage individual groups and agencies to fulfill the plan as it serves their interests.

✔ Keep the presentation simple and very clear.

# *Determining what sustainability means for government entities*

During the past several years, due to the economy, government entities have been forced to rethink what it means to be sustainable. Fundamentally, a sustainable organization has the capacity to fulfill the elected officials' mission and objectives to provide necessary public services now and into the future. Organizational sustainability isn't an end, but rather a business process that understands the resources needed and emphasizes balance between the present and the future in a dynamic and constantly changing world in order to fulfill the organization's mission.

Washoe County, located in northern Nevada, recently conducted a thorough sustainability analysis due to the widespread and continued economic decline of the region, creating instability in county government's ability to provide core services. One result from the analysis was the development of six financial sustainability metrics with minimum and maximum thresholds of allowability, or ranges of what's acceptable, based on 25 years of historical data. For example, the sustainable range of the percent of general funds budget used for salaries and benefits is between 65 and 75 percent. If the budget percentage stays within that range, a short-term stability and capacity to respond exist if changes in revenue or expenses without service disruption occur. If not, there's instability. This dashboard provides the Board of County Commissioners and senior staff with a real-time management tool to make decisions for the long-term sustainability of the organization.

## Additional resources for government entities

Tons of great resources for government strategic planning can help you in your planning efforts. Here are just a few recommendations:

✔ **International City/County Management Association:** This organization is the professional and educational organization for chief appointed managers, administrators, and assistants in cities, towns, counties, and regional entities throughout the world. On its website, you find a resource library with outstanding articles on numerous topics relevant to the public sector, including strategic planning. Some articles are open whereas others require membership. Check out the site at www.icma.org.

✔ **Good to Great and the Social Sectors: Why Business Thinking Is Not the Answer (HarperCollins):** This book was published in 2005 by Jim Collins as a supplement to his popular book *Good to Great: Why Some Companies Make the Leap . . . And Others Don't* (HarperCollins). You can also find free articles, podcasts, and exercises on his resource-rich website at www.jimcollins.com.

✔ **Internet searches:** If you want to see some examples of government strategic plans, simply search for "strategic plan" in Google or your favorite search engine. The search returns numerous agency strategic plans in the first several results pages.

# *Planning for Nonprofit Organizations*

Nonprofit staff often concentrates on those it serves and focuses less on analyzing competition and allocating resources. However, since the beginning of the Great Recession, this trend is changing. For-profit businesses compete for customers, and their very survival depends on providing services or products to satisfied, paying clients. Nonprofit organizations operate in competitive markets, where their revenues (often relying on grants or memberships) minus their costs don't yield a large surplus.

With a growing number of nonprofit organizations offering similar services, stakeholders want to ensure that the organization provides optimal results for the resources they've been given. Nonprofits are finding that success only increases the number of competitors entering the field to compete for grants. Growing competition in the nonprofit market has made grant money and membership contributions scarce, even as need and demand increase.

Today, nonprofit organizations find themselves competing for a small pool of resources. In order to compete more effectively, today's executive directors are required to understand their competitors, rethink their business processes, create a sustainable competitive advantage, implement business best practices, and increase collaboration where appropriate. I touch on these activities in the following sections.

# Redefining competition with the MacMillan Matrix

To maximize resources and funding, organizations need to focus on what they do best and outsource the rest. Easier said than done, right? The *MacMillan Matrix,* a tool developed by Wharton School of Business professor Ian MacMillan, was specifically designed to tackle this task.

The MacMillan Matrix can help you discover the program areas that are most needed in your community and that you're in the best position to provide. The MacMillan Matrix is based on the following assumptions:

- Nonprofits should avoid duplicating services to ensure that limited resources are used well and quality of service is maximized.

- Nonprofits should focus on a limited number of high-quality services, instead of providing many mediocre services.

- Nonprofits should collaborate so that a continuum of service can be provided with each partner focusing on specific pieces.

The MacMillan Matrix, therefore, helps organizations think about some very pragmatic questions:

- Are we the best organization to provide this service?

- Is competition good for our clients?

- Are we spreading ourselves too thin, without the capacity to sustain ourselves?

- Should we work cooperatively with another organization to provide services?

Using the MacMillan Matrix is a fairly straightforward process of assessing each current (or prospective) program according to four criteria: alignment with mission, program attractiveness, alternative coverage, and competitive position. I discuss these criteria in detail in the next sections.

## Alignment with mission

Services and programs that belong or fit within an organization are in *alignment with the mission.* Criteria for a good fit include the following:

- Supports the purpose and mission of the organization

- Draws on existing skills in the organization

- Shares resources and coordinates activities with programs

### Program attractiveness

*Program attractiveness* is the degree to which a program is attractive to the organization from an economic perspective, such as whether the program easily attracts resources. Here's a list of criteria that makes a program attractive:

- ✔ High appeal to groups capable of providing current and future support and stable funding
- ✔ Need from a large client base and low resistance to program
- ✔ Appeal to volunteers
- ✔ Measurable, reportable program results
- ✔ Ability to discontinue with relative ease, if necessary
- ✔ Promotion of the self-sufficiency or self-rehabilitation of client base

### Alternative coverage

*Alternative coverage* is the number of other organizations that deliver a similar program to similar constituents. If no other large, or if very few small, comparable programs are provided in the same region, the program is classified as *low coverage.* Otherwise, the coverage is *high.*

### Competitive position

*Competitive position* is the degree to which the organization has a stronger capability and potential to deliver the program than other agencies. Most programs can't be classified as being in a strong competitive position unless they have some clear basis for declaring superiority over all competitors in that program category. Criteria for a strong competitive position include the following:

- ✔ Good location and delivery system
- ✔ Large pool of loyal clients, communities, or support groups
- ✔ Past success of securing funding and ability to raise funds, particularly for this type of program
- ✔ Superior track record (or image) of service delivery
- ✔ Better quality service or service delivery than competitors with the most cost effective delivery of service
- ✔ Superiority of technical skills and organizational skills needed for the program
- ✔ Ability to conduct needed research into the program and properly monitor program performance

Five years ago, little funding existed for case management by AIDS Service Organizations. Unwilling to let clients fend for themselves in getting the help they needed, many organizations devoted staff time to this service. At the time, this was a *soul of the agency* program. These days, this program is more attractive (fundable) but has a growing alternative coverage. Therefore, organizations in a strong position to serve the clients well, with cultural competence and program expertise, should aggressively compete. Those in a weak competitive position should get out of the business.

Follow these steps and use Figure 17-1 as a guide to apply the MacMillan Matrix to your organization:

1. **Assess each of your programs in relation to the four criteria; then place each program in the MacMillan Matrix.**

   For example, a program that's a good fit is deemed attractive and strong competitively, but if it has a high alternative coverage, it's assigned to *Aggressive Competition.*

2. **Evaluate which programs are worth competing for aggressively and which ones should be divested.**

   Critically look at your programs to determine which ones to keep and which ones to eliminate.

3. **Identify whether you have any programs that are a good fit with your mission.**

   These programs should have few competitive alternatives, and your organization's offering should be very strong. MacMillan refers to these programs as the *Soul of the Agency* and describes them as difficult business but essential to the members.

 You can download a detailed overview of the MacMillan Matrix at `www.icl.org/resourcefree/macmillan-matrix` or Google "MacMillan Matrix Overview" and navigate to the Institute for Conservation Leadership.

| | | High Program Attractiveness: "Easy" Program | | Low Program Attractiveness: "Difficult" Program | |
|---|---|---|---|---|---|
| | | **Alternative Coverage** *High* | **Alternative Coverage** *Low* | **Alternative Coverage** *High* | **Alternative Coverage** *Low* |
| GOOD FIT | **Strong Competitive Position** | 1. Aggressive Competition | 2. Aggressive Growth | 5. Build up the Best Competitor | 6. "Soul of the Agency" |
| | **Weak Competitive Position** | 3. Aggressive Divestment | 4. Build Strength or Get Out | 7. Orderly Divestment | 8. "Foreign Aid" or Joint Venture |
| POOR FIT | | 9. Aggressive Divestment | | 10. Orderly Divestment | |

**Figure 17-1:** The MacMillan Matrix.

---

## Additional resources for nonprofits

As all executive directors know, the nonprofit world shares information freely and openly. Here are a few resources that help nonprofits with their strategic planning:

✔ *Strategic Planning for Nonprofit Organizations: A Practical Guide and Workbook* **(John Wiley & Sons, Inc.):** This resource was written by Michael Allison and Jude Kaye and is outstanding for nonprofit planners because it provides a comprehensive set of worksheets for all aspects of nonprofit planning.

✔ **CompassPoint's Nonprofit Genie:** This resource provides free information about nonprofit topics, including strategic planning. Check it out online at `www.compass point.com` and click Resources.

✔ **Alliance for Nonprofit Management:** This group is a professional association of individuals and organizations devoted to improving the management and governance capacity of nonprofits and to assist nonprofits in fulfilling their mission. The association's website has a host of free resources dedicated to nonprofit management. Visit `www.alliance online.org`.

---

## *Mapping out nonprofit strategies*

The following strategies are applicable to both the organizational and program levels, adapted from Alan Andreasen's and Philip Kotler's *Strategic Marketing for Nonprofit Organizations* (Prentice Hall). This list helps generate ideas and goals about how your organization can reach its vision. As you review this list, take note of what strategies you're currently employing or ones that you can.

✔ **Surplus maximization:** An organization runs in a manner that increases the amount of resources on hand. Usually, this strategy is adopted to accumulate resources for expansion or growth.

✔ **Revenue maximization:** An organization manages itself to generate the highest possible revenues, perhaps in an effort to establish a reputation or critical mass.

✔ **Usage maximization:** Organizations work to serve the highest number of users of their services. This strategy can be used to position the organization or program for funding or budgetary purposes.

✔ **Usage targeting:** An organization provides services in a manner that encourages serving a specific number or type of constituents. This strategy is used to address unmet needs of specific populations or to cover the costs associated with providing services.

✔ **Full cost recovery:** An organization manages its programs and services so that it financially breaks even, providing as much service as the finances allow. Many nonprofits adopt this strategy in an effort to provide services without entering fiscal crisis.

✔ **Partial cost recovery:** Organizations operate with a chronic deficit every year, providing services that are critical and can't be provided at a breakeven level of costs (for example, mass transit or the post office). These organizations rely on public and private foundations, individuals, and governments to cover the annual deficit.

✔ **Budget maximization:** An organization maximizes the size of its staff, services, and operating expenditures regardless of revenue or cost levels. Organizations concerned with reputation and the impact of trimming services or infrastructure on that reputation employ this strategy.

✔ **Producer satisfaction maximization:** An organization operates toward a goal of satisfying the personal and/or professional needs of a founder, staff, or board of directors instead of the established needs of external clients and customers.

✔ **Fees for service:** An organization provides services to clients for a fee. The fee is typically below market rates and doesn't cover the full cost of providing the services.

✔ **Retrenchment strategies:** An organization emphasizes efforts to reduce internal costs to offset the potential or real loss of revenues or grant monies. Examples include increasing staff workloads, increasing use of part-time or volunteer staff, eliminating services or programs, or reducing non-fixed expenses, such as training or supplies.

Whew! Is that it? I'm sure you'll have all these strategies in place by tomorrow. In all seriousness, pick one or two strategies that you think can be the most effective in your organization and use them to develop the basis of your strategic plan.

# Navigating to new frontiers

As the Boy Scouts of America (BSA) moves into its second century of developing character in youth, the executive leadership team has been rethinking its strategic focus and business model. Why? Because although the organization has roughly 300 local councils serving millions of kids through a wide network of volunteers, its membership has been slowly declining. Part of the problem was the organization's approach to strategic thinking. In the past, the BSA has done what many nonprofit organizations have done and just followed the same steps in creating its strategic plan each year, focusing on the areas that are of most interest to it and checking a box when it's done. What the BSA wasn't doing was taking an objective look at the national or council level to determine where it should really be focusing its attention.

To get the whole organization focused on the right stuff, the BSA developed 17 national performance benchmarks based on the Balanced Scorecard methodology. Called the "Journey to Excellence," this program helps staff and volunteers develop strategies and actions focused on areas that are proven to drive high performance and improve the scouting experience. Through these performance measures, the entire organization is aligned from the local to national level. Built in to the methodology is the ability to modify and adapt in order to stay relevant to young men and women as they grow up in a radically, rapidly changing environment. As Gary Butler, BSA Assistant Chief Executive for Council Operations said, "It is an exciting time for the Boy Scouts of America."

# Part VI

# The Part of Tens

The 5th Wave    By Rich Tennant

STRATEGIC PLANNING SEMINAR 2:00 BOOTH 701

## In this part . . .

**E**very *For Dummies* book has a Part of Tens. This part neatly sections off important things to know in groups of ten. In this part, you discover ten ways to keep your strategic plan off the shelf and dust free. You also uncover some pitfalls of strategic planning and ways to avoid ruining your strategic planning meetings. Lastly, I give you ten shortcuts to maintaining momentum in your strategic management process.

# Chapter 18

# Ten Tips to Keep Your Strategic Plan from Hitting the Shelf

. . . . . . . . . . . . . . . . . . . . . . . . . . . . . . . . . . . . . . . . . . .

### In This Chapter

▶ Making your strategic plan a living document

▶ Avoiding a strategic plan that gathers dust

. . . . . . . . . . . . . . . . . . . . . . . . . . . . . . . . . . . . . . . . . . .

*M*ore often than not, life and daily operations take over a well-intentioned strategic management process. If the strategic plan is one more thing people have to do, it begins feeling like a burden instead of being exciting. By embedding your strategic management into daily operations, completing items on your strategic plan becomes natural instead of something extra. This chapter covers ten quick ways to keep your strategic plan agile, preventing it from landing on the shelf and collecting dust.

## Getting Everyone Involved from the Start

Make your organization's plan everyone's plan. Start by involving everyone on your staff in the beginning of the process. If you look only to the management team, you create a recipe for failure. Employees at all levels are not only a wealth of information but also the implementers of your plan. You need them to feel part of the planning process, even if they don't have a seat at the table.

As you read the chapters in this book, you find references to group exercises and employee feedback. Use this info to help develop a strategic plan that everyone feels part of and assign every staff member a goal or objective. Then, everyone has direct responsibility for achieving a piece of the organization's strategy.

# Deleting the Fluff

The sure death of a strategic plan is entombing it in hundreds of pages of text. Less is more. Delete the nonessential text that just clutters up the page. But what are the essentials of your plan? See Chapter 1, which outlines the major pieces of your plan. Remember the size of your plan is directly inverse to your ability to implement it.

You can find a good example of a strategic plan that doesn't have any fluff on my website at www.mystrategicplan.com/examples.

Your strategic plan isn't a business plan. Your strategic plan is a guide and a road map that tells how to get from where you are to where you want to be. Every part of your plan has a role in clearly defining that journey. Unlike a business plan, you're not explaining your business to the reader. You, your staff, and your board members are the readers of the plan. Your plan isn't a sales piece but rather an action piece. It's a document that articulates what you are and *aren't* going to do.

# Appointing a Strategy Manager

Like any business process, you need a business process owner. Strategic planning is no different. Appoint someone (other than yourself) to run the strategic management process. Anoint him or her as the strategy manager who's responsible for the following:

- ✔ Keeping track of your progress through the use of a scorecard (see Chapter 14)
- ✔ Getting updates from managers and staff on goals, objectives, and action plans
- ✔ Organizing meetings and communications about the strategic plan
- ✔ Keeping the plan relevant by adapting it based on changes throughout the year

# Creating a Strategic Plan Poster (Real and Virtual)

By putting your strategic plan on one huge page, you keep your strategic plan from even touching the shelf (unless, of course, you have a really big shelf). Yes, you need backup documentation, which can be in that three-ring binder on a shelf, but put the key parts of your strategic plan on one page designed for the wall, your internal website, and social media websites. Enlarge the hard-copy page at your local print shop and hang it in your break room or common area. The poster helps keep everyone focused on your organization's strategic direction.

# Hooking Achievement into Incentives

Everyone likes to be rewarded for a job well done. Dangling a carrot out there for successfully implementing your strategic plan is a sure way to get some action. Incentives take all different shapes and colors. The green kind (ahem, money) is always welcome, but you can develop all sorts of creative perks. By paying for performance, you elevate the importance of your strategic plan. See Chapter 14 for additional considerations.

# Using a KISS

When all else fails — keep it simple, stupid. (Sorry, I don't like calling anyone stupid, but that's what the last *s* of KISS stands for.) For your strategic plan to be implemented, everyone in your organization has to understand it. Falling prey to big business lingo and confusing jargon diminishes the effectiveness of your plan. Developing a confusing strategic plan is really easy, so resist the urge.

# Holding a Monthly Strategy Meeting

Groan . . . another meeting? Well, yes and no. Replace one of your regularly scheduled staff meetings with a strategy meeting. Meetings about strategy can be exciting, and people want to be involved. The purpose of the meeting is to discuss the status of your plan. Cross off what's been completed. Troubleshoot if something isn't happening. Make changes where needed.

If your meetings are boring, spice them up a bit. Ask each employee to report on an accomplishment or two. Limit everyone's report to one minute (have someone keep time). Ask people who are having an issue or problem where they need help to list it on the board. Spend 10 to 15 minutes as a group working to solve the issue. Remember, the issues need to be related to the strategic plan; otherwise, they should be discussed at another time. Don't let the meetings run over; keep them to a set time.

You may be surprised at the enthusiasm and effectiveness of this type of meeting. People like to talk about strategy. It's exciting! It's also exciting to accomplish important initiatives. See Chapter 14 for more info about how to hold effective strategy meetings.

# Using a Scorecard

Keeping your plan alive requires constant communication, which can seem like too big a task and may just fall to the wayside. But if your staff doesn't know where it stands, it's impossible to keep implementing your plan. Some people like to play ignorant, and ignorance is bliss.

Use a scorecard to keep everyone in the loop. A scorecard provides a quick snapshot of who's contributing and who isn't. The scorecard allows you to track the monthly progress of each goal by listing the status of the goal. Ideally, you've developed measurable goals and have numbers associated with the status of each goal every month.

Think about your scorecard as your one-page progress report of every goal in your plan. Turn the scorecard into charts and graphs, and you have a quick visual that communicates your progress and is fun to look at. The scorecard may also help employees hold each other accountable for their part in meeting the strategic plan. Chapter 14 explains scorecards in detail.

# Leading by Example

Be a purposeful leader, and your people will follow. There's no better way to keep your strategy alive than through your leadership. Your complete and total commitment is critical to the success of your plan. If you pull back, even just a little, you give everyone a license to slack off. So regularly talk about your organization's strategy. Use it in conversations with clients, customers, and board members. Ask your staff questions about your plan's progress — is it working or not? When making budget decisions, point back to your plan. Does the budget fit into your plan?

# Celebrating Your Success — Whenever You Feel Like It

Too often you're so focused on tomorrow's tasks that you forget to recognize today's successes. Don't wait until the end of the year to recognize achievement. Celebrate small successes along the way! Did you achieve a big goal? Have a pizza party. Take the staff to lunch. Give everyone the day off. Go on a fun outing. No matter how big or small, celebrating successes along the way keeps everyone excited, engaged, and motivated to keep working.

# Chapter 19

# Ten Ways to Ruin Your Strategy Meetings and How to Avoid Them

*In This Chapter*

▶ Improving the success of your strategic planning sessions

▶ Knowing how to avoid typical pitfalls in your meetings

*T*he three words *strategic planning off-site* provoke reactions anywhere from sheer exuberance to ducking for cover. In many organizations, retreats have a bad reputation because stepping in to one of the many planning pitfalls is so easy. Holding effective meetings can be tough, and if you add a lot of brainpower mixed with personal agendas, you can have a recipe for disaster. That's why so many strategic planning meetings are unsuccessful. The sections in this chapter focus on the ten guaranteed ways to ruin your next meeting and what to do to avoid them in advance.

## Refusing to Use a Facilitator

If you were having a party for 100 of your closest friends, assuming money was no object, would you cook for them or hire a caterer? More than likely, you'd hire a caterer. Not because you're incapable of whipping up potato salad, burgers, and homemade fries, but because sitting back, relaxing, and enjoying the party are more fun. Besides, a caterer is trained and paid to make sure that everything goes smoothly. Why take on the extra stress?

A strategic planning meeting is no different. You or someone else in your organization are more than capable of running the meeting, but doing so isn't the best approach. By hiring a facilitator, you can be fully engaged in the strategy and planning and leave meeting process and structure to someone else. Furthermore, hiring a facilitator is better because he or she can remain totally impartial.

Make sure to find a facilitator who understands and runs strategic planning meetings regularly. You want someone who can keep the meeting on task and guide the process so you achieve the desired outcome of a strategic plan. Outline the process by

✔ Sitting down with the facilitator prior to the meeting

✔ Making sure he fully understands what success looks like to you

✔ Clearly explaining your desired outcome, what business you're in, the strategic issues you're facing, and the dynamics of your team

The best way to find a facilitator is through referrals. Tap in to your business associates or your business networks for their contacts. Check out Chapter 3 for a list of what to look for in a good facilitator.

# Neglecting to Conduct Any Research Before the Meeting

Picture this: You pick a date or series of dates for your strategic planning meetings, and the next thing you know, it's the day before the meeting. You get so caught up in the day-to-day operations that you don't have time to think strategically about your business. And thinking strategically is necessary in order to set up your strategic planning meeting effectively.

If you neglect to conduct external and internal research before the meeting, you get into your session and realize you don't have the information you need in order to make sound strategic decisions. The only way to have a solid strategy is to incorporate information about your external environment and your internal operations. The chapters in Part III help you identify the types of data and information you need to research for your strategic planning effort.

Some research is better than none. So if you find yourself in a pinch the day before or the day of the meeting, do what you can to get data about your customers' needs, your competitors' actions, and your employees' opinions. You need the right information in order to feel confident in your strategic decision making.

# Inviting Everyone

The old cliché that too many cooks spoil the broth couldn't be closer to the truth. Although it's imperative that key employees have a voice in planning, not everyone has to literally be at the meeting table. Too many people in the room can lead to chaos and confusion, resulting in a strategic plan by committee instead of through educated decisions and leadership.

If you have a lot of people who want to participate in the process, include them in a couple different ways:

✔ **Collect employees' thoughts and opinions via an employee survey.** Check out the Employee Business Purpose Questionnaire on the CD (from Chapter 5) for an example you can use in advance of your strategic planning meetings. In Chapter 5, you find a set of actions to take with the information you collect.

✔ **Hold a series of meetings.** Perhaps the first and last meetings are with your senior management team, and a couple meetings in between are with key employees and staff. In either case, you collect ideas and opinions that are valuable to developing your plan, but you reserve the right to make the final decisions about what actions you take.

How many is too many? Seven people is the optimal size of a decision-making group. Each additional member reduces effectiveness by 10 percent, according to Marcia W. Blenko, Michael C. Mankins, and Paul Rogers, authors of *Decide & Deliver: 5 Steps to Breakthrough Performance* (Harvard Business Press).

Realistically, groups tend to consist of between 10 and 15 people. If you have more people than that, you can always break up into small teams.

# Holding an Annual Retreat

Huh? Is this section about holding strategic planning meetings off-site? Yes, it is. But one common thought process in strategic planning is that you *have* to hold a retreat. Setting aside a couple days in an off-site location where everyone gathers in sweatshirts and jeans and drinks cocoa is a typical vision of a strategic planning meeting. Oftentimes, a retreat is an annual event, and all strategic decision making is reserved for that occasion.

Strategic management should be a *habit,* not an event. Hold your strategy meetings regularly (more than once a year) to realize enhanced performance. With that said, annual retreats are okay, but make sure they're not your only meetings of the year. See Chapter 14 for more discussion on this topic.

# Getting through the Agenda No Matter What

Strategic thinking is hard work. It takes a lot of mental energy to pull all the pieces of the puzzle together, see the future, make strategic decisions, and organize the plan usefully. At every strategic planning meeting I've facilitated, people are mentally exhausted by the end. Getting through the agenda is usually what it takes to have a completed plan. However, sometimes getting it all done just isn't possible. Focus on the outcomes instead of the exact agenda.

However, *do* have an agenda so everyone knows the structure of the day, but don't be so rigid that you stick to it no matter what. Remember to loosen up, have some fun, and take breaks. If you don't get through everything, plan another meeting or assign tasks for the outstanding items.

# Forgetting to Explain the Process

A good facilitator explains the strategic planning process and the expected outcome of the meeting from the get-go. Most people think they know how to develop a strategic plan, but that doesn't mean they truly can. Naturally, you don't want to insult anyone's intelligence, but take the time to review the different terms used in strategic planning and each step of the process. By making sure that everyone starts on the same page, you eliminate any confusion that may derail your meeting.

# Assuming Everyone Thinks Like You

Of course, everyone thinks like you, right? As a good leader, you know that's not the case. Unfortunately, sometimes you forget what's obvious and end up structuring a meeting based on your own preferences. In reality, stepping in to other people's shoes and ways of thinking is a difficult task. But in strategic planning, you want everyone in the room engaged.

To get everyone engaged, make sure to secure a comfortable environment. People feel the most comfortable when they're operating in their own thinking preference. Do you see any of your team members in the following descriptions?

- **Enjoys big-picture thinking:** These people get fired up talking about the mission, vision, and long-term strategies of the organization.

- **Finds big-picture discussions frustrating:** This group would rather get down to business. They want to know what you're going to do this year, who's going to do it, and when it's going to be done. These people are your goal setters and action planners.

- **Wants to analyze all possible options before making a decision:** This group wants to feel completely comfortable with the direction selected. These analyzers are great at synthesizing data from the SWOT and developing your SWOT. (Flip to Chapter 10 for all about your SWOT.) Some people think this tactic feels like the discussion is going in circles.

- **Wants to make sure that all opinions are included:** These people don't want to move on until everyone in the room has voiced his or her ideas. This group is your meeting minders. They make sure everyone is buying into the plan that's being developed.

You may not have all thinking types in your planning session, but by acknowledging that not everyone is going to be comfortable in all aspects of the planning process, you can structure the meeting and manage the discussion accordingly. To do so, first ask your employees which of the four thinking types they *most closely* identify with. Then explain which part of your agenda addresses each thinking type. In the preceding list, I indicate a part of the planning process where each type can shine.

# Ignoring the Elephant in the Room

Would you like to see a strategic planning meeting go down in flames? Forge ahead, even though you know you have some staff issues. If any key staff member is upset or has an outstanding problem, your strategic planning meeting may be disrupted. That person may sit in the meeting like a brooding elephant and finally blow his top and get the meeting off course.

The best way to handle staff concerns is to have a one-on-one discussion with every person who's attending the strategic planning session. Give your employee the opportunity to voice issues or concerns privately. Make sure that you clarify that your intent is to clear up any problems that may inhibit full participation during the strategy session.

# Ending on a Low Note

You did it! You successfully made it all the way through your strategic planning meeting. You accomplished everything you intended. You have the key pieces of your strategic plan in place. You're feeling great. Everyone is slowly packing up and heading out the door, but you sense a feeling of exhaustion and maybe a little anxiety. You're wondering why.

What just happened is that you unintentionally ended your strategic planning meeting on a low note. In most cases, you have more to cover in your meeting than you have time for. You end up rushing the last part of the meeting to get it all done. I recommend, no matter where you are in your agenda, structuring the last half-hour of the meeting to end on a high note by getting everyone excited about the new strategic direction.

The best way to get people jazzed about the plan is to have them visualize success and ensure that they're comfortable with the work product. What does success look like? Help your team feel successful by living the future today. Ask your team to draw a picture of what the company may look like if you achieve your strategic plan. How many employees? What is the office like? Where are you located? Who are your customers? What's the media saying? And so on. Then have your team explain its vision to the group. After the drawings and explanations are over, tell your staff members to hang their creations at their desks to remind them of the plan and their part in it. That way, everyone leaves the planning session feeling successful, brought into the decisions that were made, and not overworked.

# Overlooking Life after the Meeting

The absolute worst thing you can do is continue business as usual, as though you never had a strategic planning off-site. Not only have you wasted everyone's time and your money, but you've also made it nearly impossible to get people to participate in the future.

Committing time and resources to implementing the plan is almost more important than the plan itself. Don't underestimate how much effort it takes to get the plan moving. Here are a few tips:

- **Within a week after your strategic planning meeting, send a timeline that contains the next steps and deadlines for completing the plan.** Also include any notes that captured decisions from the session. Communicate this timeline to everyone in your organization so your employees know what's happening with the process.

- **Do not, under any circumstance, cancel the next meeting in your planning or implementation process.** As the leader, you're responsible for setting the example that the strategic plan is important. Canceling a meeting signifies it isn't.

- **Send the strategic plan on the deadline you set, regardless whether it's complete.** You reinforce the importance of the plan.

- **Post a visible result of the planning session in a common area.** Items to post include your mission, vision, and values statements or a poster of your strategic plan.

Flip back to Chapter 14 for more ideas on how to implement your plan.

# Chapter 20

# Ten Ways to Maintain Momentum in Your Planning Process (And Life)

. . . . . . . . . . . . . . . . . . . . . . . . . . . . . . . . . . . . . . . . . . . . . . . . .

### In This Chapter

▶ Realizing your vision of success and goals to getting there

▶ Steering clear of common roadblocks

▶ Moving your plan to completion

. . . . . . . . . . . . . . . . . . . . . . . . . . . . . . . . . . . . . . . . . . . . . . . . .

Completing your strategic plan is on your to-do list, right? But is it slipping lower and lower down the list? I know that feeling. And don't worry; you're not alone! In fact, I'd wager that everyone reading this book is struggling with the same problem. Completing your strategic plan and maintaining momentum with implementing it are arguably two of the most important things you have to do.

Creating momentum in your life, just like in business, takes *increasing* the activities that move you forward and *decreasing* those that hold you back. Sounds like a snap, but living the life you desire isn't always easy to achieve. You have habits and cycles to overcome. But by creating momentum, you can move past those habits and toward the life you want. Momentum, by its nature, requires a lot of upfront push to get the ball rolling. In this chapter, I give you ten tips to jump-start the momentum in your strategic plan and life in general.

## Create Your Picture of Success and Make It a Reality

If you can't see your vision of success, you'll never get there. As you begin working through your planning process, ask yourself the following questions:

✔ What does success look like for me *day to day?*

✔ How do I want to spend my time?

✔ How do I want to define success for myself this year?

✔ What do I expect to see differently as a result of investing our company's time in a strategic planning process?

Jot down your answers and post them where you'll see it every day.

# Pick a BHAG

A *BHAG* is a *big, hairy, audacious goal* that you want to achieve this year that will help you step into your vision of success. So what's your BHAG? Write it down along with the one thing you can do *today* to make it happen.

A study was conducted among a graduating class at Harvard University to see how many graduates had concrete goals about how much money they wanted to make. Only 3 percent had written down their goals. Ten years later, that same 3 percent was making more than the other 97 percent combined. Now that is power! Before another minute goes by, put some thought into your BHAG and get it down on paper.

# Eliminate Your Energy Drains and Recharge Yourself

Energy drains are those activities or circumstances that drag you down. And when you're dragged down, you're probably not putting too much effort into your planning process. Recharge your energy with anything that inspires you and puts you in a good mood, like an organized desk, an afternoon off to enjoy family or good weather (or both together), or lunch with a colleague. Spend time doing activities that give you energy.

First, identify all your energy drains by listing each one on a sticky note. Next to each drain you identify, stick a new post-it note with an idea for how to get rid of it. For example, a non-responsive colleague may be a drain on your energy as continual e-mails and voice mails don't produce results. A solution to eliminate that drain may be an impromptu visit to the colleague's office to figure out a better communication approach. You'll likely find that one solution can eliminate multiple drains. Group those drains together so you can clearly see your solutions. You'll find you have more spring in your step and can focus a little more clearly on those action items that will help you reach your strategic priorities.

# Conquer Your Fears — Concentrate and Be Brave

The greatest source of procrastination is often a deep-seeded fear — fear of success, change, failure, ridicule, or even just the unknown. Take a daily step to remove your fears by asking yourself, "What would I do today if I was really brave?"

Consider Brian Tracy's book *Eat That Frog* (Berrett-Koehler Publishers, Inc.), which provides the 21 most effective methods for conquering procrastination and getting more done in less time. Success comes by identifying that single most important task (or frog) that needs to be accomplished, concentrating on it to do it well, and finishing it completely. As Tracy points out, "Mark Twain once said that if the first thing you do each morning is to eat a live frog, you can go through the day with the satisfaction of knowing that that is probably the worst thing that is going to happen to you all day long." So go ahead, be brave and eat that frog!

# Take Control of Your Finances

Do you feel like you're on a treadmill, working more to pay for ever-increasing bills? Instead, trim the fat and spend a little less here and there. You'll soon free up budget dollars that you can utilize on securing needed resources that will help you manage a successful strategic plan. Or, if you have enough savings, start an employee incentive program if you don't have one already.

Start by running a Profit and Loss report to see exactly how you're spending your money. Then adjust your budget, making sure that what you purchase is in line with your business. Obviously, a business with a big focus on sales incurs more expenses for client lunches than one without. Consider decreasing every category (except maybe your rent and payroll) by 10 percent. Use the money saved to fuel your dreams instead of feeding the treadmill.

# Create a Brain Trust

Identify a handful of people in your life who you trust to help you move your life forward. Consider pulling from a wide range of backgrounds, ages, experiences, and opinions. Mentors are great sources of guidance and are often the most critical and provide the best insights. Call on them together or individually to help you move past any roadblocks and keep the momentum going.

Even if you don't have any pending issues or questions that need immediate attention, continue to meet with your mentors and spend time focusing on those tabled items that always come up in discussion but haven't been addressed. Or meet without an agenda. You may have an enlightened conversation, giving new thought and energy to your plan.

# Find the Time

One of the biggest challenges to having the life you want is finding the time to do all you want to do, whether at the office or at home. But admit it: The two areas affect each other. Track how you spend your time for a week. At the end, tally up the time spent on each activity, such as meetings, paying bills, preparing reports, checking e-mail, running errands, and so on. Look at each category. What things can you do to cut time in each area? If you struggle with preparing meeting agendas or keeping up with the books, pass the task off to someone who's better suited for the job. Or set up your spam filter or organize your inbox to make it easier to sift through the e-mails. Be creative, and you'll soon free up time that allows you to focus on what's most important, like your planning and execution process.

# Highlight Small Wins

Overlooking the short-term successes because you're looking at the mid-term or long-term horizon is an easy trap to fall into. Because strategic management is a process and an organizational journey, help your staff members stay motivated by acknowledging their progress along the way. The obvious time to highlight progress is when you're reviewing your plan during your monthly or quarterly strategy reviews. Call out the small wins by specifically identifying what was accomplished, why it's important to the strategic direction, and how the success was achieved. Additionally, point out small wins as they occur so everyone can feel the continued momentum.

# Let the Process Evolve

When the flywheel of momentum starts turning, pay attention to clues, connections, and opportunities that are presented. Be aware of environmental shifts and market changes that will affect your organization. With a little agility, allow your future to unfold and change in ways you may not have been able to imagine when you started your planning process. Remember, your strategic plan is a work in progress. Have a goal in mind but be flexible on the process of getting there. Doing so will make the process much easier.

# Be Committed

No matter what your organizational goals are or how difficult they are to achieve, creating momentum to reach them starts with commitment. Be committed to the strategic management process by starting with at least one of the ideas in this chapter, and you'll begin moving closer to your dreams. Then take on the next idea and then maybe another one. Borrow some encouragement from that famous shoe slogan and "just do it!" You'll be happier in the end and will be glad you did it.

# Appendix

# About the CD

*In This Appendix*

▶ Checking out system requirements

▶ Using the CD with Windows and Mac

▶ Exploring what you'll find on the CD

▶ Troubleshooting tips

*N*ote: *If you are using a digital or enhanced digital version of this book, this appendix does not apply.*

No book today is complete without references to the Internet or other media, and this book's no exception. Not only do I include references to online materials and examples that I've prepared to help you visualize the completed worksheets, but I also include a CD chock-full of useful resources and additional information so you can easily get started on your strategic plan. This appendix walks you through the CD that accompanies this book and also gives you the system and other technical specs you may need to get the most out of the information I've prepared for you.

# System Requirements

Make sure that your computer meets the minimum system requirements shown in the following list. If your computer doesn't match up to most of these requirements, you may have problems using the software and files on the CD. For the latest and greatest information, refer to the ReadMe file located at the root of the CD-ROM.

✔ A PC running Microsoft Windows

✔ A Macintosh running Apple OS X or later

✔ An Internet connection

✔ A CD-ROM drive

✔ Adobe Reader 7.0 or later

*Note:* Videos are viewable in an Internet browser only.

If you need more information on the basics, check out these books published by John Wiley & Sons, Inc.: *PCs For Dummies,* 11th Edition, by Dan Gookin; *Macs For Dummies,* 11th Edition, by Edward C. Baig; *iMacs For Dummies,* 6th Edition, by Mark L. Chambers; and *Windows XP For Dummies,* 2nd Edition, *Windows Vista For Dummies,* and *Windows 7 For Dummies,* all by Andy Rathbone.

# Using the CD

To install the items from the CD to your hard drive, follow these steps.

1. **Insert the CD into your computer's CD-ROM drive.**

   The license agreement appears.

   *Note to Windows users:* The interface won't launch if you have auto-run disabled. In that case, choose Start⇨Run. (For Windows Vista and Windows 7, choose Start⇨All Programs⇨Accessories⇨Run.) In the dialog box that appears, type `D:\Start.exe`. (Replace *D* with the proper letter if your CD drive uses a different letter. If you don't know the letter, see how your CD drive is listed under My Computer.) Click OK.

   *Note to Mac Users:* When the CD icon appears on your desktop, double-click the icon to open the CD and double-click the Start icon. Also, note that the content menus may not function as expected in newer versions of Safari and Firefox; however, the documents are available by navigating to the Contents folder.

2. **Read through the license agreement and then click the Accept button if you want to use the CD.**

   The CD interface appears. The interface allows you to browse the contents and install the programs with just a click of a button (or two).

# What You'll Find on the CD

In this section, I provide a summary of the software and other goodies you can find on the CD. If you need help with installing the items provided on the CD, refer to the installation instructions in the preceding section.

For each program listed here, I provide the program platform (Windows or Mac) plus the type of software. The programs fall into one of the following categories:

✔ *Shareware programs* are fully functional, free, trial versions of copyrighted programs. If you like particular programs, register with their authors for a nominal fee and receive licenses, enhanced versions, and technical support.

✔ *Freeware programs* are free, copyrighted games, applications, and utilities. You can copy them to as many computers as you like — for free — but they offer no technical support.

✔ *GNU software* is governed by its own license, which is included inside the folder of the GNU software. There are no restrictions on distribution of GNU software. See the GNU license at the root of the CD for more details.

✔ *Trial, demo,* or *evaluation* versions of software are usually limited either by time or functionality (such as not letting you save a project after you create it).

The following list is an outline of all the materials you can find on the CD, organized by chapter. I also include some links to videos on my website (www.mystrategicplan.com) for more information on a particular tool.

✔ **Chapter 3**

- **Readiness Assessment:** This questionnaire helps you assess your readiness for the strategic planning process.

- **Strategic Planning Process Checklist:** This quick guide helps keep your team on track and ensure your plan is comprehensive and complete.

✔ **Chapter 4**

- **Market Attractiveness Framework:** This worksheet guides you in your planning efforts after you determine the market attractiveness of your products or services based on their strengths.

- **Industry Structure:** Use this matrix to think about what forces surround your industry and what may be changing that will affect your company.

✔ **Chapter 5**

- **Employee Business Purpose Questionnaire:** This questionnaire helps you uncover the purpose of your business from the perspective of your employees.

- **Profit Engine Worksheet:** Use this worksheet to gain insight on the measures that drive your revenue.

- **Customer Business Purpose Questionnaire:** Use this questionnaire to gather your customers' perspectives on the purpose of your business.

- **Competitive Advantage Evaluation:** Using this tool helps you test the strength and sustainability of your competitive advantages.

- **How to Develop Competitive Advantage (video):** `www.my strategicplan.com/resources/how-to-develop-competitive-advantage/`

✔ **Chapter 6**

- **Mission Statement Worksheet**

- **Know What Game You're Playing Worksheet:** This 30-second challenge assists you in developing your mission statement.

- **Values Evaluation Worksheet**

- **Vision Evaluation Worksheet**

- **How to Write a Mission Statement (video):** `www.mystrategic plan.com/virtual-strategist/mission-statements.html`

- **How to Write a Vision Statement That Inspires (video):** `www.my strategicplan.com/virtual-strategist/vision-statements.html`

- **How to Write a Values Statement (video):** `www.mystrategic plan.com/virtual-strategist/values-statement.html`

✔ **Chapter 7**

- **SWOT Analysis Template:** Use this template to assess the internal environment of your organization

- **Intangible Assets Questionnaire:** This worksheet helps you assess your company's capabilities, skills, and resources that you need to execute plans and actions.

- **Operational Processes Questionnaire:** Answer the questions here to get a better understanding of your operational, customer, relationship, and innovation processes.

- **SWOT Analysis (video):** `www.mystrategicplan.com/resources/swot-analysis-how-to-perform-one-for-your-organization/`

✔ **Chapter 8**

- **Customer Value Calculator:** Find out how much money each of your customers is worth to you over a lifetime.

- **Business Model Diagram:** Use this diagram to build your own business model and identify what impacts or changes you need to build into your plan to bring it to life.

✔ **Chapter 9**

- **Market Segment Evaluation Worksheet:** Use this worksheet to evaluate different segments of your company and gain insight into which ones you should focus on.

- **Marketing Action Plan Worksheet:** This worksheet helps you develop an action plan that addresses the four *P*s of product, price, promotion, and place.

- **Customer Profile Worksheet:** Use this simple grid to organize your customer profile information.

- **Performing Customer Segmentation (video):** www.mystrategic plan.com/resources/performing-customer-segmentation/

✔ **Chapter 10**

- **SWOT Analysis Template:** Use this template to assess the external environment of your organization.

- **Operating Environment Questionnaire:** Answer the questions in this questionnaire to start your list of opportunities and threats in your operating environment.

- **Industry Environment Questionnaire:** Use this list of questions to start your list of opportunities and threats in your industry environment.

- **Competitor Grid:** Organize the strengths and weaknesses of your competition by using this simple grid.

✔ **Chapter 11**

- **Product/Market Grid Worksheet:** Develop and use this grid to visually see your strategic choices and prioritize and sort your options.

- **Strategy Summary Worksheet:** Summarize your strategy levels with this worksheet to ensure their consistency and harmony.

✔ **Chapter 12**

- **Impact/Effort Grid Worksheet:** Use this worksheet to sort out the best opportunities from the ones that are just good ideas.

- **Strategic Alternatives Worksheet:** Identify your strategic alternatives by using your SWOT with this worksheet.

- **Paired Comparison Analysis Worksheet:** This worksheet helps you eliminate, limit, or prioritize your alternatives when multiple demands exist on the same resources of time and money.

- **Goals Grid:** This tool helps you categorize your internal alternatives and determine goals that are worth pursuing.

- **Strategy Map Worksheet:** Use this worksheet to begin developing your strategy map.

- **Road Map Worksheet:** This worksheet helps you align your yearly goals to your company's long-term strategic objectives.

- **Strategic Planning with the Balanced Scorecard (video):** www. mystrategicplan.com/resources/strategic-planning- with-the-balanced-scorecard/

- **Choosing Your Strategic Objectives (video):** www.mystrategic plan.com/resources/choosing-your-strategic-objectives/

- **How to Set SMART Goals (video):** www.mystrategicplan.com/ resources/how-to-set-smart-goals/

✔ **Chapter 13**

- **Scorecard Worksheet:** Use this framework to begin building your scorecard.

- **Cascading Goals Worksheet:** This worksheet guides you through cascading goals to the department level.

- **Contribution Analysis Worksheet:** Use this analysis to project whether your strategy generates revenues in excess of expenses.

- **Financial Projections Worksheets:** These two worksheets help you project your financial statements.

- **How to Develop Key Performance Indicators (KPIs) (video):** www. mystrategicplan.com/resources/how-to-develop-key- performance-indicators-kpis/

- **How to Develop Action Plans (video):** www.mystrategicplan. com/resources/how-to-develop-action-plans/

✔ **Chapter 14**

- **Corporate Strategy Review Agenda Template:** Use this template to draft your own meeting agenda.

- **Common Strategic Planning Pitfalls (video):** www.mystrategic plan.com/resources/the-commont-pitfalls-of-strategic- planning-and-how-to-avoid-them/

- **The Secret to Strategic Implementation (video):** www.mystrategic plan.com/resources/the-secret-to-strategic- implementation/

✔ **Chapter 16**

- **Exit Planning Assessment:** Use this assessment to line up your exit planning activities with best practices.

✔ **Chapter 19**

- **Strategic Planning Retreats (video):** `www.mystrategicplan.com/resources/strategic-planning-retreats/`

# Troubleshooting

I tried my best to compile programs that work on most computers with the minimum system requirements. Alas, your computer may differ, and some programs may not work properly for some reason.

The two likeliest problems are that you don't have enough memory (RAM) for the programs you want to use, or you have other programs running that are affecting installation or running of a program. If you get an error message such as `Not enough memory` or `Setup cannot continue`, try one or more of the following suggestions and then try using the software again:

✔ **Turn off any antivirus software running on your computer.** Installation programs sometimes mimic virus activity and may make your computer incorrectly believe that it's being infected by a virus.

✔ **Close all running programs.** The more programs you have running, the less memory is available to other programs. Installation programs typically update files and programs; so if you keep other programs running, installation may not work properly.

✔ **Have your local computer store add more RAM to your computer.** This is, admittedly, a drastic and somewhat expensive step. However, adding more memory can really help the speed of your computer and allow more programs to run at the same time.

If you have trouble with the CD-ROM, please call Wiley Product Technical Support at 800-762-2974. Outside the United States, call 317-572-3993. You can also contact Wiley Product Technical Support at `http://support.wiley.com`. John Wiley & Sons, Inc., will provide technical support only for installation and other general quality control items. For technical support on the applications themselves, consult the program's vendor or author.

To place additional orders or to request information about other Wiley products, please call 877-762-2974.

# Index

## • A •

accelerated change, 176
accountability
  goal achievement, 242
  importance of, 264, 267
  resistance to change, 258
  strategic plan, executing, 264, 268–271
Accountable Care Organization (ACO),
    178–179
accounting software, 254
accounts payable turnover, 67
accounts receivable, 128
action item
  described, 39
  goals, cascading, 244
  planning phases, 44
  strategic priorities, 226
action plan
  creating, 243–249
  described, 243
  scenario planning, 286
adaptability, of plan, 280–281
add-on model, 141
administrative system, 310
advertising model, 141
advisor, 304
affiliate model, 141
age gap, 178
agenda, meeting
  example of, 274
  importance of, 328
  successful meetings, 273
agility, of business, 30–31
aging population, 174
agricultural society, 176
AIDS Service Organizations (nonprofit
    group), 314–315
alliance
  goals, cascading, 248
  management of, 124
Alliance for Nonprofit Management
    (professional association), 316

Allison, Michael (*Strategic Planning for
    Nonprofit Organizations: A Practical
    Guide and Workbook*), 316
alternative coverage, 314
alternative future, 288–290
AM radio, 181
Amazon (online retailer), 103, 141, 142
American Water Works Association, the
    New Jersey Section, 95
Amplitude (organizational assessment/
    employee training company), 127
Andreasen, Alan (*Strategic Marketing for
    Nonprofit Organizations*), 316
annual retreat, 264, 327
Anthropologie (retail store), 156
Arm & Hammer Baking Soda, 203
*The Art of Profitability* (Slywotzky), 146
Arthur Carhart Wilderness Training Center, 94
Articulated Plan level, 17
assumption, financial, 252
AT&T (telecommunications company),
    182–183
attainable goal, 229
attitude, negative, 25–26
attractional model, 144, 145
auction model, 141
auto manufacturer, 208
Avis (car rental company), 162

## • B •

backward integration, 208
Bain & Company (management consulting
    company), 24
bait and hook model, 142
balance sheet, 254
Balanced Scorecard. *See* scorecard
bank, 257
bargaining power, 182
barriers to entry, 72
base lining, 240
Bayer aspirin, 206
behavioral group, 154

benchmark
  defined, 130
  target selection, 239–240
  tools, 130
benefit segmentation, 153
*Best Practices for Facilitation* (The Grove
    Facilitation Guide Series), 49
BHAGs (big, hairy, audacious goals), 101,
    103, 332
bias, 258
big rock, 44
big unknown, 287
BizMiner (website), 70, 130
BizStats (website), 70, 130
Blenko, Marcia W. *(Decide & Deliver: 5 Steps
    to Breakthrough Performance)*, 327
BMW (car manufacturer), 161
board of directors, 256, 306–308
boundary principle, 221
Boy Scouts of America (youth
    organization), 94, 228, 318
brain trust, 333
brainstorming, 104
brand, 87, 120
Branson, Richard (founder of Virgin), 207
breakeven rate, 129
brick and mortar model, 142
bridge analogy, 211–212
broadband, 177
brokerage firm, 304
B2B Benchmarking Association, 130
budget
  maximization of, 317
  shortfalls, 247–248
Buffett, Warren (investor), 75
*Built to Sell: Turn Your Business into One
    You Can Sell* (Warrillow), 298
burning platform, 40
business
  characteristics, 155
  fundamental elements of, 25
  models for, 140–146
  plans, 12, 235
  target customers, 155, 157
*Business Model Generation: A Handbook
    for Visionaries, Game Changers,
    and Challengers* (Osterwalder and
    Pigneur), 146

Business Report Card (benchmarking
    tool), 130
business unit level strategy, 195–201
butterfly effect, 286
buyer, 182
buy-in, employee
  goals, cascading, 248
  need for, 30–31
  organization's mission, 31
  social sector, 306–308
  strategic planning meetings, 328–330

## • C •

calendar, 52
Calvary Baptist Church, 144–145
capital intensity, 71
cascading goals, 243–249
cash
  creators, 128–129
  drains, 129
  flow, 254, 255
celebrating success, 52, 324, 334
Center for Consumer Focus (training
    organization), 146
central control, 310
CEO
  leading by example, 324
  planning phases, 48
  role of, 46, 48
  strategic planning of, 27–28
  visibility of, 46
CEO Tools (website), 70
champion, 270
change
  business agility, 30–31
  drivers of, 289
  resistance to, 258, 278–279
  SWOT analysis, 190
channel, 143
Chatham House (analysis company),
    293–294
Chemtura (chemical business), 103
Chitimacha Tribe (Native American
    people), 94
Cisco Internet (technology company),
    292–293
Clavier, Jeff (founder of SoftTech VC), 298
clear goal, 242

climate, planning, 40–41
Clorox Company (manufacturer), 95
coaching, 271
coalition, 248
Coke (soda), 205
Collins, Jim
  *Good to Great and the Social Sectors: A*
    *Monograph to Accompany Good to*
    *Great,* 306
  *Good to Great and the Social Sectors: Why*
    *Business Thinking Is Not the Answer,* 312
comment card, 139
commodity, 182
communication
  customer feedback, 139
  guidelines for, 126
  information sharing, 166
  pitfalls of plan execution, 264
  plan, rolling out, 275–277
  strategic plan, executing, 275–278
  succession planning, 303
  technology changes, 176
  tips for success, 277
  values statement, 100
community contribution, 124, 310
comparing choices, 218–220
compensating balance, 255
compensation plan, 269–270
competition, business
  agility of business, 30–31
  financial ratio evaluation, 70–71
  ignoring, 20
  industry forces assessment, 71–72
  level of competition, 72
  market penetration, 203
  market research, 148–149
  new competitor, 179–180
  opportunities and threats, 179–187
  target markets, choosing, 157
  types of, 184
  valuation of business, 299–300
competitive advantage
  business unit level strategy, 200–201
  competitive analysis, 186
  defined, 75
  described, 38, 75–78
  evaluating, 86
  examples of, 83–84
  identifying, 79–87
  implementing, 87–89
  importance of, 78–79
  planning phases, 44–45
  sustainability, 75–76, 84–86
competitive analysis, 183–187
competitive benchmarking, 240
competitive position, 314–315
compromise, 248
concentrated growth strategy, 203
concentration level, 72
conflict, team, 50, 51
consistency, product, 86–87
construction industry, 175
contribution analysis, 253
core competency, 93, 102
corporate level strategy, 195
corporate success planning, 32
cost of goods sold
  business unit strategy, 196–198
  defined, 58
  product/service evaluation, 58
  rivalries, 183
cost structure, 143, 144
*Creating Competitive Advantage: Give*
    *Customers a Reason to Choose You*
    *Over Your Competitors* (Smith), 77–78
Creating Customer Evangelists (website), 146
creative thinking, 105–107
critical uncertainty, 289
cultural cluster, 154
cultural shift, 175
culture, organizational
  cash drains, 129
  customer satisfaction, 136, 200
  described, 13
  employees as customers, 136
  facilitator selection, 51
  government planning, 309
  organizational capital, 117–118
  planning phases, 42–43
  support of plan execution, 267
  tips for successful planning, 52
  transformational change, 279
current ratio, 64
customer
  acquiring, 123
  business models, 140–146
  cash creators, 129
  cash drains, 129

customer (*continued*)
  characteristics, 155
  competitive advantage, 81, 82–83, 88
  80/20 rule, 133
  employee as, 136, 140
  feedback from, 137–140
  intimacy, 196, 199–200
  lost, 132–133
  loyalty, analyzing, 136–140
  management processes, 123
  market penetration, 203
  neglecting, 131, 136
  planning team selection, 47
  positioning statements, 160–162
  profiles, 155–156, 167–168
  profit engine, 81
  retention, 123
  segments, 143
  selection, 123
  strategic priorities, 224
  targeting, 152–159, 162–165
  value of, 133–136
customer data
  collecting, 148–151, 165–166
  organizing, 167–168
customer needs
  marketing failures, 147
  mission statements, 93
  target markets, 157
customer relationship
  business models, 143
  business unit level strategy, 199–200
  customer management processes, 123
  helpful resources, 146
  management software, 180
customer satisfaction
  importance of, 136
  lost customers, 132
  measurement of, 137–140
  Pareto principle, 133
customer-focused metric, 137–140

• *D* •

daily operating problem, 264
dashboard, 243
data collection
  competitive advantage evaluations, 88–89
  competitive analysis, 183–187

customer feedback, 137–140
industry forces, 71–72
knowledge management, 119–120
market research, 148–151, 165–166
mission statements, writing, 96
planning phases, 42–43
planning team selection, 47
scorecard building, 241
strategic planning meetings, 326
data organization, 167–168
database, 151, 299
debt-to-equity ratio, 64–65
*Decide & Deliver: 5 Steps to Breakthrough Performance* (Blenko, Mankins, and Rogers), 327
decision maker, 154
decision-making tool
  critical uncertainty, 289
  long-term uncertainties, 290
  short-term uncertainties, 284
decline phase, of product life cycle, 164, 165
delivery, on-time, 138
demographics
  market research, 150, 154
  opportunities and threats, 178
  segmenting process, 154
DemographicsNow (website), 150
department
  goals, 245–247, 249
  identity of, 249
  strategic plan, sharing, 257
departmental customer, 136
descriptor, 154
desk calendar, 52
differentiation, of segment, 158
direct competitor, 184
direct sales model, 142
discount, 128, 182
dissatisfied customer, 132
distribution, 154, 163
distributor/retail model, 142
diverse population, 178
diversification, market, 206–207
dot-com era, 84
Dow Jones (website), 151
downsizing, 177
driving force, 287, 289, 291
Dun & Bradstreet (*Industry Norms and Key Business Ratios*), 71

DuPont (chemical business), 103
durable goods manufacturing, 175

## • *E* •

*Eat That Frog* (Tracy), 333
Economic Development Authority of
    Western Nevada, 228
economic indicator
  forecasting, 255–256
  long-term uncertainties, 287
  opportunities and threats, 173–175
*Economic Indicators For Dummies* (Griffis), 174
economies of scale, 180
Edward Jones (financial services
    company), 32–33
effectiveness, 121–127
efficiency, 121–127, 238
effort, 213, 214
80/20 rule, 133
Elephant Sanctuary (animal refuge), 94
e-mail, 88, 127
eMarketer (website), 150
employee
  attitudes of, 25–26
  audience for strategic plan, 256–257
  business's purpose, 80
  buy-in of, 30–31
  coaching, 271
  commitment of, 29, 93, 99–101
  competitive advantage implementation, 88
  as customer, 136, 140
  encouraging, 271
  engagement in meetings, 328–329
  futurecasting exercises, 105–107
  goals, cascading, 243–249
  high-value activities, 126–127
  human capital, 115–117
  invitation to meetings, 326–327
  market research, 150
  mission statements, writing, 96
  motivating, 102
  organizational capital, 117–118
  ownership of plan, 321
  pitfalls of plan execution, 264
  plan, rolling out, 276–277
  planning team selection, 46–48
  resistance to change, 258, 278–279

rewards for plan execution, 268, 269–270
  SMART goals, 229
  strategic priorities, 225–226
  support of plan execution, 266
  SWOT analysis, 190
  vision statement, creating, 104
  wasted time, 127
  well-being of, 124
Employees Business Purpose
    Questionnaire, 80
empowerment, 264
encouraging employees, 271
end date, 244
endgame, identifying, 296–297
energy drain, 332
enterprise resource planning (ERP)
    module, 259
entrepreneurial organization
  exit planning, 300–304
  goal of, 297
  importance of, 295
  legacy of business, 296
  value creation, 297–300
  value of, 297–300
  vision, 296–297
environment, operating, 173–178
environmental sustainability, 124
Eramsus, Daniel (scenario planner), 291
Erlach Computer Consulting, 122–123
ERP (enterprise resource module planning)
    module, 259
error rate, 138
Estella's Exotic Escapes (travel company), 163
E*TRADE (online brokerage company), 154
execution, of plan. *See* strategic plan,
    executing
executive sponsorship, 258
exit barrier, 182
exit planning, 300–304
expense
  cash creators, 128
  estimates, 251
  goals, cascading, 244
external priority, 217–220
external strategy, 13

## • F •

facilitator
  benefits of, 50
  costs, 49
  need for, 325–326
  selecting, 50–51
Factiva (website), 151
failure, of plan, 16, 125
false start, 28
family member, 301
Famous Footwear (retailer), 162
Fannie Mae (lending organization), 94
fear, 332–333
fees for service, 317
*Fierce Conversations: Achieving Success at Work and in Life, One Conversation at a Time* (Scott), 271
financial assessment
  defined, 39
  past performance, 63–71
  process of, 250
  successful business, 250
  viability of strategic plan, 249–256
financial control, 333
financial priority, 223–224
financial projection, 254–256
financial ratio
  benefits of, 63–64
  categories of, 64–67
  described, 63
  industry comparisons, 70–71
  three-year trends, 67–68
financial resource, 120
financial statement
  business's purpose, identifying, 80–82
  financial projections, 254–255
  past performance analysis, 63–71
*Finding Information on the Internet: A Tutorial* (University of California Berkley Library), 151
Fintel (benchmarking association), 130
flexibility, 307–308
FM radio, 181
food supply, 293–294
for sale valuation, 299
forward integration, 208
foundational training, 279
franchise model, 142

freemium model, 142
Frost & Sullivan (consulting firm), 150
full cost recovery, 317
Fundamo (mobile application), 299
futurecasting
  assumptions, identifying, 106
  defined, 105
  described, 105
  financial projections, 254–256
  mindset for, 105–106
  opportunities and threats, 172
  strategic thinking exercise, 106–107
  strategy map, 230–234
  vision statements, 102

## • G •

Gates, Bill (entrepreneur), 120
generational divide, 178
generic strategy, 196
geographic expansion, 205–206
geographic group, 154
global population, 178
globalization, 72, 174
goals
  action plans, 243–249
  attainment of, 197
  cascading, 243–249
  defined, 237
  described, 39
  of entrepreneurs, 297
  flexibility, of business, 307–308
  internal priorities, 220–226
  pitfalls of plan execution, 265
  planning phases, 44, 45
  poor examples of, 242
  purpose of, 19
  revising, 272
  rolling out, 277
  short-term, 229
  social sector, 306, 307–308
  strategy map, 230–234
  writing down, 332
Goals Grid tool, 220–221
GoDaddy (website), 117
Godin, Seth *(Purple Cow)*, 159–160
*Good to Great and the Social Sectors: A Monograph to Accompany Good to Great* (Collins), 306

_Good to Great and the Social Sectors: Why Business Thinking Is Not the Answer_ (Collins), 312
goodwill, 121
Google (website), 94
governing board, 309
government
  downsizing, 177
  planning, 308–312
GreenBook (market research directory), 151
Griffis, Michael _(Economic Indicators For Dummies)_, 174
gross profit, 58
The Grove Facilitation Guide Series _(Best Practices for Facilitation)_, 49
growth, of business
  areas of, 202
  business unit level strategy, 195–201
  customer satisfaction, 138
  importance of, 193
  market attractiveness framework, 62
  market level strategy, 202–210
  rivalry, 182
  strategic planning benefits, 28, 29–30
  target markets, choosing, 158
growth phase, of product life cycle, 164, 165
guiding principle, 97

## • H •

headline, 286
healthcare consumerism, 177–178
The Heidel House Resort, 162
Heinz (food manufacturer), 103
Herman Miller (furniture company), 98
Herrigel, Eugen _(Zen in the Art of Archery)_, 279
Hiam, Alexander _(Marketing For Dummies)_, 146
high-performance company. _See_ successful business
high-value activity, 126–127
hiring process
  intangible assets, 116
  values statement, 100–101
home healthcare service, 178
homeland security, 177
Hoover's Online (website), 151
housing start, 175

how-to principle, 221
human capital, 115–117
Hyden, Howard (founder of The Center for Customer Focus), 133

## • I •

IAF (International Association of Facilitators), 49
IBISWorld (website), 72
icons, explained, 5–6
imitation, product, 85
immediate risk, 285
Impact/Effort Grid tool, 213, 214
improvement, product, 85, 87
_Inc. Magazine,_ 27, 30, 269
Inc.com (website), 300
incentive plan. _See_ reward, employee
income statement, 80–82, 254
indirect competitor, 184
individualism, 176
industrial society, 176
industry
  association benchmarking, 240
  forces in, 71–72, 179–187
  globalization, 72, 174
_Industry Norms and Key Business Ratios_ (Dun & Bradstreet), 71
information
  versus knowledge, 119
  organizing, 167–168
  scorecard building, 241
  sharing, 166, 257
information technology (IT)
  defined, 121
  evaluating, 126
  performance management applications, 258–259
innovation, product
  competitive advantage, 87
  importance of, 124
  process of, 124–125
inspiring language, 102
intangible asset, 114–120
Intangible Assets Questionnaire, 114–115
intangible resource, 120–121
intellectual property, 121
internal benchmarking, 239

internal priority
  described, 217–218
  examples of, 225
  listing of, 220–221
internal strategy, 13
International Association of Facilitators
    (IAF), 49
International City/County Management
    Association, 312
international expansion, 206
Internet company, 141, 142
introduction phase, of product life cycle,
    164, 165
Intuit (software company), 87
inventory turnover, 66
investment, 250–251
invoice, 139
IT. *See* information technology

## • *J* •

jargon, 270, 323
job description, 303

## • *K* •

Kaplan, Robert (professor), 222
Kaye, Jude *(Strategic Planning for Nonprofit
    Organizations: A Practical Guide and
    Workbook)*, 316
Kelleher, Herb (former CEO of Southwest
    Airlines), 97
Keno, Awa (archery teacher), 279
key performance indicator (KPI)
  audience for strategic plan, 257
  defined, 241
  listing of, 239
  purpose of, 241
  strategy versus organizational reviews,
    272–273
knowledge society, 176
knowledge, tribal. *See* tribal knowledge
Kotler, Philip *(Strategic Marketing for
    Nonprofit Organizations)*, 316
KPI. *See* key performance indicator

## • *L* •

labor law, 177
leadership
  business unit level strategy, 196, 199
  defined, 118
  government planning, 308
  innovative processes, 125
  leading by example, 324
  organizational capital, 118
  strategy-focused organization, 270
legislative action, 177
LexisNexis (website), 151
Lexus (car manufacturer), 139
library, 151
life cycle stage, 71
lifetime value of a customer, 133–136
liquidation, 301
liquidity, 64
living document, plan as
  audiences for plan, 256–259
  importance of, 321
  tips for, 321–324
longevity, 87
long-range planning, 15
lost customer, 132–133

## • *M* •

Mackey, John (cofounder of Whole Foods),
    124
MacMillan Matrix tool, 313–315
management
  structure of, 266
  surveys, 24–25
management letter, 303
manager
  as coach, 271
  departments as customers, 136
  employee retention, 116
  goals, cascading, 244
  organizational capital, 118
  strategic plan contents, 257
  strategy review meetings, 273
  time-wasting activities, 33
  traits of, 31–32

mandatory meeting, 273
Mankins, Michael C. *(Decide & Deliver: 5 Steps to Breakthrough Performance)*, 327
manufacturer model, 142
map, strategy, 230–234, 257
margin, 127–130
Marine Stewardship Council (environmental organization), 94
market
  attractiveness, 60–63
  development strategy, 205–206
  diversification, 206–207
market level strategy
  business growth, 202
  defined, 195
  described, 202
  diversification, 206–207
  execution of, 208–210
  market development, 205–206
  market penetration, 203
  product development, 204–205
  vertical integration, 208
market research
  data collection, 148–151, 165–166
  data organization, 167–168
  importance of, 148
  information sharing, 166
  information sources, 149–151
  strategic planning meeting, 326
market-focused business
  described, 165–167
  opportunities and threats, 188
marketing
  action plan, 164–165
  cash drains, 129
  competitive advantage implementation, 88
  failure of, 147
  function of, 147
  market-focused mindset, 165–167
  mix, 162–163
  positioning statements, 159–162
  product life cycle, 163–165
  target markets, 152–159
*Marketing For Dummies* (Hiam), 146
MarketResearch (website), 72, 150
Marriott Hotels, 95
Mattel (toy manufacturer), 103

maturity phase, of product life cycle, 164, 165
McDonald's (restaurant chain), 103
measurable goal, 229
measure
  creating, 238–239
  defined, 238
  goals, cascading, 249
  listing of, 240
  scorecards, 241–243
  types of, 238–239
Medicare (healthcare group), 178
meeting, strategic planning
  common pitfalls, 325–330
  engagement of participants, 328–330
  enthusiasm, building, 323
  facilitation skills, 49–51
  planning team selection, 47
  postmeeting tasks, 330
  purpose of, 323
  strategy review, 272–275
  support of plan execution, 266
  SWOT analysis, 190
  task force, 274
  visible CEO, 46
Mercedes-Benz (car manufacturer), 161
Merck (pharmaceutical company), 95
middle, stuck in, 200–201
middle-class population, 174
Miller Lite (brewing company), 162
Mint.com (finance service), 299
mission
  barriers to, 92
  creeping, 93–94
  defined, 42, 92
  employee buy-in, 31
  goals, cascading, 248
  planning phases, 42
  social sector, 313
  strategic priorities, 226
mission statement
  creating, 95–97
  defined, 93
  described, 37
  elements of, 93–94
  evaluating, 95
  examples of, 94–95
missional model, 144, 145

mobile device, 176

monthly/quarterly business review (M/QBR), 39

Moody's (financial-data services), 71

Morningstar (website), 72

motivating employees, 102, 270

MyStrategicPlan (website), 257

### • *N* •

nanotechnology, 176

National CASA (nonprofit organization), 103

national expansion, 206

natural disaster, 174

needs-based segmentation, 153

net income, 29–30, 254

net profit margin, 65

Netflix (online DVD rental company), 137, 153

newsletter, 139

newspaper company, 142

Nonprofit Genie (website), 316

nonprofit organization. *See* social sector

North Slope Borough School District, 103, 109

*Northern Nevada Business Weekly* (newspaper), 162

notebook, strategy, 234–235

Novo Nordisk (diabetes care company), 103

### • *O* •

objective

described, 38

flexibility, 307–308

pitfalls of plan execution, 265

planning phases, 44, 45

purpose of, 19

revising, 272

social sector, 307–308

strategic priorities, 226

strategy map, 230–234

writing, 228–229

oil price, 174

Olsen & Associates Public Relations, 93

online customer survey, 139

online information, 185

online learning, 175

operating environment, 173–178

operating risk, 122

operation department, 122

operational process, 122–123, 197

operational review, 272–273

opportunity

analysis, 213

described, 170

environmental forces, 173–178

future plan, 172

industry competition, 179–187

summary of, 188–189

SWOT analysis, 171–172, 189–190, 213–216

order form, 139

organizational capital, 117–118

organizational chart, 117

Organizational Engagement level, 17

Organizational Transformation level, 17

Osterwalder, Alexander (business model guru)

*Business Model Generation: A Handbook for Visionaries, Game Changers, and Challengers,* 146

business models, 143, 146

outcome measure, 238–239

outline, scenario, 289

owner's vision statement, 296–297

ownership, of plan, 264, 321

### • *P* •

paired comparison analysis, 218–219

Pareto principle, 133

partial cost recovery, 317

partner, key, 143–144

past performance

financial performance, 63–71

financial projections, 255

industry forces, 71–72

portfolio analysis, 60–63

product/service analysis, 56–60

strategic issue list, 72–73

successes/failures, 56–57

Patagonia (outdoor clothing company), 118

pay-as-you-go model, 142

payment terms, 128

peer pressure, 268, 278

performance evaluation, 271

performance management system, 258–259

Pershing General Hospital, 83, 103

physical resource, 121

Pigneur, Yves (*Business Model Generation: A Handbook for Visionaries, Game Changers, and Challengers*), 146
place, 163
planning session, 49–50
planning team, 46–51
point of purchase, 139
policy board, 307
politics
  government planning, 309
  long-term uncertainties, 287
  opportunities and threats, 177–178
Porter, Michael (strategy guru), 11
portfolio, product/service, 58–63
positioning, 160
poster, strategic plan, 322–323
Post-it Brand Products (website), 50
power, 309
precise mission statement, 94
predetermined element, 289
price, service/product
  business unit level strategy, 196–198
  increase in, 60, 128
  marketing mix, 163
  portfolio analysis, 60
primary data, 151
priority setting, 217–226
proactive mode, 28–32
problem statement, 286
process, 121–127
producer satisfaction maximization, 317
product development, 204–205
production facility, 121
productivity
  financial priorities, 224
  high-value activities, 126–127
  ratio, 65–67
Product/Market Grid, 208–210
product/service
  competitive advantage, 84–87
  customer satisfaction, 138
  entrepreneurial organizations, 298
  expanded uses for, 205–206
  features, adding, 204
  leadership strategy, 196, 199
  life cycle, 163–165
  market penetration, 203
  marketing mix, 162
  past performance, 57–60

portfolio revision, 60–63
quality of, 208, 239
substitutes, 181, 184
profile, customer, 167–168
profit
  business's purpose, identifying, 80–82
  contribution analysis, 253
  engines, 80–82
  social sector, 306
  strategy map, 230–234
profit and loss report, 333
profitability
  focus on, 81
  ratio, 65
  target markets, choosing, 158
program attractiveness, 314
progress measure, 39
progress report, 265
project measure, 239
promotional activity, 163
prosperity, 176
psychographic group, 154
*Purple Cow* (Godin), 159–160
purpose, of organization
  competitive advantage, 79–80
  mission statements, 96
  vision statements, 102
PushLife (entertainment startup), 299

**• Q •**

quality, of product/service, 208, 239
question, from customer, 138
quick ratio, 64
Quicken (software), 87

**• R •**

racial demographics, 178
reactionary mode, 28–29
receivable turnover, 66
Recording for the Blind and Dyslexic (nonprofit organization), 103
recurring revenue, 142
referral, customer, 138
regulation level, 71
related diversification, 206–207
relationship management process, 123–124

report
  cash drains, 129
  goals, cascading, 249
  scorecards, 278
reputation, 121
research. *See* data collection; market
    research
resource
  business models, 143, 144
  defined, 120
  goals, cascading, 247–248
  identifying, 120–121
  lists, 120
  profit engines, 81
  support of plan execution, 266
  target markets, 157
responsible employee, 229
retaining customers, 123
retaining employees, 116–117
retreat, annual, 264, 327
retrenchment strategy, 317
return on assets (ROA), 66
return on equity (ROE), 65
return, product, 138
revenue
  calculation, 158
  estimates, 251
  financial priorities, 224
  maximizing, 316
  streams, 143
  volatility, 71
review, performance. *See* past
    performance
reward, employee
  employee retention, 117
  plan execution, 268, 269–270
  purpose of, 270, 323
  values statement, 100
riding the fence, 200–201
Right at Home (healthcare company), 178
risk level
  described, 64–65
  long-term uncertainties, 287–290
  short-term uncertainties, 284–286
rivalry, 182–183
ROA (return on assets), 66
robot, 176
ROE (return on equity), 65

Rogers, Paul *(Decide & Deliver: 5 Steps to
    Breakthrough Performance)*, 327
ROI principle, 222
rolling out plans, 259, 276–277
Rotary International (nonprofit
    organization), 95

• S •

sales
  business models, 141–142
  customer satisfaction, 138
  Pareto principle, 133
  strategic planning benefits, 29
  target markets, 158
  value of customers, 134
sales rep, 139
sales-to-assets ratio, 66
satellite radio, 181
satisfaction, customer
  importance of, 136
  lost customers, 132
  measuring, 137–140
  Pareto principle, 133
Scandinavian Airlines, 123
scenario planning
  described, 283–284
  examples of, 288
  long-term uncertainties, 287–290
  purpose of, 288
  sample scenarios, 291–294
  short-term uncertainties, 284–286
scorecard
  components of, 238
  creating, 241–243
  versus dashboard, 243
  described, 13–14, 39, 237–238
  example of, 242, 318
  guidelines for use, 274–275
  purpose of, 324
  reports, 278
  social sector, 306
  strategic priorities, 222–223
  support of plan execution, 266
Scott, Susan *(Fierce Conversations:
    Achieving Success at Work and in Life,
    One Conversation at a Time)*, 271
seasonal product, 60

secondary data, 150–151
security market, 177
segmenting
  described, 152–154
  growth strategy, 206
  target markets, choosing, 157–159
sellability, of business, 297–298
senior population, 174
shareholder, 223–224
Shell Oil (gas company), 284, 291
short-term goal, 229
simplicity, of plan, 323
Sinek, Simon *(Start With Why: How Great Leaders Inspire Everyone to Take Action)*, 296
Sirius (satellite radio), 181
Skype (Internet telephony), 177
slogan, 161
Slywotzky, Adrian *(The Art of Profitability)*, 146
SMART goal, 229
Smith, Jaynie *(Creating Competitive Advantage: Give Customers a Reason to Choose You Over Your Competitors)*, 77–78
social sector
  buy-in of board of directors, 306–308
  competition in, 184
  defined, 305
  goals, 306
  government planning, 308–312
  growth of, 305
  helpful resources, 316
  nonprofit organizations, 312–318
  profit versus sustainability, 306
  scorecard, 306
social shift
  long-term uncertainties, 287
  opportunities and threats, 175–176
soda, 205
someday list, 218, 235
Sony (entertainment company), 208
soul of the agency program, 314–315
Southwest Airlines, 95, 97, 161
Speakshop (foreign language service company), 108
specific goal, 229
spouse, communication with, 303
spreadsheet
  financial ratios, 67–68
  monthly performance, 68–70

portfolio analysis, 58–59
purpose of, 259
Standard & Poor's (financial-data services), 71, 151
Starbucks (coffeehouse chain), 87, 94, 228
start date, 244
*Start With Why: How Great Leaders Inspire Everyone to Take Action* (Sinek), 296
steering committee, 309
sticky note, 50
strategic choice
  described, 212
  identifying, 214–217
  priorities, balancing, 222–226
  priorities, creating, 217–222
  SWOT analysis, 213–216
  vision, 227–234
Strategic Differentiation level, 17
Strategic Essentials (personal coaching business), 135
strategic foundation. *See also specific foundation elements*
  described, 92–93
  examples of, 108–109
  finalizing, 107
strategic issue
  defined, 55
  industry forces, 71–72
  listing of, 72–73
  past performance, 56–60, 63–71
strategic management, 13
*Strategic Marketing for Nonprofit Organizations* (Andreasen and Kotler), 316
strategic plan
  assembling, 234–235
  benefits of, 33
  versus business plan, 235
  components of, 13–14, 36–39
  defined, 12
  evaluating, 19, 235–236
  example of, 235, 322
  frequently asked questions, 14–16
  importance of, 12
  key elements of, 14, 17–19
  lack of, 11, 17–18, 25–26
  levels of, 17
  need for, 15–16, 19–21, 26–28
  poster of, 322–323
  purpose of, 9, 322

strategic plan, executing
  accountability, 268–271
  adaptability, 280–281
  communication tips, 275–278
  described, 12–13, 39, 263
  importance of, 19, 52
  lack of implementation, 263
  pitfalls of, 264–265
  planning phases, 45–46
  postmeeting tasks, 330
  preimplementation checklist, 265–266
  resistance to change, 278–279
  steps for, 267
  support system, 266–267
  tips for success, 52
strategic plan manager
  described, 268
  role of, 322
  selection of, 48, 268–269
strategic planning
  benefits of, 28–30
  defined, 13, 15
  versus long-range planning, 15
  over planning, 52
  phases of, 41–46
  pitfalls, 258–259
  popularity of, 23–25, 160
  purpose of, 15
  readiness assessment, 40–41
  tips for success, 51–52
  top-down versus bottom-up, 52
*Strategic Planning for Nonprofit*
    *Organizations: A Practical Guide and*
    *Workbook* (Allison and Kaye), 316
strategic position
  defined, 114
  intangible assets, 115–120
  internal processes, 121–127
  planning phases, 42–43
  profit margins, 127–130
  resources, evaluating, 120–121
  SWOT tool, 114–115
strategic thinking, 16
strategy
  business unit level, 195–201
  defined, 10–11
  described, 18, 32–33, 38
  finalizing, 227–228
  levels of, 195

maps, 230–234, 257
market unit level, 202–210
notebooks, 234–235
planning phases, 43–44
routine reviews, 272–275
scenario planning, 289
summary of, 210
versus tactics, 194–195
strength, organizational
  analysis template, 114–115, 189
  business unit level strategy, 196–200
  described, 114
  portfolio revisions, 60–63
  types of, 196
strengths, weaknesses, opportunities, and
    threats analysis. *See* SWOT analysis
subscription model, 142
substitute product, 181, 184
successful business
  accidental success, 25
  celebrations of, 52, 324, 334
  choosing to be, 23
  displays of success, 56–57
  example of, 27
  financial success, 250
  Inc. 500 companies, 27
  key factors for, 170
  past performance analysis, 56–57
  tips for, 51–52
  traits of, 26–28, 31–32
succession planning
  defined, 301
  importance of, 32
  process of, 301–304
  tribal knowledge, 32
supplier
  business models, 143–144
  opportunities and threats, 181–182
  planning team selection, 47
  relationship with, 122
supply and demand, 208
support call, 139
Surfrider Foundation (environmental
    organization), 84
surplus maximization, 316
survey
  customer satisfaction, 139
  employee input for meetings, 327

planning team selection, 47
SWOT analysis, 190
Survey Monkey (survey tool), 190
Susan G. Komen for the Cure (nonprofit organization), 103
sustainable competitive advantage. *See* competitive advantage
SWOT (strengths, weaknesses, opportunities, and threats) analysis
   described, 37, 189
   input from others, 189–190
   narrowing down, 213–214
   opportunities and threats, 171–172, 189–190
   planning phases, 43
   strategic choice, 213–216
   strategic position, 114–115
   template, 114–115, 189
system-up time, 138

● *T* ●

tactics, 194–195
tangible asset. *See* resource
target
   defined, 238
   scorecard, creating, 241–243
   selection of, 239–240
target market
   business unit level strategy, 201
   creating, 152–157
   customer profiles, 156–157, 167–168
   evaluating, 157–159
   new markets, 162–165
   positioning statements, 159–162
task force, 274
tax legislation, 177, 302
teamwork
   organizational capital, 118
   support from manager, 271
   SWOT analysis, 190
technology
   changes in, 71
   goals, cascading, 248
   long-term uncertainties, 287
   opportunities and threats, 174, 176–177
telephone survey, 139
theme, 213

Thomson Research (business information company), 151
threat
   described, 170
   environmental forces, 173–178
   future plan, 172
   industry competition, 179–187
   summary of, 188–189
   SWOT analysis, 171–172, 189–190, 213–216
time, for strategic planning
   frequently asked questions about, 16
   job of CEO, 27–28
   management techniques, 333–334
   manager's use of, 33
   planning phases, 41–46
   SMART goals, 229
   tips for success, 52
   wasted time, 127, 242
timing, of exit strategy, 301
Tracy, Brian *(Eat That Frog)*, 333
Trailing 12 Months (T12M) chart, 68–70
training, employee
   intangible assets, 116
   succession planning, 303
   values statement, 100
transformational change, 279
transition planning, 300–301
tribal knowledge
   competitive advantage, 87
   defined, 4, 118
   evaluating, 118–120
   versus information, 119
   management of, 119–120
   succession planning, 32
trigger point, 286
T12M chart. *See* Trailing 12 Months chart
turnover rate, employee, 116–117
TweetDeck (mobile application), 299
24-Hour Fitness (health and fitness company), 152

● *U* ●

undercover source, of information, 185
uniqueness, of segment, 158
university library, 151
University of California Berkley Library *(Finding Information on the Internet: A Tutorial)*, 151

University of Phoenix, 95
unrelated diversification, 206, 207
U.S. Census Bureau, 150
U.S. Department of Commerce, 150
U.S. Securities and Exchange Commission, 151
usage maximization, 317
usage targeting, 317

● *V* ●

value
  business models, 141–146
  of customers, 133–136
  defined, 140–141
  entrepreneurial organizations, 297–300
  proposition, 143
Value Line (financial-data services), 71, 151
values, organizational
  creating, 98–99
  defined, 97
  elements of, 97–98
  government planning, 309
  importance of, 97
  living by, 99–101
  strategic priorities, 226
values statement
  barriers to, 92
  creating, 97–98, 99–101
  defined, 42, 92
  described, 37
  employee commitment, 99–101
  planning phases, 42
variable asset, 254
variable liability, 254
vendor. *See* supplier
vertical integration, 208
Virgin (diversified company), 207
virtual learning, 175
vision, organizational
  barriers to, 92
  defined, 42, 92
  described, 38, 101
  entrepreneurial company, 296–297
  futurecasting, 105–107
  need for, 18
  planning phases, 42
  priority setting, 222
  strategic choices, 227–234
  strategic planning benefits, 29

vision statement
  creating, 102–104
  described, 101
  elements of, 102
  entrepreneurial organizations, 296–297
  examples of, 101, 103
Visiongain (business information provider), 177
visual aid, 322–323
visualizing
  customers, 155–156
  success, 331–332
vivid description, 101–104

● *W* ●

Wack, Pierre (leader in scenario planning), 283
Wal-Mart (retailer), 94, 140, 182
Walton, Sam (founder of Wal-Mart), 140
Warrillow, John *(Built to Sell: Turn Your Business into One You Can Sell)*, 298
Washoe County, Nevada, 311
weakness, organizational, 114–115, 189
web-based application, 259
Wharton Business School, 161
Whole Foods (grocery chain), 124
W.L. Gore & Associates (manufacturer), 125
women, achievements of, 178
word-of-mouth
  importance of, 136
  value of customers, 134, 135

● *X* ●

XM Radio (satellite radio), 181

● *Y* ●

Yahoo! Answers (website), 150
yelling, 271
Yoga to the People (fitness business), 297
Yogurt Beach (yogurt shop), 223

● *Z* ●

*Zen in the Art of Archery* (Herrigel), 279
Zoomrang (survey tool), 190

# John Wiley & Sons, Inc.
# End-User License Agreement

**READ THIS.** You should carefully read these terms and conditions before opening the software packet(s) included with this book "Book". This is a license agreement "Agreement" between you and John Wiley & Sons, Inc. "WILEY". By opening the accompanying software packet(s), you acknowledge that you have read and accept the following terms and conditions. If you do not agree and do not want to be bound by such terms and conditions, promptly return the Book and the unopened software packet(s) to the place you obtained them for a full refund.

1. **License Grant.** WILEY grants to you (either an individual or entity) a nonexclusive license to use one copy of the enclosed software program(s) (collectively, the "Software") solely for your own personal or business purposes on a single computer (whether a standard computer or a workstation component of a multi-user network). The Software is in use on a computer when it is loaded into temporary memory (RAM) or installed into permanent memory (hard disk, CD-ROM, or other storage device). WILEY reserves all rights not expressly granted herein.

2. **Ownership.** WILEY is the owner of all right, title, and interest, including copyright, in and to the compilation of the Software recorded on the physical packet included with this Book "Software Media". Copyright to the individual programs recorded on the Software Media is owned by the author or other authorized copyright owner of each program. Ownership of the Software and all proprietary rights relating thereto remain with WILEY and its licensers.

3. **Restrictions on Use and Transfer.**

   **(a)** You may only (i) make one copy of the Software for backup or archival purposes, or (ii) transfer the Software to a single hard disk, provided that you keep the original for backup or archival purposes. You may not (i) rent or lease the Software, (ii) copy or reproduce the Software through a LAN or other network system or through any computer subscriber system or bulletin-board system, or (iii) modify, adapt, or create derivative works based on the Software.

   **(b)** You may not reverse engineer, decompile, or disassemble the Software. You may transfer the Software and user documentation on a permanent basis, provided that the transferee agrees to accept the terms and conditions of this Agreement and you retain no copies. If the Software is an update or has been updated, any transfer must include the most recent update and all prior versions.

4. **Restrictions on Use of Individual Programs.** You must follow the individual requirements and restrictions detailed for each individual program in the "About the CD" appendix of this Book or on the Software Media. These limitations are also contained in the individual license agreements recorded on the Software Media. These limitations may include a requirement that after using the program for a specified period of time, the user must pay a registration fee or discontinue use. By opening the Software packet(s), you agree to abide by the licenses and restrictions for these individual programs that are detailed in the "About the CD" appendix and/or on the Software Media. None of the material on this Software Media or listed in this Book may ever be redistributed, in original or modified form, for commercial purposes.

5. **Limited Warranty.**

   **(a)** WILEY warrants that the Software and Software Media are free from defects in materials and workmanship under normal use for a period of sixty (60) days from the date of purchase of this Book. If WILEY receives notification within the warranty period of defects in materials or workmanship, WILEY will replace the defective Software Media.

**(b)** WILEY AND THE AUTHOR(S) OF THE BOOK DISCLAIM ALL OTHER WARRANTIES, EXPRESS OR IMPLIED, INCLUDING WITHOUT LIMITATION IMPLIED WARRANTIES OF MERCHANTABILITY AND FITNESS FOR A PARTICULAR PURPOSE, WITH RESPECT TO THE SOFTWARE, THE PROGRAMS, THE SOURCE CODE CONTAINED THEREIN, AND/OR THE TECHNIQUES DESCRIBED IN THIS BOOK. WILEY DOES NOT WARRANT THAT THE FUNCTIONS CONTAINED IN THE SOFTWARE WILL MEET YOUR REQUIREMENTS OR THAT THE OPERATION OF THE SOFTWARE WILL BE ERROR FREE.

**(c)** This limited warranty gives you specific legal rights, and you may have other rights that vary from jurisdiction to jurisdiction.

6. **Remedies.**

**(a)** WILEY's entire liability and your exclusive remedy for defects in materials and workmanship shall be limited to replacement of the Software Media, which may be returned to WILEY with a copy of your receipt at the following address: Software Media Fulfillment Department, Attn.: *Strategic Planning Kit For Dummies,* 2nd Edition, John Wiley & Sons, Inc., 10475 Crosspoint Blvd., Indianapolis, IN 46256, or call 1-800-762-2974. Please allow four to six weeks for delivery. This Limited Warranty is void if failure of the Software Media has resulted from accident, abuse, or misapplication. Any replacement Software Media will be warranted for the remainder of the original warranty period or thirty (30) days, whichever is longer.

**(b)** In no event shall WILEY or the author be liable for any damages whatsoever (including without limitation damages for loss of business profits, business interruption, loss of business information, or any other pecuniary loss) arising from the use of or inability to use the Book or the Software, even if WILEY has been advised of the possibility of such damages.

**(c)** Because some jurisdictions do not allow the exclusion or limitation of liability for consequential or incidental damages, the above limitation or exclusion may not apply to you.

7. **U.S. Government Restricted Rights.** Use, duplication, or disclosure of the Software for or on behalf of the United States of America, its agencies and/or instrumentalities "U.S. Government" is subject to restrictions as stated in paragraph (c)(1)(ii) of the Rights in Technical Data and Computer Software clause of DFARS 252.227-7013, or subparagraphs (c) (1) and (2) of the Commercial Computer Software - Restricted Rights clause at FAR 52.227-19, and in similar clauses in the NASA FAR supplement, as applicable.

8. **General.** This Agreement constitutes the entire understanding of the parties and revokes and supersedes all prior agreements, oral or written, between them and may not be modified or amended except in a writing signed by both parties hereto that specifically refers to this Agreement. This Agreement shall take precedence over any other documents that may be in conflict herewith. If any one or more provisions contained in this Agreement are held by any court or tribunal to be invalid, illegal, or otherwise unenforceable, each and every other provision shall remain in full force and effect.

## Internet

Blogging For Dummies,
3rd Edition
978-0-470-61996-4

eBay For Dummies,
6th Edition
978-0-470-49741-8

Facebook For Dummies,
3rd Edition
978-0-470-87804-0

Web Marketing
For Dummies,
2nd Edition
978-0-470-37181-7

WordPress
For Dummies,
3rd Edition
978-0-470-59274-8

## Language & Foreign Language

French For Dummies
978-0-7645-5193-2

Italian Phrases
For Dummies
978-0-7645-7203-6

Spanish For Dummies,
2nd Edition
978-0-470-87855-2

Spanish
For Dummies,
Audio Set
978-0-470-09585-0

## Math & Science

Algebra I
For Dummies,
2nd Edition
978-0-470-55964-2

Biology For Dummies,
2nd Edition
978-0-470-59875-7

Calculus For Dummies
978-0-7645-2498-1

Chemistry For Dummies
978-0-7645-5430-8

## Microsoft Office

Excel 2010 For Dummies
978-0-470-48953-6

Office 2010 All-in-One
For Dummies
978-0-470-49748-7

Office 2010 For Dummies,
Book + DVD Bundle
978-0-470-62698-6

Word 2010 For Dummies
978-0-470-48772-3

## Music

Guitar For Dummies,
2nd Edition
978-0-7645-9904-0

iPod & iTunes For
Dummies, 8th Edition
978-0-470-87871-2

Piano Exercises
For Dummies
978-0-470-38765-8

## Parenting & Education

Parenting For Dummies,
2nd Edition
978-0-7645-5418-6

Type 1 Diabetes
For Dummies
978-0-470-17811-9

## Pets

Cats For Dummies,
2nd Edition
978-0-7645-5275-5

Dog Training For Dummies,
3rd Edition
978-0-470-60029-0

Puppies For Dummies,
2nd Edition
978-0-470-03717-1

## Religion & Inspiration

The Bible For Dummies
978-0-7645-5296-0

Catholicism For Dummies
978-0-7645-5391-2

Women in the Bible
For Dummies
978-0-7645-8475-6

## Self-Help & Relationship

Anger Management
For Dummies
978-0-470-03715-7

Overcoming Anxiety
For Dummies,
2nd Edition
978-0-470-57441-6

## Sports

Baseball
For Dummies,
3rd Edition
978-0-7645-7537-2

Basketball
For Dummies,
2nd Edition
978-0-7645-5248-9

Golf For Dummies,
3rd Edition
978-0-471-76871-5

## Web Development

Web Design
All-in-One
For Dummies
978-0-470-41796-6

Web Sites
Do-It-Yourself
For Dummies,
2nd Edition
978-0-470-56520-9

## Windows 7

Windows 7
For Dummies
978-0-470-49743-2

Windows 7
For Dummies,
Book + DVD Bundle
978-0-470-52398-8

Windows 7 All-in-One
For Dummies
978-0-470-48763-1

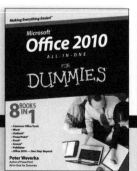

Available wherever books are sold. For more information or to order direct: U.S. customers visit www.dummies.com or call 1-877-762-2
U.K. customers visit www.wileyeurope.com or call (0) 1243 843291. Canadian customers visit www.wiley.ca or call 1-800-567-4797.

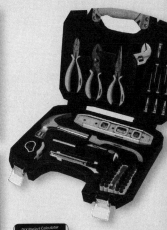

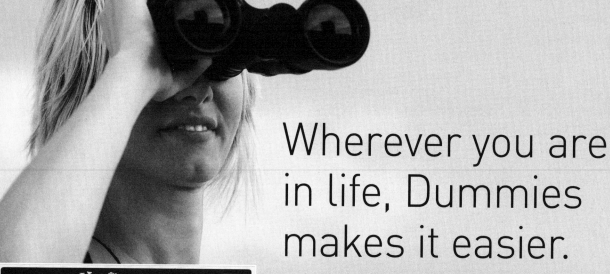

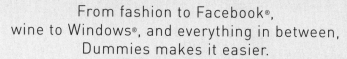